Application of Agents and Intelligent Information Technologies

Vijayan Sugumaran, Oakland University, USA

IDEA GROUP PUBLISHING

Hershey • London • Melbourne • Singapore

Acquisition Editor:	Kristin Klinger
Senior Managing Editor:	Jennifer Neidig
Managing Editor:	Sara Reed
Assistant Managing Editor:	Sharon Berger
Development Editor:	Kristin Roth
Copy Editor:	Chuck Pizar
Typesetter:	Jamie Snavely
Cover Design:	Lisa Tosheff
Printed at:	Integrated Book Technology

Published in the United States of America by
Idea Group Publishing (an imprint of Idea Group Inc.)
701 E. Chocolate Avenue
Hershey PA 17033
Tel: 717-533-8845
Fax: 717-533-8661
E-mail: cust@idea-group.com
Web site: http://www.idea-group.com

and in the United Kingdom by
Idea Group Publishing (an imprint of Idea Group Inc.)
3 Henrietta Street
Covent Garden
London WC2E 8LU
Tel: 44 20 7240 0856
Fax: 44 20 7379 3313
Web site: http://www.eurospan.co.uk

Library of Congress Cataloging-in-Publication Data

Application of agents and intelligent information technologies / Vijayan Sugumaran, editor.
p. cm.
Summary: "This book provides a comprehensive analysis of issues related to agent design, implementation, integration, deployment, evaluation, and business value; it presents research results and application of agents and other intelligent information technologies in various domains. It offers intelligent information technologies that may revolutionize the work environment as well as social computing"--Provided by publisher.
Includes bibliographical references and index.
ISBN 1-59904-265-7 (hardcover) -- ISBN 1-59904-266-5 (softcover) -- ISBN 1-59904-267-3 (ebook)
1. Expert systems (Computer science) 2. Intelligent agents (Computer software) 3. Information retrieval. 4. Artificial intelligence. 5. Online information services. I. Sugumaran, Vijayan, 1960-
QA76.76.I58A667 2006
006.3'3--dc22
2006031361

British Cataloguing in Publication Data
A Cataloguing in Publication record for this book is available from the British Library.

Applications of Agents and Intelligent Information Technologies

Table of Contents

Preface

The Web has sparked renewed interest in developing intelligent information systems that enable users to accomplish complex tasks in Web-centric environments with relative ease. Although artificially intelligent (AI) technologies such as expert systems and neural networks have been successfully used in aerospace, communication, medical, and financial applications, they have not made a significant impact on improving overall productivity due to their narrow scope. In contrast, the new breed of "intelligent information technologies" hold greater potential in that they can be applied to a large number of domains and a diverse set of problems. A generic intelligent-agent-based application, for instance, can be customized for different domains and a variety of problem scenarios. Several enabling technologies and techniques such as agent-based modeling, grid computing, data mining and knowledge discovery, data warehousing and business intelligence, fuzzy computing, machine learning and evolutionary algorithms, business components, and ontologies are being utilized in creating intelligent systems.

Intelligent-agent technology is emerging as one of the most important and rapidly advancing areas. Researchers are developing a number of agent-based applications and multi-agent systems in a variety of fields such as electronic commerce, supply-chain management, resource allocation, intelligent manufacturing, mass customization, industrial control, information retrieval and filtering, collaborative work, mobile commerce, decision support, and computer games. Research on various aspects of intelligent-agent technology and its applications is progressing at a very fast pace. Specifically, issues related to agent design, implementation, integration, deployment, evaluation and business value are actively being investigated. The authors of this book present some of the research results and application of agents and other intelligent-information technologies in various domains.

Chapter I, "OABIS: An Ontology-Based Approach to Business Rules Sourcing in Supply Chain Management Systems," by Sudha Ram and Jun Liu of the University of Arizona (USA), proposes an ontology-based approach to implementing the data-sourcing service for business rules. Business rules represent guidelines about how an enterprise should conduct its business and provide better service for customers. These rules are widely deployed in supply chains to support real-time decision making. This chapter presents a dynamically adaptable data-sourcing service for deploying business rules effectively in supply-chain management. It captures the semantics of business rules and provides an agent-enabled mechanism that dynamically maps business rules to individual database schemas in the supply chain. Data-sourcing services are important because the execution of business rules requires data to be retrieved from various data sources spread across the enterprise, including the enterprise data warehouse.

Chapter II, "Evolution and Mutation in Push Technologies: Social Concerns Resulting from the Effects of Memes on Intelligent Agents," by Julie Kendall and Kenneth Kendall, of Rutgers University (USA), raises awareness of the movement toward push technologies deploying evolutionary agents and the social implications their use entails. Push technologies are now back in vogue and RSS feeds and Podcasts are now part of many people's daily lives. Software robots, called autonomous agents, are helping users download what they want from the Internet. These agents will change as the user changes and are therefore referred to as an evolutionary agents. Evolutionary agents will also change, because memes (or messages) one agent broadcasts to another, will cause the evolutionary agent to mutate. This chapter explores the social implications of meritorious and malevolent memes exchanged by evolutionary agents. Since interactions occur among humans, evolutionary agents, and memes, the authors raise the following questions for future research regarding genetic determination of evolutionary agents. Is it possible to predict whether a meme will be meritorious or malevolent? Is it desirable to legislate the evolution of agents that are evolved from malevolent memes?

Chapter III, "Approaches and Tools to Optimize and Manage Clinical Processes," by Rainer Herrler, University of Würzburg (Germany), and Christian Heine, University of Hohenheim (Germany), shows how to optimize processes in hospitals by using agent-based simulation and agent-based information systems that can substantially increase the efficiency of hospital process management. In particular, it describes a methodology for optimization; the ingredients of the simulation; the architecture of a management system; and the integration of existing FIPA, DICOM, and HL7 standards. It also provides example scenarios to demonstrate how simulation can improve distributed scheduling and how agent-based systems can be used to manage "clinical trials."

Chapter IV, "Combining Malaria: A Complex System and Agent-Based Approach," by Narjès Bellamine-Bensaoud of University La Manouba (Tunisia) and Fatima Rateb of University College London (UK), investigates how complexity theory and more particularly how agent-based modelling and simulation can benefit the explanation of the impact of education on malaria healthcare. The proposed model takes into account the environment encompassing mainly cities, roads, hospitals, and schools. Agents, modelling the human actors, can be safe or infected by malaria according to their location in the environment. A modelled agent can also be mobile, can reproduce, and can die. Four kinds of simulation experiments over a 50-year period were conducted. The results show susceptible and immune populations in a "cyclic" fluctuation form and confirm the positive impact of both education and hospitals in combating malaria.

Chapter V, "An Intelligent Multi-Robot System Using Higher-Order Mobile Agents," by Yasushi Kambayashi of the Nippon Institute of Technology (Japan) and Munehiro Takimoto of the Tokyo University of Science (Japan), presents a framework for controlling intelligent robots connected by communication networks. This framework provides novel methods to control coordinated systems using higher-order mobile agents, which are hierarchically structured agents that can contain other mobile agents. By using higher-order mobile agents, intelligent robots in action can acquire new functionalities dynamically as well as exchange their roles with other colleague robots. The higher-order property of the mobile agents enables them to be organized hierarchically and dynamically. In addition, higher-order mobile agents require minimum communication and only need connection when they perform migration.

Chapter VI, "Instrument Validation for Strategic Business Simulation," by Chris Langdon of the University of Southern California (USA), provides a synopsis on the design science of agent-based modeling and how to adapt an agent-based research strategy for the scientific study of complex business systems. Research in information systems (IS) has begun to advance knowledge in the use of agent-based systems as a means to seek different, computational explanations for business phenomena that have eluded scientific inquiry reliant on traditional law and axiomatic explanation. The focus on business problems requires a different research approach than what is successful in computer science. One key modification is to make instrument validation explicit. This chapter extends the discussion on validation to ensure the rigor of management science research in agent-based information systems.

Chapter VII, "Challenges of the 'Global Understanding Environment' Based on Agent Mobility," by Vagan Terziyan of the University of Jyvaskyla (Finland), discusses the Global Understanding Environment as an enabling agent-driven semantic platform for implementation of the heterogeneous industrial resources, condition monitoring, and predictive maintenance. Services are semantic Web-enabled and form a service network based on internal and external agents' platforms, which can host heterogeneous mobile agents and coordinate them to perform the needed tasks. The concept of a "mobile service component" assumes not only exchanging queries and service responses but also delivery and composition of a service provider itself. A mobile service component carrier (agent) can move to a field device's local environment (embedded agent platform) and perform its activities locally. Service components improve their performance through online learning and communication with other components. This chapter presents one possible implementation framework for such Web services. It also discusses the main challenges of such an environment, which are "semantic adapters" for industrial objects, diagnostic models exchange and integration, distributed trust management, and the concept of a human as a Web service.

Chapter VIII, "Building Sound Semantic Web Frameworks for Scalable and Fault-Tolerant Systems," by Thomas Biskup, Nils Heyer and Jorge Marx Gómez, Carl von Ossietzky University Oldenburg (Germany), introduces hyperservices as a unified application model for semantic Web frameworks and proposes the WASP model as a framework for implementing them. Hyperservices are based on agent societies, provided with structured information by the semantic Web, and using Web services as a collaboration and communication interface. The WASP model adds personalization rules to modify the agents' perception and the HIVE architecture as semantic information server infrastructure within this framework. The conceptual model driven software development is proposed as a means of easy adoption to Hyperservices.

Chapter IX, "Information Parallax," by Franc Grootjen and Theo van der Weide of Radboud University Nijmegen (Netherlands), discusses a special kind of knowledge representation based on a dual view on the universe of discourse and shows how it can be used in human activities such as searching, in-depth exploration, and browsing. This chapter provides a formal definition of dualistic ontologies and exemplifies this definition with three different (well-known) kinds of ontologies, based on the vector model, formal concept analysis, and fuzzy logic respectively. The vector model leads to concepts derived by latent semantic indexing using the singular value decomposition. Both the set model and the fuzzy set model lead to formal concept analysis, in which the fuzzy set model is equipped with a parameter that controls the fine-graining of the resulting concepts. The chapter also discusses the relation between the resulting systems of concepts and demonstrates the use of this theory by introducing the dual search engine. This search engine can be employed to support various human activities.

Chapter X, "ADAM: An Automatic Approach to Database Management," by Sunitha Ramanujam and Miriam Capretz of the University of Western Ontario (Canada), presents a solution to overcome the problem of overburdened and expensive database administrators (DBAs). This chapter focuses on relational database management systems in particular and proposes a novel and innovative multiagent system (MAS) that autonomously and rationally administers and maintains databases. The multiagent system tool, called ADAM (a MAS for autonomous database administration and maintenance), offers a solution to the problem of overburdened and expensive

DBAs with the objective of making databases a cost-effective option for small- and medium-sized organizations. An implementation of the agent-based system to pro-actively or reactively identify and resolve a small sub-set of DBA tasks is discussed. Role models describing the responsibilities, permissions, activities, and protocols of the candidate agents and interaction models representing the links between the roles are explained. The Coordinated Intelligent Rational agent model is used to describe the agent architecture and a brief description of the functionalities, responsibilities, and components of each agent type in the ADAM multiagent system is presented. A prototype system implementation using JADE 2.5 and Oracle 8.1.7 is presented as evidence of the feasibility of the proposed agent-based solution for the autonomous administration and maintenance of relational databases.

Chapter XI, "Towards Distributed Association Rule Mining Privacy," by Mafruz Zaman Ashrafi, David Taniar, and Kate Smith of Monash University (Australia), proposes a methodology for privacy preserving distributed association rules genera-tion. To explore and analyze large data repositories and discover useful actionable knowledge from it, modern organizations use a technique known as data mining, which analyzes voluminous digital data and discovers hidden but useful patterns within this data. These hidden patterns have statistical meaning and may often disclose some sensitive information. As a result, privacy becomes one of the prime concerns in the data-mining research community. Since distributed data mining discovers rules by combining local models from various distributed sites, breach-ing data privacy happens more often than it does in centralized environments. The proposed approach employs a secure multiparty computation-based technique that maintains the private inputs of each participating site secret when all participat-ing sites generate the global frequent itemset. The performance evaluation shows that the overall communication cost incurred by the proposed method is less than that of count distribution (CD) and Distributed Mining Association (DMA) rule algorithms.

Chapter XII, "A Generic Internet Trading Framework for Online Auctions," by Dong-Qing Yao, Towson University (USA), Haiying Qiao, University of Maryland (USA), and Haibing Qiao, FileNet Corporation (USA), introduces a generic Internet trading framework for online auctions. A generic OR/XOR bidding language that expresses different OR/XOR combinations is adopted for web interfaces. The frame-work is implemented with free open-source technologies already successfully tested in different industries. This platform can be used to implement different electronic market mechanisms, and simulate the market behavior of interests under different experimental settings. The auction platform also provides a rule engine. Instead of coding the rules in different places such as agents, the rule engine provides central-ized rule management in conjunction with the process-flow engine. This alleviates the auction developer or agent developer from the burden of implementing these rules in a number of places.

Chapter XIII, "Monitoring and Enforcing Online Auction Ethics," by Diana Kao of the University of Windsor (Canada) and Shouhong Wang of the University of Massachusetts Dartmouth (USA), discusses ethics-related issues that are relevant in online auctions and recommends a code of ethics that could be applied to online auctions. Although using a different mode for conducting auction activities, online auctions should abide by the same code of ethics outlined in the face-to-face auction environment. The unique features of online auctions present an opportunity to address how ethical conduct should be supported, monitored, and enforced in an online auction environment. With technology being the backbone of online auction, information systems serve as a useful tool in facilitating ethics enforcement. This chapter presents a model for an information system that supports and enhances ethical conduct in an online auction environment.

Chapter XIV, "Mail Server Management with Intelligent Agents," by Charles Willow of Monmouth University (USA), presents an agent-based solution for managing mail servers. One of the difficulties faced by IS managers is accurately forecasting the memory needs of the organization. In particular, managers are often confronted with maintaining a certain threshold amount of memory for a prolonged period. However, this constraint requires more than technical and managerial resolutions, encompassing knowledge management for the group, eliciting tacit knowledge from the end users, and requiring pattern and time series analyses of utilization for various applications. This chapter summarizes current methods for managing server memory by incorporating intelligent agents. Specifically, a new framework for building a set of automated intelligent agents with neural networks is proposed using the client-server architecture. The emphasis is on collecting the needs of the organization and acquiring the application usage patterns for each client involved in real time. The proposed framework takes into account platform independence, portability, and modularity.

Chapter XV, "Predicting Protein Secondary Structure Using Artificial Neural Networks and Information Theory," by Saad Osman Abdalla Subair of Al-Ghurair Univetsity (UAE), and Safaai Deris of the University of Technology Malaysia (Malaysia), describes a new method for predicting protein secondary structure from amino-acid sequences. Protein secondary structure prediction is a fundamental step in determining the 3D structure of a protein. The newly developed method utilizes the knowledge of GOR-V information theory and the power of neural networks to classify a novel protein sequence in one of its three secondary structure classes—helices, strands, and coils. The NN-GORV-I method is further improved by applying a filtering mechanism to the searched database and hence named NN-GORV-II. The Cuff and Barton 513 protein data set is used for training and testing the prediction methods under the same hardware platform, and environment. The developed prediction methods are rigorously analyzed and tested together with other five well-known prediction methods to allow for easy comparison.

Agent-based applications and intelligent information technologies are beginning to be widely used by individuals and organizations alike. Many mission-critical applications are being developed for the purpose of improving productivity and gaining competitive advantage and facilitating growth and success for both organizations and individuals. Effective use of intelligent information technologies becomes a necessary goal for all, and this may be accomplished by learning from the research and advances of others within the intelligent-information-technologies field. An outstanding collection of the latest research associated with intelligent agents and information technologies has been presented in this book. Use of intelligent-information technologies has the potential to revolutionize the work environment as well as social computing.

Vijayan Sugumaran

Editor-in-Chief

Application of Agents and Intelligent Information Technologies

Vijayan Sugumaran *is an associate professor of management information systems in the Department of Decision and Information Sciences at Oakland University, Rochester, Michigan, USA. His research interests are in the areas of ontologies and Semantic Web, intelligent-agent and multiagent systems, component-based software development, knowledge-based systems, and data & information modeling. His most recent publications have appeared in ACM Transactions on Database Systems, IEEE Transactions on Engineering Management, Communications of the ACM, Healthcare Management Science, Data and Knowledge Engineering, The DATABASE for Advances in Information Systems, Information Systems Journal, Journal of Information Systems and E-Business Management, Expert Systems with Applications, and Logistics Information Management. Besides serving as the editor-in-chief of the International Journal of Intelligent Information Technologies, he also serves on the editorial board of seven other journals. Dr. Sugumaran is the Chair of the Intelligent Information Systems track for the Information Resources Management Association International Conference (IRMA 2001, 2002, 2005, 2006, 2007) and the Intelligent Agent and Multi-Agent Systems in Business minitrack for the Americas Conference on Information Systems (AMCIS 1999–2006). He served as Chair of the e-Commerce track for Decision Science Institute's Annual Conference, 2004. He also regularly serves as a program committee member for numerous national and international conferences.*

Acknowledgments

The editor would like to acknowledge the help of all involved in the collation and review process of the book, without whose support the project could not have been completed. I wish to thank all the authors for their great insights and excellent contributions to this book. Thanks to the publishing team at Idea Group Inc., for their constant support throughout the whole process. In particular, special thanks to Mehdi Khosrow-Pour, Jan Travers, Lynley Lapp, and Kristin Roth for their great help in taking this project to fruition.

Chapter I

OABIS:
An Ontology-Based Approach to Business Rules Sourcing in Supply Chain Management Systems

Sudha Ram, University of Arizona, USA

Jun Liu, University of Arizona, USA

Abstract

In recent years, business-rule management has become an important component of enterprise information systems. Business rules are guidelines for how an enterprise should conduct its business and provide better service to customers. Business rules are being widely deployed in supply chains to support real-time decision-making. The research reported in this chapter is aimed at designing a dynamically adaptable data-sourcing service for deploying business rules effectively in supply-chain management. Such a data sourcing service is important since execution of business rules requires data to be retrieved from various data sources spread across the enterprise, including the enterprise data warehouse. We propose an ontology-based approach to implement the data-sourcing service for business rules. Our approach captures semantics of business rules and provides an agent-enabled mechanism that dynamically maps business rules to individual database schemas in the supply chain.

Introduction

Business rules are an important asset of any enterprise: They represent decisions that are made to achieve business objectives and reflect the business policies of an enterprise (Rosca & Greenspan, 2002). Nowadays, the need to incorporate business rules into information systems is becoming imperative due to the rapid development of **e-business**. Many companies embrace e-business because it helps reduce inventories, lower cycle times, lower cost of sales and marketing, and create new sales opportunities (Motiwalla, Khan, & Xu, 2005). However, e-business has led to a radical shift in how business is conducted as it entails access to far more information, creates new channels for products, and provides multiple alternatives for outsourcing. All these raise serious challenges related to real-time decision-making and sharing and management of data for supply chains. To obtain a competitive edge and to take full advantage of the new opportunities offered by e-business, **supply chains** need to respond quickly to new business opportunities and make smart business decisions based on voluminous data shared among supply-chain partners. As a result, deploying business rules to support **supply-chain decision-making** has become a major issue that affects the competitiveness of an enterprise.

In the last decade, business-rule management has become an important component of information systems. Traditionally, business rules have been scattered and hard-coded in different applications. Today's new technologies for managing and executing business rules such as rule engines (Rosca & Greenspan, 2002) and business-rule repositories (Herbst, 1996, 1997; Von Halle, 2001) follow the principle of "externalizing business rules" (Date, 2000) and manage business rules in a separate module to support centralized supply-chain decision-making. Isolating business rules from individual applications enables business people to easily find and modify the pertinent rules when a policy change is needed, thereby providing the ability to make business decisions based on the real-time market situation. However, it also creates a need for integrating business-rules systems with other applications in the supply chain. Consequently, a business-rules service requires software components that interface with databases and other supply-chain applications to be effective. As an example, a software component that sources data for business rules is important.

Business rules are data-based (Ross, 1997). Validation of business rules using supply-chain simulation should be based on current information regarding inventory, order rates, product data, and so on. Execution of business rules also requires data to be retrieved from multiple information sources because the logic of business rules must operate on data stored in the information sources. Therefore, there is a need for a mechanism that retrieves (sources) the most recent data from multiple data sources to support business-rules management. However, since business rules often represent the strategic or tactical decisions of a business, business experts usually specify business rules in natural language so that they can provide complete and appropriate business requirements without being restricted by the models of the existing databases. Moreover, to stay competitive in the current emerging competitive environment, supply-chain-management systems must pursue data sharing and coordination across organizational boundaries—that is, not only within the enterprise, but also between enterprises and across industry boundaries. As a result, a "semantic gap" between business rules and local database schemas arises when we link business rules specified using natural language to distributed information sources with autonomously developed local schemas both within and across enterprises, which makes **business-rule data souring** a complex issue.

In this chapter, we propose an **O**ntology-based **A**pproach to **B**us**I**ness rules **S**ourcing (OABIS) to enable efficient supply-chain decision-making. To address the problem of the semantic gap mentioned above, we utilize a domain-specific ontology to establish semantic interoperability between business rules and schemas of underlying distributed information sources. Furthermore, today's rapidly changing business environment requires supply-chain operations to be automatic and scalable as much as possible. As a result, our research focuses on proposing a dynamic and automatic business rules management approach that can swiftly and smoothly adjust to changes made to both business rules and local schemas by establishing dynamic mappings between business terms in business rules and data objects in local schemas with little human intervention.

The rest of the chapter is organized as follows. In the "A Motivating Senario" section, we motivate the need for sourcing business rules using a scenario from a manufacturing organization and identify some challenging issues. The "OABIS" section, presents our ontology-based approach in detail. We show the overall structure of OABIS first, and then describe its components in detail. We briefly describe related work in the next section. In the "Discussion" section, we compare our current work with previous research and summarize its contributions. Finally, we conclude the paper and point out directions for future research.

A Motivating Scenario

Consider the following scenario for a large semiconductor manufacturing company in the management of its supply chain. The biggest challenge facing the company is that late order changes happen very often, and order changes account for approximately

20% of its total order request. To ensure that it has on-hand the specific products that the customers are favoring at a particular point, in spite of the order changes, the company deploys a delivery-planning module in its supply chain that accepts order-change requests and then reassigns shipping points for orders that were in jeopardy of not being fulfilled. A decision-support agent embedded in the delivery-planning module makes order-reallocation decisions (see Figure 1). After receiving order-change requests from an upstream supply-chain node, the decision-support agent determines the importance of the order, evaluates the supplier's capability to fulfill the order, and then creates an order-delivery plan and submits a request to the ERP system to reassign the shipping point for the order. As shown in Figure 1, two sets of business rules, that is, "order importance rules" and "supplier capability rules," are deployed to support decision making. The decision-support agent utilizes order-importance rules to evaluate the importance of a specific order and supplier-capability rules to determine the supplier's capacity to fulfill the order. An example of an order importance rule is "if order-criticality is very-low and order-size is small then order-importance is very-low," and an example of a supplier-capability rules can be "if supplier-inventory-availability is available and supplier-responsiveness is good then supplier-delivery-capability is good." The data required to execute these rules and make decisions is obtained (sourced) from a number of distributed sources within and between enterprises. Once a set of rules is executed and a decision is made, the data generated from the decision (e.g., a new shipping point) is fed back into one or more information sources, such as the ERP system.

As illustrated by this scenario, a business-rules data-sourcing service is indispensable because execution of the business rules requires data to be retrieved from various data sources spread across the enterprise. As discussed above, development of e-business and e-supply chains has resulted in unprecedented opportunities in data-driven knowledge acquisition and real-time supply-chain decision-making. However, the effective use of increasing amounts of data from disparate information sources present several challenges in practices:

- Data repositories are large in size, dynamic, and distributed. Consequently, it is neither desirable nor feasible to gather all of the data in a centralized location. Hence, there is a need for a method that automatically extracts the relevant information from distributed sources whenever a business rule is executed.

- Data sources are autonomously owned and operated. Each data source implicitly or explicitly uses its own ontology (i.e., concepts, attributes, and relationships) to represent data (Sowa, 1999). As a result, a business-rules sourcing service requires a mechanism that bridges the semantic mismatches between business rules and various data sources.

Figure 1. The decision process of the delivery-planning module

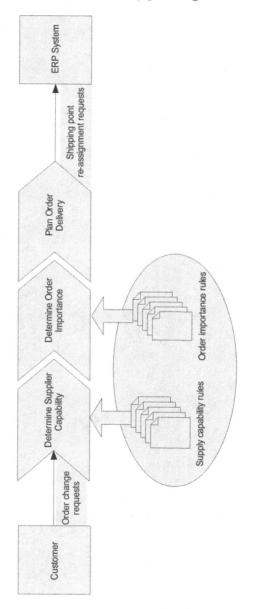

Figure 2. Architecture of OABIS

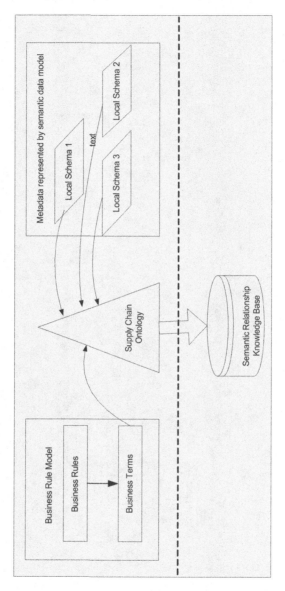

Having elucidated the challenging issues, we discuss how our approach addresses these issues in the following sections.

Oabis: An Ontology-Based Approach to Business-Rules Sourcing

OABIS links business-rules systems with information sources such as the enterprise data warehouse, the ERP system, and relational databases that store the most recent supply-chain data. An overview of OABIS is presented in Figure 2. It consists of the following components.

- *A business-rules model* that captures semantics of business rules and describes what constitutes a business rule.

- A set of *local database schemas* of distributed information sources represented using a semantic data model.

- *A supply-chain ontology* that captures various concepts and relationships between the concepts in the domain of supply-chain management. In OABIS, it is used to represent the semantics of business rules and local information schemas.

- *An agent-enabled mapping mechanism* that generates mappings between local database schemas and the supply-chain ontology as well as mappings between business rules and the ontology.

- *A semantic relationship knowledge base* that identifies and stores semantic relationships between components in different information models. Exploiting the stored semantic relationships, we derive mappings between business rules and data objects, usually attributes, in local database schemas.

Figure 3. Example of a business rule

> If **customer-rating** is below average and **inventory-availability** is low
> then **order-lead time** is long

Figure 4. Classification of business terms

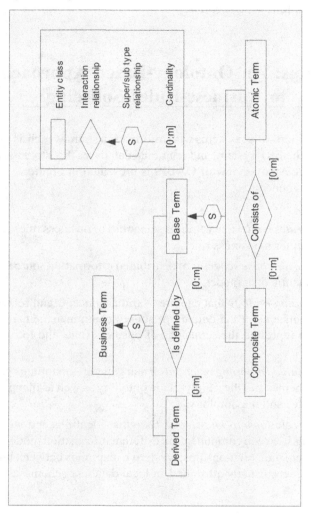

The Business Rules Model

Our business-rules model describes specifically what constitutes a **business rule**. We adopt the Business Rule Group's idea that business rules are formed of **business terms**, which are words or phrases that have specific meaning for a business in some designated context (The Business Rule Group, 2000). An example of a business rule formulated in our model with business terms highlighted (in bold) is shown

Figure 5. Part of the supply-chain ontology

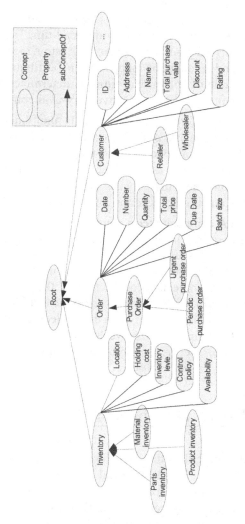

in Figure 3. This business rule consists of three business terms: "customer-rating," "inventory-availability," and "order-lead time".

We classify business terms based on their semantics. This classification is shown in Figure 4. According to our classification, business terms used in business rules are either base terms or derived terms, and base terms can be further classified into atomic terms and composite terms. Different mapping schemes will be applied to different types of business terms, which are described as follows.

- **Derived terms:** A derived term is defined by multiple base terms, indicating that the value for this term is determined by values of a set of base terms. As a result, we do not create direct mappings between a derived term and data objects in a database schema. The term "order-lead-time" in the business-rule example above is derived from the base terms "customer-rating" and "inventory-availability," and it cannot be mapped to any attribute in local schemas, meaning that the value of "order-lead-time" is determined by the values of the base terms "customer-rating" and "inventory-availability."

- **Atomic terms:** Atomic terms are semantically undividable. Although an atomic term normally consists of a single word, it can also be a multiword term. For example, the atomic term "lead-time" consists of multiple words but is captured in thesauri such as WordNet as a single expression. In general, we create a one-to-one mapping between an atomic term and a data object, which can either be an entity class or an attribute in local database schemas.

- **Composite terms:** A composite term consists of multiple atomic terms. For example, "customer-rating" is a composite term composed of the atomic terms "customer" and "rating." This is different from derived terms whose value is determined by values of the associated base terms, in that, a composite term is normally mapped to data objects in local schemas. To obtain an accurate mapping for a composite term, we first map its component atomic terms separately and then find an appropriate mapping to a data object, usually an attribute, in local schemas for the composite term. We describe this mapping in more detail later since most business terms used in business rules are composite terms.

Local Database Schemas

A local database schema describes the data stored in autonomous, local systems participating in a supply chain. In OABIS, local database schemas are represented in the form of the unifying semantic model (USM) (Ram, 1995; Ram, Park & Ball, 1999). The **USM** extends the **entity-relationship (ER) model** (Chen, 1976) by capturing more complex semantics in modeling constructs such as "super/subclass" and "aggregate/group" relationships. The reader is referred to Ram (1995), for details on the USM constructs. The primary purpose of designing local database schemas using a semantic data model is to make the semantics (hidden in a relational model) explicit. As shown in subsequent sections, we attempt to capture various schema-level semantic relationships. Developing local schemas using such a semantic model as the USM explicitly captures relationships among data objects using a semantically rich set of modeling constructs.

Figure 6. Examples of schema-ontology and rule-ontology mappings

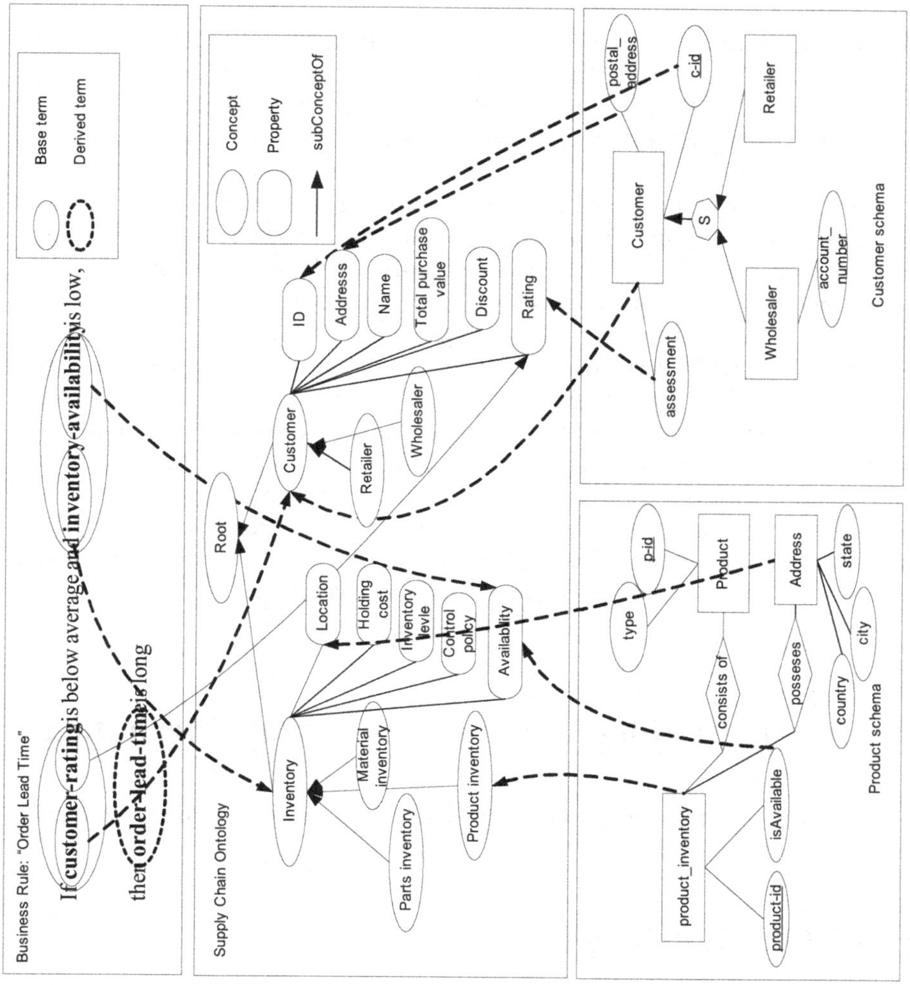

We assume that entity classes and their attributes and/or relationships in a database are represented by meaningful terms when a local information source is added. Thus, knowledge about the semantic relationships between the terms can indicate the real-world correspondence between data objects in different database schemas.

A Supply-Chain Ontology

We construct a supply-chain ontology to specify shared knowledge about the domain of supply-chain management. Existing supply-chain ontologies such as Frankovic, Budinska, and Dang (2003) and Fayez, Rabelo, and Mollaghasemi (2005) can also be used. According to Gruber (1995), **ontology** is a "formal explicit specification of conceptualization." The main advantage for having such a formal specification is to facilitate knowledge-sharing and re-use among the various parties involved in an application domain. With respect to the interoperability problem, ontologies enable the identification and association of semantically corresponding objects in heterogeneous information sources. They represent declarative specifications of concepts and various semantic relationships among the concepts in a domain of discourse. In OABIS, our supply-chain ontology covers different supply-chain functions such as new product development, operations, distribution, and customer service. Using the SCOR model, the only widely accepted knowledge model within the supply-chain community, as its core, we built our supply-chain ontology by defining various supply-chain concepts, subconcepts, properties, and relationships between the concepts independent of any existing application schemas. A part of our ontology is shown in Figure 5. Due to space limitation, it displays only some concepts and properties for orders, inventory, and customers.

An Agent-Enabled Semantic Mapping Mechanism

In this section, we present an agent-agent enabled mechanism that links the various components of our system.

Rule-Ontology Mappings

When a business rule is added to the business-rules repository, the semantic mapping **agent** identifies business terms in the rule and maps the identified **business terms** to elements (including concepts and properties) in the supply-chain ontology.

The mapping between the business rule "If customer-rating is below average and inventory-availability is low, then order-lead time is long" and our supply-chain ontology are graphically illustrated in the upper part of Figure 6. Note that to simplify the example, we have shown only a small part of our supply-chain ontology in Figure 6. The dotted arrowhead lines indicate the mappings between business terms and the corresponding supply-chain-ontology elements

In this example, "inventory-availability" is a composite term consisting of the atomic terms "inventory" and "availability." We map "inventory" and "availability" separately. We also create one-to-one mappings for atomic business terms "customer" and "rating."

Schema-Ontology Mappings

After an information source is added to the system, a mapping agent is launched to semi-automatically generate mappings between the local data schema and the supply-chain ontology. It also modifies the extant schema-ontology mappings and issues change notifications whenever a modification to an existing database schema leads to changes in established mappings.

Figure 6 includes two local database schemas and displays mappings between data objects in local schemas and elements in the supply chain ontology. For example, the entity "product_inventory" in the product inventory schema is mapped to the concept "product inventory" in the ontology, and the entity "address" is mapped to "location," a property of the concept "inventory" in the ontology.

We do acknowledge that in many cases, it is difficult to automate the mapping process and a domain expert may be needed to create the mappings. However, OABIS uses **WordNet**, a generic thesaurus, to provide a way to automate the semantic mappings in some circumstances. Distinct from the supply chain ontology that captures domain-specific knowledge, a thesaurus such as WordNet provides lexical knowledge that can be used to provide initial mappings between two different terms. WordNet categorizes words of the English language into synonym sets called synsets. By consulting WordNet, our mapping agent can generate initial mappings for a term representing a data object by identifying its synonyms in the ontology. Domain knowledge is then used to verify and finalize the mapping. As an example, for the entity "address" in the product schema, the combined use of the ontology and WordNet will automatically identify two candidate elements in the ontology: the property "location" of the concept "inventory" and the property "address" of "customer." The domain expert can then select the correct one.

The Semantic-Relationship Knowledge Base

This knowledge base is a key module in OABIS because it identifies various semantic relationships between elements in different information sources. Exploiting the semantic relationships captured in the knowledge base, we pinpoint the data object in a local schema to which a business term should be linked. We then extract information from distributed data source to support business rules execution and decision-making.

Semantic Relationships

We propose a set of relationships, named semantic relationships between the elements in different components (including the business-rules model, the supply-chain ontology, and local database schemas). Consider two different elements *A* and *B*. We can derive three possible relationships between *A* and *B* as follows:

1.   **Semantic Equivalence** (*SEM_EQ*) is defined between *A* and *B* when they are considered semantically equivalent and therefore can be used interchangeably without changes in the meaning. In the example shown in Figure 6, we have the following relationship "product schema: address" *SEM_EQ* "Supply chain ontology: location."

2.   **Semantic Subclass** *(SEM_SUB)* is defined between *A* and *B* when *B* has a broader and more general meaning than *A*. As an example, "customer schema: wholesaler" *SEM_SUB* "customer schema: customer" since "wholesaler" is a subconcept of "customer."

3.   **Semantic Relation** *(SEM_REL)* is defined between *A* and *B* when they are related in some way other than being equivalent or a subclass. In our example, the composite term "inventory_availability" consists of "inventory" and "availability," and there is a *SEM_REL* relationship between these two atomic terms. Also, in the product schema, "product_inventory" *SEM_REL* "product" since there exists a binary relationship "consists" between them, and "product" *SEM_REL* "type" since "type" is an attribute of "product." Notice that we do not make a distinction between relationships and attributes here because a concept can be modeled as an entity in one schema and an attribute in another.

Semantic-Relationship Extraction and Inference

Three levels of semantic relationships are extracted and added to the semantic relationship knowledge base sequentially.

1.   **Schema-level relationships:** We first add semantic relationships existing at the database schema level. As mentioned above, in OABIS, local database schemas are represented using the USM, a semantic model that captures semantic relationships such as *SEM_SUB* and *SEM_REL*. Therefore, we extract

schema-level relationships by exploiting the local schema represented by the USM without the need for further analysis.

2. **Ontology-based relationships:** We identify a *SEM_EQ* relationship between a business term and an element in the ontology that are mapped to each other by the mapping agent. Based on the relationships between concepts captured in the ontology, we derive semantic relationships between the business term and other components in the ontology. For instance, the business term "inventory" is mapped to the concept "inventory" in the ontology; therefore, we define a *SEM_EQ* relationship between them. Also, the concept "product_inventory" *SEM_SUB* the business term "inventory" since "product_inventory" is a sub-concept of "inventory" in the ontology. The semantic relationships between a data object in a local information source and elements in the ontology can also be identified in a similar fashion.

3. **Inferred relationships:** We infer new relationships between atomic business terms in business rules and data objects in local schemas by considering both schema-level relationships and ontology-based relationships. We define the following inference rules. Assume that A, B, C are elements in different sources.

    *   **Rule 1:** If A *SEM_EQ* B and B *SEM_EQ* C, then A *SEM_EQ* C.
    *   **Rule 2:** If A *SEM_EQ* B and B *SEM_SUB* C, then A *SEM_SUB* C.
    *   **Rule 3:** If A *SEM_SUB* B and B *SEM_SUB* C, then A *SEM_SUB* C.
    *   **Rule 4:** If A *SEM_EQ* B and B *SEM_REL* C, then A *SEM_REL* C.
    *   **Rule 5:** If A *SEM_SUB* B and B *SEM_REL* C, then A *SEM_REL* C.

As an example, we derive a *SEM_SUB* relationship between the entity "Wholesaler" and the business term "customer" based on Rule 2 and a *SEM_EQ* relationship between the attribute "assessment" and the term "rating" based on Rule 1.

Mappings Between Composite Terms and Database Objects

After identifying semantically related data objects in a database schema for each atomic term in a composite business term, we create an exact mapping between the composite **business term** with a data object, usually an attribute, if there are semantic relationships existing between the object and each of the atomic terms. In our example, the composite term "customer-rating" is mapped to the attribute "assessment" in the customer schema because the atomic term "customer" *SEM-REL* "assessment" according to Rule 3 and the atomic term "rating" *SEM-EQ* "assessment" according to Rule 1. In contrast, the composite term "inventory-availability" cannot be directly mapped to the attribute "isAvailable" in the product schema even though the atomic term "availability" *SEM-EQ* "isAvailable." This is because there is no semantic relationship existing between the other atomic term "inventory" and "isAvailable" since the entity "product_inventory" *SEM-SUB* the business term "inventory" and hence Rule 5 cannot be applied. Thus, simply mapping the business term "inventory availability" to "product inventory.isAvailable" may result in loss of information and consequences that are perhaps even more serious. In such cases, OABIS elicits human interaction to determine whether the mapping is acceptable.

Related Work

In recent years, business rules have received a lot of attention in literature as offering solutions to many information technology problems (Rosca & Greenspan, 2002). Substantial efforts were put into discovering a robust and powerful method for representation of business rules in a data model. As opposed to static business rules that can be expressed in **entity-relationship (ER)** models, dynamic business rules are not supported because ER models do not allow an explicit representation of events, conditions, or actions. Consequently, several extensions to the ER and other business-rules modeling methods (Halpin, 2001; Kardasis & Loucopoulos, 2004; Ram & Khatri, 2004; Ross, 1997) have been proposed. Our approach is similar to prior research (Ram & Khatri, 2004; Rosca & Greenspan, 2002) in the sense that it focuses on integrating business rules with data models. However, it is significantly different from them in that it supports specification of business rules in natural language and loosely couples business rules and data models with a mapping mechanism.

Moreover, the need for externalizing business rules and managing them in a central repository has long been recognized (Date, 2000; Von Halle, 2001), since business rules support and manage changes in the business environment. However, a business rules repository needs to interact with other components of information systems (IS) to be effective. Not much literature is available with respect to establishing explicit links between business rules and other IS applications to ease the process of decision-making. Rosca and Greenspan (2002) and Rosca and Wild (2002) propose a business-rule deployment architecture that consists of three interconnected components: business-rule models, an enterprise model, and a decision-support model, thus supporting the evolution of business rules in the face of changing regulatory environment and competitive markets. Bajec and Krisper (2005) emphasize the need for an explicit link between each business-rule instance as exists in a business environment and its implementation in one or more application systems. Similar to the previous research, our work focuses on linking business rules with other components in the supply chain, providing a mechanism to keep the organization's

IS aligned with the business environment. Our unique contribution in this research is that it proposes a dynamically adaptable data sourcing approach for business-rules execution by integrating business rules with various information sources in a supply chain. The issue of data sourcing for business rules has not been addressed in previous research.

Another important area that influences our research is ontology-aided semantic data integration. Prior related research in this area includes Arens, Hsu and Knoblock, (1996); Gruber (1995); He and Ling (2006); Mena, Kashyap, Sheth and Illarramendi (2000); and Ram and Park (2004)). Our research creates mappings between business terms and data objects in schemas by identifying semantic relationships between them. Similar methods have been employed by MOMIS (Bergamaschi, Castano, De Capitani di Vimercati, Montanari, & Vincini, 1998; Bergamaschi, Castano, Vincini & Beneventano, 2001) and OBSERVER (Mena, Kashyap, Sheth & Illarramendi, 2000) to fulfill different objectives. Aiming to produce a global schema for database integration, MOMIS creates a common thesaurus by extracting terminological relationships from database schemas. A module related to this perspective in OBSERVER is the Inter-Ontology Relationships Manager (the IRM). It keeps track of the relationships between terms in different ontologies, thereby creating mappings between ontologies. Our methodology of identifying semantic relationships is different from the ones proposed in OBSERVER and MOMIS. In OABIS, identifying semantic relationships is a much more complicated as we extract schema-level relationships, derive relationships between business terms and ontology components by scanning through rule-ontology mappings, and then infer relationships between business terms and data objects by investigating both schema-level and ontology-based relationships. Moreover, OABIS utilizes WordNet to provide lexical knowledge for creating initial semantic mappings, thus semi-automating the process of semantic mapping. In contrast, manual identification of relationships between terms in different sources is required in both OBSERVER and MOMIS.

Discussion

OABIS employs a domain ontology rather than a global data model for semantic mappings. In our previous work (Ram & Liu, 2005), we proposed mappings between business rules and data objects using an enterprise schema to represent data spread across multiple information stores and applications including the enterprise data warehouse and the ERP system. However, in an e-business environment, supply-chain decision-making often requires interorganizational data sharing and coordination, and it is extremely difficult to create and maintain such an enterprise schema. Moreover, the ontology-based approach is advantageous over the one using a global schema in that the former fully supports the autonomy of local information sources, whereas the global schema approach is not designed to be independent of particular schemas and applications.

Ouksel and Ahmed (1999) posit that ontologies are not a panacea for data integration due to the limitations of ontologies in dynamically identifying semantic heterogeneity. However, they also point out that despite their drawbacks, ontologies are very useful in semantic reconciliation as they can serve to establish initial mappings between terms of a local and a remote information system. Our design of the business rule data sourcing system focuses on associating terms in business rules with attributes in local schemas rather than revolving data-level and schema-level conflicts existing among heterogeneous information sources. Therefore, the ontology-based approach we employed is a perfect fit for dealing with the problem of business-rules data sourcing.

Besides providing a distinct ontology-based approach to semantic interoperability between business rules and local database schemas, OABIS aims to make several key contributions summarized below.

First, OABIS is one of the first attempts to provide a practical approach to business-rules data sourcing. As business rules represent the strategic or tactical decisions of a business (Rosca & Greenspan, 2002), organizations have recognized the need for business experts to specify rules in natural language without being restricted by the schemas of existing databases. However, natural-language specification of business rules often results in a "semantic gap" between the business rules system and the underlying information sources (Shao & Pound, 1999; Von Halle, 2001). This makes business-rules data sourcing a challenge. Our approach bridges this "semantic gap" by creating semantic mappings between business rules and local database schemas, thus enabling the business-rules system to provide data for business-rule execution in a seamless way. Using our approach, experts can specify business rules using terms they are familiar with, without the need to refer to any existing database schemas. Moreover, the decentralized structure of our approach enables local information sources to retain significant autonomy such that they can be easily added or removed without affecting the rest of the system.

Second, our approach to business-rules data sourcing is semi-automatic with limited human intervention. It helps minimize human intervention in supply-chain systems, which is important because today's rapidly changing business environment requires supply-chain systems to adjust to changes as quickly as possible. We use WordNet and a supply-chain ontology to provide both lexical and domain-related knowledge required to capture semantics of terms used in business rules and data objects in database schemas. OABIS semi-automatically identifies data objects in local database schemas that are semantically related to the business terms.

Third, our approach creates dynamic mappings between business rules and local database schemas. Static mappings between business terms and data objects in local schemas are infeasible for supply chain systems because the information sources involved may be extremely dynamic, and changes to local schemas may invalidate the mappings. Mappings established via our approach are dynamic because they can easily adapt to changes made to both the business rules and the information sources. A change to a business rule simply requires updating the corresponding mappings between the relevant business terms and elements in the ontology. Adding a new information source is also a simple process. It requires providing a local schema of the sources and relating data objects in the local schema to entries in the ontology. OABIS automatically identifies semantic relationships and creates the mapping between the schema and related rules.

Conclusion and Future Work

In summary, we have proposed OABIS, an ontology-based approach to create dynamic mappings between business rules and local database schemas. We believe our approach benefits the business expert and the data analysts in different ways: (1) instead of forcing business expert to formulate business rules according to an existing information model, they use terms that are familiar to them and then map the business terms to the elements in a supply-chain ontology; (2) when a local information source is added to the supply chain, the database analyst simply maps the local schema to the ontology, eliminating the need to learn details about the rest of the system.

The limitation of our approach lies in that some human intervention is still required when we create schema-ontology and rules-ontology mappings. Therefore, in ongoing research, we are investigating techniques to create automated mappings via agent negotiations. In addition, we are conducting a case study to document the benefits of our approach.

References

Arens, Y., Hsu, C., & Knoblock, C. (1996). Query processing in the SIMS information mediator. In M. Huhns & M. Singh (Eds.) *Readings in agents* (pp. 82-90) San Francisco: Morgan Kaufmann

Bajec, M., & Krisper, M. (2005). A methodology and tool support for managing business rules in organizations. *Information Systems, 30*, 423-443.

Bergamaschi, S., Castano, S., De Capitani di Vimercati, S., Montanari, S., & Vincini, M. (1998). An intelligent approach to information integration. In N. Guarino

(Ed.) *Proceedings of the 1ˢᵗ International Conference on Formal Ontology in Information Systems (FOIS 1998)*, Trento, Italy (pp. 253-267). IOS Press.

Bergamaschi, S., Castano, S., Vincini, M. Beneventano, D. (2001). Semantic integration of heterogeneous information sources. *Data and Knowledge Engineering, 36*(3), 215-249.

Business Rule Group, The. (2000). *Defining business rules—what are they really?* Published by author.

Chen, P. (1976). The entity-relationship model—toward a unified view of data. *ACM Transaction of Database Systems, 1*(1), 9-36.

Date, C. J. (2000). *What not how—the business rules approach to application development*, Addison-Wesley.

Fayez, M., Rabelo, L., Mollaghasemi, M. (2005). Ontologies for supply chain simulation modeling. In M. Kuhl, N. Steiger, F. Armstrong, & J. Joines (Eds.) *Proceedings of the Winter Simulation Conference* (pp. 2364-2370). Monterey, CA. Dec 4-7, 2005.

Frankovic, B., Budinska, I., & Dang, T. (2003, February 12-14). Ontological framework for supply chain modeling and management. In *Proceedings of 1ˢᵗ Slovakian-Hungarian Joint Symposium on Applied Machine Intelligence. (SAMI 2003)*, Herlany, Slovakia (pp. 131-138).

Gruber, T. (1995). Toward principles for the design of ontologies used for knowledge sharing. In N. Guarino & R. Poli (Eds.), *Formal ontology in conceptual analysis and knowledge representation.* Kluwer Academic Publishers.

Halpin, T. (2001). *Information modeling and relational databases: From conceptual analysis to logical design.* Morgan Kaufmann.

He, Q., & Ling, T. W. (2006). An ontology based approach to the integration of entity-relationship schemas. *Data and Knowledge Engineering, 58*(3). 299-326.

Herbst, H. (1996). Business rules in systems analysis: A meta-model and repository system. *Information Systems, 21*(2), 147-166.

Herbst, H. (1997). *Business rule-oriented conceptual modeling.* Heidelberg: Physica-Verlag; New York: Springer Verlag.

Kardasis, P., & Loucopoulos, P. (2004). Expressing and organizing business rules. *Information and Software Technology, 46*, 701-718.

Mena, E., Kashyap, V., Sheth, A., & Illarramendi, A. (2000). OBSERVER: An approach for query processing in global information systems based on interoperation across pre-existing ontologies. *International Journal on Distributed and Parallel Databases, 8*(2), 223-271.

Motiwalla, L., Khan, M. R., & Xu, S. (2005). An intra- and inter-industry analysis of e-business effectiveness. *Information & Management, 42*(5), 651-667.

Ouksel, A., & Ahmed, L. (1999). Ontologies are not the panacea in data integration: A flexible coordinator to mediate context construction. *Distributed and Parallel Databases, 7*(1), 7-35.

Ram, S. (1995). Intelligent database design using the unifying semantic model. *Information and Management, 29*(4), 191-206.

Ram, S., & Khatri, V. (2005). A comprehensive framework for modeling set-based business rules during conceptual database design. *Information Systems, 30*(2), 89-118.

Ram, S., & Liu, J. (2005, January). An agent based approach for sourcing business rules in supply chain management. *International Journal of Intelligent Information Technologies 1*(1), 1-16.

Ram, S., & Park, J. (2004). Semantic conflict resolution ontology (SCROL): An ontology for detecting and resolving data and schema-level semantic conflicts. *IEEE Transactions on Knowledge and Data Engineering, 16*(2), 189-202.

Ram, S., Park, J., & Ball, G. (1999). Semantic-model support for geographic information systems. *IEEE Computer, 32*(5), 74-81.

Rosca, D., & Greenspan, S. (2002). Enterprise modeling and decision-support for automating the business rules lifecycle. *Automated Software Engineering, 9*, 361-404.

Rosca, D., & Wild, C. (2002). Towards a flexible deployment of business rules. *Expert Systems with Applications, 22*, 385-394.

Ross, R. (1997). *The business rule book: Business rule solutions.* Boston: Database Research Group.

Shao, J., & Pound, C. J. (1999). Extracting business rules from information systems. *BT Technology Journal, 17*(4), 179-186.

Sowa, J. (1999). *Knowledge representation: Logical, philosophical, and computational foundations.* New York: PWS Publishing Co.

Von Halle, B. (2001). *Business rules applied.* Wiley & Sons.

Chapter II

Evolution and Mutation in Push Technologies:
Social Concerns Resulting from the Effects of Memes on Intelligent Agents

Julie E. Kendall, Rutgers University, USA

Kenneth E. Kendall, Rutgers University, USA

Abstract

PointCast was a magic carpet of content providers. Imagine that of all the information that users needed to complete their work would suddenly appear on their desktops. Although PointCast and other technologies did not survive the hype that surrounded their introduction, push technologies are now back in vogue. RSS feeds and podcasts are now part of many people's daily lives. Software robots, called autonomous agents, are helping users download what they want from the Internet. The next helpful software agent will be more akin to a butler who anticipates all of the user's needs today, tomorrow, and in the future. This agent will change as the user changes and is therefore referred to as an evolutionary agent. Evolutionary agents will also change because memes (or messages) one agent broadcasts to another will cause the evolutionary agent to mutate. In this chapter, we explore the social implications of meritorious and malevolent memes exchanged by evolutionary agents. We also discover that interactions occur among humans, evolutionary agents, and memes. Finally, we raise a series of questions for future research regarding genetic determination of evolutionary agents; if it is possible to predict whether a meme will be meritorious or malevolent; and whether it is desirable to legislate the evolution of agents that are evolved from malevolent memes. This chapter contributes to the awareness of the movement toward push technologies deploying evolutionary agents and the social implications their use entails.

Introduction

First, there was PointCast. PointCast was computer software that delivered news, weather, and other content. It was introduced with great fanfare, hyperbole, and enthusiasm. Some authors went so far in their predictions about the supremacy of PointCast and other push technologies as to declare that Web browsers had been made obsolete (Wolf, 2004).

PointCast was touted to be a great idea, but after rejecting an offer of $350 million from Rupert Murdoch's News Corp., PointCast soon disappeared. Users ignored it, and many universities and corporations banned it because it ate up too much bandwidth. Perhaps they were worried that reading all the pushed content would result in nonproductive time as well. One of the problems with PointCast was that a user could download channels, but not individual stories. It was not capable of searching effectively for keywords.

In the late 1990s, push technologies were actually proclaimed to be dead by many research and popular-press authors (Pflug, 1997). Others said that there was simply a lack of quality content (Bing, 1997) while, at the same time other authors were blaming the failure on providers offering too much content (Cronin, 1997). Still another researcher stated publicly that Webcasting at Apple was little more than Webcasting as an Infomercial to promote their own software and hardware (Johnson, 1997a). For a complete discussion and classification of push technologies see Kendall and Kendall (1999).

The advent of new techniques like RSS readers and podcasting seems like a revolution, but both had roots in PointCast and other push-delivery systems. On many Web sites, orange buttons, marked XML (or sometimes RSS) indicate that users can subscribe to a new type of push technology called RSS, which stands for really simple syndication. What RSS does is help the provider package the information along with the date, title, and link, so it can be easily put in a standard format and quickly downloaded as well (now at rapid, broadband speeds). Once it arrives, it can be read with an RSS reader.

This approach calls for some cooperation from content providers. They need to develop feeds that are used for syndication. In this way, each user has the opportunity to specifically choose the feeds (also called channels) they want to watch. In Web-based push systems, intelligent agents typically are used to filter out or personalize messages that may not be appropriate. Agents allow a user to set up a profile, something that makes it easier to screen out unwanted content. Profiles work because the user is asked to set up predetermined criteria.

Autonomous agents are those agents that act on their own without immediate, direct input from users. An agent, for example can fill in new profile details for the user based on what the user has done in the past. An example of a simple autonomous agent is TiVo, the box that automatically records television programs it "thinks" the viewer would like to watch. Agents can change as well. Agents that change based on what they observe about a user's behavior are called evolutionary agents (Kendall, 1996).

In this chapter, we explore how evolutionary agents can and often do change, what it means to change, and identify potential consequences if evolutionary agents mutate. In this chapter, we introduce the concept of memes, or messages that evolutionary agents use to communicate with each other. We then explain how they influence evolutionary agents into mutating into another form. The discussion then centers on the social consequences of good (meritorious) and bad (malevolent) memes. Finally, we suggest what will happen in the future generations of evolutionary agents and memes and their impact on humans.

Autonomous Agents Facilitate Delivery of User *Wants*

In push technologies, information can be delivered to users in many ways. At one end of the spectrum, there is broadcasting, where no attempt is made to distinguish among potential recipients. An example of this is updating virus signatures. As long as a user's subscription is active, the user gets the same information other users receive. Another type of push technology (Kendall & Kendall, 1999) delivers only the content that users think they want. By selecting channels and keywords, the user can receive only the information they desire.

A third type of push technology uses an autonomous agent, a software robot of sorts, to deliver the information users actually want. Autonomous agents often develop their rules with user profiles, data mining, and recommendation systems. An example of a user profile is an instruction to "always try to get an aisle seat on an airplane." Data mining (Codd, 1995; Gray & Watson, 1998; Watson & Haley, 1997) may be used to predict a user's preference based on a user's history. Collaborative filtering and recommendation systems are often used to suggest content, such as a list of books a user might want to purchase (Stohr & Viswanathan, 1999). Autonomous agents therefore find cheaper airfares, worthwhile books to purchase, software to support current decisions, stock tips, and other opportunities. Autonomous agents try to match up the content the push provider wants to send with what it believes the user wants to receive. This assumes that an agent can actually *know* what the user wants.

Evolutionary Agents Facilitate Delivery of User *Needs*

In the last section, we discussed the autonomous agent. Still another type of push technology will soon allow the user to appoint a different type of agent that will seek out and deliver only the information the user actually needs. This may be significantly different from what the user wants. A user may not think that he or she needs information that an agent will discover. Furthermore, a user may want something, but not need it to make the decision at hand.

Evolutionary agents facilitate the delivery of content by first observing the behavior of an individual over time. The evolutionary agent then notices not only those

Figure 1. Evolutionary agents approach analysis and design differently from autonomous agents

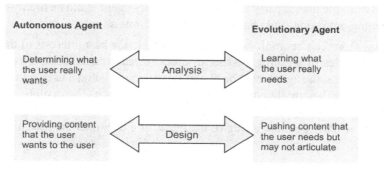

patterns observed by the autonomous agent but, in addition, the changes in these patterns. After all, individuals can and do change. Education transforms their thinking, opinions of friends and family affect their thinking, and random events change a person's attitude. Individuals may also be recruited or even evangelized so that they see everything in a new light. Evolutionary agents will monitor these changes and act in view of that. Evolutionary agents deliver what the user *needs*, not merely what the user *wants*. Another way to explain the difference between an autonomous agent and an evolutionary agent is to examine what each agent does in the analysis and design phases as shown in Figure 1.

Evolutionary agents are continually monitoring the user. While considered to be spyware to some, the evolutionary agent observes what the user has been doing so it can evolve based on the Web pages the user has just visited, the time spent on each page, and the number of times the page is revisited. It will share the results with other agents and then these agents will be allowed to evolve based on how other agents judge the results. You may have noticed that search engines already assign relevance ratings.

Advances in the study of genetic agents in artificial intelligence make this a reality. Evolutionary agents can and do change spontaneously. An entire generation can occur each time the user visits another Web site to make a purchase, accepts a EULA, or even signs up for a free newsletter.

One advantage of an evolutionary agent is that it can possess the foresight to protect a user from seeing what a user may not want to see (Kendall, 1996). An intelligent agent can be more effective in screening out pornography, for example, than software that uses a blacklist approach. Just as data mining tries to screen out information about products that users have no intention of buying, evolutionary agents can screen out information not needed for a decision. This can be viewed as an improvement.

This means that certain topics or philosophies can be filtered out as well. If a liberal prefers not to be bombarded with conservative viewpoints, the agent can recognize this and protect the user. The same can be said for the conservative who wants to be shielded from the liberal party line. An evolutionary agent could be highly effective in screening out propaganda harboring a particular bias.

Shielding a user can be ironic because it might be in the best interests of the person to see *both* sides of a political issue. In order to really understand what the user needs, not wants, the agent must be evolutionary, sensing that a user actually needs a political view they might not normally seek on their own. The evolutionary agent becomes a personal butler that is concerned about the user to such a degree that the agent may actually be more aware of the needs of a user than the user himself.

Figure 2. Three key differences between evolutionary agents and autonomous agents emphasize how evolutionary agents change

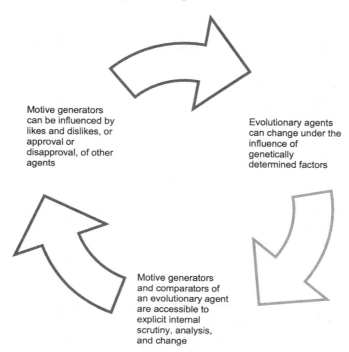

Motive generators can be influenced by likes and dislikes, or approval or disapproval, of other agents

Evolutionary agents can change under the influence of genetically determined factors

Motive generators and comparators of an evolutionary agent are accessible to explicit internal scrutiny, analysis, and change

Agents Rely on Memes to Evolve

Autonomous and evolutionary agents manifest three differences that are essential when designing evolutionary agents. By examining the differences, we can see clearly how evolutionary agents change. These differences include (1) evolutionary agents can change and do so when influenced by genetically determined factors (2) an evolutionary agent contains motive generators and comparators that are accessible to explicit internal scrutiny, analysis, and change and (3) other agents can influence the motive generators via their likes and dislikes, or approval or disapproval, of other agents.

Examining the first principle listed, we see that it implies that based on a prepro-grammed set of rules or instructions, an agent can change of its own accord. The

Figure 3. Brodie (1996) identifies four types of memes

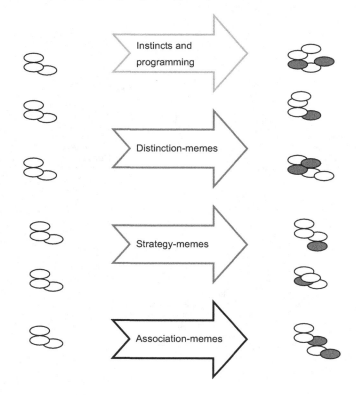

second difference implies that an agent can change via some kind of self-examination. Also, it can be seen that this suggests that an agent can evolve in response to information it receives or judgments originating from external sources. Other agents are the most probable source of this information.

In order for these evolutionary agents to dramatically alter their behavior, a message must be sent to the agent. In this section, we explore a particular kind of message, called a meme, that one agent broadcasts to another.

Memes are messages that make their ways into minds, and then from there, they can influence subsequent occurrences. In this instance, we are discussing the mind of an evolutionary agent. Memes make duplicates, or copies of themselves, and thus perpetuatually enter into an increasing number of different minds. In this case, an analogy can be built between a meme and an elementary form of a virus.

Memory aids and memory traps can all be part of a meme. Humans are susceptible to memes such as rhymes, advertising jingles, catchy tunes or phrases, marketing slogans, and so on. Infectious ideas are also present in memes, making the possibility of exposure to danger startlingly quite clear.

A meme that spreads easily from mind to mind can be considered a successful one. A meme was characterized as a "virus of the mind" (Brodie, 1996, p. 36) that influences the behavior of people infected with the meme in a clever way, such that they help to perpetuate the virus.

Four types of memes distinguished by Brodie (1996) include: (1) instincts and programming; (2) distinction-memes; (3) strategy-memes and (4) association-memes (pp. 40-44). Reflecting on the four types of memes, some stand out as essential for survival, while some are necessary for spurring us on to career and lifelong success. One can see that the combining of instincts and programming is an unfortunate characterization, since the essences dividing them are wide.

For example, some of the functions that we would classify as "instincts," those not consciously controlled (those controlled by the autonomic system), are inborn behavior for living creatures. Therefore, as infants we do not learn to breathe, to digest, or to perspire, we are already able to do so. All creatures exhibit instinctual behaviors such as salmon swimming upstream to spawn, birds flying south for the winter and so on.

Distinction is easily drawn between inborn behaviors and those that are learned, such as touching our hand to a hot burner on a lighted stove and then pulling it away rapidly in response to the pain. The lesson learned is actionable; we will not put our hand on a hot burner again. By contrast, programming is something we are taught or teach ourselves. It is not inborn to us.

On the next level up, distinction-memes serve useful functions, helping us to classify, categorize, organize, and label things. This level is elevated in sophistication in comparison to the foregoing classification of instincts and programming memes. Further, not every animal is capable of using distinction memes.

Strategy-memes are still further up the hierarchy of order and thought. Memes at this level assist in accomplishing complex activities such as driving an automobile. Fortunately, employing strategy-memes means that we do not have to learn how to drive every time we sit down behind the wheel. As a driver, we remember some strategy-memes that serve to organize our thoughts around how to drive safely (the memes tell us some driving techniques are better than others) and we are able to successfully navigate our way out of the car park.

On the highest level are association-memes, which are memes serving to link two or more memes together. A familiar fragrance can bring back a powerful memory of a person, place, season, or event in an onslaught of remembrance. Each individual possesses his or her own group of linkages. Many critics decry the way advertisers attempt to link memes together, often trying to link sex with their products, for instance.

While Brodie equates memes with "viruses of the mind," it is worthwhile to raise the question of whether there is truly a distinction between memes and viruses. If a distinction cannot be made, then our discussion could conceivably focus on viruses alone.

A virus can be defined as something that follows a predetermined series of instructions that then employs an external copy machine to enable it to make copies of itself. In the computing world, the term "virus" carries a connotation of something that is vicious or evil. In a familiar example, a computer virus is defined as a program that is designed to produce copies of itself on other computers.

One can reason that a meme can mutate, either in a good way or a bad way, and replicate itself without the external copying mechanism. An evolutionary agent possesses this basic characteristic.

However, evolution is not complete with replication alone. Rather, evolution requires both replication and innovation. Innovation is a positive characterization of mutation, and the concept of evolution has a powerfully positive connotation in its own right.

Considered in the Darwinian conceptualization, evolution deals directly with the concept of "fitness," as understood by the phrase "survival of the fittest." Extending these concepts, Dawkins (1987) introduces the idea of the "selfish gene." He asserts that evolution occurs because it is in the interest of a gene and its well-being, not our well-being.

Analogous to the changes occurring in a species responding to an upward trend in climate temperature, a meme typically depends on a stimulus to further evolve. Memes evolve due to responses to a crisis, to a problem, to a danger or even due to an opportunity that is posed. On the other hand, memes could evolve because of self-examination or observations of likes and dislikes. The approbation or disapproval registered by external judges can also serve as a spur to evolution. An evolutionary agent might react to other evolutionary agents and thus evolve because of that reaction.

Memes and Web-Based Agents

Advertisers sponsor Webcasts using memes in push technology to devise memorable songs, ideas, and slogans that resonate and reside with users of the medium at least long enough for them to purchase a product or service that has been encoded in a particular meme. Web agents can use memes to mutate and viruses to replicate and spread content. Successful reproduction of messages can alter behavior in a way that a push provider (such as an advertiser, a politician, or a proponent of a social movement) desires.

It is useful to think of higher forms of push technologies (such as the delta-push technologies described by Kendall & Kendall, 1999) as evolving memes. Preparing widely dispersed segments of a native population for an impending natural disaster such as a tsunami is an example of an advantageous use of evolutionary agents passing memes. There are other serious social uses of evolutionary agents that call for a concentrated effort in response to a momentous, rapidly changing, problem domain that are worth considering. Mounting a concentrated effort for solving a potentially widespread urban transportation strike; or unifying factions in looking for a common solution to a violent, escalating conflict within a short period might also prove to be worthwhile uses of agents.

Over time, and as evolutionary agents evolve, they will accomplish an increasing amount of work, taking over chores that were often drudgery to those tasked with them. For example, evolutionary agents surfing the Web can make finding the cheapest airfare, retrieving the time of the football match next Saturday, or locating a spare part to repair an ageing automobile a brief foray onto the Web, rather than a long, frustrating journey replete with broken links and irrelevant results.

Reid (1996) describes this use of specific, evolutionary pull technology versus ineffective push technology this way:

> The efficiency of pushed channel misses, priced-out content, and available-but-not ubiquitous pushed information can be reduced by placing content on a shelf from which anybody can pull it. ...The Web is precisely that shelf, its audience's interests in it becomes its distributor, and the frictionless ether its channel. (p. 11)

Memes can embody either meritorious or malevolent values. Memes originally thought to be meritorious, may be revealed as evil later on. One example of this type of revelation is when a person programs their mind, psychologically investing in a specific political agenda, only to become gradually wakened to the fact that the politics involved are odious. Propaganda memes exemplified here can be utterly destructive of a person's beliefs and ultimately their value system.

The familiar tale of the sorcerer's apprentice is a handy illustration of what happens when push technologies replicate harmful memes without controls in place. The apprentice is empowered to command an intelligent agent (an enchanted broom) to perform a specific action (filling a cistern). The broom obligingly continues its actions, sans feedback, and unrestrained until the water carried can flood a room.

In this tale, the agent's dogged repetition of the task finally means that the outcome of engaging with the technology will be detrimental.

Users can become infected with malevolent memes in many ways. These include a type of conditioning, wherein they customarily interact with push information systems such as monthly newsletters, or by innocently choosing to pull apparently "useful" concepts or ideas from the Web, only to encounter a Trojan horse. Memes can spread by casually pushing a message to another user, or by using an attractive site to pull the user there for purposes of evangelization.

Meritorious Memes

Responses to evolutionary agents will vary. Many users will view evolutionary agents positively, as saviors, since they will deliver only what a user needs. While users condemn the tyranny of information overload, often in the unwelcome form of spam in their e-mail inbox, they paradoxically thirst for ever more information by searching the Web. Characterizing this apparent contradiction even before the age of the Web, Heim (1993, p. 17) states, "With a mind-set fixed on information, our attention span shortens. We collect fragments. We become mentally poorer in overall meaning."

Evolutionary agents might be able to rescue users from the great amount of unwanted information. Perhaps meritorious memes will succeed and individuals will be spared of useless information. Reid (1996) reminds us that:

> *All pushed information inevitably reaches many people who just aren't interested in it. Consider the Sunday newspaper...The many misses of pushed communication mean that every spot on hit is expensive to reach, and this expense prices a tremendous amount of would-be content out of the distribution channel.* (p. 10)

Reid has also characterized the steady barrage of broadcast information (minus customization or personalization) as a "wasted expression." Evolutionary agents bearing meritorious memes sensitive to user information needs and mindful of the disposition of overloaded users may win out.

Malevolent Memes

As we reflect on the nature of memes, we recall that they are a basic unit of cultural transmission or imitation (Dawkins, 1987, p. 27). Memes can run the gamut from malevolent to meritorious or anything in between. The virus, or virtual copy machine, is imperfect, which means that mutations occur and the copy is modified. It is only fair to observe that mutations can improve a meme or make it defective. The key point is that neither the meme nor the virus is perfect. Problems arise because the content and process involved in memes is not pure in heart and the virus reproduces memes imperfectly.

The danger is clear. Memes can be destructive. Push technologies can be characterized by examining what happens when evolutionary agents of the future push memes that mutate, affecting and infecting other agents, other users, corporations and societies that are susceptible, with no available remedy to mitigate the power of the destructive meme. An unsettling scenario would depict an evolutionary agent that spawned a malevolent meme bearing sectarian hatred, directly inflaming a group's passions to the point of war, rising against multiple targets, perhaps even brutally turning on its own citizens in a paroxysm of hate.

Push technologies using evolutionary agents may create messages, and the situations for reception of those messages, that are so engaging that they effectively eradicate all other memes or even all other forms of thinking. Many authors believe that extreme cases of malevolent memes can result in "social fragmentation and the production of incompatible social segments" (Marshall, 1998, p.4).

It is worth considering tactical as well as strategic approaches to remedying problems with malevolent memes. Remedies can be fashioned that create a culture of awareness of the effects, attributes, problems, and responsibilities inherent in the deployment of evolutionary agents via push technology. We recommend that individuals and organizations start small, and work on many tangible problems, the artful solving of which will demonstrate tangible results and help bring to light the possibilities available for tackling larger themes. As adoption of remedies and resolutions become more widespread, they can also be centrally funded.

Society can address the experiences of users unaccustomed to advanced, evolutionary agents that push memes, whether they are good or evil. Approaches include underscoring the value of such technology along with cultural education to help reframe users' perceptions of how information technology is revolutionizing the entire society (Kendall & Kendall, 2000).

In order to alleviate the worrisome aspects of push technologies society should cultivate greater understanding of and appreciation of the current culture. Postman (1985) states:

> *To be unaware that a technology comes equipped with a program for social change, to maintain that technology is neutral, to make the assumption that technology is always a friend to culture, is, at this late hour, stupidity plain and simple.* (p. 157)

Another researcher describes the problem as that of curtailing user control without a giveback of linear narrative found in the content and technology of traditional broadcasting (Johnson, 1997b). Put another way, push technology, including evolutionary agents, are ubiquitous, but they are not disruptive of routine tasks. Therefore, technologies can sit on a "desktop;" where they are superficially present, but they are not engaging the user with a narrative structure.

Indeed, the very ubiquity of push media means that their capacity for good story telling is diminished. Persuasive sources point to the importance of narrative in all we do, for all human beings, including adults. For more reflections on the adoption of new push technologies and how they might affect narrative structure in organizations, see Kendall and Kendall (1995).

Proper education is a second potential remedy. All users need to know about the design, use, and impacts of evolutionary agents in push technology. Educating them regarding how the adoption and use of new media will change the structure of our discourse is vital. Decision makers in corporations and other organizational users should be among the first to be educated about the importance of balance when using new media.

Current providers of push content also require education on the impacts of evolutionary agents. Once versed in the power of memes, they will grasp how essential it is to push coherent stories that coalesce in a meaningful way, rather than leaving scattered shards of information at the bottom of a newscast or carelessly strewn on the side of a graphic.

Conclusion

We introduced the concept of evolutionary agents embedded in push technologies that are capable of rapid evolution. We highlighted some of the key differences between autonomous and evolutionary agents. Evolutionary agents have indeed arrived and are being embraced by designers of push technologies and content providers. Evolutionary agents are here to stay.

Evolutionary agents evolve by their encounters with messages they exchange with other agents. Messages can also be called memes. Recall that memes were defined as a basic unit of cultural transmission or imitation. Memes can be either meritorious or malevolent.

It may be useful to redefine the memes that evolutionary agents exchange, so that they can in turn become highly relevant to managers encountering them in their push systems. It is this aspect of emblematic usefulness along with the capacity for *both* human and machine control that is one of the most important implications of memes for managers and how they work.

According to Lissack (2004):

> *If an environmental niche has an important managerial role, paying attention to its symbols and affordances can also be important. Memes are stripped of their casual role and instead become semantic tokens capable of evoking ascribed meanings. It is the process of evoking and the efficacy of the meme as the trigger for attention, recall, and petition of the ascribed meaning that gives memes relevance to managers.* (p. 2)

The nature of memes translates into a phenomenon that does not work within traditional lines of authority and responsibility. (These have typically been the building blocks of analysis for this type of study.) Instead, we note that memes permeate what seems impermeable, running freely across well-entrenched boundaries, making new acquaintances, rudely intruding on others.

Humans require the skill to retain the possibility of control of memes that could easily mutate out of control. Hence, the law of requisite variety, familiar from general systems theory, is well remembered by those designers developing evolutionary agents. That is, for every way for a meme to go out of control, there must be an equal number of ways to control it. These can and should consist of both human- and machine-centered approaches.

Indeed the most potent combination for a solution would be one that takes advantage of both human and machine capabilities to stop a malevolent mutation of a meme from spreading. The intelligent agent may, after all, know best, but the human is the one being served through most of their interactions with the evolutionary agent, and not vice versa.

In the final section, we suggest fruitful research directions as well as featuring pressing research questions arising out of the advent of evolutionary agents and the memes that they exchange via push technologies in a social setting.

Future Research Directions

Many research questions remain. The fields of push technologies, evolutionary agents, and memes are still in their infancy. Developers continue creating push technologies at a surprising rate. New generations of users, citizens and leaders of developing countries, and many other people who have not previously had access to push technologies will be coming on board in ever increasing numbers, at an ever-increasing rate for the near future.

Other researchers will want to study these questions using both quantitative and qualitative methods. The complexity, breadth, and gravity of several of the ethical and social issues surrounding push technologies, evolutionary agents, memes, and new populations of users signal the necessity of a systematic, interdisciplinary, and reasoned approach to their study. As our push technologies increase, the quality of our methods to study them, and the rate at which we do so, must both improve concomitantly. It would be a serious error to address these topics without adopting novel approaches to meet the increased rapidity of their introduction.

How can one tell whether a meme is meritorious or malevolent? A corollary of this question is: How can one tell the difference between them? Both of these questions deserve reflection and research.

Can one predict whether a meme will evolve into either a meritorious or malevolent meme? Answering this question will be important, since the answer will also help inform the question of whether one can control the evolution of memes, or whether this will be random.

In our chapter, we identified three key design elements of evolutionary agents. We need to determine how much of an evolutionary agent's behavior is genetically determined. How much does the evolution of an intelligent agent depend on its original design?

How much should the evolution of evolutionary agents depend on internal scrutiny, analysis, and change? Moreover, how much does their evolution depend, instead, on their interaction with other evolutionary agents?

Problems of spam and e-mail provide the basis for some further research questions about memes and evolutionary agents. Humans are currently invoking unwanted spam and viruses. We can create legislation that stops humans from doing this, but what will happen when evolutionary agents create spam? Can we stop them from evolving with malevolent memes? Is it desirable or even possible to pass legislation to control the evolution of memes and evolutionary agents? What will happen if an evil evolutionary agent arrives cloaked as a friendly agent? The severity of the problem then escalates and our abilities to cope are taxed.

There are many important research directions to pursue in examining the relationships of evolutionary agents, push technologies, and memes to society. The challenge is to respond rapidly yet wisely to their ever-burgeoning ranks.

References

Bing, M. (1997). Implementing Webcasting as a communication tool. *Database, 20*(6), 42-44.

Brodie, R. (1996). *Virus of the mind.* Seattle, WA: Integral Press.

Codd, E. F. (1995, April 13). Twelve rules for on-line analytic processing. *Computerworld,* 84-87.

Cronin, M. (1997, September 29). Using the Web to push key data to decision makers. *Fortune, 136*(6), 254.

Dawkins, R. (1987). *The blind watchmaker: Why the evidence reveals a universe without design.* New York: W. W. Norton & Company, Inc.

Gray, P., & Watson, H. J. (1998). *Decision support in the data warehouse.* Upper Saddle River, NJ: Prentice Hall.

Heim, M. (1993). *The metaphysics of virtual reality.* New York: Oxford University Press.

Johnson, M. R. (1997a). *Part 6: Webcasting as event reproduction.* Webcasting: What is it and what should it be? Retrieved March 4, 2006, from http://www.mindspring.com/~cityzoo/mjohnson/papers/webcasting/event_reproduction.html

Johnson, M. R. (1997b). *Part 1: Introduction.* Webcasting: What is it and what should it be? Retrieved March 4, 2006, from http://www.mindspring.com/~cityzoo/mjohnson/papers/webcasting/introduction.html

Kendall, J. E., & Kendall, K. E. (1995, June). The impact of using hypertext-based information systems on organizational narrative: Changing the structure of stories. In D. M. Olson (Ed.), *Proceedings of the Third International Meeting of the Decision Sciences Institute,* Puebla, Mexico.

Kendall, J. E., & Kendall, K. E. (1999, April 23). Information delivery systems: An exploration of Web push and pull technologies, with K. E. Kendall. *Communications of AIS, 1,* Article 14.

Kendall, J. E., & Kendall K. E. (2000). Individual, organizational, and societal perspectives on information delivery systems: Bright and dark sides to push and pull technologies. In R. Baskerville, J. Stage, & J. I. DeGross (Eds.), *IS2000: The Social and Organizational Perspective on Research and Practice in Information Technology* (pp. 179-193). Boston: Kluwer Academic Publishers.

Kendall, K. (1996, Fall). Artificial intelligence and Götterdämerung: The evolutionary paradigm of the future. *The DATA BASE for Advances in Information Systems, 27*(4), 99-115.

Lissack, M. R. (2004). The redefinition of memes: Ascribing meaning to an empty cliché. *Journal of Memetics—Evolutionary Models of Information Transmission, 8*(1). Retrieved July 8, 2004, from http://jom-emit.cfpm.org/2004/vol8/lissack_mr.html

Marshall, G. (1998). *The Internet and memetics.* Retrieved February 27, 2006, from http://pespmc1.vub.ac.be/Conf/MemePap/Marshall.html

Pflug, O. (1997, January). Push technology: Dead on arrival. *Computerworld, 31*(4), 37.

Postman, N. (1985). *Amusing ourselves to death: Public discourse in the age of show business.* New York: Penguin Books.

Reid, R. H. (1996). *Architects of the Web: 1,000 days that built the future of business.* New York: John Wiley & Sons, Inc.

Stohr, E. A., & Viswanathan, S. (1999). Recommendation systems: Decision support for the information economy. In K. E. Kendall (Ed.), *Emerging information technologies: Improving decisions, cooperation, and infrastructure* (pp. 21-44). Thousand Oaks, CA: SAGE Publications, Inc.

Watson, H. J., & Haley, B. (1997). A framework for data warehousing. *Data Warehousing Journal, 2*(1), 10-17.

Wolf, G. (2004, May). Bye-bye, browsers: Push media is back! *Wired, 12*(05), 34.

Chapter III

Approaches and Tools to Optimize and Manage Clinical Processes

Rainer Herrler, University of Würzburg, Germany

Christian Heine, University of Hohenheim, Germany

Abstract

There are several continuing challenges within the health-care domain. On the one hand, there is a greater need for individualized, patient-oriented processes in diagnostics, therapy, nursing, and administration; and on the other hand, hospitals have extremely distributed decision processes and strong local (individual) autonomy with a high degree of situational dynamics. This research focuses on how to optimize processes in hospitals by using agent-based simulation and agent-based information systems that can substantially increase the efficiency of hospital process management. In particular, we describe a methodology for optimization; the ingredients of the simulation and the architecture of a management system; and the integration of existing FIPA, DICOM, and HL7 standards. We discuss example scenarios to show how simulation can improve distributed scheduling and how agent-based systems can be used to manage "clinical trials." This research is part of the German Priority Research Program (SPP) 1083 "Intelligent Agents and their application in business scenarios."

Introduction

Over the last few years, the cost of health services in Germany has become an important area of economic analysis. The budget for German health care increased to €239 Billion during the year, 2003 and there is a constant growth of 5-10 % every year (see Figure 1). Thus, the current expense of health care is forcing the German government to take a closer look at the macroeconomic cost structures within this industry and find new ways to minimize the overall cost. Information technology is expected to play a major role in the reduction of expenses and the stabilization of health-care budgets. With a view to curb expenditure , the biggest IT project for German health care was recently started, which has introduced a new electronic eHealth-Card. One of the major problems that needs to be addressed is hospital logistics, which is rather complex and highly distributed. Efficient patient logistics in hospitals can reduce patient stay time in hospitals, optimizing load of medical devices and thus reducing treatment costs. Considerable research is underway in this area, which is designed to analyze the domain as well as to develop software systems, particularly for management and control of information flows and business processes. The approaches to this domain are two-fold. On the one hand, simulation systems are used for analyzing the domain, planning, and re-engineering of business processes. On the other hand, development of management and control systems for information flow and business processes is of interest. The increasing importance of information systems is interlinked with specifics of the (German) health-care domain—such as highly fragmented, disparate professional groups—which complicates or particularly blocks the integration of innovative service processes as well as new and more efficient information systems.

Several important questions have been examined by the German Priority Research Program (SPP 1083) since 2000. The main goal of SPP 1083 is to investigate the utilization of agent technologies within large realistic business scenarios and

Figure 1. Development of health-care costs in Germany (Federal Statistical Office)

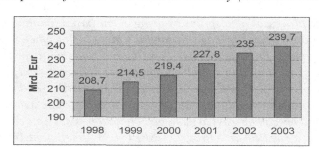

the identification of further research needs. Basic supposition of the SPP is that agent-based development and connection of decentralized information systems generates important benefits by supporting interorganizational business processes and organizational flexibility. Examination of these hypotheses is supported by the development of large agent-based software systems.

In this chapter, we introduce the essential questions, the research approach and results of the project "ADAPT," which is part of the previously mentioned SPP 1083. We discuss the systems developed for simulation and application and their integration into the large Agent.Hospital Framework. In addition, we address questions on how to realize large-scale agent-based distributed service networks that support health-care standards like HL7 or DICOM. An example scenario in the "Clinical Trials" section illustrates our approach. At the end of the chapter, we discuss the shortcomings and give an outlook on further research steps and implementation activities.

Research Problem and Main Objectives

The overall objective of our research is to substantially increase the efficiency of hospital processes. The main problem in optimization is that the processes as well as the systems are inherently distributed and the effects of changes are difficult to foresee. Under these circumstances, agent technology is the appropriate solution. Optimization by agents can be reached in two ways: (1) optimization potential can be identified by agent-based simulation experiments, and (2) flexible agent-based information systems can optimize the real system. Integrating both of these components, simulation models can be used as a test bed for the development of agent applications. Our empirical studies have identified the following critical success factors that help achieve the objectives of being able to optimize the system:

- Completeness and topicality of information available to (human) actors
- Knowledge about the actual patient status helps trigger other changes
- Adequate representation of the variety and the dynamics of inter-/intraprocess interactions

Based on our experience, we contend that a lot of domain knowledge and interdependencies are necessary to create an appropriate agent-based system. On the other hand, even more knowledge would be needed by conventional information systems. The adaptive abilities of agents allow dealing with even uncertain conditions and distributed knowledge.

In cooperation with the clinical partners, the ADAPT project (Heine, Herrler, Petsch, & Anhalt, 2003) tried to optimize the processes as well as the information flow between the participating oncology and radiation-therapy departments. Because of this, resource allocation, time scheduling, and tactical planning should improve with respect to efficiency and control. The experiences gained should allow us to draw conclusions about the usability as well as the advantages of agent-based software. The specific motives and goals of this research are:

- **Improvement of distributed appointment scheduling:** Appointment scheduling for treatment and examination tasks in hospitals is inherently distributed between various organizational units and there are many interdependencies between the processes and the actors. This fact makes it very difficult to determine the effects of single improvement actions and to optimize the process. Patient scheduling in general practice is mainly dominated by manual negotiation and simple ad hoc solutions that are suboptimal and can be optimized. Therefore, one aim of the ADAPT project was to create a powerful simulation tool that is capable of depicting various hospital scenarios in a kind of virtual hospital. Using this simulation environment the clinical management is able to make experiments for proving optimization ideas and finally to improve scheduling and coordination of patients, medical staff, and equipment.

- **Support for decisions about participation in clinical trials:** Clinical trials obligate the participating hospitals to perform prescribed treatments and examinations. As one of the benefits, the cost calculation should show whether the incurred liabilities are covered or not. According to this, the ADAPT system should allow cost-benefit estimations based on simulations, which take into account medical considerations and individual preferences. Agent technology is used to handle the high level of environmental dynamics as well as the complex and restrictive requirements of clinical trials. Utilization and trial-specific statements are supported by realistic simulation results.

- **Operationalization of study protocols:** Due to the complexity and regimentation of trials, a tremendous effort is needed for the coordination of all the actors and equipments involved. A continuing goal of the ADAPT project is to advance the agent-based simulation system towards a real-time assistance system that enables online resource allocation. Supporting the operational processes by coordinating the flow of information (adapted to the individual medical pathway) using agent technology should result in a higher level of process efficiency.

Related Work

Simulation is yet much more spread in the manufacturing domain than in health care. Reasons might be that hospitals have neglected cost pressure for many years and clinical processes are usually more complex and more varied than manufacturing processes. Nevertheless, one can find some approaches for hospital simulations in the literature and there are even commercial applications. Task scheduling and efficient resource utilization are very promising fields for optimization and therefore tackled very often. For example, Erdem, Demirel, and Onut (2003) use simulation for the evaluation of a novel appointment system in an outpatient clinic. Agent-based approaches for task scheduling in hospitals have also been presented by Decker and Li (1998) and Paulussen et al. (2004). These systems were also evaluated using simulation. Other approaches (Alvaraz & Centeno, 1999; Riley, 1999) were initially designed for the usage as a decision-support system. Within these systems, different strategies can be evaluated respecting the given circumstances. Already in 2001 there was an ambitious project (Sibbel & Urban, 2001) for creating an agent-based hospital simulation system that had the aim of creating a visual general-purpose construction kit.

Many providers of commercial simulation systems (e.g., Flexsim or Promodel) have realized the need for simulation in health care and are offering specialized extensions. The major problem of many existing models and systems for hospital simulation is that they do not represent the patient process in its whole complexity. Often, a very reduced and simplified set of the actual processes is used. This is critical, because the load of resources may also be influenced by the neglected tasks, and interdependencies between processes may play an important role.

Simulation

Basic Description of the Simulation Model
for Patient Scheduling

Before we describe the technical realization of the framework, we will first discuss the basic model. Important agent types and their abilities and the simulated processes will be described. As always in modeling, a certain abstraction level has to be chosen. This level is highly dependent on the aim of simulation. During the examination and execution of task scheduling, some aspects can be neglected. Therefore, we currently do not want to simulate the work of single persons but the occupation of organizational entities. Patients and organizational entities are the only actors in the model. Other important model elements are the knowledge of how to schedule and the typical processes that have to be performed. These elements might vary depending on the patient's disease.

- **Organizational entities:** Hospitals differ in the amount and configuration of their comprised organizational entities. Entities are usually responsible for certain services and are autonomous in their planning. Concerning patient treatment, there are three types of entities. *Wards* (e.g, a gastroenterological ward) are responsible for long-term treatment and everyday care. *Functional units* (e.g., x-ray unit or sonography) provide special short-term treatment or examination tasks. *Laboratories* perform analyses of samples (e.g., blood samples). Whereas knowledge about processes within wards is difficult to acquire in detail, process optimization between the organizational units is of limited complexity and therefore very promising for simulation. To realize this, the number and types of organizational entities have to be specified for each hospital. Typical parameters are a services list that describes which tasks are to be performed in a unit, capacities that describe how many patients or samples can be processed at the same time, and the working hours that describe when the unit is opened and able to perform medical actions. Sophisticated models might also include probabilities for resource breakdown and flexible rules for working overtime.

- **Patients:** Another basic ingredient of a hospital simulation is the patient. Patients are the cause for work in the organizational entities, and the average length of a patient stay is one of the central evaluation criteria. Patients can be seen as generic agents that are associated with different clinical pathways determined by their initial diagnosis. The pathway needs to be formally described and contains all necessary medical tasks, constraints for execution, and possible options for alternative treatment. Some pathways associated with severe diagnoses can be treated as emergency. This will be a signal for functional units to execute according tasks with a higher priority. Many aspects of the clinical treatment like simultaneous actions or multiple diseases have to be respected in a suitable pathway representation. In addition to the pathways, a realistic frequency distribution of diseases has to be specified. This *patient mix*, as well as a patient arrival rate, has to be specified in an arbitrary manner.

- **Execution strategies:** There are many possibilities in how the pathways are executed. This is highly dependent on organizational and infrastructural circumstances, and the method of execution often changes with the introduction of new information technology. There are three types of execution strategies. The first one is a simple *queuing strategy* where patient tasks (or samples) are executed in the order of occurrence, and a task is just started only if the preceding task is finished. This strategy is applicable if the tasks are very short or the patient's presence is not required. Most common is the *call strategy*. This means the tasks are registered at the functional unit and the patient is waiting for a call to come to the functional unit. Important and expensive tasks are often *scheduled in advance*. Appointments are made as early as possible and even before the execution of preceding tasks is finished. Execution strategies are typically bound to the functional units and have to be specified for every unit.

- **Clinical pathways:** Sometimes also referred to as clinical guidelines, clinical pathways describe the patient processes or task structures in a standardized manner. The introduction of diagnosis related groups (DRGs) for reasons of quality assurance and accounting forced health-care officials and physicians to formalize pathways. This change generally improved the availability of systematic process descriptions, and—as a side effect—the results can be utilized for automated task scheduling and for the creation of realistic simulation models. Nevertheless, physicians are usually reluctant to strongly formalize processes. The medical domain is manifold, and formal representations from computer science or economic science lack expressivity or are too complicated. That is the reason why pathways are often described textually following a structured template. Sometimes descriptive diagrams are used but often without a strong semantics. These semiformal pathway representations are a first step but further formalization has to be made to utilize these pathways in simulation and planning. Due to the specific requirements of the project, a new pathway representation and visual editors were developed (Herrler & Puppe, 2005) and a set of the most common pathways of internal medicine have been implemented for the simulations.

SeSAm

ShEll for Simulated Agent systeMs (SeSAm) (Klügl, 2001) is an integrated environment for modeling and simulating multiagent systems. SeSAm is Open Source Software and has been developed at the University of Würzburg. The first prototype of SeSAm was realized in LISP in 1995 and was specialized to ant simulation or biological simulations in general. Over the years, SeSAm grew to a general-purpose simulation tool and was reimplemented in JAVA starting in the year 2000 (Oechslein, 2004). SeSAm provides powerful modeling functions for the easy construction of complex models. As a special feature, a visual modeling user interface supports domain-experts without programming skills in creating simulation models. It allows the construction of agents and their environment respecting their properties, abilities, and behavior. Different agent classes can be created and their properties and abilities can be defined by just adding agent specific attributes and modular features.

Figure 2. Example for UML behavior modeling in SeSAm

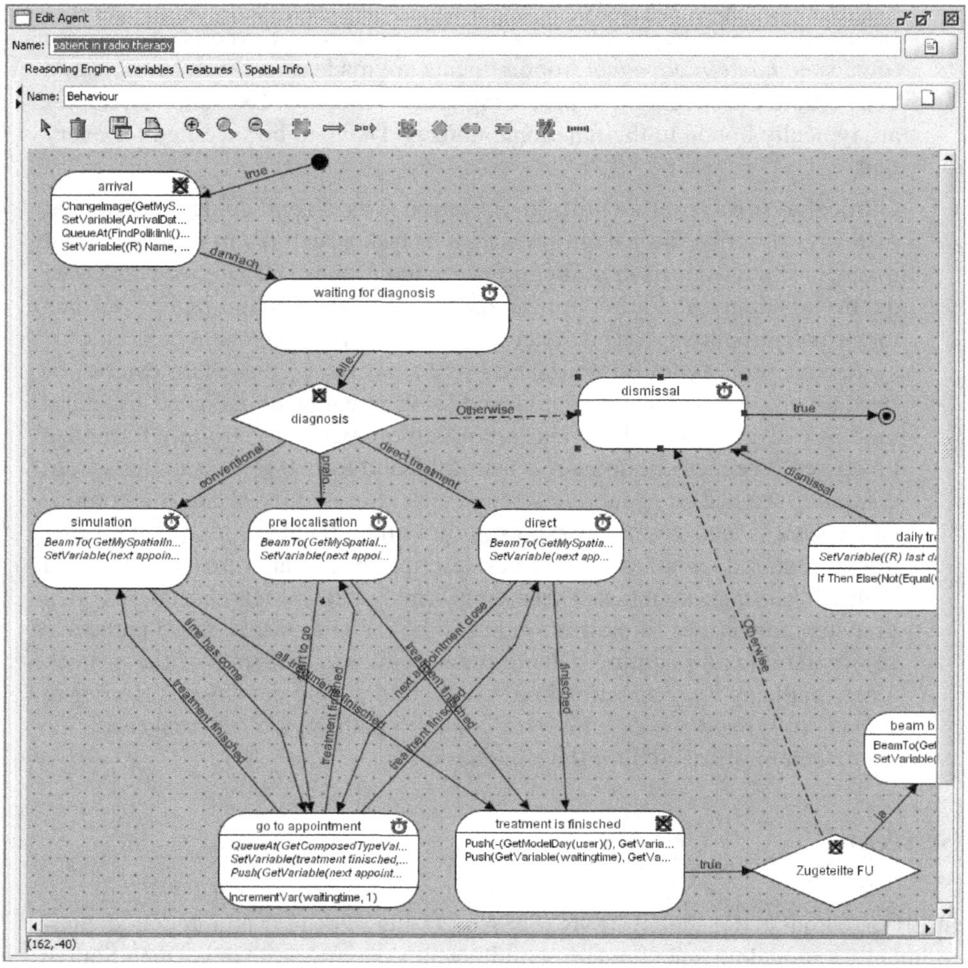

There is already a useful set of basic functions available (e.g., Move, SendMessage, GetAllObjectsOnPosition) and the user can extend the given set. The behavior of the agent can be described by composing these functions according to complex instructions and using these in a visually constructed activity graph (see Figure 2). The UML activity graphs (Oechslein, Klügl, Herrler, & Puppe 2002) are easy understandable and a well-known notation, but even if one is not familiar with UML, the graphical description looks very intuitive. Activity diagrams consist of activities and transition rules. The activities represent states containing a series of actions. These are executed until an exit rule activates the next activity. After modeling the agent classes, simulation situations can be created. Situations are snapshots of a scenario that describes which agents are to be present at the start of the simulation and how they are configured. Usually placing the agents on a two-dimensional map and defining their initial attribute values defines a situation. Several situations can be stored in one model.

After modeling, the resulting model representation is compiled and can be simulated. Compilation as well as simulation is integrated in the SeSAm environment. The simulation state can be observed during execution. It is possible to pause and resume the simulation and to control an agent's states. Results can be derived from the simulation by integration online (Block- or Series-charts) and offline analysis (Output to ".csv") features.

In recent time, several additional features to support handling more models that are complex were integrated in the environment. Among various other features, the environment allows hierarchical modeling at the level of function description as well as on the level of behavior description. Basic function primitives can be composed to more complex user-defined primitives, and parts of the activity graph can be melted together into compound activities. To simplify testing and finding errors in the model, it is possible to create rules for invariant states—similar to assertions in modern programming languages. Even re-factoring methods, which became quite popular in software engineering, are supported. In summary, modelers can get the power of a programming language without having to learn any syntactic notions.

SeSAm is not just useful for making simulation experiments in a closed world. To support the connection to external agent systems additional extensions were required. Therefore, new features to support communication as well as ontologies were added. Here, general standards were adhered in order to ensure interopera-

Figure 3. Engineering agent systems in a simulated environment vs. application in real world

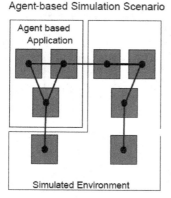
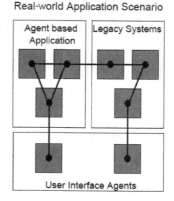

tion with other systems. The new plug-ins provide FIPA-compliant communication primitives and a possibility to import ontologies modeled with the standard ontology tool, Protege 2000.

In our view, agent-based applications are part of an environment containing real-world agents like users and other systems (possibly agent systems). In agent software development, isolated tests are usually very difficult; instead, tests have to be carried out under the conditions of this environment. Our goal was to extend SeSAm in a way that it could be used as a test-bed for agent-based software without remodeling the agent for interacting with the simulated environment (Klügl, Herrler, & Oechslein, 2003). Then, creating models of the global system becomes rather intuitive. Figure 3 shows a sketch of this approach. An agent-based application is integrated in an environment consisting of additional information systems and users, which can be seen as agents. Simulated agents in SeSAm replace all agents from the real-world environment. The level of detail of the simulation is dependent on the requirements of the agent system. Due to the representation of the real world in the simulated

Figure 4. Graphical analysis of simulated processes

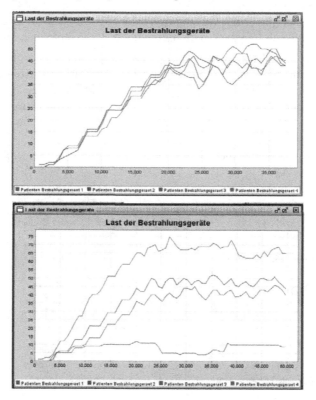

test-bed, the developed components can be tested both under realistic as well as extreme conditions. This usually cannot be done in the real world for reasons of security and prohibitive costs. Especially in the health-care domain, practical testing of prototypical software is usually dangerous. In this context, SeSAm offers powerful capabilities for experimentation support like the distribution of simulation runs on several hosts and online graphical analysis of the simulation results like the ones shown in Figure 4.

SeSAm Hospital Extensions

According to the basic model described before, general-purpose tool SeSAm was extended to a specific simulation tool for hospital patient scheduling. Due to the modular design of SeSAm and many interfaces for plug-in extensions, additional features for predefined agent types such as functional unit-agents, patient-agents, or reception-agents can be realized. In contrast to working with the basic SeSAm environment, the user deals just with configuration parameters and does not have to specify the actual behavior of the agent. The aim of providing generic but configurable agent classes is to enable the user to build simulation models quick and comfortable.

In the following basic elements of the kit are described in more detail:

- **Pathway Modeling Tool:** An editor for pathway libraries was implemented and integrated to SeSAm. This editor can also be used as a small stand-alone tool that can be given to physicians. New pathway libraries are saved as XML files and can be feed into the SeSAm simulation (see Figure 5).

- **Time-Feature:** Since the basic SeSAm-Simulator simulates tick by tick, it does not provide a concrete time model. Usually the representation time advance is part of the model. To reduce modeling work, a module for adjustable time was integrated into the environment. The user can specify the relation between a simulation tick and simulated minutes. This relation can also be modified dynamically (e.g., the simulation is less precise during night or skips weekends). This variable time advance can speed up the simulation.

- **TimeTable-Feature:** This feature can be attached to patient agents as well as to functional units. It is used to store confirmed appointments. Primitive behavior functions allow setting and removing new appointments, to ask for the next appointment or to get all appointments of a specific date. During the simulation, a graphical timetable shows the current appointments of the selected agent (see Figure 5).

- **ServiceProvider-Feature:** This feature can be attached to functional units for treatment and examination as well as to laboratories. It provides a new user

Figure 5. The components of the toolkit around a simulation scene

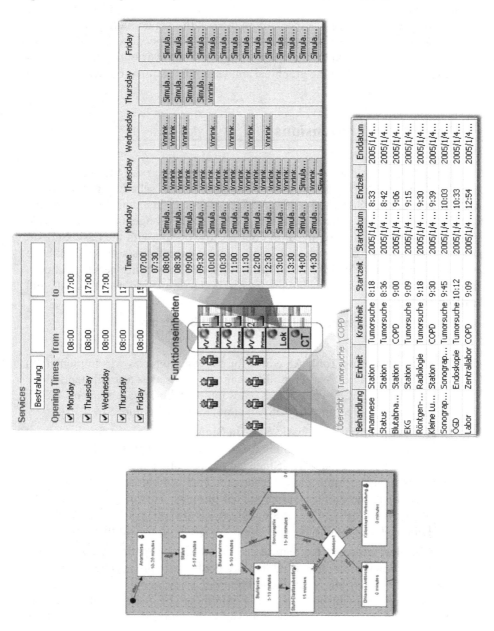

interface for modeling a list of services and opening hours (see Figure 5). The agent is registered at a central yellow pages service, where other agents can ask for units that provide a requested service. They can request an appointment at the found functional unit or queue there immediately (see Figure 5)

- **Patient-Feature:** This feature has to be added to patient-agents. It allows the selection of a pathway from a pathway-library. Primitive behavior functions allow to set the state of a task (preconditions fulfilled, task finished) and to determine the next possible tasks. So according to the implemented strategy, the tasks of the patient can be executed. Additionally the patient feature contains the medical record, showing a protocol of all executed tasks (see Figure 5)

By using these features for modeling, one can create hospital models very effectively. Model adaptation to a new hospital means just to specify the number and configuration of agents in a situation. Most parts of the model can be modified after a short period of working with the tool. Only changing the execution strategy is yet more complicated, but can also be realized with SeSAm's abilities for visual programming.

Implementation of a Scheduling Scenario

In this section, an example model of a clinic for radiation therapy is presented in detail. After a general description of the domain and the model, possible examination questions are shown. Regarding the treatment of cancer, radiation therapy plays an important role along with surgery and chemotherapy. Ambulatory patients are usually sent by their local general practitioner. After their arrival, a couple of appointments are made for examinations and adjustment of radiation devices. The scheduling of the first appointments is most critical because it has to be performed at short notice and many constraints (e.g., minimum delay between examinations) have to be considered. After the first examination in the outpatient department, one of three possible treatment plans (i.e, clinical paths) is selected. The path determines which treatment tasks (listed in Table 1) are executed in which order. Different functional units or resources are responsible for task execution: a radioscopy device, where a suitable patient position for radiation can be determined, a further unit to make x-ray pictures and finally there are four devices for radiation therapy, each having its own schedule. The first exposure in these units is for adjustment and takes longer than the following daily exposures and there are reserved time intervals for adjustment. As soon as the patients have passed the adjustment, the phase of daily exposures starts for an average treatment time of 30 days. A medical assistant is responsible for the scheduling after the patient's admission. He sends appointment requests to the different functional units and keeps an eye on the compliance of the

Figure 6. Runtime visualization showing the animated map, timetables, and online analysis

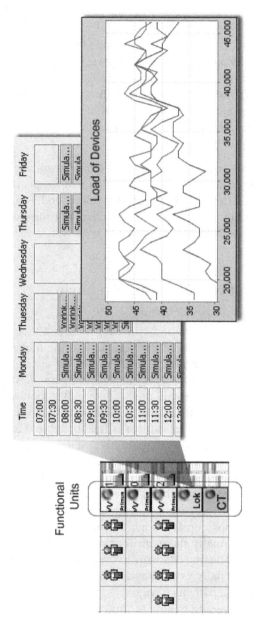

path constraints. Since the times given in Table 1 are average times, the execution time of single tasks may differ from the pre-planned schedule.

A simulation model depicting this scenario was built based on the SeSAm Hospital Framework (see Figure 6). It simulates the described scheduling and treatment in the radiation therapy department. The simulation generates patients with random paths. The modeler can specify the arrival rate and the random distribution of the paths. Furthermore, he can modify the number and opening hours of functional units. By running the simulation, evaluation parameters like average stay time, patient throughput, and the average load of devices can be measured and shown as a series chart (see Figure 6).

For the validation of the model, an actual state model has to be created and resulting evaluation parameters are to be compared with the reality. In the simulation of the radiation therapy, we were able to reproduce real-world phenomena like periodical oscillations of the load of certain devices and the maximum patient quantity were consistent with the reality.

Having validated the actual state model, different simulation experiments can be performed, comparing the original model with alternative settings. Possible questions for a comparison are:

- **Calculation of the maximum load:** Modifying the arrival rate can influence the amount of patients. So one can determine which amount of patients can be treated at a given resource configuration.

- **Effects of buffer times:** Buffer times in the schedule allow a flexible reaction on unexpected changes (e.g., device breakdown or emergencies). On the other hand, buffer times might also have negative effects on patient throughput, if the general load is very high.

- **Strategies for dealing with device breakdowns:** If one of the four radiation devices breaks, the available time slots for treatment are reduced. Two strategies might countervail this shortage: A second shift can be introduced at one of the working devices, or all working devices extend their opening hours and the staff is apportioned to the rest.

Table 1. Model parameter for radiation therapy

Planned task	Required resources (amount)	Estimated duration	Number per day	Opening hours
Prelocalization	Simulator (1)	~ 20 min	~ 20	8:00-17:00
Simulation		~ 30 min		
CT	CT (1)	~ 30 min	~13	8:00-15:00
Radiation	Radiation device (4)	~ 15 min	max. 16	10:00-11:00

The analysis component of SeSAm allows saving series charts of chosen model parameters. Alternatively, one can watch the online visualization in different types of charts (e.g., block charts, series charts, pie chart). Effects of model changes on the average waiting time of a patient or the load of devices can be easily observed. This shall be illustrated by an example: In a simulation experiment, we recorded the average and maximum stay times of the current situation. We observed an average treatment time (from admission until all examinations are finished) of about 3 days up to a maximum of 10 days (including weekends). The results of the simulation were consistent with observations in reality. Because the treatment times are not constantly growing, we conclude that this resource configuration can handle the current patient arrival rate. The simulation of alternative configurations has shown that the clinic can treat up to three additional patients a day resulting in a slight increase of the average stay time. If more than three additional patients would arrive, other changes—for example, extending working hours—have to be made to compensate the increased patient number. Similar experiments concerning other questions are quickly realized.

Integrated Scenario Agent.Hospital

To evaluate the agent systems that have been developed and to show that they interoperate in a sophisticated way, a complex and realistic evaluation scenario is needed. Therefore, the "hospital logistics" working group of SPP 1083 including the ADAPT-project developed an extensive model called *Agent.Hospital (Kirn, Heine, Herrler, & Krempels,2003)*. This model is based on an open framework for numerous health-care actors. The basic architecture of the framework is shown in Figure 7. The *Agent.Hospital* framework contains several detailed health-care models, different kinds of service agents, and agent-based platforms. Within *Agent.Hospital,* one can evaluate modeling methods or examine configuration problems as well as agent-based negotiation strategies and coordination algorithms.

In the context of the Priority Research program (SPP 1083) the research partners involved in the "hospital logistics" working group integrated the partial hospital logistics models created by the individual projects. Due to the high number of participating research groups, a wide spectrum of relevant clinical processes could be offered. Relevant organizational structures, processes, and necessary data models were analyzed, formalized, and modeled at several hospitals. To be able to integrate a number of separate partial models, it was necessary to define numerous gateways between these models (see Figure 7) and to develop a common ontology for interaction through these gateways. Additionally, basic process patterns had to be defined (for instance planning and execution of clinical trials with oncological patients). At the conceptual level, *Agent.Hospital* consists of partial models, process patterns,

Figure 7. Application diagram of the Agent.Hospital framework with several selected supply chains

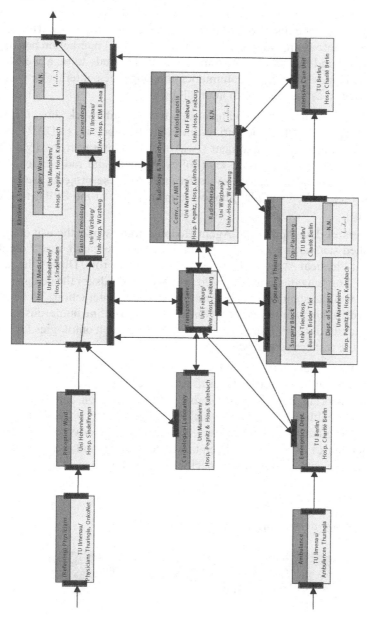

gateway specifications, and shared ontologies. The *resulting framework* is an overall conceptual model *based on t*he integration of project specific partial models.

In *Agent.Hospital* several clinics, departments, and wards are defined as service provider and consumer units. In our framework, the services offered and the services requested are denoted simply as services. For a meaningful interaction between the service provider and the service consumer unit, there needs to be a well-defined interface based on existing agent communication languages, interaction protocols, content languages, as well as common ontologies.

Currently, the following supply chains of the overall framework shown in Figure 7 have been implemented: clinical trials and radio therapeutics (ADAPT), rescue patient (AGIL), lung-cancer treatment (ASAinlog), angina pectoris (MedPAge), gallstone therapy, surgerical processes (Policy Agents), and radiological-service processes (EMIKA). More details and references to these projects are provided via the RealAgentS Web site, the public groupware tool of the SPP (http://www.realagents.org).

For the successful development of Agent.Hospital framework, the use of existing and established standards was very important. In agent research, the "Foundation for Intelligent Physical Agents" (FIPA) plays the leading role. During the last few years, the FIPA organization has proposed primary standards for the design of agent platforms as well as standards for communication and interaction. To be able to integrate the different agent systems it was necessary to define numerous gateways using these standards (see Figure 8) and to develop common ontologies for interactions among the respective gateway agents.

Intelligent software agents in any application have to be integrated into an existing (often proprietary) information system infrastructure. Therefore, the aim of the hospital-logistics working group is the implementation, evaluation, and documentation of agent-based health-care services, which are supposed to be the foundation for future FIPA—*Application Specifications*. Since 2002, the priority research program 1083 is a member of FIPA and has been tasked to develop and evaluate examples and to refine the existing application specifications in health care.

Figure 8. Gateway-agent concept (Krempels et al., 2003)

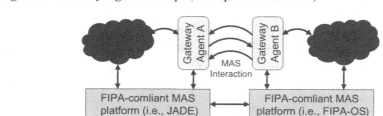

Besides working with FIPA, the SPP 1083 has initiated cooperation with the association of information system producers in health care (VHGit), to develop specifications for interfaces between specialized applications (e.g., practice systems, patient record, etc.). Further more, the SPP contributes to *Agentcities* (Willmott et al., 2003), an open, worldwide net of FIPA-compliant agent platforms, using which different agent-based services—often in the development stage—are provided. Currently there are more than 140 agent platforms that are members of *Agentcities* with a high concentration in Europe and several platforms in the USA, Australia, and the Near East.

Within Agentcities, a lot of different application domains exist, for instance eHealth, manufacturing control, digital libraries, travel services, and so on. The ultimate aim of this initiative is to support the commercial as well as academic efforts for the development of agent-based applications and to make it possible to compose dynamic, intelligent, and autonomous agents as well as complex service agents. *One goal of Agent.Hospital* was to become a part of *Agentcities*. Therefore, new *Agentcities* platforms have been set up in five German cities. They are connected by a central directory service (Agent.HospitalDF) in Aachen, which registers all participating service agents.

Different infrastructural services and tools have been set up or developed to realize Agent.Hospital:

- **Agent.Hospital Directory Facilitator (AHDF):** a common and centralized yellow pages service for the agents within Agent.Hospital. It provides a Web interface for online monitoring and several other extended functions like availability testing.

- **Agent.Hospital Event Service (AHES):** an event service realized by an agent. It can be used for event-based simulation of multiagent systems in the health-care domain.

- **Agent.Hospital Actor Agent (AHAA):** another common component to all the involved projects is the Actor agent. Instances of the actor agent represent real actors in Agent.Hospital scenarios.

- **Agent.Hospital Simulation Model (AHSim):** an executable simulation model describing a typical patient process providing interfaces for agent-based application systems.

- **Agent.Hospital Ontology Repository (AHOR):** a repository providing health-care specific task ontologies (Becker, Heine, Herrler, & Krempels, 2003) on demand. The shared ontologies are a basis for mutual understanding of the systems.

- **Agent.Hospital CVS (AHCVS):** a concurrent version system containing the source files of the service and interface agents.

Management of Clinical Trials

An important field in health care is the medical treatment of cancer. Typically, these treatments are very expensive and new clinical trials are conducted to test the effectiveness of various new drugs and treatment protocols. Clinical trials are carefully controlled studies in which oncology experts evaluate better and more cost-effective ways to treat, prevent, or diagnose cancer. Increasing the number of qualified patients who are enrolled in clinical trials, as they represent an opportunity for patients with cancer to receive the best possible care is important.

Figure 9. Exemplary part of the clinical-trial scenario with interactions between different multiagent systems

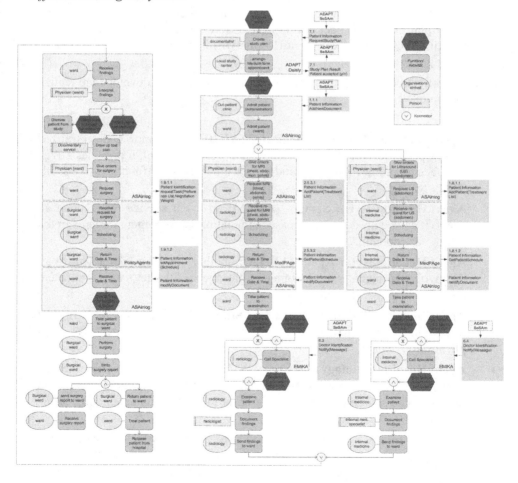

Clinical trials are also extremely valuable because they answer important questions that will help to continually improve cancer care and decrease the risk of cancer development. Before a new therapy or medical treatment can be put into daily clinical practice, many trials have to be run. These trials are detailed plans for medical treatments, for instance a clinical trial protocol can describe at which point of time, in which quantum, and how medications or therapies have to be executed. However, clinical trials are not performed in linearity; instead their concrete structures depend on specific patient constitutions, laboratory results, and so on. Clinical trials can be described using the graph metaphor, each node representing a particular state of a particular study. Typical sample sizes for clinical trials require about 150 to 200 patients which make it necessary in general that several hospitals cooperate in performing such trials (multicentric trials). Figure 9 exemplifies the process aspects of the integrated clinical-trial scenario. The simulation according to the process description is directed by SeSAm and utilizes several agent-based services provided by the SPP 1083. At the beginning of a clinical trial, various tasks for diagnosis and treatment have to be coordinated and resources have to be scheduled and if necessary

Figure 10. HL7 Schedule Request Message structure (SRM) in the clinical trial scenario

```
     SRM^S01-S11^SRM_S01      Schedule Request Message

     MSH                      Message Header
     ARQ                      Appointment Request Information
     [ APR ]                  Appointment Preferences
     [ { NTE } ]              Notes and Comments
     [ { PID                  Patient Identification
         [ PV1 ]              Patient Visit
         [ PV2 ]              Patient Visit - Additional Info
         [ { OBX } ]          Observation/Result
         [ { DG1 } ]          Diagnosis
       }
     ]
     { RGS                    Resource Group Segment
       [ { AIS                Appointment Information - Service
         [ APR ]              Appointment Preferences
         [ { NTE } ]          Notes and Comments
       }
       ]
       [ { AIG                Appointment Information - General Resource
         [ APR ]              Appointment Preferences
         [ { NTE } ]          Notes and Comments
       }
       ]
       [ { AIL                Appointment Information - Location Resource
         [ APR ]              Appointment Preferences
         [ { NTE } ]          Notes and Comments
       }
       ]
       [ { AIP                Appointment Information - Personnel Resource
         [ APR ]              Appointment Preferences
         [ { NTE } ]          Notes and Comments
       }
       ]
     }
```

Figure 11. SRM Message for an MRT examination

```
MSH|^~\&|||||20030101||SRM^S01|1234|1234|2.4
ARQ|0001|0002||||||0010^radiological
examination^ROUTINE|NORMAL|120|min|200303150800^200303201700|P
riorität||||4711^Mayer^Hans^^Dr.||||4712^Otto^Karl^^Dr.
PID|1111|2222|3333|4444|Mustermann^Hans|Mustermann|19500521|M
DG1|001|I9|786.5|CRANIAL PAINS|199401010730|W
DG1|002|I9|412|OLD MYOCARDIAL INFARCTION|199401010730|W
AIL|1234|||0100^MRT
```

communicated to the corresponding units. Figure 8 shows an example with computer tomography (CT) and magnetoresonance-tomography (MRT) examinations as well as the execution of a surgery.

At first, the suitability of the patient for the clinical study will be checked (age, gender, blood count, etc.). If the patient fulfils the preconditions for the trial for instance, an MRT examination is necessary. Planning of this examination means that different service agents try to negotiate mandatory appointments. However, these agent-based negotiations are constrained by the existing timetable of the corresponding hospital information system. To interact with this information system (precondition is HL7 compliance) the HL7 agent generates specific "HL7 Schedule Messages" like SRM (Schedule Request Message). Figure 10 shows the HL7 Schedule Request Message structure. Based on this message structure, the actual Schedule Message (SRM^S01) is generated, which is shown in Figure 11. The responsible HL7 Agent is able to receive, edit, process, and send such HL7 Messages to standards compliant hospital information systems (HIS). Currently, detailed tests with different HIS have been planned. The agents communicate in a FIPA compliant way and transmit the HL7 as well as the DICOM Messages as content of the FIPA-ACL messages (Agent Communication Language).

A Screenshot of the HL7 Message Agent interface is shown in Figure 12. Relevant message segments and fields can be edited by the user and sent to the next responsible agent or hospital information system.

After the MRT examination, several HL7 messages have to be sent pertaining to the results of the examination in the current scenario. But the transfer of radiological image data is historically grown and still not supported by HL7. The transfer of image data for instance from the MRT modality to viewing workstations, digital archives or a remote radiologist for a second opinion is supported by the DICOM standard (our basic assumption is that all systems are DICOM compliant with specific conformance statements).

Figure 12. HL7 Message Agent for interactions with HL7-compliant HIS

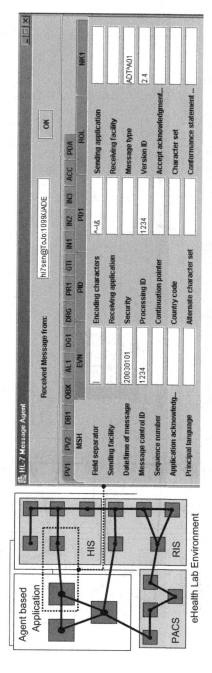

Figure 13. DICOM Message Agent for interaction with DICOM-compliant PACS/ RIS, and so on

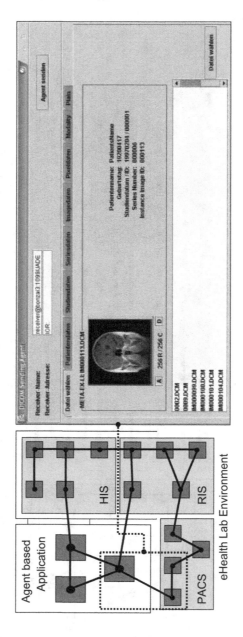

The Screenshot of the DICOM Message Agent interface shows the viewing and editing (if allowed) functions (Figure 13). The agent can send the DICOM image data with all header information to the next responsible agent or archiving system.

All these interactions have first been tested in a simulated environment provided by SeSAm and in the second step implemented and tested in connection with real hospital information systems in the secure laboratory environment called "eHealth Lab" (http://www.ehealthlab.de/index_e.html).

Summary and Outlook

Agent technology is able to handle the high level of environmental dynamics as well as complex and restrictive requirements of clinical processes. The aim of ADAPT is to optimize the planning and management of clinical processes as well as provide decision support in the context of clinical trials. In order to accomplish this, realistic simulation results are needed. In this research, we have employed a multiagent based simulation because conventional simulation has been shown to be not sufficient (Klügl, Oechslein, Puppe, & Dornhaus, 2002). As far as multiagent modeling is concerned, we have improved existing modeling techniques to handle complex models with intelligent actors. Another unique aspect of our approach to materializing realistic simulation scenarios is the integration of partial models within the Agent.Hospital initiative. FIPA compliance and subsequent use of ontologies facilitate this interoperation and also enables the development of agent systems, which can be deployed from the simulation environment to an existing information system infrastructure.

The prototype system development has been completed. There are already demo systems, which can explicate the possibilities of our approach. While the initial feedback is very encouraging, we still have to demonstrate the practical use of our system. Our immediate goal is to bring the agent systems to a controlled real-life experiment and show that the results of simulation and the system can be practically used in the management and control of clinical trials. We are at the point where we have gotten the initial results from the simulation and now we can evaluate the experimental agent systems and deploy them to existing information system infrastructure in the near future. Both applications (simulation/management) will be evaluated with respect to specific advantages of agent-based software over traditional systems.

References

Alvarez A. M., & Centeno, M. A. (1999). Enhancing simulation models for emergency rooms using VBA. In *Proceedings of the 1999 Winter Simulation Conference,* (pp. 1685-1693).

Becker, M., Heine, C., Herrler, R., Krempels, K.H. (2003) An ontology for hospital scenarios, In A. Moreno, & J. Nealon (Eds.), *Applications of software agent technology in the health care domain Whitestein series in software agent technologies (WSSAT)* (pp.87-103). Basel.

Decker, K., & Li, J. (1998). Coordinated hospital patient scheduling. In *Proceedings of the Third International Conference on Multi-Agent Systems (ICMAS98)* (pp. 104-111).

Erdem, H. I., Demirel, T., & Onut, S. (2002). An efficient appointment system design for outpatient clinic using computer simulation. In *Proceedings of the 2002 Summer Computer Simulation Conference*, San Diego, (pp. 299-304).

Heine, C., Herrler, R., Petsch, M., & Anhalt, C. (2003). ADAPT—adaptive multi agent process planning and coordination of clinical trials. In *AMCIS 2003 Proceedings*, Tampa, FL (pp.1823-1834).

Herrler, R., & Puppe, F. (2005). Evaluation and optimization of clinical processes with multi-agent simulation. In *Proceedings of the Workshop on Agents Applied in Healthcare, IJCAI 2005,* Edinbourgh.

Kirn, S., Heine, C., Herrler, R., & Krempels, K. H. (2003). Agent.Hospital—agent-based open framework for clinical applications. In G. Kotsis & S. Reddy (Eds.), *Twelfth IEEE International Workshops on Enabling Technologies: Infrastructure for Collaborative Enterprises (WET ICE 2003 Post-Proceedings)* (pp. 36-41). Los Alamitos, CA: CS Press.

Klügl, F. (2001, April). *Multagentensimulation—Konzepte, werkzeuge, anwendungen (Multi-agent simulation—concepts, tools, application)*. Addison Wesley.

Klügl, F., Herrler, R., & Oechslein, C. (2003). From simulated to real environments: How to use SeSAm for software development. In M. Schillo et al. (Eds.) *Multiagent System Technologies—1ˢᵗ German Conference (MATES03)* (LNAI 2831, pp. 13-24).

Klügl, F., Oechslein, C., Puppe, F., & Dornhaus, A. (2002). Multi-Agent Modelling in Comparison to Standard Modeling. In F. J. Barros & N. Giambiasi (Eds.), *Artificial Intelligence, Simulation and Planning in High Autonomy Systems (AIS2002)* (pp. 105-110). SCS Publishing House.

Krempels, K.-H., Nimis, J., Braubach, L., Pokahr, A., Herrler, R., & Scholz, T. (2003). Entwicklung intelligenter multi-multiagentensysteme—Werkzeugunterstützung, lösungen und offene Fragen (Development of intelligent multiagent systems—tool-support, solutions and open questions). In K. Dittrich, W. König, A. Oberweis, K. Rannenberg, & W. Wahlster (Eds.), *INFORMATIK 2003 Innovative Informatikanwendungen, GI-Edition Lecture Notes in Informatics, 1,* 34. Bonn, Germany: Köllen Publisher.

Oechslein, C. (2004). *Methodology for multi agent simulations with integrated specification and implementation language* (German). München: Germany: Shaker Verlag.

Oechslein, C., Klügl, F., Herrler, R., & Puppe, F. (2002). UML for behavior-oriented multi-agent simulations. In B. Dunin-Keplicz & E. Nawarecki (Eds.), *From Theory to Practice in Multi-Agent Systems LNAI; Second International Workshop of Central and Eastern Europe on Multi-Agent Systems (CEEMAS 2001), Revised Papers.* Heidelberg, Germany: Springer.

Paulussen, T. O., Pokahr, A., Braubach, L., Zöller, A., Lamersdorf, W., & Heinzl, A. (2004). Dynamic patient scheduling in hospitals. *Multikonferenz Wirtschaftsinformatik, Agent technology in business applications.* Essen.

Riley, L. A. (1999). Applied simulation as a decision support system tool: The design of a new internal medicine facility. In *Proceedings of the 32nd Hawaii International Conference on System Sciences* (pp. 22-27).

Sibbel, R., & Urban, C. (2001). Agentbased modelling and simulation for hospital management. In N. J. Saam & B. Schmidt (Eds.), *Cooperative agents* (pp. 183-202). Boston: Kluwer Academic Publishers.

Willmott, S., Constantinescu, I., Dale, J., Somacher, M., Marinheiro, R., Mota, L., et al. (2003). *Agentcities network architecture recommendation.* Retrieved January 27, 2003, from http://www.agentcities.org/rec/00001/actf-rec-00001a.pdf

Chapter IV

Combating Malaria:
A Complex System and Agent-Based Approach

Narjès Bellamine-BenSaoud, University La Monouba, Tunisia

Fatima Rateb, University College London, UK

Abstract

In this chapter, we investigate how complexity theory and more particularly how agent-based modeling and simulation can benefit the explanation of the impact of education on malaria health care in Haiti. Our model includes: (1) the environment, encompassing mainly cities, roads, hospitals and schools; (2) the agents, modeling the human actors, who can be safe or infected by malaria disease according to their location in the environment; and (3) a modelled agent can also be mobile or not, can reproduce, and can die. We run four kinds of experiments over a 50-year period each. Our main emerging results are growing total agent, susceptible, and immune populations in a "cyclic" fluctuation form. Furthermore, we confirm the positive impact of both education and hospitals in combating malaria disease.

Introduction

The spread of disease has always been a great hazard threatening public health. In fact, there have been epidemics since the beginning of recorded history (Brauer, 2004). More than ever, multidisciplinary research on the spread of epidemics is becoming a key issue, where medical specialists are collaborating with modeling (mathematic, informatics, etc.) researches in order to first understand, explain emergent diseases, and ultimately contribute to design solutions and strategies to fight against such epidemics.

We focus, in this chapter, on malaria spread and we aim to assess the impact of the education of both hospital staff and laypeople on malaria health care. Henceforth, we refer to **education** as the acquisition of malaria awareness by the human population. In order to achieve this goal, we have adopted the complexity paradigm and then considered agent-based modeling and simulation to develop a virtual environment representing malaria spread in Haiti.

Our main objectives of this computational-modeling approach are to understand, answer, and solve different questions and problems concerning vector-based disease spread and more particularly malaria. Our first aim is to understand malaria spread among humans by including education as well as hospitals (as a means of combating malaria). Consequently, our first and immediate questions are: How do hospitals combat malaria spread? How does education enable humans to fight against malaria? More broadly, we are interested in exploring how agent-based modeling and simulation could support humanitarian actions by helping decision makers develop efficient strategies to face malaria threats and diseases in general. Our model, presented in the following sections, aims to encompass the malaria problem in Haiti.

In the remaining part of this section, we introduce the global malaria problem, followed by the complexity paradigm and the agent-based modeling adopted. This is followed by an insight into the current malaria situation in Haiti, the country we have chosen for our study.

The rest of the paper is organised as follows: "State of the Art" section introduces current efforts in the field of malaria modeling; the following section discusses the model; then the virtual experiments and their results are presented; the "Discussion" part gives some conclusions and a brief analysis; finally, "Future Work" discusses ideas for future research.

Malaria

Malaria is an infectious and vector-borne disease caused by a parasite (plasmodium) and transmitted between humans by the bites of mosquitoes (female anopheles being the parasite vector). The malaria parasite lives in both mosquito and human. A parasite-carrier mosquito infects a human by its bite and similarly, a human who hosts the parasite can transmit it to a mosquito. Mosquitoes are not affected by the parasite.

Malaria affects greatly social and economic development in the world. The World Health Organization (WHO) in 2005 estimated the global burden, where approximately 2.2 billion people were at risk of contracting the parasite, and 270 to 400 million were already infected. Endemic areas are characterised by "ideal" mosquito habitats, which are largely where water is present, the temperature is at least 18°C, and there is little pollution (Baudon, 2000). Many third-world rural areas meet these conditions. Efforts to eradicate this deadly disease have included using DDT to minimise the vector population, and administering antimalarial drugs to susceptible people, as prevention. However, both methods have proved only temporarily effective. The former was first adopted in the mid-1950s with a subsequent significant global decrease in mosquito population. This was soon to become a failure when a resurgence of malaria was detected because of anopheles developing a resistance to the insecticide (Krogstad, 1996; WHO, 1996). The latter prophylaxis was the use of chloroquine as an antimalarial drug. Resistance of *Plasmodium falciparum* (the more prevalent and deadly of the four existing parasite species) to chloroquine emerged due to the massive usage of the drug (Payne, 1987). Therefore, a novel way of combating this plague would have to be devised.

Complex Systems and Agent-Based Modeling

Various definitions of **complex systems** exist: a system whose key parameter throughput is increased beyond a certain threshold (Hübler, 2005); a system at the edge of order and chaos (Crutchfield, 2002); the property of a language expression that makes it difficult to formulate its overall behaviour, even when given almost complete information about its atomic components and their interrelations (Edmonds, 1999); a system that does not have pure superposition of phenomena and processes (Keyser, 2000); systems that are composed of a large number of parts that interact in a nonsimple way and in where the whole is more than the sum of the parts (Simon, 1969).

Pavard (2002) describes a complex sociotechnical system to be one for which it is difficult, if not impossible, to restrict its description to a limited number of parameters or characterising variables without losing its essential global functional properties. Indeed, from this definition, four characteristics of such a system appear: nondeterminism; limited functional decomposability; distributed nature of information and representation; and emergence and self-organisation. These properties show that dealing with a complex system entails dealing with the impossibility to anticipate precisely its behaviour despite knowing completely the function of its constituents.

This, combined with nonlinear behaviour means that it is quite problematic if not impossible to use a mathematical or statistical approach for its analysis (Bagni et al., 2002; Pavard & Dugdale, 2002). Carley (2002) refers to complexity theory as not a theory but rather a paradigm, a set of procedures and techniques, and an approach to complex systems. It involves the study of many actors and their interactions (Axelrod, 1997).

The world exhibits many examples of complexity that are contrasted with the simplicity of the basic laws of physics. An example can be seen in climate, which is considered a complex field, however one knows that spring is after winter every year. This experience has not yielded new laws of physics, but has instead set lessons about appropriate ways of approaching complex systems (Goldenfeld & Kadanoff, 1999).

It is recognized that computer simulation, especially **agent-based simulation**, is valuable for studying complex systems. Because the study of large numbers of actors with changing patterns of interactions often becomes too difficult for a mathematical solution, a primary research tool of complexity theory is computer simulation. The trick is to specify how the agents interact, and then observe properties that occur at the level of the whole society (Axelrod, 1997).

Studying complex systems through multiagent systems has yielded useful results such as: the evolutionary population dynamics of settlement systems in the search of emerging spatial regularities (Aschan-Leygonie, Mathian, & Saunders 2000); demographic phenomena through its roots in individual choice behaviour and social interactions (Jaeger & Janssen, 2001); simulations of crowd behaviour aiming to understand its dynamic and consequent control (Gomez & Rowe, 2003; Hamagami, Koakutsu, & Hirate 2003). The goal of agent-based modeling is to enrich our understanding of fundamental processes that may appear in a variety of applications. This requires adhering to the Keep It Simple Stupid (KISS) principle (Axelrod, 1997).

Haiti

The level of poverty in Haiti is approximately 65% (PAHO, 2001), a socioeconomic factor affecting access to public health care. Not only is an adequate health infrastructure not fully developed, but "individual" poverty also hinders access to health care. Not having the financial resources to travel to the place of care or not judging it necessary to seek medical care aggravates this further.

Malaria is considered a public health problem in Haiti (PAHO, 2001), especially in rural areas. Malaria education, or its lack thereof, plays an extremely important role in the "healing" process. It is primordial for effective and efficient treatment that malaria be diagnosed at an early stage (Baume & Kachur, 1999). In order for this to apply, the population must be completely aware of its symptoms and act consequently. Symptoms which can be easily mistaken for another disease include: high fever, vomiting, convulsions, and anaemia. Not only must the population attribute specific symptoms to malaria, but they must also seek the correct medical attention. The first problem to tackle is educating the population, which could be done through national schooling. However, school attendance by children from lower-income families is limited by the cost of school fees and curtailed by child labour.

State of the Art: Modeling Diseases

The beginning of mathematical epidemiology was a simple nonlinear dynamic system (Kermack & McKendrick, 1927). This model considers the class S of individuals susceptible to the disease, that is, not yet infected, and the class I of infected individuals, assumed infective and able to spread the disease by contact with the susceptible population (Brauer, 2004).

Subsequently, more models and extensions are developed based on Kermack and McKendrick's (1927) model. They add mainly the Exposed and Recovered classes for human populations. This family of models is referred to as the SEIR (susceptible-exposed-infected-recovered [or immune]) models.

Another way of viewing the problem is with spatial point-pattern analysis and its application in geographical epidemiology as seen in Gatrell, Bailey, Diggle, and Rowlingson (1996). They used information on the spacing of the points to characterise pattern. These spatial point patterns were then represented statistically, their first- and second-order properties characterised through concepts of intensity. The concepts used in this research draw on the classic work of John Snow in Victorian London, linking the clustering of cholera deaths around a pump in Soho.

More recent disease-transmission research has integrated **agent-based modeling** (ABM) with both network theory and geographic information systems (GIS). Simoes (2005) focuses on an agent-based model with a human-mobility-network model superimposed on a SEIR model. The study relies on the results of simulating different scenarios comparing differences in the spatial structure of the mobility network and geographical distribution of individuals. Similarly, Yang and Atkinson (2005) look at a specific disease-transmission scenario in a UK university. They use both ABM and GIS to incorporate a variation of the SIR model as well as control measures such as immunisation and isolation, where the risk of transmission varies from place to place depending on the concentration of students.

Developed at Los Alamos National Laboratory, Transportation Analysis Simulation System (TRANSIMS) is an agent-based system simulating the movement of people and vehicles in the transportation network of a large metropolitan area. It was designed to provide more accurate information on issues such as traffic impacts, energy consumption, traffic safety, and emergency evacuation, amongst others. EPISIMS is a simulator developed from TRANSIMS that enables the inclusion of disease-evolution scenarios. This has been used to answer questions such as: How can an outbreak be contained before it becomes an epidemic, and what disease surveillance strategies should be implemented? (Eubank et al., 2004).

The research presented above emphasises the morbidity of diseases in general. Similarly, the following demonstrate approaches to the global malaria problem, using ABM, from two angles. Janssen and Martens (1997) focus on the adaptiveness of mosquitoes to insecticides and malaria parasites to antimalarial drugs. This work aims to find a solution to controlling the spread of the disease by understanding the mechanism that renders this prophylaxis useless. Similarly, the same result is sought by Carnahan, Costantini, Toure, and Taylor (1997) but by studying the problem at a different level: the dispersal of anopheles. Here, there is a focus on understanding the behaviour of malaria-transmitting mosquitoes, their geographical displacement, with the aim to consequently monitor their movements and thus reduce the number of malaria cases. At the same level, but from the human standpoint, Hay, Noor, Nelson, and Tatem (2005) aim to map the human population at risk at the global, continental, and national scales to help guide priority setting in international health financing. This is quite an important aspect as estimates of the burden of disease caused by malaria are crucial for informing malaria-control programmes (Snow, Guerra, Noor, Myint, & Hay, 2005).

Furthermore, Ngwa and Shu (2000) consider the vector-borne disease by developing a mosquito susceptible-exposed-infected (SEI) model in addition to their SEIR human cycle.

People enter the Susceptible class either through birth or migration. When an Infected mosquito bites a susceptible human there is a finite probability that the parasite will be passed on to the human and the person will move to the Exposed class. After a latency period, the exposed humans become Infected. If not dead, infected humans recover and move to the Recovered class. The recovered humans are immune a specified period after which they return to the Susceptible class. Mosquitoes enter the Susceptible class through birth. Susceptible mosquitoes are Infected either spontaneously according to a certain probability or through contacts with Infected and Recovered humans. Then they pass through the Exposed and Infected classes. The mosquito remains Infected for life.

Model Overview

Our model attempts to encompass the present malaria situation in Haiti and includes additional information we have deemed relevant to the parasite problem.

We have implemented a computer simulator, which can be considered as a virtual environment, having the following properties:

1.   It can take into account the human agents, their properties, and behaviours (birth, death, mobility, education, etc.) as well their potential malaria contamination.

2.   It includes the environment representing the geographical space with its sub-areas (cities, roads, schools, hospitals) affecting differently the contamination process.

3.   It can support experimentation of various scenarios where number of agents, schools, hospitals, simulation duration, and so on can be suitably chosen.

4.   It is a generic tool offering reusable modules that may be adapted for any geographical region and any vector-borne disease.

In this section, we present the model overview.

The Environment

Since our application case is Haiti, we model the environment as a schematic map of Haiti with a graphical terrain granularity sufficient to represent that which affects the dynamics of what we intend to model. This granularity is such that the simulation space is divided into microenvironments: sea, hospitals, land, mountains, cities, roads, and schools. All of these microenvironments have a direct impact on our agents and hence the simulations we run.

The Mosquito Population

Our model represents only the parasite carriers of the entire anophele population, unlike in Janssen and Martens (1997). We do not model seasonal mosquito population variations. All of our modelled mosquitoes pose a malaria threat to the human (agent) population concerned.

We have decided not to model mosquitoes as an agent whose behaviour is affected by its interaction with both the environment and other agents. Their presence in the model is stochastic, embedded in the environment we create. The probability of an agent contracting malaria varies according to conditions the seven microenvironments present; the probability of an agent contracting malaria differs. We can observe for example that land (rural areas) is the ideal breeding ground for mosquitoes. This is contrary to mountains where despite the adequate water level and lack of

Table 1. Mosquito contamination probabilities

Microenvironment	Contamination Probabilities
Land	2.00%
Road	1.00%
City	0.66%
Mountain	0.50%

Note: Microenvironments not included are those with 0% probabilities

pollution, elevation lowers ambient temperature, making it an unsuitable mosquito habitat (Lindsay & Martens, 1998). We consequently say that the highest probability of malaria infection is in land, and decreasingly in road; city; and mountain. No contamination occurs in a hospital or school. This stochastic order abides to the information given on such habitats (Baudon, 2000), see Table 1.

The Human Population

Human actors are modelled as reactive agents spread in the environment and catching infection according to probabilities varying from microenvironment to another.

Each agent is characterized mainly by:

- **Sex:** The sex of an agent is not explicit. This factor only affects our model when breeding occurs.

- **Age:** We have included natural death as well as death caused by malaria. The average life span for men and women in Haiti is 51.9 and 53.3 years respectively (WHO, 2005). In order to accommodate these data, bearing in mind that our agent population is sexless, we have set a maximum age of 52 years. If an agent survives malaria, it dies when attaining that age.

- **Breeding:** We have embodied the sexless property by using a random-number generator allowing an agent to reproduce 50% of the time, as the male to female ratio is approximately 1:1 in Haiti. The above condition in combination with the following must be satisfied before an agent can reproduce: minimum age of 14 years, maximum age of 49 years, not have reproduced more than 4 times, and have at least an interval of 1 year after reproduction (WHO, 2005).

- **Mobility and Speed:** We have endowed some of our agents with the ability to be mobile, and if so, a fraction with a car. This translates into those mobile exiting their city of origin with greater ease than those not mobile. Similarly,

Figure 1. Agent state cycle

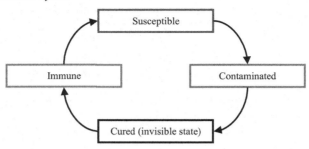

car owners can move throughout the country at a greater speed, especially on roads, than those without a vehicle. The speed of contaminated agent is diminished by 50%, due to weakness caused by the parasite.

- **Level of education:** Baume and Kachur (1999) stress the importance of educating the population with the recognition of malaria symptoms and the gravity of not acting consequently. We have introduced this facet of the problem by creating an "education scale" where agents have education points ranging from 1 to 20. Points represent the time agents take to attribute existing symptoms to malaria, where a contaminated agent with 1 education point waits longer before heading towards a hospital than its counterpart with 20 points, who as soon as it is contaminated seeks medical attention. The maximum waiting period is 29 days, because 30 days after contamination, an agent outside a hospital dies. Points are cumulative only. Schools are distributed throughout our Haiti map, both in rural and urban areas. The utility of a school lies in that agents moving randomly arrive at a school and leave with more malaria awareness. They enter the school, if they do not have 20 points and are not contaminated. They remain for a period of three days, after which they gain an education point. Education's role is seen in the model when the contaminated agent, because of lack of malaria awareness, does not recognise symptoms in time and hence cannot reach a hospital.

- **Health state:** Each agent can go through the malaria cycle of being Susceptible (when they are susceptible to contracting malaria), becoming Contaminated, and consequently either dying of lack of treatment or becoming cured as a consequence of a hospital visit (see Figure 1). These states are dependent on the interaction of agents with their surrounding environment. The model emulates the contamination process stochastically through its environment. Only those agents whose state is susceptible can be contaminated when in a microenvironment and according to the probabilities.

- **Natural inoculation:** occurs through continuous repetitive contamination, where a person cured from malaria is immune to the parasite for an average of one year (Baudon, 2000). As there must be mosquito-person contact, and a greater number of anopheles are found in rural areas, the initial immune and contaminated populations are all mobile. Contaminated agents are to wait an amount of time, depending on the education they have, as discussed above. If a contaminated agent has a maximum education of 20, the shortest distance between itself and the existing hospitals will be calculated. Subsequently the agent will start heading towards medical attention. Those contaminated who have reached a hospital in time, will remain there for a period of 20 days, the average malaria recovery time (Malaria Foundation International, 2000), and subsequently the agent's state changes to Immune (during 1 year). In our model, death strikes when a period of 30 days has elapsed after symptoms appear, the average interval (Malaria Foundation International).

Agent-Based Malaria Simulator MalSim

Our agent-based **Malaria Simulator MalSim** is developed using the programmable modeling environment starlogo.[1] A snapshot of the simulation graphical user interface can be seen in Figure 2.

The simulator provides an overview plan allowing the visualization of continuous agent evolution. The agents move throughout the environment and their health states change accordingly (appropriate colour codes are assigned to each agent

Figure 2: MalSim interface: Starlogo main display and some graphics

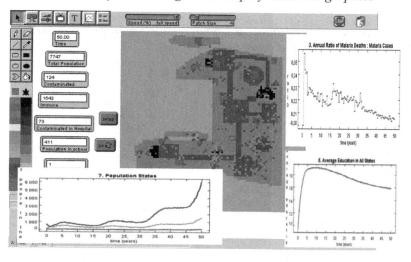

health state). Graphs trace over time relevant measures enabling us to follow the **simulation steps:** the total number of population, the number of agent population in each state (Susceptible, Contaminated, and Immune), the total death cases, the ratio of annual contamination, and so on. Simulator parameters and their values for each step are saved into files for further statistical analysis.

Virtual Experiments and Results

We present here the performed virtual experiments and their main results answering the following questions:

1.   What is the effect of **hospitals** on malaria spread over a long period?
2.   What is the effect of **schools** on malaria spread over a long period?

In order to answer these questions, we have designed four scenarios where numbers of schools and hospitals are different. Henceforth, our four scenarios will be denominated in the following manner: Experiment A (0 schools and 0 hospitals); Experiment B (0 schools and 3 hospitals); Experiment C (20 schools and 3 hospitals) and Experiment D (20 schools and 5 hospitals).

For all experiments, added to the calibration values (mentioned in the model description), we consider 1000 agents as the initial human population evenly distributed in the five cities in our Haiti map.

Figure 3. Experiment A (0 hospitals, 0 schools) results: agent population per state, whole population growth, and death cases over time

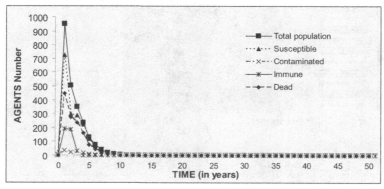

With this set of scenarios, we investigate the model behaviour during a period of 50 years (instead of 10 years as in Rateb et al., 2005).

No Hospitals, No Schools (Experiment A)

This experiment shows (see Figure 3) that the total population decreases and reaches zero after 15 years. This means that, although the population breeds, without any treatment a whole population can disappear after certain period.

Figure 4. Total agent population

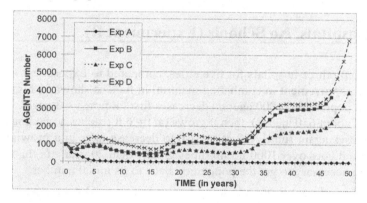

Figure 5. Mortality rates

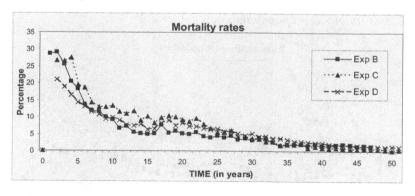

Figure 6. Total agent population for experiments B and C for the first 20 years

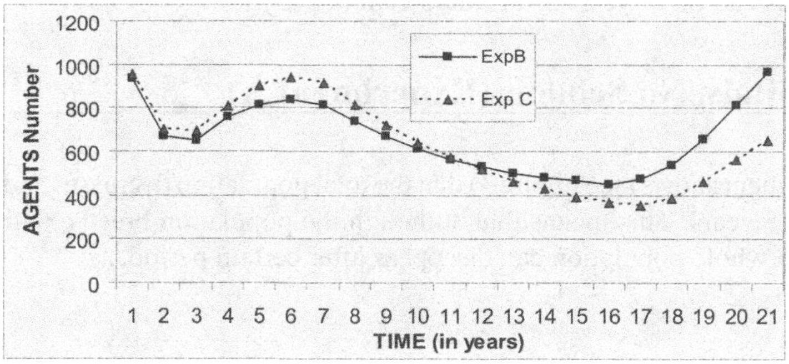

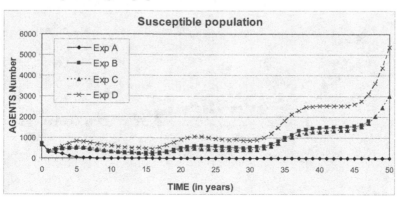

Three Hospitals, No Schools (Experiment B)

By adding only three hospitals for five cities, compared to Experiment A, we notice a great improvement in combating malaria. In fact, as shown in Figure 4, the initial agent population (1000 agents) decreases first (at time t = 3 years, it reaches a minima of about 650 agents), then it grows (at t = 6 it reaches a maxima of about 850), decreases again (until 450 at t =16), to decrease later in a growing "wave like" form and goes over 1000 for all times greater than 20 years. In this scenario, 20 years are necessary to get the population back to its initial number.

Also, with Experiment B, the mortality rate[2] (see Figure 5) is at most 30%; even though this value is high, it is much lower than the results of Experiment A for which mortality rapidly reaches 100%.

Figure 7. Susceptible-agent population

Figure 8. Contaminated-agent population

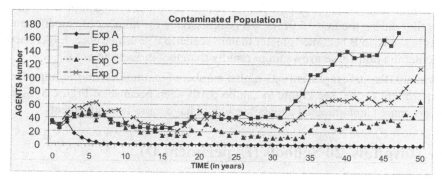

Three Hospitals, 20 Schools (Experiment C)

By adding schools, contrarily to our initial thoughts, we notice first (see Figure 4) that the whole agent population evolution with Experiment C has similar global behaviour to Experiment B (global evolution with local fluctuations).

Nonetheless, the Experiment C results, compared to those of Experiment B, do not show a continuous improvement in terms of malaria fighting. In fact, as shown in Figure 6, during the first 10 years, the total population is greater with Experiment C than with B. After the 12th year, Experiment B's total population becomes and remains greater than that of Experiment C (as illustrated in Figure 4).

For Experiment C, the mortality rate is close to the mortality rate of Experiment B. This can be explained by the fact that we have the same number of hospitals.

Figure 9. Immune-agent population

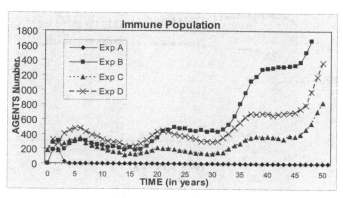

Figure 7 shows that the number of susceptible agents for experiments B and C are close to each other during the whole period. However, contaminated population sizes are similar during the first 15 years, but progressively the number of contaminated agents in scenario B becomes greater than in scenario C. Furthermore, Experiment B's contamination curve grows more rapidly than that in Experiment C.

Experiment B's curve representing a higher number of immune agents in comparison to Experiment C one, see Figure 9, can be partly seen because of Figure 8. Since there are more Contaminated agents, we would have more Immune agents.

Five Hospitals, 20 Schools (Experiment D)

Figure 4 shows that with Experiment D the agent population number over time is greater than all other experiments. In addition, the safe-population graph is the highest, Figure 7.

For this experiment, contamination looks greater than for Experiment B for the first 25 years, and becomes smaller for the remaining period.

Although a greater contamination, the Immune-agent population in Experiment D is the highest of all the experiments for the first 20 years. This can be explained by the fact that there are more hospitals and consequently more malaria cases are treated.

For the remaining period, as contamination is lower than with B, immunization is also lower.

Figure10. Average education level over time

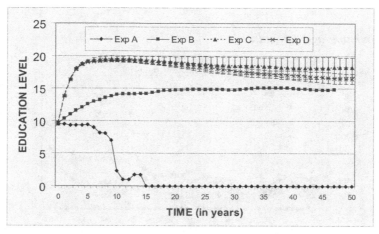

At the beginning, the mortality rate in Experiment D is lowest. This can be explained by both the rapid average education-level increase (see Figure 10) and the highest number of hospitals. Not only do contaminated agents rapidly become aware of their disease, but they also rapidly find nearby hospitals for medical attention.

Discussion

Our work is novel as there has not been research undertaken on vector-borne diseases studied with Agent-Based Modeling in a complex-system approach. This is given so that our model incorporates the closing of the Susceptible-Contaminated-Immune loop where after a person is cured from malaria, it remains immune before returning to a susceptible state. Apart from Rateb et al.'s (2005) model of malaria awareness, there is little information available showing the impact of education on health care. In fact, in Rateb et al., we have researched the effect of malaria awareness on human mortality due to malaria where models of malaria contagion, birth-death and awareness acquisition, were grouped and simulations were run for different situations for a 10-year period. In this chapter, after recalibrating our model with up-to-date data on Haiti, we conducted a new series of simulation runs over a 50-year period in order to investigate whether the previous findings are maintained for a longer period.

The new results emerging after this new series of simulation is that, by adding hospitals only (Experiment B) or hospitals and schools (Experiment C and Experiment D), we surprisingly find curves having similar behaviours. In fact, for each scenario, the total living population increases then decreases in a periodic manner. Approximately every 15 years, there is a local behaviour where the curve increases-decreases and with a global increase in a wave-like form.

This emerging cyclic-like behaviour, observed with the total agent-population curves, is also present for Susceptible-agent population and Immune-agent population curves. This emerging behaviour was not noticed when running simulations for a 10-year period.

By comparing the total agent populations for Experiment B and Experiment C, we notice that during the first 10 years, Experiment C shows better evolution results and then Experiment B improves and remains greater until the end. This may be explained by the average education curves (Figure 10) showing that the fact of adding schools (Experiment C and Experiment D) influences rapidly on the population awareness reaching a maximum near to 20 (top value in the education scale) and then decreases slowly; whereas for Experiment B, the education awareness increases slowly and continues to increase.

Figure 11. Morbidity over time

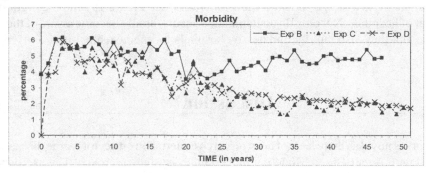

As for these three scenarios (B, C, and D) and on a long-term level, the average education is stable and high (greater than 14 over a scale of 20), the whole population grows, and the mortality rate decreases.

By comparing morbidity[3] in the three scenarios (B, C, and D), experiment B is the worst, with the highest morbidity rate; whereas for experiments C and D, morbidity decreases globally.

The morbidity graph in Figure 11 confirms that schools as well as hospitals improve the combating of malaria.

As a conclusion, from this set of virtual experiments, we can state that:

1.   First, hospitals are necessary to fight against malaria. In fact, just by adding three hospitals to our environment, the whole evolution of agent population changes. In fact, the mortality is highly reduced and even the population number grows globally.

2.   Second, schools and hospitals positively influence the fight against malaria, mainly on a mid-term (first 10 years) level.

Even with running our simulation over 50 years, we have shown that education is not sufficient in our model. Therefore, we still need to revise our model mainly with respect to education modeling. Also, perhaps we need to study a 100-year period (since 50 remains close to an agent's average life span) and can investigate deeper the "generation change" and malaria evolution, since they would inherit the parasite and not the education level.

Future Work

Due to our very time consuming modeling and simulating efforts, we consider that we still have to both improve our model and deepen our investigation by simulation. Consequently, our future work can be drawn on various levels. First, and in order to reach more realism with our model, we can implement a new model including the SEIR cycle for humans and the addition of the mosquito transitions through S-E-I states; this means mainly including mosquitoes as agents able to get infected after biting an infected human. Rural population dynamics as well as climatic seasons may be included too in order to emulate the fluctuations in mosquito population and hence consequent malaria contamination spread. Second, we can extend the model to consider additional and new means supporting the combat against malaria such as bed nets. Third, with respect to public awareness, we have to revise our modeling way considering mainly long periods. Fourth, additional socioeconomic factors should be included such as road infrastructure and transportation. Finally, and in response to our ultimate goals, our simulator can be revised and extended to become a generic tool usable to simulate any vector-borne disease and/or any geographical area. Connecting it to a geographical information system would be an interesting step towards supporting the malaria combat in any part of the world.

Acknowledgments

Many thanks to Prof. B. Pavard and to all those who helped the authors in achieving these results. Sincere thanks go to the book editors.

References

Axelrod, R. (1997). *The complexity of cooperation: Agent based models of competition and collaboration*. Princeton, NJ: Princeton University Press.

Anderson, R. M., & May, R. M. (1991). *Infectious diseases of humans: Dynamics and control*. Oxford, England: Oxford University Press.

Aschan-Leygonie, C., Mathian, H., & Saunders, L. (2000). A spatial microsimulation of population dynamics in southern france: A model integrating individual decisions and spatial constraints. In G. Ballot & G. Weisbuch (Eds.). *Applications of simulations to social sciences* (pp. 109-125). HERMES Science Publishing Ltd.

Bagni, R., Berchi, R., & Cariello, P. (2002, June). A comparison of simulation models applied to epidemics. *Journal of Artificial Societies and Social Simulation, 5*(3). Retrieved October 12, 2006 from http://jasss.soc.surrey.ac.uk/5/3/5.html

Brauer, F. (2004, November). What does mathematics have to do with SARS? *Pi in the Sky Magazine*, (8) December 2004, 10-13.

Baudon, D. (2000, July-September). Les paludismes en Afrique Subsaharienne. *Afrique Contemporaine, Numéro spécial, La santé en Afrique: Anciens et nouveaux défis, 195*, 36-45. La Documentation française.

Baume, C., & Kachur, S. P. (1999). Améliorer la Prise en charge communautaire du paludisme infantile: Comment la recherche comportementale peut-elle aider? *Technical Report Support for Analysis and Research in Africa (SARA) Project (Report PN-ACJ-022)*. Academy for Educational Development (AED), United States Agency for International Development (USAID).

Carley, K. (2001). Intra-organizationl complexity and computation. In Baum, J. C. (Ed.), *Companion to organizations*. Oxford, UK: Blackwell.

Carnahan, J., Li, S., Costantini, C., Toure, Y. T., & Taylor, C. E. (1997). Computer simulation of dispersal by Anopheles gambiae in West Africa. In *Artificial Life V* (pp. 387-394). MIT Press.

Crutchfield, J. P. (2002). What lies between order and chaos? In J. Casti (Ed.), *Art and complexity* (pp. 31-45). Oxford, UK: Oxford University Press.

Edmonds, B. (1999). What is complexity? The philosophy of complexity *per se* with applications to some examples in evolution. In F. Heylighen & D. Aerts (Eds.), *The evolution of complexity* (pp. 1-18). Dordrecht: Kluwer..

Eubank, S., Guclu, H., Kumar, V., Marathe, M., Srinivasan, A., Toroczkai, Z., & Wang, N. (2004). Modeling disease outbreaks in realistic urban social networks. *Nature, 429*, 180-184.

Gatrell, A. C., Bailey, T. C., Diggle, P. J., & Rowlingson, B. S. (1996). Spatial point pattern analysis and its application in geographical epidemiology. *Transactions of the Institute of British Geographers, 21*(1), 256-274.

Goldenfeld, N., & Kadanoff, L. P. (1999, April 2). Simple lessons from complexity. *Science, 284*, 87-89.

Gomez, R., & Rowe, J. E. (2003). An agent-based simulation of crowd movement. In D. Al-Dabass (Ed.) *Proceedings of UK Simulation Conference*. London: UK Simulation Society.

Hamagami, T., & Hirata, H. (2003). Method of crowd simulation by using multiagent on cellular automata. In *Proceedings of IEEE/WIC international conference on intellegent agent technology (IAT2003)* (pp. 46-52).

Hay, S. I., Noor, A. M., Nelson, A, & Tatem, A. J. (2005). The accuracy of human population maps for public health application. *Tropical Medicine and International Health, 10*(10), 1073-1086.

Hübler, A. W. (2005). Predicting complex systems with a holistic approach. *Complexity, 10*(3), 11-16.

Jaeger, W., & Janssen, M. A. (2001). *Diffusion processes in demographic transitions: a prospect on using multi agent simulation to explore the role of cognitive strategies and social interactions* (Tech. Rep. No. 01B40). University of Groningen, SOM (Systems, Organisation and Management).

Janssen, M. A., & Martens, W. J. M. (1997). Modeling malaria as a complex adaptive system. In *Artificial Life III* (pp. 213-236). MIT Press.

Kermack, W. O., & McKendrick, A. G. (1927). A contribution to the mathematical theory of epidemics. In *Proceedings of the Royal Society of London, Series A, 115*, 700-721.

Keyser, D. (2000). Emergent properties and behavior of the atmosphere. In B.-Y. Yaneer (Ed.), In *Proc. Intl. Conf. Complex Systems* (pp. 33-41). Cambridge, MA: Advanced Book Program, Perseus Books.

Krogstad, D. J. (1996). Malaria as a reemerging disease. *Epidemiological Reviews, 18*(1), 77-89.

Lindsay, S. W., & Martens, W. J. M. (1998). Malaria in the African highlands: Past, present and future. *Bulletin of the World Health Organization, 76*(1), 33-45.

Malaria Foundation International. (2000). Retrieved June 2000 from http://www.malaria.org.

Ngwa, G. A., & Shu, W. S. (2000). A mathematical model for endemic malaria with variable human and mosquito populations. *Mathematical and Computer Modelling, 32*, 747-763

Pan American Health Organization (PAHO). (2001). Basic country health profiles. Retrieved on October 12, 2006 from http://www.paho.org/english/sha/prflhai.htm

Pavard, B. (2002, June-July). Complexity paradigm as a framework for the study of cooperative systems. *COSI Summer School on Modelling and Designing Complex Organisational Systems*, Chania, Greece.

Pavard, B., & Dugdale, J. (2002). An introduction to complexity in social science. *COSI project*. Retrieved December, 2001, from http://www.irit.fr/COSI/training/complexity-tutorial/complexity-tutorial.htm

Payne, D. (1987). Spread of chloroquine resistance in plasmodium falciparum." *Parasitology Today, 3*, 241-246.

Rateb, F., Pavard, B., Bellamine-Bensaoud, N., Merelo, J. J. & Arenas, M. G. (2005, April-June). Modelling malaria with multi-agent systems. *International Journal of Intelligent Information Technologies, 1*(2), 17-27.

Simoes, J. (2005). Modelling the spreading of infectious diseases using social mobility networks. In S. E. Batty (Ed.), *Proceedings of the 9th International Conference Computers in Urban Planning and Urban Management (CUPUM)* (p. 43). London: University College London.

Simon, H. A. (1969). *The sciences of the artificial.* Cambridge, MA: MIT Press.

Snow, R. W., Guerra, C. A., Noor, A. M., Myint, H. Y., & Hay, S. I. (2005). Malaria risk. *Nature, 437*(7056), e4-e5.

World Health Organization (WHO). (2005). *Health situation in the Americas: Basic indicators.* Retrieved October 12, 2006, from http://www.paho.org/english/dd/ais/BI-brochure-2005.pdf

World Health Organization (WHO). (1996). Fighting disease fostering development. *The World Health Report.* Geneva, Switzerland: Author.

Yang, Y., & Atkinson, P. M. (2005, April). Integrated ABM and GIS modeling of infectious disease transmission. In R. Billen, J. Drummond, D. Forrest, & E. João (Eds.), *Proceedings of the GIS research UK (GISRUK 2005)* (pp. 27-29). Glasgow, Scotland: University of Glasgow.

Endnotes

[1] http://education.mit.edu/starlogo

[2] We compute mortality rate as the ratio of dead agents to the total agent population per year

[3] We define morbidity as the ratio of the number of contaminated agents to the sum of susceptible and immune agents

Chapter V

An Intelligent Multi-Robot System Using Higher-Order Mobile Agents

Yasushi Kambayashi, Nippon Institute of Technology, Japan

Munehiro Takimoto, Tokyo University of Science, Japan

Abstract

This chapter presents a framework for controlling intelligent robots connected by communication networks. This framework provides novel methods to control co-ordinated systems using higher-order mobile agents. Higher-order mobile agents are hierarchically structured agents that can contain other mobile agents. By using higher-order mobile agents, intelligent robots in action can acquire new function-alities dynamically as well as exchange their roles with other colleague robots. The higher-order property of the mobile agents enables them to be organized hierarchi-cally and dynamically. In addition to the advantages described above, higher-order mobile agents require minimum communication. They only need connection to be established when they perform migration.

Introduction

In the last decade, robot systems have made rapid progress in not only their behaviors but also in the way they are controlled. In particular, control systems based on multiagent methodologies enable a controlled robot to learn to adapt to the circumstances around it through its own interactions. Furthermore, multiagent systems introduced modularity, reconfigurability, and extensibility to control systems, which had been traditionally monolithic. They have made easier the development of control systems on distributed environments such as intelligent multirobot systems.

On the other hand, excessive interactions among agents in the multiagent system may cause problems in the multirobot environment. Consider a multirobot system where each robot is controlled by an agent, and interactions among robots are achieved through a communication network such as a wireless LAN. Since the circumstances around the robot change as the robots move, the condition of each connection among the various robots also changes. In this environment, when some of the connections in the network are disabled, the system may not be able to maintain consistency among the states of the robots. Such a problem has a tendency to increase as the number of interactions increases.

In order to lessen the problems of excessive communication, mobile-agent methodologies have been developed for distributed environments. In the mobile-agent system, each agent can actively migrate from one site to another site. Since a mobile agent can bring the necessary functionalities with it and perform its tasks autonomously, it can reduce the necessity for interaction with other sites. In the minimal case, a mobile agent requires that the connection be established only when it performs migration (Binder, Hulaas, & Villazon, 2001). This property is useful for controlling robots that have to work in a remote site with unreliable communication or intermittent communication. The concept of a mobile agent also creates the possibility that new functions and knowledge can be introduced to the entire multiagent system from a host or controller outside the system via a single accessible member of the intelligent multirobot system.

The structure of the balance of this chapter is as follows. In the second section, we describe related works. The third section describes our development of the higher-order mobile agents. The fourth section describes the dynamic extension concept of our higher-order mobile-agent system. Dynamic extension is the key feature that supports the ability to add new functionalities to intelligent robots in action. The fifth section demonstrates the feasibility of our system with two examples of intelligent multirobot systems in which robots play the game of TAG and search for an object cooperatively. Finally, the sixth section discusses future research directions and conclusions.

Related Works

The traditional structure for the construction of intelligent robots is to make large, often monolithic, artificial-intelligence software systems. The ALVINN autonomous driving system is one of the most successful such developments (Pomerleau, 1994). Putting intelligence into robots is, however, not an easy task. An intelligent robot that is able to work in the real world needs a large-scale knowledge base. The ALVINN system employs neural networks to acquire the knowledge semiautomatically (Pomerleau, 1989). One of the limitations of neural networks is that it is assumed that the system is used in the same environment as that in which it was trained. When the intelligent robot is expected to work in an unknown space or an extremely dynamic environment, it is not realistic to assume that the neural network is appropriately trained or can acquire additional knowledge with sufficient rapidity. Indeed, many intelligent robots lack a mechanism to adapt to a previously unknown environment.

On the other hand, multiagent robotic systems are recently becoming popular in RoboCup or MIROSOT (Murphy, 2002, pp. 301-302). In traditional multiagent systems, robots communicate with each other to achieve cooperative behaviors. The ALLIANCE architecture, developed in Oak Ridge National Laboratory, showed that multiagents could achieve cooperative intelligent systems (Parker, 1998). The architecture is, however, mainly designed to support self-adaptability. The robots in the system are expected to behave without external interference, and they show some intelligent behaviors. The observed intelligence, however, is limited due to the simple mechanism called motivation. Robots' behaviors are regulated by only two rules: robot impatience and robot acquiescence. These rules are initially defined and do not evolve. In contrast, the goal of our system is to introduce intelligence and knowledge into the robots after they start to work (Kambayashi & Takimoto, 2005). Therefore, our system does not have any learning mechanism or knowledge-acquiring mechanism. All the necessary knowledge is sent as mobile agents from other robots or the host computer.

An interesting research work of a multiagent robot-control system was conducted at Tokyo University of Science (Nishiyama, Ohwada, & Mizoguchi, 1998). Their work focused on the language aspect of robot-control systems using multiagents. They employed a hierarchical model of robot agents where the root agent indirectly manages all the agents. The lowest agents are physical devices and each has only one supervisor agent. Communications are performed through superagent channels and subagent channels. Each robot has a hierarchically structured set of agents and the structure is rigidly constructed at the initial time. Therefore, the structure of the control software is predetermined, and there is no concept of dynamic configuration of the structure of agents. The framework we present in this chapter provides dynamic restructuring of the set of agents and provides more flexibility in the hierarchically structured control software.

For the communication aspect, they employ agent negotiation. In contrast, we employ agent migration so that our model can more suitably fit in a realistic multirobot environment where the communication should be expected to be intermittent.

One notable feature of the system of Nishiyama et al. (1998) is the description language, called Multiagent Robot Language (MRL). This language is based on the committed-choice concurrent logic programming language and compiled into guarded Horn clauses (Shapiro, 1987; Ueda, 1986). This feature has advantages of transparency of the agent descriptions over systems that are based on Java. The efficiency problem of logic programming is overcome by recompiling into C language.

The work most closely related to ours is the distributed port-based adaptable agent architecture developed at Carnegie Mellon University (Pham, Dixon, Jackson, & Khosla, 2000), designed for real-time control applications (Stewart & Khosla, 1996). The port-based agents (PBAs) are mobile software modules that have input ports and output ports. All PBAs have the map of the port addresses so that they can move other robots and combine themselves with other PBAs to compose larger modules. Software composition is clearly possible using port-based modules. However, the dynamic extension capability of our mobile control system is another strategy for the composition of larger software.

The usefulness of PBA architecture is demonstrated by the Millibot project also at Carnegie Mellon University (Grabowski, Navarro-Serment, Paredis, & Khosla, 2000). In a robotics mapping application, a PBA is used to control the mapping robots, and when the working robot has a hardware failure, the PBA on the robot detects it and moves to an idle robot.

The framework we present in this chapter is an exploration of the applications of mobile agents and software composition through mobility and extensibility. The construction of robot control software by mobile agents and its dynamic extension is not only novel but also flexible due to dynamic inheritance. It may be superior for extensibility of working software.

Higher-Order Mobile Agent

The model of our system is cooperative work by a pool of heterogeneous robots. Possible applications are rescue and surveillance. In such applications, the environments are expected to be adverse and it would be not easy for robots to move around. Mobile agents, however, can easily move from one robot to another to find the most suitable robot, that is, most conveniently located or most adequately equipped to achieve the system goal. For example, if a robot finds it cannot go beyond a large gap and it knows a colleague robot is on the other side of the gap, then the mobile agent on the robot can migrate to the colleague robot to continue its task.

Therefore, the ability of the agent to move from one robot to another contributes to flexibility, energy efficiency, and scalability in the use of the robot resources.

- **As an example of flexibility:** Suppose a multirobot system consists of small heterogeneous mobile robots that are scattered in a field. Each robot has some general capability such as mobility, and some specific capability such as an infrared cameras, ultrasound system, or long arms. The mobile agents can select from among such heterogeneous mobile robots to achieve a specific goal. A mobile agent with a specific purpose can migrate to each robot one by one to find the most physically suitable one to perform the purpose.

- **To illustrate energy efficiency:** A mobile agent can migrate to the robot that is most conveniently located to a given task, for example, the closest robot to a physical object such as soccer ball. Since agent migration is much easier than robot motion, this capability saves power-consumption. Also, notice that agents on a robot can be killed as soon as they finish their tasks. If each agent has a policy choosing idle robots rather than busy ones in addition to these migration strategies, it would result in more efficient use of robot resources.

- **To illustrate scalability:** If any robot cannot achieve the purpose alone, the agent can migrate to several robots to make them cooperate to perform the goal. This means that if the current robot system lacks some capabilities, we can complement it by adding some robots with new capabilities and coordinating mobile agents.

The mobile agent system we use to control robots is based on a system called MobileSpaces developed by Satoh (2000). MobileSpaces is based on the mobile ambients computational model proposed by Cardelli and Gordon (1998). Mobile-Spaces provide the basic framework for mobile agents. It is built on the Java virtual machine, and agents are programmed in Java language. We are reimplementing our system with a descriptive language based on a functional language, Objective Caml (Chailloux, Manoury, & Pagano, 2000), in order to regain transparency of agent descriptions (Kambayashi & Takimoto, 2004).

Based on the observations mentioned above, we have developed a framework for constructing intelligent multirobots controlled by higher-order mobile agents where the higher-order property of the mobile agents means that they can be organized hierarchically and dynamically. Each mobile agent can be a container of other mobile agents and can migrate to other agents. This migration to an agent enables the migrated agent to acquire new functions as well as to permit the robot that receives the migrated agent to acquire new functions.

This higher-order property gives significant advantages to control systems based on traditional mobile agents. When agents migrate, not only the program code of the agent but also the state of the agent can be transferred to the destination. Consider robots moving around in a situation where there are obstacles. In this case, avoiding collision with obstacles or other robots can be regarded as common behavior for every robot. Such common behavior can be achieved by migration of the agent that rotates a robot in response to signals from collision-sensors. After that, in order to realize complete behavior, an agent for the main behavior has only to migrate to the agent with the common behavior. This means that the main behavior can be described without considering obstacles, and therefore, the higher-order property contributes to not only increasing scalability due to dynamic extension but also decreasing development cost due to separation of functions.

The higher-order mobile agents are mobile agents whose destination can be other mobile agents as well as places in traditional agent systems. Moreover, since the extended agent behaves as a single agent and it can migrate to another agent with the containing agents, communications through remote connections can be reduced further. We implemented two examples to prove our framework's effectiveness. Although they are toy program examples, they provide intuitive understanding leading to practical use.

Two unique features are worth emphasizing with respect to our robot-control system: (1) Each mobile agent can contain one or more mobile agents (hierarchical construction), and (2) each mobile agent can migrate to any other mobile agent (interagent migration).

Thus, migration to another agent results in a nesting structure of agents. Agents in the other agent are still autonomous agents that can behave independently. When an agent migrates to another agent, the newly arrived agent is called the child agent, and the container agent is called the parent agent. In the same sense, nested agents

Figure 1. When agent C migrates from agent A to agent B, the contained agent D also migrates from A to B

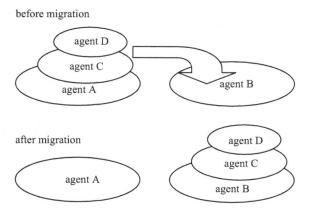

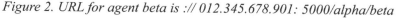

Figure 2. URL for agent beta is :// 012.345.678.901: 5000/alpha/beta

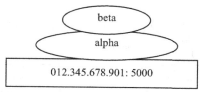

are called descendent agents and nesting agents are called ancestral agents. Parent agents give their resources and services to their child agents so that an agent or a group of agents acquires whatever its parent provides. Figure 1 illustrates the situation that agent C migrates from agent A to agent B and the child agent D also migrates from agent A to agent B. Each place (an address space designated by IP address and Port number) has a special stationary agent MATP, and MATP does serialization and other necessary processing for migration.

When the system has decided to transfer an agent, the agent is passed to the stationary agent MATP. MATP marshals the agent and its descendent agents into a bit-stream. MATP then transfers the bit-stream to the destination computer by using an HTTP-like application-layer protocol for agent transmission over TCP/IP communication. On the receiver side, another MATP receives the bit-stream and then reconstructs an agent and its descendent agents. The transferred bit-stream is formed in Java's JAR file format, and MATP uses the Java object serialization package for marshaling agents.

The first feature allows a mobile application to be constructed by organizing more than one agent. The second feature allows a group of agents to be treated as a single agent. By using these two features, we can construct a mobile application as the combination of mobile agents. We can send the base agent to a remote site, and then we can add new features and functions to the base agent by sending other agents later, while the base agent is running.

We use a special addressing term similar to the Internet URL to specify agents in a hierarchical structure. In this chapter, we continue to call these addresses URLs. Figure 2 depicts a situation where an agent alpha that contains the other agent beta is on a machine whose IP address is 012.345.678.901 and uses port number 5000. In this case, URL for agent beta is ":://012.345.678.901:5000/alpha/beta."

Dynamic Extension

MobileSpaces provides the basic mechanism for agent migration and remote-method invocation. When an agent wants to invoke a method in another agent, the calling

Figure 3. Dynamic extension by migration of the child agent with new features

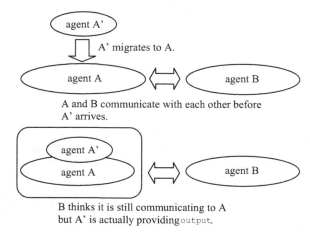

agent specifies the called agent by URL and sends a message object to the agent. It lacks, however, the feature that an agent can dynamically extend its functionality. For intelligent multirobot control, we add a dynamic extension feature to customize functions of intelligent robots while they are running.

Suppose an agent A is working somewhere and we want to extend its capability. One way is to replace that agent with a new agent B. On the other hand in our system, we only need to send an agent A' with the new feature to the agent A. In this case, the method in agent A' overrides that method in the agent A. While the agent A' is the child of A, the agent A behaves with the extended feature. If the agent A' leaves the agent A, the agent A behaves with the original feature. All the other agents do not have to be aware of the change of the agent A. In Figure 3, after an agent A' migrates to an agent A the other agent B still communicates to the agent A without knowing about the migration of A'. The agents A and A' behave just as a single agent for the agent B.

It is necessary to define how this override capability is to be implemented. For that, we use the concept of the "signature" of a function. The signature is the extended type of a function. When it is said that two functions have the same signature, it means that they have the same name, the same number of the same type of formal parameters, and the same return type. For example, if it is necessary to extend the output method in the agent A, the agent A' with new output method with the same signature is to be sent into the agent A. The agent A checks all the incoming messages and passes those implemented in A' to the agent A' for output request as shown in Figure 4. For output request, the agent A' uses its own output method instead of the output method in the parent agent A. Thus, the agent migration achieves the same semantics as dynamic inheritance (Abadi & Cardelli, 1996, pp. 46-47).

Figure 4. Every message to A is checked against the supercede list that A received with A'. If the method corresponding to the request is implemented in A', the message is passed by A to A'.

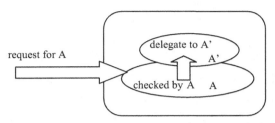

Figure 5. Agent A' migrates into A, and tries to represent for communication to B. Agent A can still send messages to B, and these may interfere the messages from A'.

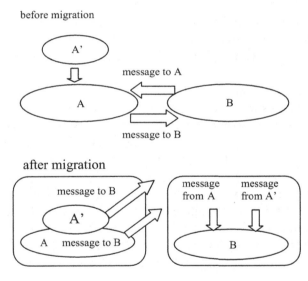

The agent A' is also designed to communicate to B. Since A and A' are agents with their own threads, the agent A can still send messages to B after the arrival of A'. Therefore, it is possible that the message sending of A would interfere with the message sending of A' as shown in Figure 5.

In order to manage this problem, each agent has a mechanism to suppress its parent's message sending. It is hard for A to anticipate which of its messages may be suppressed in the future. On the other hand, it is easy for A' to have a list of messages to be suppressed ("supercede list").

Figure 6. The `sender` *agent*

```
public class sender extends Agent
   implements Runnable, Serializable, StatusListner, StructureListner {
   Transient private Thread th;
        …
    setName("sender");
        …
   public void run() {
     int count=0;
     try {
      while (true) {
         count++;
         Thread.sleep(1000);
         Message msg = new Message("output");
         Msg.setArg(count);
         getService(new AgentURL("://reporter/"), msg);
       }
     } catch (Exception e) {System.out.println(e)}
```

Therefore, the child agent (that extends the parent) is given the supercede list when it is created. The list consists of pairs of URL and method name that the parent agent may not send. When the child agent A' migrates into the parent agent A, the child agent A' passes the supercede list to the parent agent A.

When an agent tries to send a message to another agent, it checks the supercede lists in the child agents recursively. If the agent finds that the message it is trying to send has been superceded, it refrains from sending it. When a child agent leaves its parent agent, the supercede list that was passed by the child agent is erased so that the parent agent can resume sending those messages.

Let us construct an example of dynamic extension using a simple scenario of a sender agent (Figure 6) that sends a message to the reporter agent (Figure 7), which displays the contents of that message. The `getService` method in `sender` agent sends the message that tells how many seconds have passed since the sender was created. Initially, let us create the sender agent to send once per second a message where the variable `count` has a value equal to the number of seconds since the

Figure 7. The `reporter` *agent*

```
public class reporter extends Agent
   implements Runnable, Serializable, StatusListner, StructureListner {
   Transient private Thread th;
        …
    setName("reporter");
        …
   public void output(int count) {
     System.out.println(count);
   }
```

sender agent was created, and the method `output` in the reporter agent is called once a second and display the current content of `count`. Then we create an extending agent `reporter2` (Figure 8) and cause it to migrate into the reporter agent and override the `output` method. The difference between `reporter` and `reporter2` is the latter's `output` method displays enhanced messages. The sender agent sends the same message to the reporter agent, but now the `reporter` agent has a supercede list that tells it to refrain invoking that method and to delegate that message to its child agent, `reporter2`. Therefore, the arrived message is forwarded to the extending agent `reporter2` and `reporter2`'s `output` method is invoked so that enhanced messages are displayed as shown in Figure 9.

Now we create another extending agent `sender2` that extends the sender agent. `Sender2` is the same as sender but sends a message once per 10 seconds. When we make this extending agent migrate into the sender agent, it starts to send messages once per 10 seconds. The original sender is, however, still working and issuing its message once a second.

This is not the desired outcome. In order to prevent this interference, `sender2` must have a supercede list that tells which methods in the parent agent are supposed to be suppressed. The `addRefusal` method invocation in `sender2` agent does this task (see Figure 10). The user of this agent is expected to set the URL and method

Figure 8. The `reporter2` *agent*

```
public class reporter2 extends Agent
  implements Runnable, Serializable, StatusListner, StructureListner {
  Transient private Thread th;
    ...
    setName("reporter2");
    ...
  public void output(int count) {
    System.out.println(count+" seconds passed after
                  the sender created.);
  }
```

Figure 9. Upon arrival of `reporter2`, *the new output method is used*

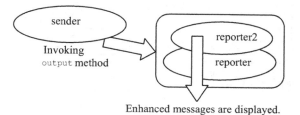

Enhanced messages are displayed.

Figure 10. `addRefusal` *method invocation*

```
addRefusal(new AgentURL(":://reporter/"), "output",
           new Class[]{int.class});
```

name by using this method. Note that the URL is "`://reporter/`", not "`://re-porter2.`" `Sender2` does not know the reporter agent has been extended.

For example, once `sender2` has arrived in `sender` agent with the proper super-cede list, `sender`'s message (output invocation) is suppressed by `sender2` and the reporter agent receives the output message once per 10 seconds as shown in Figure 11.

After that, if the child agent of the `reporter` agent, `reporter2`, leaves the agent `reporter` so that `reporter` has no child, the output request from `sender2` causes `reporter`'s `output` method to be invoked and the nonenhanced messages are displayed again. Then, the state of `reporter`, the target agent of `sender` and `sender2`, is changed, but `sender` and `sender2` do not need to know about it. What `sender` and `sender2` know is that they are sending messages to the `re-porter` agent.

Note that the behavior of the sender agent before the reporter's extension is the same as that after `reporter`'s extension, as is that of after the extension is cancelled (when the child agent leaves).

Similarly, when the child agent, `sender2`, of the `sender` agent leaves from `sender`, `sender` is allowed to send messages, and `reporter` displays the output once a second.

Figure 11. Upon arrival of `sender2`, `sender`*'s* `output` *method is suppressed, and* `sender2`*'s is used*

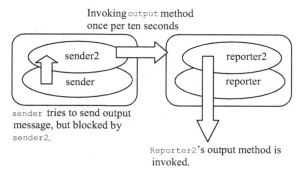

Thus, the extension and restriction of agents can be achieved dynamically by the other agents' migration. It is not necessary to statically compose the agent program. It is even not necessary to stop the running agent. This should be a desirable feature of intelligent multirobot control programming.

Robot-Control Example

In this section, we demonstrate that the model of higher-order mobile agents with dynamic extension is suitable for the composition of software to control intelligent multirobots.

Intelligent multirobots are expected to work in distributed environments where communication is relatively unstable and therefore where fully remote control is hard to achieve. In addition, we cannot expect that we know everything in the environment beforehand. Therefore, intelligent robot control software needs to have the following features: (1) It should be autonomous to some extent. (2) It should be extensible to accommodate the working environment. 3) It should be replaceable while in action. Our higher-order mobile agent with dynamic extension satisfies all these functional requirements.

Our control software consists of autonomous mobile agents. Once an agent migrates to a remote site, it requires minimal communication to the original site. Mobile agents are higher-order so that the user can construct a larger agent by hierarchical composition of smaller agents. Finally, if we find that the constructed software is not satisfactory, we can replace the unsuitable component (an agent) with new component (another agent) by using agent migrations.

The Robot

We employed the Palm Pilot Robot Kit (PPRK) by ACRONAME, Inc. (information available at http://www.acroname.com) as the platform for our prototype system. Each robot has three servomotors with tires. Four AA batteries supply the power. A robot has a servo motor controller board that accepts RS-232 serial data from a host computer. We use Toshiba Libretto notebook computers for the host computers. Each robot holds one notebook computer as its host computer. Our control agents migrate to these host computers by wireless LAN (see Figure 12).

Figure 12. Robot control agents are working on ACRONAME Palm Pilot Robot Kit

The Controller Agents for TAG

In the beginning, two agents migrate to the host computer to give the basic behavior of the robot. One is the `operate` agent, and the other is the `wall` agent.

`Operate` agent can read and write serial data, and behaves as the interface between PPRK on-board controller and the intelligent software agent. `Wall` agent receives sensor data from `operate` agent and sends messages such as go-forward, turn-left/

Figure 13. Structure of the controller agents; the base agent MATP is not shown

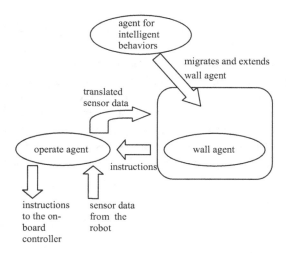

right, and stop to `operate` agent. `Operate` agent translates instructions corresponding to these messages into serial data and sends it to the on-board controller.

In order to achieve these functions, the `operate` agent has methods to obtain and to release a serial port, to read the sensor data as well as to instruct the robot movement. To read sensor data, an event listener is required. The registration of the event listener is done as a part of obtaining the serial port.

The sole task of `wall` agent is to avoid collisions. When it receives sensor data indicating something exists in front of it (wall or another robot), it issues instructions to turn around. This simple collision avoidance algorithm is implemented in `think` method in the `wall` agent.

In order to give the robots more intelligent behavior, we extend this `wall` agent by dynamic extension. In our example, two agents, `chase` and `escape`, extend `wall` agent. Robots with `escape` agent try to avoid the chaser as well as the wall, while the robot with `chase` agent looks for other robots and tries to catch one of them. As a result, they play the game of TAG. Figure 13 shows the structure of the agents that control the robot.

The `escape` and `chase` agents have their own `think` methods so that they can extend `wall` agent to make the behaviors of the robots more intelligent. The `think` method of `escape` agents can distinguish the other robots from the wall, and instruct different behaviors. It can move as close as 30 cm if it finds the wall in front of it, but it should not move as close as 60 cm if it finds a robot in front of it, because the other robot may be the chaser.

The `chase` agent has two methods. One is its own `think` method and the other is `arrive` method. The `think` method of `chase` agents can also distinguish the other

Figure 14. think *method in the* chase *agent*

```
public void think(int dist1, int dist2) {
  if (dist2<=10) {
    Context cx;
    cx = getContext();
    try {
      cx.move(new AgentURL(":://wall/chase/",
          new AgentURL(nextAddress));
    } catch(Exception e) {System.out.println(e);}
  }
  Message msg;
  if (dist2<100) {
    msg = new Message("forward");
  } else {
    msg = new Message("turn");
  }
  try {
    getService(new AgentURL(":://operate/", msg);
  } catch(Exception e) {System.out.println(e);}
}
```

Figure 15. The chaser catches the escapee and they swap their roles

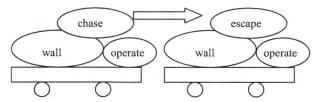

(a) When the chaser catches the escapee, the `chase` agent migrates to the `wall` agent on the escapee.

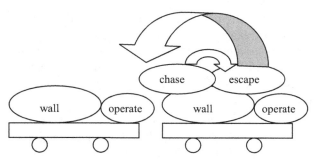

(b) Migrated `chase` agent makes the `escape` agent migrate back to where the `chase` agent came.

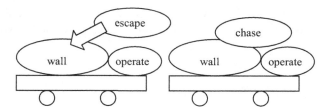

(c) The `escape` agent is moved by the `chase` agent, and the exchange of the roles is over.

robots from the wall, and instruct different behaviors. If the robot with `chase` agent finds another robot, it chases the robot and tries to catch it. For our purposes, if the chaser gets as close as 10 cm to another robot, the chaser judges the other robot to be caught. Figure 14 shows the `think` method of the `chase` agent.

When the robot with `chase` agent catches another robot, it migrates its `chase` agent to the `wall` agent on the caught robot, so that the roles of chaser and escapee can be exchanged with each other as shown in Figure 15. This is done by the `move` method invocation in the `think` method of the `chase` agent as shown in Figure

Figure 16. `Arrive` *method in the* `chase` *agent*

```
public void arrive(StructureEvent e) {
  Context cx;
  cx = getContext();
  try {
    cx.move(new AgentURL(":://wall/escape/",
            new AgentURL(nextAddress));
  } catch(Exception x) {System.out.println(x);}
}
```

14. Upon arrival in the `wall` agent on the caught robot, the `chase` agent causes the `escape` agent to be migrated back to the `wall` agent on the robot from which the `chase` agent originated. This is achieved by the `arrive` method in the `chase` agent. Figure 16 shows the `arrive` method.

The `chase` agent initiates and controls the exchange of the roles. Therefore, other agents—for example, the `escape` and `wall` agents—do not have to know anything about the role exchange. In addition, messages from the `operate` agent are delegated to the child agents—that is, the `escape` or `chase` agent—the `operate` agent do not need to know whether it communicates with the `wall` agent, the `escape` agent, or the `chase` agent. While `chase` and `escape` agents are migrating to swap themselves, the robot is controlled by the `wall` agent, which avoids collision. This simplicity is achieved directly with higher-order mobile agents.

The Controller Agents for Target Searcher

In the previous section, we have shown a simple example of two robots that swapped behaviors through migration of agents. This way of constructing control software demonstrates the reuse of components. It certainly reduces the cost of developing systems. From the design point of view, however, such a system requires more sophisticated analyses than a simple object-oriented system. The designer must determine which agents can be reusable and which functions should be included in the migrating agents. In this section, we show an example of cooperative target search that can be employed for practical applications.

Let us consider how to program robots to find a target. For such a task, the most efficient solution would be to make all robots search for the target simultaneously. If the targets were comparatively fewer than the robots, however, most robots would move around in vain, consuming power without finding anything. This problem can be more serious in our model where any robots can be shared by any agents, because the robots to which an agent is going to migrate may be already occupied

Figure 17. The `search` *agent's behaviors*

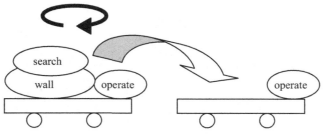

(a) The `search` agent rotates a robot. At this time, if it cannot find the target, it migrates to another robot.

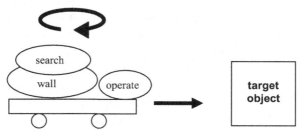

(b), If a target is found as a result of rotation, the `search` agent makes the robot move toward it.

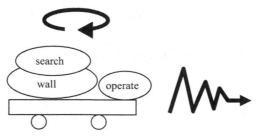

(c) If the last robot cannot find the target after the rotation, the `search` agent makes the wall agent active to make the robot perform random-move.

with another task. Thus, this searching strategy could result in increasing the total costs for the aggregate of the multirobots.

On the other hand, our strategy of using higher-order mobile agents achieves a power-preserving search without sacrificing efficiency, that is, only one robot is in action. The core of our idea is finding the nearest robot to the target by using agent migration. Initially, an agent is dispatched from the host machine to a nearby robot in the multirobots system. Then, the agent hops around the robots one by one and checks the robot's vision in order to locate the target until it reaches the robot that is closest to the target. Until this stage, robots in the multirobot system do not move; only the mobile agent migrates around so that robots can save power.

Once the agent finds the target, it migrates to the closest robot and makes the robot move toward the target. This strategy is obviously not as efficient as that of having all robots search for a target simultaneously. The migration time, however, is negligible compared to robot motion and the efficiency of power preservation offsets the slight search inefficiency. In our multirobot case, the robots' vision does not cover 360 degrees so that a robot has to rotate to check its circumstance. Rotating a robot at its current position may capture the target and another robot closer to the target. Then the agent migrates to the more conveniently located robot. Take note that the rotation requires much less movement of the wheels than exploration, and it contributes the power saving.

Details of our searching algorithm are the following: (1) an agent chooses an arbitrary robot to which it migrates and performs the migration, (2) as the agent arrives on the robot, it makes that robot rotate as shown by Figure 17a, (3) if the target is found, the agent makes the robot move to that direction as shown in Figure 17b; otherwise, go back to the step 1, and (4) at this stage, if all robots have been tried without finding the target, the agent makes the last robot do random-walk until it can find a target as shown by Figure 17c.

This algorithm can be implemented as a `search` agent with a `think` method to execute these steps as well as the TAG example. It is worthwhile to notice that the wall agent of TAG can be reused. If the `search` agent can control the `wall` agent, all that the `search` agent has to do against the `wall` agent is to make it hibernate until reaching step 4, and then it wakens the `wall` agent. We achieve this implementation by designing the `search` agent as a child agent of the wall agent. The `search` agent migrates to the `wall` agent, so that these two agents are composed into one agent. After that, the combined agent traverses each robot. In principle, the `search` agent does not have to take the `wall` agent to other robots, since all the robots have the `wall` agents. However, the current system is a prototype and the cooperation with other tasks is yet to be perfected; thus, control agents migrate with the `wall` agent.

Conclusion and Future Direction

We have presented a novel framework for controlling intelligent multirobots. The framework helps users to construct intelligent robot-control software by migration of the mobile agents. Since the migrating agents are higher-order, the control software can be hierarchically assembled while they are running. Dynamically extending control software by the migration of mobile agents enables us to make base control software relatively simple, and to add functionalities one by one, as we know the working environment. Thus, we do not have to make the intelligent robot smart from the beginning or make the robot learn by itself. We can send intelligence later as new agents.

We implemented a team of TAG-playing robots and a team of cooperative search robots to show the effectiveness of our framework. Even though our examples are toy programs, our framework is scalable. The creation of a practical system is accomplished by adding more mobile agents to the base system.

Our future directions for research will include the addition of security features, refinement of the implementation of dynamic extension, additional proof of concept for dynamic addition of new functionality, additional work on scheduling of conflicting tasks, and the introduction of self-adaptability to identify, adapt, and overcome barriers encountered during operation in difficult real environments. We also are implementing a descriptive language based on a functional language, Objective Caml, in order to achieve transparency of agent description.

Acknowledgments

Masato Kurio and Mayu Mizuno contributed to discussions and implementation of the system. Kimiko Gosney gave us useful comments.

References

Abadi, M., & Cardelli, L. (1996). *A theory of objects*. Berlin; Heidelberg; New York: Springer-Verlag.

Binder, W. J., Hulaas, G., & Villazon, A. (2001). Portable resource control in the J-SEAL2 mobile agent system. In *Proceedings of International Conference on Autonomous Agents* (pp. 222-223).

Cardelli, L., & Gordon, A. D. (1998). Mobile ambients. In *Foundations of Software Science and Computational Structures* (LNCS 1378, pp. 140-155). Berlin; Heidelberg; New York: Springer-Verlag.

Chailloux, E., Manoury, P., & Pagano, B. (2000). *Developement d'Applications avec Objective Caml*. Paris: O'Relly.

Grabowski, R., Navarro-Serment, L. E., Paredis, C. J. J., & Khosla, P. K. (2000). Heterogeneous teams of modular robots for mapping and exploration. *Autonomous Robots, 8*(3), 293-308.

Kambayashi, Y., & Takimoto, M. (2004). A functional language for mobile agents with dynamic extension. In *Knowledge-Base Intelligent Information and Engineering Systems* (LNAI 3214, pp. 1010-1017). Berlin; Heidelberg; New York: Springer-Verlag.

Kambayashi, Y., & Takimoto, M. (2005). Higher-order mobile agents for controlling intelligent robots. *International Journal of Intelligent Information Technologies, 1*(2), 28-42.

Murphy, R. R. (2000). *Introduction to AI robotics.* Cambridge, MA: MIT Press.

Nishiyama, H., Ohwada, H., & Mizoguchi, F. (1998). A multiagent robot language for communication and concurrency control. In *Proceedings of International Conference on Multi-Agent Systems* (pp. 206-213).

Parker, L. E. (1998). ALLIANCE: An architecture for fault tolerant multirobot cooperation. *IEEE Transaction on Robotics and Automation, 14(*2), 220-240.

Pham, T. Q., Dixon, K. R., Jackson, J. R., & Khosla, P. K. (2000). Software systems facilitating self-adaptive control software. In *Proceedings of IEEE International Conference on Intelligent Robots and Systems* (pp. 1094-1100).

Pomerleau, D. A. (1989). ALVINN: An autonomous land vehicle in a neural network. In *Advances in Neural Information Processing System 1* (pp. 305-313). San Francisco: Morgan Kaufmann.

Pomerleau, D. A. (1994). Defense and civilian applications of the ALVINN robot driving System. In *Proceedings of 1994 Government Microcircuit Applications Conference* (pp. 358-362).

Satoh, I. (2000). MobileSpaces: A framework for building adaptive distributed applications using a hierarchical mobile agent system. In *Proceedings of IEEE International Conference on Distributed Computing Systems* (pp. 161-168).

Shapiro, E. (1987). *Concurrent prolog: Collected papers.* Cambridge, MA: MIT Press.

Stewart, D. B., & Khosla, P. K. (1996). The chimera methodology: Designing dynamically reconfigurable and reusable real-time software using port-based objects. *International Journal of Software Engineering and Knowledge Engineering, 6*(2), 249-277.

Ueda, K. (1986). *Guarded horn clauses.* Unpublished doctoral dissertation, University of Tokyo.

Chapter VI

Instrument Validation for Strategic Business Simulation

Chris Schlueter Langdon, University of Southern California, USA

Abstract

This paper aims to provide a synopsis on the design science of agent-based modeling and how to adapt an agent-based research strategy for the scientific study of complex business systems. Research in information systems (IS) has begun to advance knowledge in the use of agent-based systems as a means to seek different computational explanations for business phenomena that have eluded scientific inquiry reliant on traditional, specifically, law and axiomatic explanation (Kimbrough, 2003). The focus on business problems requires a different research approach than what is successful in computer science. One key modification is to make instrument validation explicit. This chapter extends a discussion of emerging insights on the subject to ensure the rigor of management science research in agent-based IS (Schlueter Langdon, 2005a).

Foundation in Economics

The design science paradigm is foundational to the information systems (IS) discipline. It "seeks to extend the boundaries of human and organizational capabilities by creating new and innovative artifacts" (Hevner, March, Park, & Ram, 2004, p. 75). This includes research on agent-based IS. Work on intelligent agents has been explicitly identified as "a way to deal with the staggering variety and volume of data in distributed and heterogeneous environments" (March, Hevner, & Ram, 2000, p. 334). In today's world of instant, anytime, anywhere communications everything appears to be connected with everything else. Innovation in information technology appears to be constantly connecting stand-alone objects into distributed systems or business ecosystems. While the Internet has improved interconnectivity globally in the 1990s, Web-services computing has begun to improve interoperability between spatially and functionally disparate elements. As one consequence, decision-making in business has become more complicated. Specifically, today's connectedness has made recognition of interaction effects or feedback loops a crucial requirement in business planning. Often, business strategies that make perfect sense at the company or individual level can aggregate up to industry-level conditions, which can have the adverse effect and for all incumbents. A primitive but instructional example is ad spending: Companies often increase advertising activities and expenditures to boost sales to create a profit. However, if all competitors do the same, the strategy will fail. Instead of higher profits, the outcome will likely be higher cost and lower margins for everyone.

Agent-based research strategies have been identified as particularly suitable for the study of distributed systems and services (e.g., Sikora & Shaw, 1998). Despite its innovativeness, the core underpinnings of agent-based information systems (ABIS), including computational simulation, are from the same traditional disciplines that undergird work in so many other management-science areas. One of the best-hidden secrets in ABIS is that much of its foundation is based on theory and Nobel-prize winning work in economics. From the conceptualization of an "agent" to laboratory experiments and even computational simulation, all correspond with theory and work in economics.

Agent Metaphor

The "agent" metaphor used to anchor ABIS research is compliant with linguistics and rooted in economics. The Merriam-Webster Collegiate Dictionary defines "agent" as "one that acts or exerts power; something that produces or is capable of producing an effect; a means or instrument by which a guiding intelligence achieves a result." Holland (1995), an artificial intelligence scholar and pioneer of genetic algorithms and complex adaptive systems, borrowed the term "agents" from economics "to refer to active elements without invoking specific contexts" (pp. 6-7). The field of economics that Holland was referring to is agency theory, which explains how to best organize the relationship between one party—the principal—who determines the work, and another party—the agent—who undertakes the work (Grossman & Hart, 1983; Ross, 1973; and for a survey, see Sappington, 1991). Agency theory analyzes the costs of resolving two types of conflicts that can arise between principals and agents under conditions of incomplete information and uncertainty: adverse selection and moral hazard. Adverse selection is the condition under which the principal cannot ascertain if the agent accurately represents his ability to do the work for which he is being paid. Moral hazard is the condition under which the principal cannot be sure if the agent has put forth maximal effort (Eisenhardt, 1989). In ABIS, an agent is understood as a representation of a decision unit or, in general, a knowledge processor and (when implemented) a software module. An agent is created to perform a task or set of tasks, and it features some combination of the following selected properties: autonomy, activity, communicability, adaptability, and mobility (Prietula, Carley, & Gasser, 1998, provide a rich overview of the computational modeling of organizations). Depending upon the combination of tasks and the environment, the literature distinguishes between various categories of agents (Wooldridge & Jennings, 1995).

Agent-Based Information Systems

The notion of agent-based IS subsumes the research strategy of agent-based modeling and laboratory experiments using computational methods. It follows the tradition of laboratory experiments as a tool in empirical economics established by Smith. He was awarded a Nobel prize for pioneering tests of predictions from economic theory by way of laboratory experiments (Kagel & Roth, 1995; Smith, 1962). Smith "initiated the use of the laboratory as a 'wind tunnel' (a laboratory setup used to test prototypes for aircraft) in order to study the performance of proposed institutional mechanisms for deregulation, privatization, and the provision of public goods" (The Royal Swedish Academy of Sciences, 2002, p. 9; Smith, 2002).

Simulation

Simulation in agent-based IS has benefited from Simon's Nobel-prize winning work in economics, who has been credited with creating the disciplines of behavioral economics and the cognitive sciences. Simon (1996) understood simulation as "a technique for understanding and predicting the behavior of systems" (p. 13). At its core, he referred to it as the creation of the artificial (as opposed to the natural) things that are synthesized by human beings, may imitate appearances in nature, and can be characterized in terms of functions, goals, and adaptation.

Reliability of Results and Instrument Validation

Rigor is a *conditio sine qua none* in scientific research. A key aspect of scientific rigor is validity. Validity refers to getting results that accurately reflect the concept being measured (for a typology of validation, see Cronbach & Meehl, 1955; "If (all B are C) and (A is B), then (A is C)" is an argument form whose logic is valid). In choosing laboratory experiments as a research method and simulation as a research instrument, the challenges with validity of research are twofold. Because ABIS is an innovative approach and less traditional yet than structural equation modeling (SEM), for example, it should first be exposed to particular scrutiny including an explicit test of instrument validity (i.e., Boudreau, Gefen, & Straub, 2001, p. 12; Carley, 1995; Carley & Prietula, 1994). Second, architectural compliance of the artifact with theories and previously validated frameworks is limited by the means of implementation available. Without appropriate software capabilities, certain theoretically required elements and conditions might be impossible to implement despite best intentions.

In order to pinpoint opportunities to strengthen instrument validation a generic approach to strategic simulation is considered. Figure 1 depicts a strategic simulation approach or in more general terms, a business intelligence modeling schedule with its distinct phases (Schlueter Langdon, 2005b).

The starting point of a strategic simulation project is typically a business scenario—an account or synopsis of a phenomenon and a projected course of action. Often important issues have already been crystallized into a set of questions or even first research hypotheses at this stage. During the next phase, a model is drafted to represent the most relevant processes with a set of variables and a set of logical and quantitative relationships between them. Specifically, independent variables are separated from dependent ones and mediating and moderating effects are recognized based on theory and best practice. In order to simplify model construction and to allow for a focus on the main effects certain assumptions are introduced. While these assumptions simplify the model, they also create an idealized or stylized framework, which is known to be false in some detail. Such procedure is justified because simplification of the model aids the accuracy of results.

The next phase is concerned with the construction of a formal model and its implementation (see Figure 1). It may involve standard spreadsheet software, statistical tools or even customized software applications. In any case, it is advisable to follow

Figure 1. Generic business intelligence modeling approach

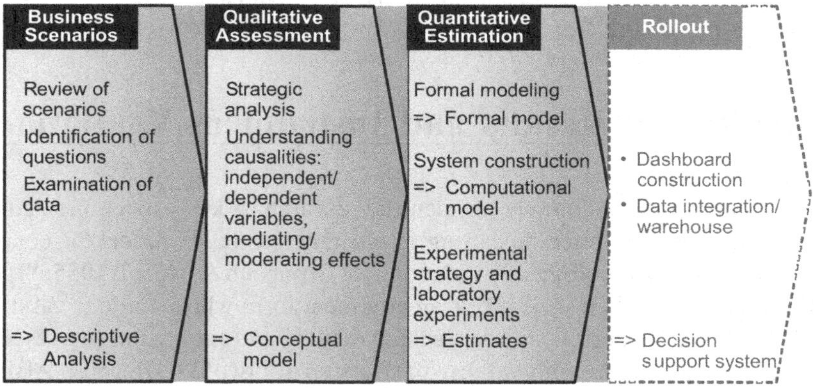

standard software or information-systems development practice to ensure a tight fit between model requirements and system capabilities. This means adhering to generally accepted systems lifecycle-development concepts (SLDCs). Examples include the waterfall model, rapid application development, and the spiral model (Beam, 1988; Hoffer et al., 1999). We argue that instrument validation should be an integral part of the quantitative estimation phase (as indicated in Figure 1) in order for it to be most effective and convincing.

Modeling Strategy: Use of Established Complex Adaptive System (CAS) and Multiagent System (MAS) Frameworks

In order to ensure internal validity of the model—whether something is actually being measured that is supposed to be measured—a multistep research strategy can be devised. In short, the conceptual model should be "docked" with research models in the literature (Burton, 1998) and its computational implementation should be aligned and in correspondence with established computational models (Axtell, Axelrod, Epstein, & Cohen 1996; Burton & Obel, 1995). In a first step, the research problem should be decomposed into simple elements. In case of a supply chain problem, the supply chain could be broken into firms, as the unit of analysis, and types of interaction (Burton, 1998; Burton & Obel, 1995; Swaminathan, Smith, & Sadeh, 1998, pp. 610-612). Second, decomposition should be aligned with the appropriate literature. Using the supply-chain example again, decomposition could mimic traditional models of tiered or convergent supply-chain topologies as well as supply-chain strategies (e.g., vertical integration, Malone & Smith, 1988; or competing on quantities, Corbett & Karmarkar, 2001). Third, because decomposition is simple, and, according to the literature, both the behavior of agent types as well as their interdependencies are already well understood. Both can, therefore, be based on the literature. In the supply-chain example, pricing behavior could be based on microeconomic cost theory. In other words, cause-and-effect relationships that are embedded in the conceptual model can be taken from theory. This ensures causality in terms of two dimensions: temporal (the cause precedes the effect) and covariation of the cause and effect. Fourth, the implementation of the conceptual research model as a computational model would benefit from adherence to modeling and design principles that have already been validated. Key contributions include Sikora and Shaw's (1998) multiagent system (MAS) framework and Holland's (1995) complex adaptive system (CAS) design principles.

A multiagent system (MAS) "allows for the different modules, objects, or processes (i.e., agents) to maintain their local control by treating them as autonomous agents, while at the same time providing them with a means for achieving the desired coordination" (Sikora & Shaw, 1998, p. 72). A complex adaptive system is a multiagent system with a particular set of mechanisms and properties in which:

> *a major part of the environment of any given adaptive agent consists of other adaptive agents, so that a portion of any agent's efforts at adaptation is spent adapting to other adaptive agents.* (Holland, 1995, p. 10)

Holland (1995) provided a detailed framework for CAS design that includes three mechanisms and four properties common to all CASs (pp. 10-40). The three mechanisms include building blocks, internal models, and tagging. The four common properties are aggregation, nonlinearity, diversity, and flows. Of those mechanisms and properties, "building blocks" and "aggregation" have emerged as popular choices. Detailed examples can be found in Schlueter Langdon and Sikora (2006) and Schlueter Langdon and Shaw (1998).

Building Blocks

The CAS design mechanism of building blocks refers to the decomposition of a complex scene into a few distinct categories of components and relationships (Holland, 1995, pp. 34-37). Building blocks can be reused and combined to create relevant, perpetually novel scenes. With decomposition and the repeated use of building blocks, novelty arises through combination. Even with only a few sets of categories of building blocks and rules for combining them, an exponentially large number of different configurations can be assembled. Consider the following example: With only two different types of agents, such as firms (e.g., manufacturers and distributors), and 10 variations of each type, such as 10 different degrees of vertical integration, as many as 2^{10} or 1024 different combinations or industry scenarios could be created. Hewitt (1991) stated:

> *Our hypothesis is that by organizing large-scale systems into composable units, each of which provides support for operations, membership liaison, accounting, and management, we will be able to construct large-scale systems that are more scalable, robust, and manageable.* (pp. 99-100)

The challenge with building blocks is the decomposition of a complex scene into as few relevant categories of components and rules for combining them as possible. If this can be achieved, building blocks can provide great scalability and efficiency with reconfiguration. Actual building blocks can be perceived as agents with their embedded functions or methods, while relationships can be considered as dependencies in the context of multiagent systems (Sikora & Shaw, 1998).

Aggregation

Building blocks become even more powerful when applied to aggregated or tiered designs (see Figure 1). Aggregation "concerns the emergence of complex, large-scale behaviors from the aggregate interactions of less complex agents" (Holland, 1995, p. 11). This design property allows for patterns of higher-level events to derive from the settings of lower-level building blocks. A higher-level event, such as a change in industry structure, can be observed emerging from lower-level conditions and dynamics of interaction (see Figure 1). Aggregation corresponds to the concept of subagents in Sikora and Shaw's (1998) multiagent system framework.

Implementation Strategy: Mitigating Machine Bias

Designing a simulation research model that is grounded in theory is only one part of the instrument validation challenge. The other part is its appropriate and theory compliant implementation (see Figure 1).

Hurdles to such implementation are many; some of the most persistent ones include lack of machine randomness and machine concurrency. Both problems are severe, because they can cause a bias that threatens the validity of the results of any simulation experiment. Therefore, any implementation would have to explicitly address how both problems, a lack of machine randomness and a lack of machine concurrency, have been mitigated.

Randomness

Randomness implies "being or relating to a set or to an element of a set each of whose elements has equal probability of occurrence" (Merriam-Webster OnLine). On a computer, everything is artificial and completely predictable, including randomness, which is generated algorithmically through what is often referred to as pseudorandom-number generators. The solution to a lack of machine randomness is seed management. Typically, random-number generators require a start value or "seed" to begin generating a string of "random" numbers. The same seed will always generate the same sequence of random numbers. This is good, because if the seed is conserved, results can be repeated. It is bad because there is no randomness. The solution is to vary the seed value randomly and keep track of this variation. This way results remain repeatable and random at the same time.

Concurrency

The problem of lack of machine randomness is often compounded by a lack of concurrency, the lack of "the simultaneous occurrence of events or circumstances" (Merriam-Webster OnLine). On a computer, instructions are executed sequentially, line by line. This is obviously a problem if a model requires simultaneous actions of its agents. One solution to a lack of concurrency is to vary the invocation sequence of software agents randomly. As a result, actions remain sequential but results are no longer path dependent.

Object Orientation

Object-oriented programming has greatly enhanced the capabilities of simulation tool kits and has therefore provided an opportunity to implement architectures that can comply with validated frameworks. Object-orientation has two primary objectives, which fit well with the properties of multiagent-system frameworks: first, the development of reusable components and second, the development of implementations with greater flexibility for adaptation. The latter advance corresponds well with the requirements of CAS. In order to achieve these objectives, object-oriented languages and tools support the following three key concepts: First, encapsulation—this means internalizing or hiding the functions or methods of an agent, as well as data, which consists of instance variables and method variables (the actual, "living" representation of an agent in a simulation run is called an instance); second, inheritance—the ability to extend the capabilities of the system by exception, or, in other words, to have one subclass of agents receive (i.e., inherit) capabilities from its superclass; Third, polymorphism, which allows a single command or message to evoke many different responses, each from a different agent. With polymorphism, the message-sending agent does not need to know the specifics of the receiving agent's function or method. Furthermore, new functions and even agents can be added without changing the message passing mechanism.

One simulation system that takes advantage of object-orientation is the Swarm system developed at the Santa Fe Institute. Several exploratory studies have confirmed that the system corresponds well with MAS/CAS modeling requirements (Lin, Tan, & Shaw, 1999).

Swarm is a general-purpose object-oriented (written in Objective C) multiagent simulation software application developed at the Santa Fe Institute (Hiebeler, 1994; Minar, Burkhart, Langton, & Askenazi, 1996). It is particularly well suited for the study of complex adaptive systems, since it allows for discrete event simulation of the interactions between heterogeneous agents, such as firms and markets, and a collective environment (Schlueter Langdon, Bruhn, & Shaw, 2000; Terna, 2002). Furthermore, because it is object-oriented, the system ensures that multiple representations or instances of the same type can be created.

Conclusion and Discussion

ABIS are next-generation analytical methods that are quickly emerging to complement conventional, linear-research instruments to aid analysis in areas that exhibit complex, dynamic, nonlinear, and emergent behavior, such as digital business transformation and business ecosystem competition. While agent methods and intelligent agents have been a field of study in computer science for some time, its importance has just recently received recognition in the management sciences. For example, one of the best-hidden secrets in ABIS is that much of its underpinnings are based on theory and Nobel-prize winning work in economics (besides the obvious foundation in computer science). This paper synthesized thinking on one important issue in ABIS to simplify agent-based analysis—instrument validation. Instrument validation is a *conditio sine qua none*, particularly for a lesser-known scientific methods like ABIS. Often, it is omitted or unnecessarily complicated with implementation and software development details. Validation can be kept clear and simple following the four-step approach derived from the literature: First, decompose a problem into simple elements; second, align decomposition with the literature; third, because decomposition is simple and according to the literature, both, the behavior of the elements as well as their dependencies are already well understood and, therefore, can also be based on the literature; fourth, implement elements and dependencies (or the conceptual model) by adhering to generally accepted ABIS modeling and design principles for ABIS. Key hurdles to theory compliant implementation of models are the lack of machine randomness and lack of machine concurrency.

Compliance with this four-step approach should ensure that a discussion of validation remains accessible even to scientists outside of the ABIS community, which would further broaden the appeal of ABIS.

Acknowledgments

The manuscript has benefited from thoughtful suggestions and comments of the many AIS SIGABIS contributors and anonymous reviewers. The author gratefully acknowledges discussions with and advice from John Holland, Mike Shaw, Riyaz Sikora, Steve Kimbrough, Piramuthu Selwyn, Vijay Sugumaran, and Alok Chaturvedi.

References

Axtell, R., Axelrod, R., Epstein, J., & Cohen, M. (1996). Aligning simulation models: A case study and results. *Computational and Mathematical Organization Theory, 1*(2), 123-141.

Bakos, J. Y. (1985). Toward a more precise concept of information technology. In *Proceedings of the International Conference on Information Systems*, Indianapolis, IN (pp. 17-24).

Boehm, B. (1988, May). A spiral model of software development and enhancement. *IEEE Computer, 21*(5), 61-72.

Boudreau, M. C., Gefen, D., & Straub, D. W. (2001). Validation in information systems research: A state-of-the-art assessment. *MIS Quarterly, 25*(1), 2-16.

Burton, R. (1998). Validating and docking. In M. J. Prietula, K. M. Carley, & L. Gasser (Eds), *Simulating organizations: Computational models of institutions and groups* (pp. 215-228). Cambridge, MA: The MIT Press.

Burton, R. M., & Obel, B. (1995). The validity of computational models in organization science: From model realism to purpose of the model. *Computational and Mathematical Organization Theory, 1*(1), 57-71.

Carley, K. M., & Prietula, M. J. (Eds). (1994). *Computational organization theory.* Hillsdale, NJ: Lawrence Erlbaum Associates.

Carley, K. M. (1995). Computational and mathematical organization theory: Perspective and directions. *Computational and Mathematical Organization Theory, 1*(1), 39-56.

Corbett, J, C., & Karmarkar, U. S. (2001, July). Competition and structure in serial supply chains with deterministic demand. *Management Science, 47*(7), 966-978.

Cronbach, L. J., & Meehl, P. E. (1955). Construct validity in psychological tests. *Psychological Bulletin,* (52), 281-302.

Dewett, T., & Jones, G. R. (2001). The role of information technology in the organization: A review, model, and assessment. *Journal of Management, 27*, 313-346.

Eisenhardt, K. M. (1989). Agency theory: An assessment and review. *The Academy Of Management Review, 14*(1), 57-75.

Grossman, S., & Hart, O. (1983). An analysis of the principal-agent problem. *Econometrica, 51*, 7-45.

Hevner, A. R., March, S. T., Park, J., & Ram, S. (2004). Design science in information systems research. *MIS Quarterly, 28*(1), 75-106.

Hewitt, C. (1991). Open information systems semantics for distributed artificial intelligence. *Artificial Intelligence, 47*, 79-106.

Hiebeler, D. (1994). *The Swarm simulation system and individual-based modeling* (Tech. Rep. No. 94-12-065). Santa Fe, NM: Santa Fe Institute.

Holland, J. H. (1995). *Hidden order: How adaptation builds complexity*. Reading, MA: Helix, Addison-Wesley.

Hoffer, J. A., et al. (1999). *Modern systems analysis & design*. Reading, MA: Addison Wesley.

Kagel, J. H., & Roth, A. E. (Eds.). (1995). *Handbook of experimental economics*. Princeton, NJ: Princeton University Press.

Kimbrough, S. O. (2003). Computational modeling and explanation. In H. K. Bhargava, and N. Ye (Eds.), *Computational modeling and problem solving in the networked world*. Boston; London: Kluwer Academic Publishers.

Lin, F.-R., Tan, G. W., & Shaw, M. J. (1999). Multiagent enterprise modeling. *Journal of Organizational Computing and Electronic Commerce, 9*(1), 7-32.

Malone, T. W. (1987, October). Modeling coordination in organizations and markets. *Management Science, 33*(10), 1317-1332.

Malone, T. W., & Smith, S. A. (1988, May-June). Modeling the performance of organizational structures. *Operations Research, 36*(3), 421-436.

March, S. T., Hevner, A. R., & Ram, S. (2000). Research commentary: An agenda for information technology research in heterogeneous and distributed environments. *Information Systems Research, 11*(4), 327-341.

Minar, N., Burkhart, R., Langton, C., & Askenazi, M. (1996). *The Swarm simulation system: A toolkit for building multi-agent simulations* (Tech. Rep. No. 96-04-2). Santa Fe, NM: Santa Fe Institute.

Prietula, M. J., Carley, K. M., & Gasser, L. (1998). A computational approach to organizations and organizing. In M. J. Prietula, K. M. Carley, & L. Gasser (Eds.), *Simulating organizations: Computational models of institutions and groups* (pp. xiii-xix). Cambridge, MA: The MIT Press.

Ross, S. (1973). The economic theory of agency: The principal's problem. *American Economic Review, 63*, 134-139.

Royal Swedish Academy of Sciences, The. (2002, December 17). *Foundations of behavioral and experimental economics: Daniel Kahneman and Vernon Smith. Advanced information on the prize in economic sciences* (electronic document). Retrieved August 1, 2003, from http://www.nobel.se/economics/laureates/2002/ecoadv02.pdf

Rust, J. (1996, July 31-August 3). *Dealing with the complexity of economic calculations.* Paper presented at the Workshop on Fundamental Limits to Knowledge in Economics. Santa Fe, NM: Santa Fe Institute.

Sappington, D. (1991). Incentives in principal-agent relationships. *Journal of Economic Perspectives, 5*, 45-66.

Schlueter Langdon, C., & Shaw, M. J. (1998, April). An organizational ecosystems simulator applied to electronic commerce. In *Proceedings of CIST/INFORMS Conference*, Montreal, Canada (pp. 259-270).

Schlueter Langdon, C., Bruhn, P., & Shaw, M. J. (2000). Online supply chain modeling and simulation. In F. Luna, & B. Stefansson (Eds.). *Economic simulations in Swarm: Agent-based modeling and object oriented programming* (251-272). Boston: Kluwer Academic Publishers.

Schlueter Langdon, C., & Sikora, R. (2006). Conceptualizing coordination and competition in a two-tier serial supply chain as a complex adaptive system. *Journal of Information Systems and E-Business, 4*(1), 71-81.

Schlueter Langdon, C. (2005a, July-September). Agent-based modeling for simulation of complex business systems: Research design and validation strategies. *International Journal of Intelligent Information Technologies, 1*(3), 1-11.

Schlueter Langdon, C. (2005b). *Assessing economic feasibility of E-business investments.* White Paper (Version 3.0). Redondo Beach, CA: Pacific Coast Research.

Sikora, R., & Shaw, M. J. (1998, November). A multi-agent framework for the coordination and integration of information systems. *Management Science, 44*(11), 65-78.

Simon, H. A. (1996). *The sciences of the artificial* (3rd ed.). Cambridge, MA: MIT Press.

Smith, V. L. (1962). An experimental study of competitive market behavior. *Journal of Political Economy, 70*, 111-137.

Smith, V. (2002). *Constructivist and ecological rationality in economics*. Stockholm. Retrieved September 29, 2006 from http://nobelprize.org/economics/laureates/2002/smith-lecture.html

Swaminathan, J. M., Smith, S. F., & Sadeh, N. M. (1998, Summer). Modeling supply chain dynamics: A multiagent approach. *Decision Sciences, 29*(3), 607-632.

Terna, P. (2002). Economic simulations in Swarm: Agent-based modeling and object-oriented programming, by Benedikt Stefansson and Francesco Luna: A review and some comments about "agent based modeling." *The Electronic Journal of Evolutionary Modeling and Economic Dynamics* (1013). Retrieved from http://www.e-jemed.org/1013/index.php

Wooldridge, M. J., & Jennings, N. R. (1995). Agent theories, architectures, and languages—a survey. In *Proceedings of the ECAI-94 Workshop on Agent Theory, Architectures, and Languages* (pp. 1-21). Heidelberg, Germany: Springer.

Chapter VII

Challenges of the "Global Understanding Environment" Based on Agent Mobility

Vagan Terziyan, University of Jyvaskyla, Finland

Abstract

Among traditional users of Web resources, industry also has a growing set of smart industrial devices with embedded intelligence. Just as humans do, smart industrial devices need online services—for example, for condition monitoring, remote diagnostics, maintenance, and so on. In this chapter, we present one possible implementation framework for such Web services. Assume that such services should be Semantic-Web-enabled and form a service network based on internal and external agents' platforms, which can host heterogeneous mobile agents and coordinate them to perform needed tasks. The concept of a "mobile-service component" assumes not only the exchange of queries and service responses but also the delivery and composition of a service provider itself. A mobile-service component carrier (agent) can move to a field device's local environment (embedded agent platform) and perform its activities locally. Service components improve their performance through online learning and communication with other components. Heterogeneous service components' discovery is based on semantic P2P search. In this chapter, we discuss the Global Understanding Environment as an enabling agent-driven semantic platform for implementation of the heterogeneous industrial resources, condition monitoring, and predictive maintenance. The main challenges of such an environment are presented, which are "semantic adapters" for industrial objects, diagnostic models, exchange and integration, distributed trust management, and the concept of a human as a Web service.

Introduction

The intersection of Web service, Semantic Web and enterprise integration technologies are recently drawing enormous attention throughout academia and industry (Bussler, Fensel, & Sadeh, 2003). The expectation is that Web-service technology in conjunction with Semantic Web services will make enterprise integration dynamically possible for various enterprises compared to the "traditional" technologies (electronic-data interchange or value-added networks).

The Semantic Web is an initiative of the World Wide Web Consortium with the goal of extending the current Web to facilitate Web automation, universally accessible content, and the "Web of Trust." Tim Berners-Lee, Hendler, and Lassila (2001) has a vision of a Semantic Web, which has machine-understandable semantics of information and trillions of specialized reasoning services that provide support in automated task achievement based on the accessible information. Management of resources in the Semantic Web is impossible without use of ontologies, which can be considered as high-level metadata about semantics of Web data and knowledge (Chandrasekaran, Josephson, & Benjamins, 1999). DAML-S (OWL-S) or DAML for Services (Ankolekar et al., 2002; Paolucci, Kawamura, Payne, & Sycara, 2002) provides an upper ontology for describing properties and capabilities of Web services in an unambiguous, computer-interpretable markup language, which enables automation of service use by agents and reasoning about service properties and capabilities. There is also a growing interest in the use of ontologies in agent systems as a means to facilitate interoperability among diverse software components (Ontologies, 2003). The problems related to that are being highlighted by a number of recent large-scale initiatives (e.g., agentcities, grid computing, the Semantic Web and Web services). A common trend across these initiatives is the growing need to support the synergy between ontology and agent technology.

The key to Web services is on-the-fly software composition using loosely coupled, reusable software components (Fensel, Bussler, & Maedche, 2002). Still, more work needs to be done before the Web service infrastructure can make this vision come true. Among most important European efforts in this area, one can mention the

SWWS (Semantic Web and Web Services, swws.semanticweb.org) project, which is intended to provide a comprehensive Web service description, discovery, and mediation framework. Another global effort in that area is the Adaptive Services Grid (http://asg-platform.org/) project, the aim of which is to develop a proof-of-concept prototype of an open platform for adaptive-services discovery, creation, composition, and enactment. To achieve its goal, the project uses the knowledge and expertise of major European research institutions with significant contributions from the software, telecommunications, and telematics industry.

Usually a Web service is accessed by human users or by applications on behalf of human users. However, there already exists a growing group of Web service "users," which are smart industrial devices, robots, or any other objects equipped by "embedded intelligence." There is a need to launch special Web services for such smart industrial devices. Such services will provide necessary online information provisioning for the devices, allow the heterogeneous devices to communicate and exchange data and knowledge with each other and even support co-operation between different devices. There are many open questions to be answered within this research area.

In this chapter, we are trying to discuss the way of implementing emerging Semantic Web and Web service technologies to a real industrial domain, which is field-device management. The goal of this chapter is to discuss a possible implementation framework to Web services that automatically follow up and predict the performance and maintenance needs of field devices.

This chapter is an extended version of Terziyan (2005). Since last publication, many of the concepts described here have been implemented by the Industrial Ontologies Group (http://www.cs.jyu.fi/ai/OntoGroup/index.html) within the framework of the SmartResource Project (http://www.cs.jyu.fi/ai/OntoGroup/SmartResource_details. htm) and presented in the list of references. However, many challenges remains to be targeted and they are discussed in separate a section of this paper.

The rest of the chapter is organized as follows. The next section briefly introduces our concepts of an intelligent agent and mobility. The "'Mobile And Distributed Brains' Architectures" section presents two alternative architectures for distributed problem solving based on mobile agents. The following section describes the domain of field-device maintenance and ways of implementing agents in it. The next section discusses implementation issues related to the Web service network (OntoServ.Net) of smart devices based on integration of Semantic Web services and multiagent technologies. The "Global Understanding Environment and Its Challenges" section describes the concept of a Global Understanding Environment as a possible platform for implementation and provides the description of its main challenges. The final section concludes the chapter.

Agents, Semantic Balance, and Mobility

In spite of existence of so many definitions for the concept of an intelligent agent, we will use our own one. The definition will be based on the concept of Semantic Balance (Terziyan & Puuronen, 1999). In Figure 1, the concept of internal and external environments is illustrated.

We consider an intelligent agent as an entity that is able to *keep continuous balance between its internal and external environments* in such a way that, in the case of unbalance agent, it can choose a behavioral option from the following list:

- *make a change within external environment* to be in balance with the internal one;

- *make a change within internal environment* to be in balance with the external one;

- find out and *move to another place* within the external environment where balance occurs without any changes;

- *communicate* with one or more other agents (human or artificial) to be able *to create a community*, where the internal environment will be able to be in balance with the external one;

- *adjust sensors* by filtering the set of acquired features from the external environment to achieve balance between the internal environment and the deliberately distorted pattern of the external one. This can be informally interpreted in the

Figure 1. Internal and external environments of an agent

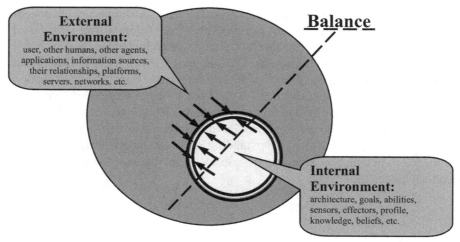

following way: "if you are not able either to change the environment or adapt yourself to it, then just try not to notice thingsthat make you unhappy."

The above means that an agent:

1. is **goal-oriented**, because it should have at least one goal—to *keep continuous balance between its internal and external environments*;
2. is **creative** because of the ability to *change the external environment*;
3. is **adaptive** because of the ability to *change the internal environment*;
4. is **mobile** because of the ability to *move to another place*;
5. is **social** because of the ability to *communicate to create a community;*
6. is **self-protective** because of the ability to *protect the "mental health"* by sensing only a "suitable" part of the environment.

Thus, we see the mobility is an important adaptation ability of an intelligent agent.

"Mobile and Distributed Brains" Architectures

Assume that there is certain intelligent task (e.g., remote diagnostics of a device based on sensor data) that appears somewhere in the Web. Assume also that intelligent components ("distributed brains") necessary to perform this task are distributed over the Web, for example, in the form of Web services. Assume finally that there is also an intelligent engine able to perform integration of autonomous components for solving complex tasks.

Consider following two architectures for this distributed problem solving:

- **Mobile engine architecture.** To integrate distributed service components into one transaction to solve the task, the intelligent engine (e.g., mobile transaction-management agent) makes necessary visits to all distributed platforms that host these services and provides all necessary choreography. An option here is mobility , which can be replaced by remote access to the components.

- **Mobile components architecture.** Alternatively, the components needed for performing the task move to the platform where engine is resized and choreography is performed locally. According to business models around the concept of a Web service, it is natural to assume that services (intelligent components in our case) should be "self-interested" and whenever they move, they should serve according the interests of their creators. This means that a very appropriate concept for such components is the concept of mobile agents. An agent is self-interested entity, which can act according to certain goals whenever it appears.

Both architectures can be considered as appropriate for implementation of the environment for distributed condition monitoring and remote-diagnostics Web services for field devices, which is discussed in the following sections of this chapter.

Field-Device Management and Agent Technologies

The expectations from smart field devices include advanced diagnostics and predictive maintenance capabilities. The concerns in this area are to develop a diagnostics system that automatically follows up the performance and maintenance needs of field devices also offering easy access to this information. The emerging agent and communication technologies give new possibilities also in this field. Field-device management in general consists of many areas of which the most important are:

- Selection
- Configuration
- Condition monitoring
- Maintenance

Valuable information is created during each phase of device management and it would be beneficial to save it into a single database. This information can be utilized in many ways during the lifetime of the devices, especially as life cycle cost (or lifetime cost) of all assets is getting nowadays more and more attention. Accordingly, the concept of life-cycle management of assets has become very popular (Pyötsiä & Cederlöf, 1999).

Field Agent is a software component that automatically follows the "health" of field devices. This agent can be either embedded to a device (Lawrence, 2003) or resized at the local network. It is autonomous, it communicates with its environment and other Field Agents, and it is capable of learning new things and delivering new information to other Field Agents. It delivers reports and alarms to the user by means of existing and well-known technologies such as intranet and e-mail messages. Field-device performance has a strong influence on process performance

Figure 2. Agent-based symptom recognition in device monitoring

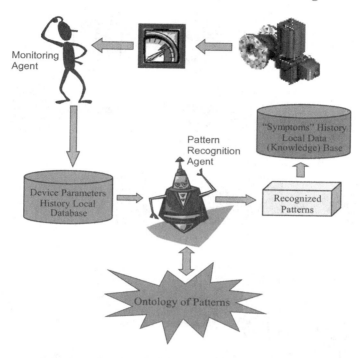

and reliable operation in more distributed process-automation architecture based on FieldBus communication (Metso, 2003; Sensodec, 2003). In this situation, easy online access to the knowledge describing field-device performance and maintenance needs is crucial. There is also a growing need to provide automatic access to this knowledge not only to humans but also to other devices, applications, expert systems, agents, and so on, which can use this knowledge for different purposes of further device diagnostics and maintenance. In addition, the reuse of collected and shared knowledge is important for other field agents to manage maintenance in similar cases.

While monitoring a field device via one information channel (Figure 2) one can get useful information about some dimension of the device state, then derive online some useful patterns from this information, which can be considered to be "symptoms" of the device "health," and finally recognize these symptoms using the "Ontology of Patterns."

If one monitors a device via several information channels (Figure 3), then appropriate Field Agent Infrastructure allows not only deriving and recognizing "symptoms"

Figure 3. Agent-based diagnostics of field devices

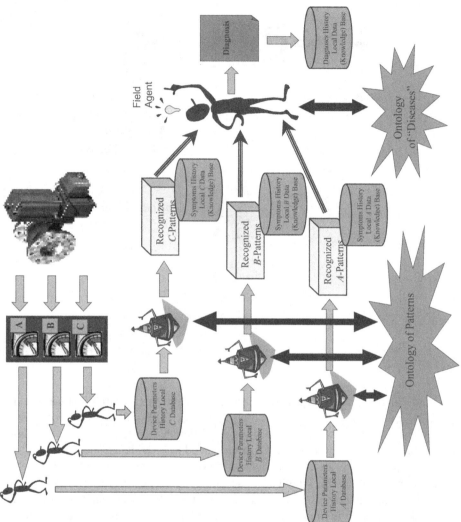

of the device's "health," but also deriving and recognizing a disease itself using the "Ontology of Diseases." In any case history data, derived patterns, and diagnoses can be stored and used locally; however, there should be a possibility to easily access this information and also to share it with other agents for reuse purposes.

There are at least two cases when such distributed infrastructure is reasonable. The first one is when we are monitoring a group of distributed devices, which are physically and logically disjoint, however they all are of the same type. In this case, any history of derived patterns and diagnoses from one device can be useful to better interpret current state of any other device from the group.

The second case relates to the monitoring of a group of distributed devices of a different type, which are considered as a system of physically or logically interacting components. In such a case, it would be extremely important for every field agent to use outcomes from other field agents as a context for interpretation of the produced diagnosis. Thus, in these two cases appropriate field agents should communicate with each other (e.g., in peer-to-peer manner) to share locally stored online and historical information and thus to improve the performance of the diagnostic algorithms, allowing even the co-operative use of heterogeneous field devices produced by different companies, which share common communication standards and ontologies.

We are considering a case when (predictive) maintenance activities can be performed not only by humans but also by embedded automatics controlled by agents. We also assume that the newest Semantic Web and Intelligent Web Services concepts can be applied to the problems of interoperability among field devices and will result to essential improvement of field device maintenance performance.

OntoSERV.NET Implementation Issues

Industrial Ontologies Group (http://www.cs.jyu.fi/OntoGroup) developed the OntoServ.Net concept as a large-scale automated industrial environment for assets management. First, we must consider maintenance of assets, but, in general, this concept can be applied for process control, improvement of operating efficiency, field-performance diagnostics, and so on as well. Better maintenance provided by OntoServ.Net considers maintenance-information integration, better availability of operational data, and a shift from reactive and preventive maintenance towards predictive and proactive maintenance, which meansreduced Total Life Cycle Cost of machines. OntoServ.Net is also a network of industrial partners, which can share maintenance methods and information developed during the work of separate machines (device, equipment, installation). Improved locally, maintenance experience can be shared.

In addition, it is assumed that there are special commercial maintenance (diagnostics) services supported either by manufactures of machines, or by third parties. Browsing a device's internal state is extended to an automatic diagnostics and recovery within a network of maintenance services or even within network of platforms hosting several maintenance services. The role of a maintenance service is to organize gathering and integration of field data to learn based on it, and secondly, support its "clients" (field devices) providing remote diagnostics and maintenance services. Implementation of such large-scale environment as OntoServ.Net presents many problems to be solved. The challenge here is standardization of maintenance data across various software systems within OntoServ.Net and existing industrial systems.

Ontology-Based Standardization of Maintenance Data

We are focusing on maintenance data, which comes from field devices. For remote diagnostics (in the case of predictive maintenance, for instance), these data need to be sent to some other place beyond a local computing system (whether it be a computer or embedded system). We assume that a maintenance network without centralized control requires some global standard for data representation in order to provide compatibility of network nodes.

We consider standardization based on ontological description of data. An ontology-based approach stands here as an alternative to development of a maintenance-specific set of standards/vocabularies/procedures for information exchange. We use an ontology concept and data-representation framework, which was developed within Semantic Web activities. Ontology-based information management is going to be more flexible and scalable, and it has potential to become a next-generation standard of information exchange in the Internet. An ontology-engineering phase includes development of upper-ontology (schema for ontology) and development of ontology itself, which includes specific data about maintenance domain (such as device descriptions, diagnostic-methods descriptions, etc.) Concrete data is annotated in terms of upper- and common ontology. Here, ontology provides a basis for a well-understood "common language" to be used between devices and systems.

If considering field devices as data sources, then information to be annotated is sensors' data, control parameters, and other data that presents a relevant state of the device for the maintenance process. A special piece of device-specific software (*OntoAdapter*) is used for translation of *raw diagnostic data* into *standardized maintenance data*. This adapter can be integrated into a legacy system used for device management or can be developed independently from existing software if such a solution is appropriate and possible.

Type of software, which uses data being described in an ontological way, can vary depending on needs. It can be a data browser, control panel of an operator, computing system, database storage, and so on. Because of the way data is represented, it will never be processed incorrectly, since software can check itself whether data semantics, as annotated, is the same or compatible, as data processing unit needs.

Additional benefit comes from data annotation for software development even if there is no need to deliver information outside of an origin computing system; there is no longer a need to develop special formats of maintenance-data exchange between applications, since they are already presented in common standard by means of ontology. Software can be developed in modular, scalable manner with support of this standard (ontology). Such commitment to the shared (upper-) ontology will provide compatibility of software.

Ontology-Based Diagnostics Based on Maintenance Data

It is assumed that there are special commercial diagnostic units (maintenance services) supported either by manufactures of machines or by third parties. Browsing a device's internal state is extended to automatic diagnostics and recovery within a network of maintenance services. As already mentioned, the role of maintenance service, firstly, is to organize the gathering and integration of field data and learning based on it, and secondly, to support its "clients" (field devices) providing remote diagnostics services.

Considering aspects of maintenance-network development, the following statements are true:

1. There are diagnostic software components (also mentioned as *classifiers* or *diagnostic units*), which perform predictive/proactive diagnostics. These diagnostic units obtain maintenance data delivered to them either locally, or from a remote source, and provide a diagnosis as an output.

3. The diagnosis provided by classifier can be of several types: which class of state an observed device has, what kind of in-depth diagnostics it is, and which [maintenance] actions/activities are required.

3. Diagnostic units are specialized in certain aspects of maintenance diagnostics, so a device usually needs support from a set of different diagnostic units, which operate and can be replaced independently.

4. Diagnostic units (components), in general, are not device-specific and perform similar diagnostic tasks in variety of device monitoring systems.

5. Diagnostic units are platform-compatible and developed separately from maintained devices; thus, they can be used on any platform within OntoServ. Net.

6. Once a diagnostic unit possesses the ability to learn, the maintenance experience it got will be available for diagnostics of other devices. It is done by means of running a copy of classifier on other maintenance platforms or presenting its experience in a way that will allow reusing it by other diagnostic units. Of special interest is the presented capabilities of integration of such information obtained "worldwide" and applied effectively for individual devices.

7.   A maintenance platform is a computing environment in which maintenance services (diagnostic units, etc.) are installed. It supports device-specific interfaces for connecting devices, on one side, maintenance managing core with installed maintenance services and, on theother side, supports connection to a maintenance network consisting of maintenance platforms of other devices and maintenance platform of *maintenance services*—specialized centres for remote maintenance. Such services can be implemented based on agent technology (e.g., Gibbins, Harris, & Shadbolt, 2003). Taking into account the openness of the system, the issues of security and trust management are considered as exceptionally important (Kagal, Finin, & Peng, 2001);

8.   Maintenance platform manages maintenance information exchange between devices and diagnostic units resided locally and elsewhere in the maintenance network. It also supports search of required network resources, upgrades of installed software, supports mobility feature for maintenance services.

Since the available set of classifiers can vary, type of the classifiers (their purpose) is specified in order to allow their selection in cases, when there is a necessity. Every classifier has its description attached—information concerning its capabilities. Description also contains information on how to use a classifier, what inputs it requires, and what output it provides.

The preliminary classification mechanism of a maintenance platform takes into account which services (classifiers) are available now, and selects those that declare themselves as able to deal with the class of problems derived from the preclassification phase. Here, preclassification is akin to human-operator work, which can detect some abnormal device behaviour and use analysis tools in order to find out the source of the problem.

It is supposed that some historical maintenance data is available and it is used to automatically learn what kind of maintenance actions should be performed. Learned knowledge in this model supports a rather simple, but automated, reasoning mechanism, which implements preliminary diagnostics of a device state and can identify certain deviations from a normal operational state and run appropriate diagnostic service.

Industrial Ontologies Group proposes to involve the descriptions of available maintenance resources in maintenance-data processing (classifier services, as it was shown) and explicit representation of knowledge for initial data preprocessing.

Service descriptions allow changing a service set easily. Diagnostic knowledge, first, allows automated maintenance system activity and, second, makes it possible to reuse learned knowledge (presented in a specific classification model as data, rules, etc.) in a newly installed device that has no historical data yet can use classification ontology of some other device of the same type.

We use application of Semantic Web technology for maintenance-data description, service-component description, and representation of classification knowledge. Those descriptive data pieces have to be in some common format for the whole maintenance system. *RDF* and its derivatives are going to be a perfect basis for that.

Ontology-Based Diagnostic Services Integration

To be able to integrate heterogeneous resources and services over the Web, we have to describe them in a common way based on common Ontology. In considering resources in an industrial product's maintenance domain, we distinguish such resources as: smart devices, which are represented like services of their alarm or control systems (or some software interface); sets of diagnostic services or classifiers; platforms, which are represented like clusters or a collection of elements; humans, which can be represented by some special service; large enterprise's systems; and so on. This ontology-based annotation must comprise not only a resource's description (parameters, inputs, outputs), but also many other necessary things, which concern their goals, intentions, interaction's aspects, and so on. "Ontology-based" means that we have to create ontologies to be used for all of such resources.

Each service represents a three-level resource: input parameters, "black box" (service engine), and output parameters. Since all services are heterogeneous, we have a need to describe each resource (service) via common ontology and create a common shell (OntoShell), which will provide such common description and will make transparent real-service realization. OntoShell is a main core of such an integration environment. Now that OntoShell has been elaborating in the scalable and modular manner, it also may represent a mediation platform for the set of adapted, semantically annotated resources (cluster of OntoShells). OntoShell is a shell (frame) for these resources, which is a mechanism for making ontological description and providing interoperability. One of the important OntoShell parts is an OntoAdapter for resources. If we are talking about transformation of existing resources to semantically enable ones, then we have to develop the mechanisms for accessing the resources. Since the resources are developed based on different specific standards on both content (WSDL, C/C++ (dll), Java, SQL Server, DCOM, CORBA, etc.) and transport levels (TCP, HTTP, RMI, etc.). In this case, we have to design and develop corresponding software modules (OntoAdapters) for semantic, content, and transport levels. Construction blocks will fill OntoShell depending on resource's description.

Set of services represents a three-level automated diagnostic system. First level is represented by the alarm system of a device (WatchDog), which signalizes about changes of the normal device state. Main maintenance diagnostic system (service) forms second level of the system via the preliminary (initial) diagnostics. It contains preliminary diagnosis classification via the ontology of the device condition. The result of such initial classification is making decision what kind of the classifier (diagnostic service) has to make further data processing. This system initiates the third level of diagnostic for making decision about precise diagnosis. Request of the further classification is being sent to respective classifiers of the local centralized diagnostic system directly taking into account a probability of a classifier's belonging to the class of the problem.

Semantic Peer-to-Peer Discovery of Maintenance Services

Within the OntoSert.Net concept, a peer-to-peer architecture of a global network of maintenance Web services is assumed. The architecture provides support for registration of maintenance-service profiles based on ontology shared within the network. The profiles are registered in a local repository. The architecture includes a platform steward module, which implements a semantic search engine. The engine searches among local maintenance services for those whose profile corresponds to a query according to semantic match procedure. A steward also implements peer-to-peer functionalities like query forwarding and sending, neighbour registration, and so on.

When platform steward makes a decision about the necessity of using of external maintenance services, it sends a formalized query to the neighbour platforms. Such necessity can occur if the requested maintenance service is absent on the local platform or cannot provide sufficient performance, or if a steward needs "opinions" of other classifying services, for example, during learning. If the neighbours cannot satisfy the query, they forward it to their own neighbours and so on. Thus, the query can roam through many platforms in a global network and the probability to find the required service is very high.

When some platform receives a query, which it can satisfy, it sends the response to the query initiator about its location. The query initiator can collect some number of such responses—a list of potential partners.

To increase the efficiency of the search of maintenance Semantic Web services and their automated nature (initiators of the search are smart devices) the system should inherit the concepts of Semantic Web. That means:

1. Development of common ontology for the global network that contains a classification of "maintenance services" in a hierarchical tree and an explicit definition of relations between such classes. Another option might be to provide possibilities to manage several pre-existing ontologies, as in Mena, Illarramendi, Kashyap, and Sheth (2000).

2. Every platform creates a local repository of profiles of available Maintenance Services based on ontology.

3. Each Platform Steward must have Semantic Search Engine, which will find a semantic match between query and each profile in the local repository.

4. Each platform steward must have a Semantic Query Engine, which composes formalized queries.

Thus, we are using combination of centralized architecture for service discovery within the platforms of services and peer-to-peer architecture for service discovery across the platforms (e.g., Arumugam, Sheth, & Arpinar, 2002). A platform steward provides centralized capabilities when it manages service discovery within its internal platform, and in the same time it can behave in peer-to-peer manner when interacts with external service platforms.

Global Understanding Environment and Its Challenges

The main objective of the Industrial Ontologies Group is to contribute to fast adoption of Semantic Web and related technologies to local and global industries. It includes research and development aimed to design a Global Understanding Environment (GUN) as the next generation of Web-based platforms by making heterogeneous industrial resources (files, documents, services, devices, business processes, systems, organizations, human experts, etc.) Web-accessible and proactive and cooperative in a sense that they will be able to automatically plan their own behavior; monitor and correct their own state; communicate and negotiate among themselves depending on their role in a business process; and utilize remote experts, Web-services, software agents, and various Web applications. Three fundamentals of such a platform are interoperability, automation, and integration. Interoperability in GUN requires utilization of Semantic Web standards, RDF-based metadata, and ontologies and semantic adapters for the resources. Automation in GUN requires proactivity of resources based on applying the agent technologies. Integration in GUN requires ontology-based business process modeling and integration and multiagent technologies for coordination of business processes over resources.

The Global Understanding Environment Concept

GUN (Kaykova, Khriyenko, Kovtun, et al., 2005; Terziyan, 2003) is a concept we use to name a Web-based resource "welfare" environment, which provides a global system for automated "care" over (industrial) Web resources with the help of heterogeneous, proactive, intelligent, and interoperable Web-services. The main

Figure 4. Layers of the GUN architecture (Kaykova, Khriyenko, Kovtun, et al. 2005)

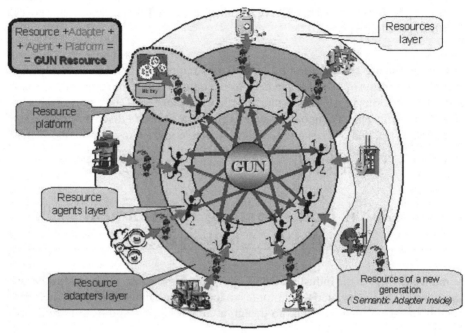

players in GUN are the following resources: service consumers (or components of service consumers), service providers (or components of service providers), decision-makers (or components of decision makers). All these resources can be artificial (tangible or intangible) or natural (human or other). It is supposed that the "service consumers" will be able: (a) to proactively monitor their own state over time and changing context; (b) to discover appropriate "decision makers" and order from them remote diagnostics of their own condition, and then the "decision makers" will automatically decide, which maintenance ("treatment") services are applied to that condition; (c) to discover appropriate "service providers" and order from them the required maintenance. The main layers of the GUN architecture are shown in Figure 4.

Industrial resources (e.g., devices, experts, software components, etc.) can be linked to the Semantic Web-based environment via adapters (or interfaces), which include (if necessary) sensors with digital output, data structuring (e.g., XML) and semantic adapter components (XML to Semantic Web). Agents are assumed to be assigned to each resource and are able to monitor semantically, reach data coming from the adapter about states of the resource, decide if more deep diagnostics of the state are needed, discover other agents in the environment that represent "decision makers," and exchange information (agent-to-agent communication with semantically enriched content language) to get diagnoses and decide if a maintenance is needed. It is assumed that "decision making" Web services will be implemented based on various machine learning algorithms and will be able to learn based on samples of data taken from various "service consumers" and labeled by experts. Implementation of agent technologies within a GUN framework allows mobility of service components between various platforms, decentralized service discovery, FIPA communication protocols utilization, and MAS-like integration/composition of services.

Three Components of GUN According to SmartResource Project Vision

The SmartResource project, which was mentioned above, in its research and development efforts analyzes Global Understanding Environment decomposing it into three frameworks:

1.   **General Adaptation Framework (GAF)**, for Interoperability (First project year—2004).GAF provides a framework to describe domain resources (declarative knowledge). It includes Resource State/Condition Description Framework (RscDF), appropriate RscDF-based domain ontology, appropriate RscDF Engine and the family of so called "Semantic Adapters for Resource" to provide an opportunity to transform data from a variety of possible resource-data representation standards and formats to RscDF and back. For more details about RscDF and GAF see Kaykova, Khriyenko, Naumenko, Terziyan, and Zharko (2005) and Kaykova, Khriyenko, Kovtun, et al. (2005).

2.   **General Proactivity Framework (GPF)**, for Automation (Second project year—2005).GPF provides a framework to describe individual behaviors (procedural knowledge). It includes Resource Goal/Behavior Description Framework (RgbDF), appropriate RgbDF-based domain ontology, appropriate RgbDF engine and a family of "Semantic Adapters for Behavior" to provide an opportunity to transform data from a variety of possible behavior representation standards and formats to RgbDF and back. See more on RgbDF in Khriyenko, Terziyan, and Zharko (2005).

3.   **General Networking Framework (GNF),** for Integration (Third project year—2006).GNF provides a framework for knowledge integration (both declarative and procedural) to describe group behavior within a business process. It includes Resource Process/Integration Description Framework (RpiDF), appropriate RpiDF-based domain ontology, appropriate RpiDF engine and a family of "Semantic Adapters for Business Process" to provide an opportunity

to transform data from a variety of business-process-representation standards and formats to RpiDF and back.

Finally, GUN Ontology will be a result of an integration of RscDF-based domain ontology, RgbDF-based domain ontology, and RpiDF-based domain ontology and should be able to include various available models for describing all GAF-, GPF-, and GNF-related domains. The basis for interoperability among RscDF, RgbDF, and RpiDF is a universal triplet-based model provided by RDF and two additional properties of a triplet (true_in_context and false_in_context).

The General Networking Framework considers an opportunity of ontological modeling of business processes as integration of component behavioral models of various business actors (agents representing smart resources in the Web) in such a way that this integration will constitute the behavioral model of an agent responsible for the "alliance" of the components. This means that such a "corporate" agent will monitor behaviors of the proactive components against the constraints provided by the integration scenario. Such a model is naturally recursive and this means that the corporate agent can be a component in a more complex business process and will be monitored itself by an agent from the more higher level of hierarchy. Hierarchy of agents can be considered as possible mapping from the part-of ontological hierarchy of the domain resources.

The above motivates the main research objective of SmartResource project in 2006: "Design of a General Networking Framework as a platform for integration individual behaviors of proactive smart resources into a business process with opportunity to manage the reliability of components by certification, personal trust evaluations and exchange."

As a business case for GNF, we will consider the expansion of an industrial maintenance case from previous project years by allowing multiple industrial devices, Web services, and maintenance experts into the business-process modeling.

The roadmap of further research and development assumes complex interactions between multiple distributed agents—representatives of Web services, human experts, and smart devices. Advanced features of the SmartResource environment cause this necessity:

- One industrial smart device exploits several Web services (composition) for more precise diagnostics;
- One Web service provides diagnostics for multiple smart devices: knowledge reuse cases;
- Learning a Web service utilizes multiple sources of training sets (many smart devices);

- One smart device provides training sets from its history to multiple learning Web services;

- Exchange of underlying diagnostic models between Web services;

- One smart device requests opinions about its conditions and diagnoses from multiple human experts to increase quality of decisions;

- One human expert provides diagnostic service to multiple devices (efficient reuse of knowledge).

An additional important aspect that will be studied and analyzed in the third project year is trust. This aspect inevitably arises in environments where multiple customers interact remotely with service providers whose authenticity, credibility, and reliability have to be verified. In general, two strategies regarding trust have to be analyzed:

- Exchange of opinions about authenticity and quality of Web services (QoS) and human experts between smart devices (controlled by their companies' owners);

- Certification of the Web services and human experts by nationally or internationally-known authorities.

GUN Challenges

The GUN vision being very general, there are many opportunities to be checked and open issues to be studied. Below, some of the GUN challenges are listed. These have not been studied deeply yet or only preliminary studies are available.

Standardized Adapters for Heterogeneous Resources

It is a really challenging task to adapt extremely heterogeneous real-world resources to the Web environment. The task must be solved by creating a set of reusable (hardware and software) components for the adapters (see Figure 5) and a smart way of how to automatically design an adapter for some resource by combining existing components based on the resource semantic description. In Kaykova, Khriyenko, Kovtun, et al. (2005) a General Adaptation Framework has been discussed to target the problem. Resource Adapters based on General Adaptation Framework are supposed:

- to enable to connect industrial resources to the GUN Environment;
- to add semantics to the resource data;
- to encode data into RscDF, which enables semantic description of dynamic and context-sensitive resources;
- to be build from hardware, software, and even "human" components;

General Adaptation Framework provides tools and technology for semiautomated adapters created from reusable components and templates based on Semantic Technology.

Semantic Annotation, Exchange, Integration, and Mobility of Diagnostic Models and Decision Engines

As mentioned above, the GUN environment is supposed to have decision-making resources, which are based on certain machine learning algorithms. Getting data from some external industrial resources (devices, machines, etc.), such algorithms are able to build models for diagnostics and performance prediction of these devices. Natural heterogeneity and distribution of these algorithms and models result to another important challenge of the GUN environment, which is to provide an opportunity for automated algorithms (learning and decision engines) and models discovery, sharing, reuse, interoperability, invocation, integration, and composition. For some ontology and markup for learning algorithms should be developed as well as the ontology and markup for learned models.

An example is shown in Figures 6 through 9. A Bayesian network (Figure 6) has

Figure 5. Architecture of an adapter linking any industrial resource to a GUN environment

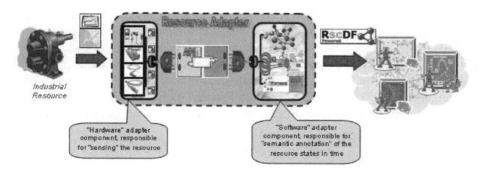

Figure 6. Sample of a Bayesian Network model (graphical, formal, symbolic, and semantic representations)

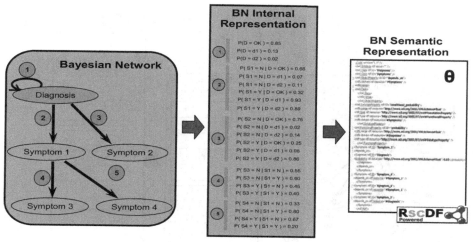

been learned based on training data from some industrial device. The appropriate GUN resource (e.g., Web service) has produced this model according to a Bayesian learning algorithm and now keeps it in some internal format (e.g., as it is shown in the picture). It is evident that other external services (even the ones that also provide Bayesian learning and reasoning) will not necessary "understand" that model because of possibly a different format of representation. Imagine that two heterogeneous Bayesian reasoners have studied the same object based on different subsets of data and got different Bayesian models as a result. Is there any way to integrate these two models without relearning so that each of the reasoners can use the more advanced integrated model? This can be done if the representation of both models is done according to the same standard. Just for that, it is reasonable to develop semantic markup (e.g., as shown in Figure 6) for various model representations as well as the ontology of the models itself. In this case, an integration of the models from a similar class can in principle be done automatically without involvement of the original training data.

The problem of integration becomes much more complicated if it involves the models from different classes. For example, a Bayesian learner on one hand observed the same part of object data, and on the other hand neural-network learner observed some other part of the same object data (see Figure 7). Even if both models were semantically marked-up and integrated, neither a Bayesian reasoning engine nor a neural-network reasoning engine can be applied to be able to run such a hybrid. This means that to enable to run integrated models, a universal reasoning engine should be developed, which will be able to integrate semantically annotated heterogeneous

Figure 7. Sample of a neural-network model (graphical, formal, symbolic, and semantic representations)

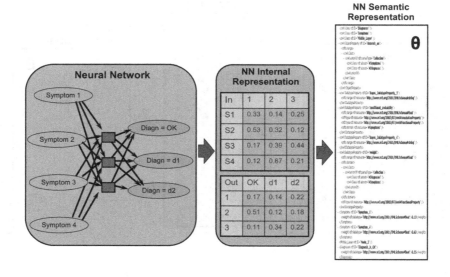

Figure 8. Sample of a Bayesian network reasoning engine internal and semantic representation

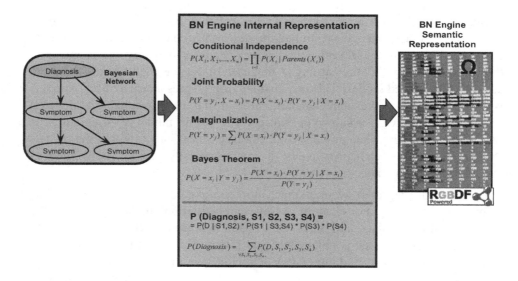

Figure 9. "Mobile Learner" in a GUN environment

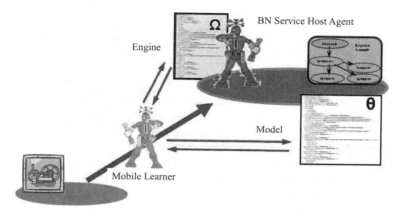

engines. The sample of a Bayesian network reasoning engine internal and semantic representation is given in Figure 8.

Thus, the challenge discussed above includes ontology and markup for a learned-models description, ontology, and markup for the decision (reasoning) engines description and appropriate tools for models and engines automatic discovery, exchange, integration, or composition.

Such implementation may allow also mobility of the decision-making entities within a GUN network. Imagine a mobile agent whose functionality is to move from a platform, learn models from different sources, and also implement learned models later in different places (see example in Figure 9).

Such an agent:

- Is a shell (engine);
- Can learn a learning algorithm (metalearning);
- Can learn a model based on data and learning algorithm;
- Can "swallow" and run existing model;
- Can learn contexts;
- Can reason based on the model, data, and context;
- Can move to "universities" (special platforms with appropriate Web services) for learning;
- Self-interested;
- Can take care of a GUN resource;
- Its learning ability is ontology-based.

Figure 10. Sample scenario for "Mobile Model" concept: Annotated resource data is sent to a service

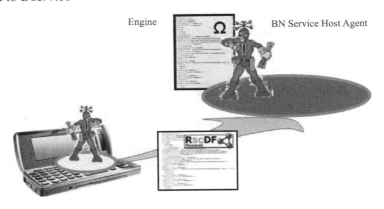

Figure 11. Sample scenario for "Mobile Model" concept: Service learns a model from data

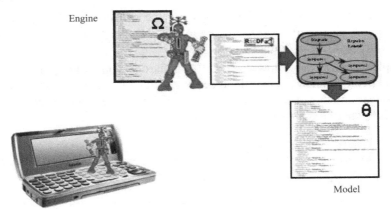

There is also a sense to talk about "mobile models," which is a similar but not the same concept as the mobile learner. A mobile model is useful for various personalized Web services for mobile users. User data is being collected in the mobile-client terminal and by portions that go to the server; the server learns a model based on this data; the model "goes" back to the mobile client and runs on it. The sample scenario can be as follows: (1) the log of online data from some GUN resource is collected locally; (2) collected data after semantic enrichment is sent to special machine-learning Web service (e.g., for Bayesian learning as shown in Figure 10); (3) based on this data the service creates a model and transfers it to a semantic format (Figure 11); (4) nominated by the platform agent with learned model and appropriate engine moves to the original client platform (Figure 12); (5) the "guest" agent will perform further diagnostics of the original resource locally.

Learning Distributed Trust

Another challenge is to manage "trust" in a GUN environment. This is especially important due to extensive use of numerous decision-making services (for condition monitoring, diagnostics, prediction, maintenance planning, etc.). In cases when a resource is making a choice as to which decision-making service it should send its query, the knowledge about services performance in the past would be quite important. Trust of some service requestor to some service provider can be considered as a personalized prediction of service performance (quality, precision, etc.) partly based on the success history of previous interactions between the requestor and the provider and also partly based on known or communicated trust evaluations from other requestors or trust-certification authorities.

The challenge of learning distributed trust contains:

- Automated certification of GUN Resources;
- Trust calculation;
- Trust monitoring, diagnostics, and maintenance;

Figure 12. Sample scenario for "Mobile Model" concept: Agent with model and engine moves to the original client platform

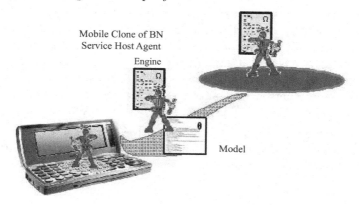

- Trust models learning;
- Trust prediction;
- Trust sharing and exchange;
- Smart P2P environments based on trust;
- Trust-related security and privacy issues.

Consider the sample scenario from Figure 13. Assume some industrial GUN resource (device) has collected on a local GUN platform-labelled data (e.g., personal history faulty states descriptions labelled by experts with appropriate diagnoses). The following procedure is the one widely used in the machine-learning field known as learning ensembles of classifiers. The local platform agent divides the data into two subsets: a training-sample set and a test-sample set. The training set is given to several external services so that they are able to adjust their models or learn the new diagnostic model specifically for that device from the scratch. External services can in principle support different learning algorithms (e.g. neural, fuzzy, Bayesian, genetic, etc.). After all contacted services report that they have learned, the device provides them another piece of labelled data, that is, a training set with hidden actual diagnoses. Services are requested to provide the diagnoses for given cases. A device agent compares received outcomes from services with known (actual) diagnoses and calculates for each service the performance value (e.g., percentage of correctly classified cases from the test set) and considers these values as personalized ranks of services, which determine the trust of the "device" towards appropriate service providers. The ranks can be used in the future to diagnose new states of the device either by selecting the best-ranked service from available ones or by integrating outcomes from several services as weighted (based on ranks) voting among them. This approach should increase diagnostic performance in comparison to randomly selected service or simple averaging of outcomes from several services.

Consider another scenario in Figure 14. Here, in addition to "personal" trust evaluation, the client (e.g., industrial device) can use also professional evaluation of services performance from special certification service. It is reasonable that the device manufacturer provides such a certification service to check all external services, which pretend to provide reliable diagnostics. The advantage of the evaluation provided by a certification service is availability of quite a complete set of training and testing data collected from a number of the same types of devices. However, it is also true that the advantage of personal evaluation (previous scenario) is based on personalized model creation (data might be incomplete but belongs to own history).

Consider one more scenario in Figure 15. Here, the case is shown when some client (device) has not done personal evaluations of some services but has tried to get such values from the "colleagues" in the network (other devices of the same type,

Figure 13. Sample scenario for "Learning Distributed Trust" concept: Service learns trust values by providing training and test samples of data for various services to use these values later for smart service integration

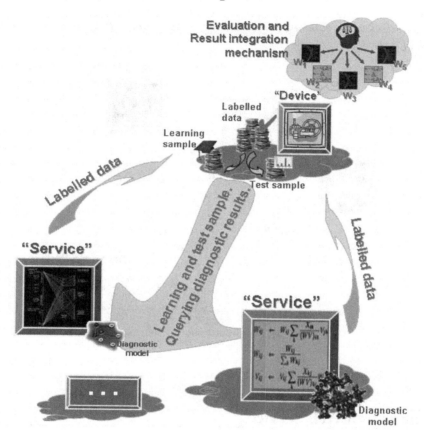

which already evaluated the services in question). The trust towards the colleagues itself should be taken into account and combined to the values of trust towards services they share.

Actually the complete trust evaluation of a client towards some service is some kind of smart combination of (a) personal evaluation, (b) evaluation obtained from a certification service, (c) evaluation communicated from the colleagues (clients of the same type).

Figure 14. Sample scenario for a "Certification Service" concept: Certification service learns trust values by providing complete training and test samples of data. Clients (devices) can access certification service and request a trust certificate concerning the service they are going to use. In combination with the previous scenario, a device can combine personal trust values and certified values to compute rank of a service.

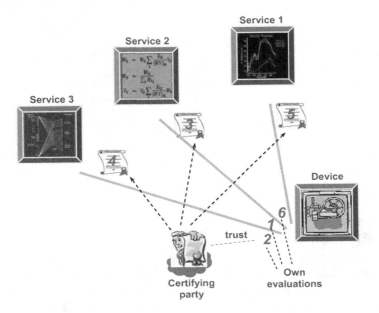

Human as a Web Service

Another interesting challenge of GUN is that a human can play the role of Web service. Because different categories of industrial resources (e.g., devices and maintenance experts) can be adapted to GUN environment with adapters and provided by agents, it may happen that the device can be a service requestor (e.g., require diagnostic based on a measured state of parameters) and a human can be a service provider (e.g., the one who can provide a diagnosis based on state description online). The challenge here is how to take into account human specifics to manage such architectures (e.g., Figure 16) in a reliable way and also how to enable automated discovery, sharing, reuse, interoperability, invocation, integration, and composition of online human resources in the Web.

Figure 15. Sample scenario for the "trust exchange" concept: The device imports trust values concerning services 1 and 2 from the "colleagues" (Devices 1 and 2). The device should also take into account the trust values towards colleagues if known.

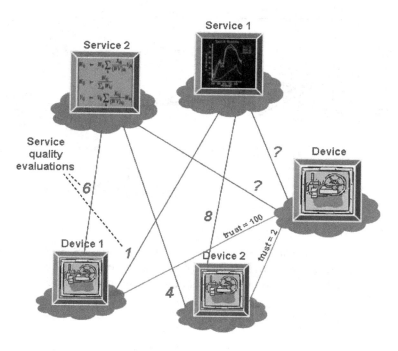

Conclusion

The goal of this paper is to provide a possible implementation framework for Web services that automatically follow up and predict the maintenance needs of field devices. The concept of a "mobile-service component" supposes that any component can be executed at any platform from the service network, including a service requestor side. This allows the delivery of not only service results but also a service itself. Mobile service component carrier (agent) can move to a field device's local environment (embedded agent platform) and perform its activities locally. Service components improve their performance through online learning and communication with other components. Heterogeneous service components' discovery is based on semantic P2P search. This chapter contains very basic challenges related to Web

Figure 16. "Human as a Web service" concept

services for smart devices and partly related implementation issues. Some preliminary results of the project in this area are mentioned and referenced. Still more research efforts are needed to prove some of the concepts mentioned in this chapter.

Acknowledgments

The author is grateful to Tekes (National Technology Agency of Finland) and co-operating companies (Agora Center, TeliaSonera, TietoEnator, Metso Automation, ABB, JSP) for the grant that supports the activities of the SmartResource project.

References

Ankolekar, A., Burstein, M., Hobbs, J., Lassila, O., Martin, D., McDermott, D., et al. (2002). DAML-S: Web service description for the Semantic Web. In *Proceedings of the First International Semantic Web Conference (ISWC)*, (pp. 348-363).

Arumugam, M., Sheth, A., & Arpinar, B. (2002). The peer-to-peer Semantic Web: A distributed environment for sharing semantic knowledge on the Web. In

Proceedings of the International Workshop on Real World RDF and Semantic Web Applications, Hawaii.

Berners-Lee, T., Hendler, J., & Lassila, O. (2001). The Semantic Web. *Scientific American, 284*(5), 34–43.

Bussler, C., Fensel, D., & Sadeh, N. (2003). *Semantic Web services and their role in enterprise application integration and e-commerce.* Retrieved February 15, 2006, from http://www.gvsu.edu/ssb/ijec/announcements/semantic.doc

Chandrasekaran, B., Josephson, J., & Benjamins, R. (1999). What are ontologies, and why do we need them? *IEEE Intelligent Systems*, 20-26.

Fensel, D., Bussler, C., & Maedche, A. (2002). A conceptual architecture of Semantic Web enabled Web services. *ACM Special Interest Group on Management of Data, 31*(4), 24-29.

Gibbins, N., Harris, S., & Shadbolt, N. (2003). Agent-based Semantic Web services. In *Proceedings of the 12th International World Wide Web Conference* (pp. 455-462).

Kagal, L., Finin, T., & Peng, Y. (2001). A dramework for distributed trust management. In *Proceedings of the IJCAI-01 Workshop on Autonomy, Delegation and Control* (pp. 1-11).

Kaykova, O., Khriyenko, O., Kovtun, D., Naumenko, A., Terziyan, V. & Zharko, A. (2005)., General adaption framework: Enabling interoperability for industrial Web resources. *International Journal on Semantic Web and Information Systems, 1*(3), 31-63.

Kaykova, O., Khriyenko, O., Naumenko, A., Terziyan, V. & Zharko, A. (2005). RSCDF: A dynamic and context-sensitive metadata description framework for industrial resources. *Eastern-European Journal of Enterprise Technologies, 3*(2), 55-78.

Kaykova, O., Khriyenko, O., Terziyan, V. & Zharko, A. (2005, August 25-27). RGBDF: Resource goal and behaviour description framework. In M. Bramer & V. Terziyan (Eds.), *Industrial Applications of Semantic Web, Proceedings of the 1st International IFIP/WG12.5 Working Conference (IASW-2005)* (pp. 83-99). Jyvaskyla, Finland: Springer, IFIP.

Lawrence, J. (2003). Embedded FIPA agents. In *Agentcities: Agent Technology Exhibition, Barcelona.* Retrieved February 15, 2006 from http://www.agentcities.org/EUNET/ID3/ documents/exh_program.pdf

Mena, E., Illarramendi, A., Kashyap, V., & Sheth, A. (2000). OBSERVER: An approach for query processing in global information systems based on interoperation across pre-existing ontologies. *International Journal on Distributed and Parallel Databases, 8*(2), 223-271.

Metso. (2003). *Neles FieldBrowser™ system for field device predictive mainte-nance.* Metso Automation Tech. Bulletin. Retrieved February 15, 2006 from http://www.metsoautomation.com/

Ontologies. (2003). *Ontologies in agent systems.* Retrieved February 15, 2006 from http://oas.otago.ac.nz/OAS2003

Paolucci, M., Kawamura, T., Payne, T., & Sycara, K. (2002). Importing the Semantic Web in UDDI. In *Proceedings of Web Services, E-business and Semantic Web Workshop* (pp. 225-236).

Pyötsiä, J., & Cederlöf, H. (1999). Advanced diagnostic concept using intelligent field agents. In *ISA Proceedings.*

Sensodec (2003). *Sensodec 6C for paper: Metso Automation Tech. Bulletin.* Retrieved on February 15, 2006 from http://www.metsoautomation.com/

Terziyan, V. (2003). Semantic Web services for smart devices in a "global under-standing environment." In R. Meersman and Z. Tari (eds.), *On the Move to Meaningful Internet Systems 2003: OTM 2003 Workshops* (LNCS 2889, pp. 279-291). Springer-Verlag.

Terziyan, V. (2005). Semantic Web services for smart devices based on mobile agents. *International Journal of Intelligent Information Technologies, 1*(2), 43-55.

Terziyan, V., & Puuronen, S., (1999). *Knowledge acquisition based on semantic balance of internal and external knowledge* (LNAI 1611, pp. 353-361).

Chapter VIII

Building Sound Semantic Web Frameworks for Scalable and Fault-Tolerant Systems

Thomas Biskup, Carl von Ossietzky University Oldenburg, Germany

Nils Heyer, Carl von Ossietzky University Oldenburg, Germany

Jorge Marx Gómez, Carl von Ossietzky University Oldenburg, Germany

Abstract

This chapter introduces hyperservices as a unified application model for Semantic Web frameworks and proposes the WASP model as a framework for implementing them. Hyperservices are based on agent societies, provided with structured information by the Semantic Web, and using Web services as a collaboration and communication interface. The WASP model adds personalization rules to modify the agents' perception and the HIVE architecture as Semantic Information Server infrastructure within this framework. Finally, conceptual model driven software development is proposed as a means of easy adoption to hyperservices.

Overview

The Semantic Web and its effects are a mainstream catalyst for current Web development. Its influence is felt across many areas of research and business development: agent systems, knowledge-management frameworks, ontology definitions, and other areas all are refined by new ideas from Semantic Web research (and vice versa). Since many complex topics now are combined with the goal of building the "Next Generation Internet", it becomes increasingly important to build sound and flexible frameworks lest small research and development teams are overwhelmed by the multitude of choices, complex technologies, and the interfaces between those individual building blocks. Additionally operation-level support needs to be integrated in future architectures at a very basic level in order to provide a stable, scalable, and fault-tolerant basic architecture.

Research shows that the underlying methodology for defining Semantic Web-oriented frameworks can be defined very well. This chapter will explain the main streams which will be integrated towards the Semantic Web and more importantly show—based on a thorough requirements analysis—how Semantic Web-oriented systems must be built in order to create scalable, fault-tolerant, and extensible systems.

The following steps will lead to a refined methodological rules system that should govern all underlying concerns to build Semantic Web-centric frameworks and systems:

- The main research streams and technologies making up the Semantic Web are identified. Their interrelations and resulting requirements for frameworks and systems are shown.

- An in-depth requirements analysis concerning the architecture of Semantic Web systems and the must-have features of such features provides the ground for the definition of the corner stones of future Semantic Web systems. Specifically the requirements to be fulfilled by fault-tolerant, extensible, and scalable systems are shown.

- An approach to build multiplatform Semantic Web frameworks based on the core technologies of agents, ontologies, Web services, and personalization frameworks is explained. This approach is generic enough to encompass most currently existing frameworks and lends itself towards the integration of emerging standards. A new type of service—a hyperservice—is derived from integrating these core technologies into a new type of service infrastructure.

- Hints about using model-driven software development (MDSD) to build complex systems from standards-based simple building blocks will be given. Specifically we will explain the basics of a new MDSD philosophy we have developed (so-called conceptual model-driven software development/CMDSD) which greatly simplifies the system specification process and in the context of the Semantic Web can take advantage of semantic service descriptions.

An Overview of Emerging Semantic Web Technologies

First, we will give an overview of existing Semantic Web research and describe the current underlying problems that need to be solved in the future to let the Semantic Web become a living reality. Currently, we face a major gap between the reality of the Web—a disjoined and tangled mass of loosely coupled information resources—and the vision for the Web—a tightly integrated and openly structured information network with machine-readable data that allows autonomous agencies to create new applications empowered by this wealth of information. Current research shows that we can hope to achieve this goal, but there are many obstacles left to be mastered. We propose a framework to allow researchers and developers to choose the level of detail, the type of technologies, and the extent of computing power they want to utilize for their proposed solutions. We focus on a flexible abstraction layer, pattern-oriented architecture, and open interfaces to build on the successful foundations of the Web: ease of use, flexibility, and almost unlimited expression power. Agents are the central paradigm for software development using this architecture.

The Web—Now and Then

The World Wide Web Consortium (W3C) pushes the Semantic Web (Berners-Lee, 1998; Berners-Lee, Hendler, & Lassila, 2001) as a valuable vision to build the future foundation for a true information society. The efforts are supported by a multitude of research efforts.

Nonetheless, progress is slow and even if research would yield results at much greater speed (which does not seem reasonable since the open questions are rather challenging and tax the current state of the art research attempts), the results still need to be implemented. Current research hints at much more expressive and thus more powerful means to represent data and information—but the price is added complexity required to build the representations.

The World Wide Web was successful because people were enabled to share information overnight—with simple technology. This allowed for the enormous growth in information resources we now face, and this pattern most likely should be reproduced to guarantee the further growth of the Web Berners-Lee, 2000).

The Web of Systems

The World Wide Web in its current form is the largest information system ever built by humans—and it probably is one of the least structured information systems built. There are billions of Web pages (not counting other resources like images, videos, sounds, CGI interfaces to large databases, etc.) and almost none of them are structured in a standardized way. These pages mostly are built with HTML and coupled in a very loose manner—links lead into oblivion as often as they do not. And even existing links do not provide much semantic information (e.g., what is the meaning of a specific link except "someone thought that two information resources should be connected in some way"). Most information is presented in a way that allows humans to use it—although access to this information usually is a problem because it becomes harder and harder to find the few titbits of information in the existing mess of data.

Thus, we argue that we need to find ways to evolve from the current World Wide Web (a Web of systems—so named because there are many individual systems that usually are only connected by the simplest means, namely hyperlinks) to something more.

It would be foolish and dangerous to try too much at once. At the same time, it would be as foolish and dangerous to create artificial boundaries and introduce building blocks that limit our power of expressiveness. Thus, we propose to search for architectures and frameworks that support gradual evolution without limiting the final goal. We find practical examples that support the viability of this approach: Modular programming has spawned object-oriented programming to be able to control complexity with more natural concepts. For certain problem areas, agent-oriented systems have been discovered to be an immensely powerful and very natural concept for defining solutions (Ciancarini & Wooldridge, 2001). Now the industry momentum offers a huge chance to solve one of the basic problems of agent societies: Communication by Web services promises to do away with the artificial system boundaries currently inhibiting large-scale distributed autonomous agent systems.

The Web of Services

Web services have created a lot of recent buzz with business software companies. Web services (Christensen, Curbera, Meredith, & Weerawarana, 2001; Gottschalk, Graham, Kreger, & Snell, 2002)—while surrounded by a lot of hype—offer a standard means to communicate between disparate systems and applications with absolute disregard for programming languages, computer hardware, and system-specific communication protocols. Based on eXtensible Mark-up Language (XML) (see

Biskup & Marx Gómez, 2005) this new and exciting standard promises a new way of defining interfaces—without stickling to implementation details and basic technical questions. Together with hypertext transfer protocol (HTTP) (see Gourley & Totty, 2002) and simple object access protocol (SOAP) (see Mitra, 2001) as protocols we face an enormous opportunity to bring together previously separated building blocks for the next generation Internet. XML is the unifying data representation standard that could be used to encode any kind of information. HTTP and SOAP are simple yet flexible protocols that allow a system-independent communication between heterogeneous systems. More generally, the basic notion of application-level protocols is very important to be able to conceptualize a working architecture for a true Web of services. While it currently is very difficult to connect different Web-based systems, future interfaces could greatly benefit from these standards (e.g. when trying to combine a flight information system and a hotel booking system).

A Web of Services thus becomes a tangible possibility—a network of still loosely connected services but with one new and exciting feature: a standardized way of communicating with those services, to send requests and to receive results. This could be the next important step for Web technologies—because Web services possess many powerful features ideally suited for industrial use and commercial success stories. This also could build the momentum to ensure the widespread use of a—in our point of view—very important technology. Current developments support this theory; most new API versions and programming systems supply some sort of Web services integration (from ancient languages like COBOL to the most recent developments like .NET).

The Web of Semantics

All aforementioned efforts target one underlying and ever-present goal: the Semantic Web—an information network of machine-readable data that allows autonomous agencies to gather data, turn it into information, reason about it, and come to conclusions. Intelligent agents will traverse this information network to fuel new and exciting services (e.g., Joy, 2000; McIlraith, Son, & Zeng, 2001; Metcalfe, 2000). Humans will never be able to fully utilize the mass of data collected in the World Wide Web. Thus, we need to find new ways to turn all the data into something more than a loosely connected set of HTML pages. The basic building blocks for the Semantic Web are made up by

- **Semistructured data:** XML has been accepted as the means of choice to represent platform-independent data in a semi-structured way that allows for an open-ended way of describing data (Bray, Paoli, Maler, Sperberg-McQueen,

& Paoli, 2000). Based on plain text (but powered by Unicode), XML enriches pure data with metadata to allow machines to use the data more effectively and in ways not initially coded into the data format.

- **Machine readable data:** The current proposal for this building block relies on XML as a means of expression and has been named RDF (Resource Description Framework, see Lassila, 2000; Brickley & Guha, 2000). It should be noted that that RDF has various means of representation but XML seems to be the most natural for the World Wide Web and the most widely used right now. RDF allows describing resources, properties of resources and relations between resources. RDF can be extended to create languages that are more complicated and at the same time provides powerful foundations for reasoning (based on first-order logic). Interestingly, RDF takes a very pragmatic approach to provide a viable solution for information representation; it right away allows for inconsistence, incorrectness, and incompleteness in the represented information and takes it as given that data can lead to situations where agents will not be able to come to a decisive or correct conclusion. This pragmatism adheres to the concepts that established the current Web—ease of use with an allowance for mistakes.

- **Ontologies** as a means to describe the relations between objects and to define standard hierarchies as descriptions of "the world." A lot of research is concerned with the question of what should be in an ontology language in order to once more find the best way of combining computing and expression power with ease of use. Ontology languages like SHOE (Heflin, Hendler, & Luke, 1999), DAML (Hendler & McGuiness, 2000) and DAML+OIL (2000) hint at the power of future metadata structures.

So far, major concerns in the World Wide Web community were to standardize the encoding of data and information. Retrieval, automated reasoning about information, connection of services and basically all other means of exploiting this information pool were only moderately successful. The Web spawned a variety of search engines and metasearch engines but these, together with shop systems and Web directories, cover the efficient means of access to the World Wide Web for humans. There were some experiments with agents and agent societies (Brickley & Guha, 2000) but so far these attempts failed to become widespread successes due to the lack of a unified information infrastructure and lack of standardized interfaces—the common gateway interface (CGI) is hardly sufficient to build even semicomplex applications in an abstract and elegant way. Other experiments (e.g., De Bruijn, Fensel, Keller, & Lara, 2005; Harper & Bechhofer, 2005) hint at different exciting possibilities to enhance the knowledge acquisition process for users but still lack the unified foundation required to build a whole generation of such service enhancements. The need for such a foundation is proven by some extensive first-generation systems (e.g., Lin,

Harding, & Teoh 2005), which show the basic building blocks that will be required again and again and thus are the primary target for standardization attempts.

To cope with this situation we propose a new model regarding future applications building on the foundations mentioned so far—a unit of abstraction we have named hyperservices.

Hyperservices: A Unified Application Model

We believe that the next important step will be to find a unifying, language- and system-independent architecture that allows for a convergence in current research areas surrounding the Semantic Web. When we talk about Web-based applications, we mean, "based on Web technologies." Web technologies have been widely accepted and have managed to bring together disparate system structures.

Looking at the components currently available, a unified application model based on agent societies seems to be in reach: The Semantic Web allows one to reason about information by structuring information appropriately. This provides the basis for "intelligent" agents (with "intelligence" on a pragmatic hands-on level). Web services introduce the interface for collaboration among systems. Agents are the natural extension to achieve autonomous systems (Benjamins, 2002). Currently, we face a multitude of ontology languages (e.g., Benjamins, Fensel, & Asunción, 1998) and many models and theories to map information to efficient data models and retrieval algorithms—but these means will only see wide-spread use if they become easy to communicate to future users (e.g., programmers), based on standard architectures and easy to integrate in existing systems. Integration still is one of the main problems faced by current computer science (from the business perspective) but the Web can only remain successful if it manages to stay commercially interesting (whether by drawing enough people to it to supply Internet Providers with customers or by introducing truly successful E-Business models is not that important). Thus, the integration of these new models into existing structures will be the most important task from a business point of view.

Topics under current discussion (e.g., agent societies and the Semantic Web) will not be able to replace classic information systems (e.g., tax accounting, enterprise-resource planning, and logistics). However, if built in the right way they will be able to enrich classic systems by providing benefit. They will open up a new venue of information systems—built around the necessity to decide between precision and speed. The sheer size of the Web and its constant flux will make it impossible to store nearly enough data in local systems to allow for efficient information systems (in the classic sense). Thus, it seems much more likely that future information systems will be built around the idea of (semi-) autonomous agents wandering across the Web, collecting information, reasoning about it, and yielding results—either continuously or after specified resource limits (e.g., time, bandwidth, or a financial budget) have been exhausted (e.g., Hendler, 2001).

The WASP Model

We propose a unified model that has been inspired by currently successful component models like, for example, Enterprise JavaBeans and COM. If a way of expressing standard application scenarios can be found that at the same time provides enough structure (to speed up application development) and leaves enough room (to take into account concurrent models, warring philosophies, and the general lack of precision in the underlying data in the Web environment) an important step has been made towards a truly usable Semantic Web.

We are convinced that it will not be possible to find the one true way—but, for example, Enterprise JavaBeans have shown a viable approach: Start small and target the most pressing issues and then grow to finally encompass most possible scenarios.

Thus our basic philosophy for a unified framework is founded on four building blocks which in our point of view will be absolute necessities to populate the future Web with more powerful applications:

- Web services as a means of providing a unified communication interfaces between applications and agencies (UDDI, 2001; Christensen et al., 2001; Dale, 2002).

- Agents as a natural and central means to represent typical tasks and solutions for a distributed and constantly changing information environment.

- Semantic Web technologies as a means to provide data and information in a consistent manner that allows retrieval and reasoning.

- Personalization technologies to customize processes to the needs of the individual user—an absolute necessary concerning the current (and future) size of the World Wide Web lest it becomes impossible to separate useless from useful information.

Agents will be the central building block of this architecture because they implement the actual business logic. Web services are the natural means of communication and collaboration for agents working under the described model, the Semantic Web is the environment (world) for these agents and the personalization rules can be used to make up or modify the beliefs of the agents. Thus, the described components integrate very nicely and in a very natural manner into the underlying agent paradigm.

The WASP framework (the acronym representing the basic building blocks of Web services, Agents, Semantic Web technologies, and Personalization) will account for a variety of necessities explained in the next sections. In contrast to existing major endeavours in this area (e.g., O'Brien & Nicol, 1998; Object Management Group, n.d.; Finin, Labrou, & Mayfield, 1997 for more details) we plan to provide an architecture that focuses on:

- proactive information agents that collect information and provide results by using an inference mechanism to reason about the existing information.

- high-level technical support for the application developer (e.g., communication, distribution, data storage),

- tight integration of Web technologies (RDF, Web services, DAML, SOAP, etc.),

- independence from specific kinds of implementations (e.g., no specific communication language will be enforced),

- focus on agents relying on the Semantic Web as the dominant information source.

Thus, the following central paradigms will be of greatest importance.

Open Interfaces

Since it is impossible to enforce one true operating system, one true programming language or one true CPU architecture for the network underlying the World Wide Web it is of paramount importance to provide a powerful means of communication between the interacting agencies. SOAP and HTTP (as underlying protocols) together with Web services (as a means of interface specification) seem to be natural choices. The framework will provide a layer of abstraction to be able to disconnect from these particular technologies, should, for example, other protocols become more important.

Service Agencies

Agents seem to be a very natural way for describing typical scenarios of Web usage. They are the machine representation of human beings who right now have to do most of the work manually. Thus, the WASP framework will provide the means to define a variety of agents—mobile, autonomous, reactive, and so on. To enhance the usefulness of the framework it is set up to allow agents to be self-describing—thus automatically turning agents into services that can be used by others and integrated via standard interfaces. This allows for widespread service dissemination and easy integration with other systems.

It will be especially important to integrate current agent research into this framework layer; efforts like DARPA Agent Mark-up Language (DAML) allow for powerful modeling means to devise agents and agencies.

Data and Information Gathering

The framework must provide for a means to accumulate data, compare it, and reason about it. Data might be persistent (to allow for agents with increasing reasoning power) or transient (to model short-effect tasks) and data should be interchangeable between different agents. It must be possible to integrate ontologies to allow for a solidified view of the "world" (in regards to the agent or agents).

Personalization Integration

It must be easy to integrate personalization technologies. At the most basic level it should be possible to specify user preferences and dislikes and to integrate them in the reasoning and retrieval process to improve the quality of the returned information.

The HIVE:
Semantic Web Brokering Simplified for WASP Agents

Web servers have been the technical foundation for the success of the World Wide Web. Applications servers have been a successful model in abstracting from the everyday chores of building complex applications and thus form the basis for modern large-scale business applications. Thus, it seems natural to evolve to Semantic Information Servers that provide a corresponding environment for Semantic Web agents specialized on utilizing the Semantic Web resources to provide information services to the end user.

Application servers offer persistence, transactions, distributed processing, and scalability if the software complies with a predefined component model (e.g., Java 2 Enterprise Edition/J2EE). This allows developers to focus on the actual task, for example, implementing the business logic for a complex transaction portal. In our view, a similar model is required for Semantic Web applications based on agent societies. Different layers of abstractions will allow concentrating on functional

Figure 1. HIVE architecture

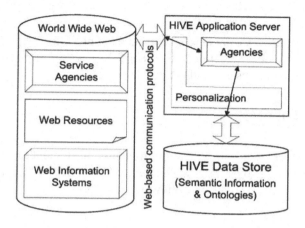

requirements and help to abstract from the details of the implementation. In the same way a J2EE application server takes away the details of persistence from the developer, a semantic information server can abstract from the details of, for example, storing semantic information, retrieving it, and reasoning about it. This holds true for other areas as well (e.g., information recovery from the Web, resource management for agents, and communication between members of local and remote agencies). Within the WASP framework, we intend to call the semantic information servers a HIVE (not an acronym but rather a play of words continuing the WASP idea).

These ideas result in the infrastructure diagram in Figure 1.

Important Semantic Web Research Areas

In this section, we intend to describe but a few of the more important current research topics that need to be solved to further the development of Semantic Web services:

- Ontology integration and translation is a major problem for interconnecting distributed services and systems (Gruber, 1993; Heflin, Hendler, & Luke, 1999; Heflin & Hendler, 2000): How can differing ontologies for related topics be mapped on each other?

- Web service orchestration, interoperation, and transaction handling needs to be standardized (UDDI, 2001; Web services Choreography Requirements, 2003; Web services Transaction, 2002).

- Standards to allow for personalization need to find wide acceptance (Platform for Internet Content Selection, n.d.; Stahl & Völter (2005) for currently available yet still rarely used standards).

Remaining Challenges

Besides the technical questions that currently enjoy most attention, a multitude of additional topics needs to be investigated before distributed agent systems and the Semantic Web become truly viable. A few of them are:

- **Cost challenges:** Who is going to pay for the resources being used in distributed agent networks? It is safe to assume that such agent services will be a lot more cost intensive than the "simple Web information platforms of today" (e.g., Web servers).

- **Pricing challenges:** Already now, there is a tendency to commercialize high-quality services. How will future information systems be rated in terms of usage fees if the component services of some complex service (e.g., the logistics service, the currency-conversion service, and the mapping service for a complex online order service) each incur fees but the user of the complex will not necessarily add to the income of the complex service provider (e.g., because the user decides against buying something after getting the shipment information)?

- **Business challenges:** What are viable business models for Semantic Web agencies and services?

- **Quality challenges:** How will services be able to guarantee a certain level of quality if they rely on the data collected in the Semantic Web—an information storage that will be as inaccurate as the currently available World Wide Web (mostly because everyone will be able to put up whatever he or she deems correct and appropriate)?

- **Trust challenges:** How can one be sure that not only the quality of results gained by Semantic Web analysis is sufficient for the individual but also correct at all?

- **Workflow challenges:** How can complex workflows (like booking a complete holiday trip) be orchestrated when dynamic service directories, user preferences, potentially faulty information, and other factors need to be considered?

- **Performance challenges:** How must services be constructed to be able to retrieve useful data in a timely manner from the Semantic Web—a Web that is infinitely more complex to search compared to current search engines and technologies due to the far more involved complexity created by allowing inferences, conclusions, and reasoning about information?

- **Security challenges:** How can personal and private information be protected from prying eyes? What new security challenges arise from the architectural decisions made for the WASP framework?

- **Legal challenges:** Who will be held responsible for incorrect, imprecise, or faulty information derived from or modified by Semantic Web content?

- **Architectural challenges:** What are the best-of-breed software infrastructures/application architectures to allow for a rapid dissemination of the technologies involved? How can user and developer acceptance be increased?

Requirements Analysis Concerning Semantic Web Architectures

As explained in our example Semantic Web architecture, different technology layers usually will be found in a Semantic Web based system. In this section, we will continue the example by analyzing the essential requirements to be fulfilled both by our but also by similar architectures in order to be Semantic Web ready. We will start at the bottom-most layer (the database tier) and work upward from there. Differences compared to standard enterprise architectures will be explained in the individual sections.

Requirements for the HIVE Data Store

The HIVE Data Store will store and evaluate data gained by analyzing Semantic Web resources. To provide a useful and extensible model the following functional and technical requirements must be taken into account:\

- The HIVE Data Store should be independent from the specific type of storage (DBMS, RDF store, flat file, some kind of network service). Thus, it will be possible to choose the best type of storage for a given situation. Additionally, this is a basic requirement to be able to exchange data–s3tore implementations as technology and research continue to evolve.

- The HIVE Data Store must not assume that data is correct, complete, or unambiguous. The Internet by design is a place where data is provided in a spontaneous and improvised manner. Thus, the Data Store must be able to cope with such data. This is also a major difference from classical enterprise systems where usually utmost care is taken to insert only verified, correct, and unambiguous data into databases.

- The HIVE Data Store must provide inference support. The true value of the Semantic Web can be used only by analyzing the gathered data and drawing conclusions. Thus, inference support is paramount. Nonetheless, there must not be any assumptions about the specific inference approaches being used, again to allow flexibility and configurability.

- The HIVE Data Store must be able to access data from a variety of sources. This is necessary due to the size and varied nature of the underlying information sources. The Internet itself is just too large to be kept on one server or a whole farm of servers, and while in most cases an application will not need to access all the information available on the Internet, for some of the more exciting Semantic Web applications it will be a necessity to be at least potentially able to access all available information.

- The HIVE Data Store must be able to integrate ontologies into its repository. Ontologies are the basic mechanism for defining the meaning of concepts modeled in, for example, RDF structures. An important add-on functionality will be the ability to compare ontologies and map them onto each other to be able to integrate differing ontologies designed for the same problem area.

- The HIVE Data Store must include a facility to manage the credibility of sensitive information. Mission-critical data must only be accepted from sources that are able to authenticate themselves and prove their credibility (e.g., with certificates or similar mechanisms).

- The HIVE Data Store should be able to organize itself physically, manage its resources and to restructure information based on dynamic changes of the environment. This is an optional but highly recommended functionality as it is to be expected that the Data Store of a widely used system will grow with leaps and bounds. To remain efficient and to conserve resources the Data Store itself has to take responsibility for this.

- The HIVE Data Store must explicitly consider data-retention periods, along with models and algorithms for purging. Otherwise, the data cached there will rapidly become stale and will overload the database.

- The HIVE Data Store must provide a management facility so that external users can examine the state of the server, the data, and the rules accumulated in the store. Additionally, typical functionality must be provided to configure the data sources and to control resource allocation of the store. It should be noted that the management facility might have a very different outlook depending on the underlying storage mechanism being used for the specific server.

To be able to incorporate these widely varying requirements, an abstraction layer will be required through which all HIVE Data Store access operations will be routed. This will allow the addition of functionality as required (e.g., by defining a HIVE Data Store proxy that collects requests, runs through a caching layer to increase performance, and then delegates unanswered requests to the actual physical or distributed Data Store).

Requirements for the HIVE Agent Server

The HIVE Application Server is responsible for running the various agents that implement the business logic side of the framework and access all other components to achieve their goals. The following functional and technical requirements need to be taken into account:

- The HIVE Agent Server must provide a runtime environment for varying agents that share a common interface as defined by the WASP framework. There must be support for both mobile and static agents to allow for a wide range of application scenarios.

- The HIVE Agent Server must provide a security layer that controls resource access for all agents operating on the server. This is an absolute necessity for servers incorporating mobile agents and allowing mobile agents to migrate from one server to another.

- The HIVE Agent Server must provide access to the HIVE Data Store in an abstracted and generalized manner. Agents must not be required to know about the details of data storage or inference.

- The HIVE Agent Server must provide access to the "outside world" so that the sensors of the agents involved can operate. The HIVE Agent Server may modify perceived data based on personalization and security rules.

- The HIVE Agent Server must allow for communication using a variety of agent communication languages (ACLs) to be able to integrate a variety of agent systems. This probably will include the necessity to provide translation services between different agent communication languages in order to allow communication between agents of different breeds.

- The HIVE Agent Server must provide a management facility so that external users can examine the state of the server and the agents running on it. The

Figure 2. Scope of intelligent agents (Adapted from Gilbert et al., 1995)

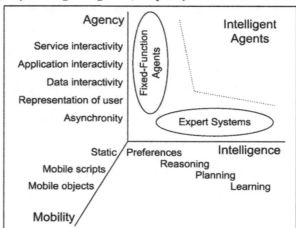

management facility must include all kinds of standard management functionality to allocate resources, control permission, direct agents, and so on.

- The WASP Agent Interface must be structured so that existing agent frameworks can be easily integrated into the system while there also must be enough room to develop new concepts and architectures. Additionally the interface must be extensible, so that incremental extensions may be made both forward and backward compatible, allowing upgrades to clients or servers in either order.

Interestingly the requirements concerning the actual agents are very small—when examining, for example, the proposed scope of software agents in Gilbert et al. (1995) the only functional requirement that must be provided by the HIVE Agent Server is mobility. Everything related to the intelligence aspects of agents can be modelled in the HIVE Data Store and the agent implementation. All other aspects are determined by the actual agent implementation.

Requirements for the HIVE Personalization Layer

The HIVE Personalization layer modifies both the perceived external environment (e.g., the Internet and other servers) and the perceived internal environment (especially the information gathered in the HIVE Data Stores). To provide a meaningful level of personalization the following functionalities are of utmost importance:

- The HIVE Personalization Layer must provide permission-based personalization so that the perceived environment adjusts based upon the permissions of each individual agent. Permissions will have to be modeled on a per-server, per-agent, and per-user basis in order to be fully effective.

- The HIVE Personalization Layer must be able to handle agent-specific inference rules in order to modify and control the inference process based on agent preferences.

- The HIVE Personalization Layer must be able to handle user-specific inference rules in order to modify and control the inference process based on agent preferences.

Requirements for the HIVE Communication Layer

The HIVE Communication Layer connects the HIVE Agents with external systems (e.g., the Internet, other servers, etc.).

The argumentation in the sections above shows that the HIVE Communication Layer also should serve another important purpose: The various components of the WASP Framework need to be connected in a system-independent and flexible way by using the HIVE Communication Layer not only for intersystem but also for intrasystem communication several powerful synergy effects can be utilized:

- **Communication uses but one protocol layer:** This makes it much simpler to distribute agents, objects, and servers since no separate protocols are required for communication and information exchange. The implementation of the HIVE server itself is simplified, too.

- **Intrasystem services** (e.g., resource management, process supervision, etc.) can—if wanted—be modeled as agents to use the infrastructure provided by the WASP framework to implement the WASP framework itself. This is analogous to database systems that store database metainformation in their own database structures or compilers used to compile themselves and serves as a good proof of the concept for the simplicity and validity of the architecture, once implemented.

- **The communication layer must integrate mechanisms** to transparently handle both scalability of the system as a whole and to increase the fault tolerance when concerned with individual requests.

To be able to fulfil these expectations a number of functional requirements must be considered:

- The HIVE Communication Layer must be implemented with a system-independent protocol and communication API. It must be possible to exchange atomic and complex information objects. Web services and the associated communication protocols (e.g., SOAP) will serve nicely as a basis for the HIVE Communication Layer.

- The HIVE Communication Layer must be able to communicate with external systems through a standard protocol. Otherwise, communication would be too limited for a reasonable system trying to support Semantic Web applications.

- The HIVE Communication Layer must provide some means to execute a lookup for external services and resources. Services like UDDI (Heflin & Hendler, 2000) and maybe also LDAP are typical candidates to be integrated. Although this might seem like a rather minor and trivial point at first (especially given the fact that more or less established technologies like LDAP and UDDI already exist) it must be stressed that the integration of a powerful lookup service for other services and resources is of major importance—especially so when considering the stress on "fault tolerance" and "scalability."

Scalability is rather easy to achieve in some respects if a lookup mechanism exists. Requests for services on one hand can be dispatched to service endpoints based on a variety of load-balancing strategies and algorithms—only imagination limits the possible scenarios ranging from simple round-robin algorithms to elaborate agent-based schemes where agents monitor the CPU load on connected systems and use that information to control the dispatching of further incoming requests. Hardware-based load balancing mechanisms can also be easily integrated as the endpoint of a service can represent a façade for a server cluster with a hardware load balancer handling the incoming requests. Naturally, these techniques can also be combined.

To be able to effectively handle faults several approaches can be implemented. The important concern is whether service faults on the actual service level (e.g., complete service failures due to unavailable servers, etc.) or on the logical level (e.g., service errors, etc.) are examined. The communication layer can easily enhance the fault tolerance of a hyperservice-based system on the service level. A simple protocol handler extension can be integrated in order to allow the resubmission of service requests if a service endpoint fails to respond. This behaviour can be enhanced by integrating a regular availability check into the service/resource registry to be able to filter out or deactivate temporarily unavailable endpoints and thus reduce the overall network load. Errors on the logical level cannot be handled in a transparent level in the HIVE communication layer without extensive semantic descriptions of the services themselves. Since the idea of the HIVE architecture is to provide a simple and extensible architecture for now no logic fault handling at all will be integrated into the communication layer. Future research will have to show whether such extensions can be integrated in a simple yet effective manner.

Finally, it is important to note that—as the internal HIVE services also can and should make use of the service and resource registries—the HIVE system itself transparently benefits from the integration of the features concerning fault handling and scalability as described above.

- The HIVE Communication Layer must be system- and programming-language independent. Again, Web services and the associated protocols nicely fit this requirement.
- The HIVE Communication Layer must use standardized protocols to be able to connect to as many systems as possible.

Common Requirements

Finally, there are some common requirements that are shared by all frameworks—for example, compositionality, reusability, and extensibility—that must be taken into account. Of special importance for the WASP framework is language independence (even if the reference implementation might use a specific language like Java or C#), in order to be able to connect as many systems as possible. Since these requirements are not unique or special to the presented topic, we will not elaborate on them any further within the bounds of this chapter.

Conclusion to the Requirements Analysis

In order to make the Semantic Web as accessible as possible, a highly abstracted framework with open interfaces and simple overall concepts is very important—especially since the underlying technologies mentioned above individually already require a high level of expertise to be able to use them effectively. We have shown that such an infrastructure framework is defined by a manageable amount of requirements and that available standards (ready or just evolving) already cover a lot of ground.

How to Build
Multiplatform Semantic Web Frameworks

In this section, we will explain basic technological patterns to enable building multiplatform Semantic Web frameworks. Configuration and instrumentation of such systems will be a focus. For other areas (e.g., actual business-logic implementation), the explanations given in the previous sections hold: Web services, agents, and ontologies will be the driving technologies with implementation details being governed both by the implementation platform (e.g. J2EE or Microsoft .NET) and emerging standards (Web service transactions, Web services reliability, etc.).

Conceptual Summary

First, we will summarize once more the philosophical concepts behind the functional layers presented in the previous sections before describing a configuration framework for Semantic Web Architecture based systems.

Conceptualization of the HIVE Data Store

The HIVE Data Store will store and evaluate data gained by analyzing Semantic Web resources. Features include independence from the specific type of storage (DBMS, RDF store, flat file, some kind of network service); the ability to exchange data-store implementations as technology and research continue to evolve; robust handling of incorrect, incomplete, and ambiguous data; inference support and configurability; means of access to a wide variety of data sources; ontology integration; and a range of administrative functions. To be able to incorporate these widely varying requirements, an abstraction layer will be required through which all HIVE Data Store access operations will be routed.

Conceptualization of the HIVE Agent Server

The HIVE Application Server is responsible for running the various agents that implement the business logic side of the framework and access all other components to achieve their goals. Features include the abstraction from specific agent implementations (allowing a mixture of agent types to operate under the same hood), support for both mobile and static agents, security support, resource control, abstracted access to the HIVE Data Store, unified access to the "outside world," translators for agent communication languages (ACLs). The unified means of accessing agents from the outside will be through Web services—specifically to the outside we make no difference between agents and services because in our opinion successful and complex services over time might naturally evolve into agents if the appropriate infrastructure is provided (Foster, Jennings, & Kesselmann, 2004) for an extended discussion of this point).

Conceptualization of the HIVE Personalization Layer

The HIVE Personalization layer modifies both the perceived external environment (e.g., the Internet and other servers) and the perceived internal environment (especially the information gathered in the HIVE Data Stores) by providing permission-based, per-server, per-agent, and per-user personalization so that the perceived environment adjusts based upon the specific settings for agents or agent types.

Conceptualization of the HIVE Communication Layer

To be able to connect the components described above the HIVE Communication Layer must be implemented with a system-independent protocol and communication API. It must be possible to exchange atomic and complex information objects. Web services and the associated communication protocols (e.g., SOAP) will serve nicely as a basis for the HIVE Communication Layer. The HIVE Communication Layer also must provide some means to execute a lookup for external services and resources. Services like UDDI (UDDI, 2001) and maybe LDAP are typical candidates to be integrated, although the communication API will abstract from the specific type of lookup service. To be system- and programming-language independent, Web services will be used as the most appropriate standardized protocol available. The basic strategies for fault handling and increasing scalability have been integrated into the communication layer architecture to provide a very nonintrusive support for the future users of this architecture. Here, the concept of registries and façades serve as the basic building blocks to create a scalable and fault-tolerant system, although fault handling is so far only conceptualized on the system level and not on the level of logical operations.

Setting Up a Configurable Core System

As discussed in Biskup, Marx Gómez, and Rautenstrauch (2005) and Biskup and Marx Gómez (2004a) we try to keep the overall system as flexible as possible. The

Figure 3.

```
<hive>
  <registries>
    <connect-to-registry name="…">
       <inquire>…</inquire>
       <publish>…</publish>

       …

    </connect-to-registry>

    …

    <start-registry name="…" implementation="impl">
       <executable>…</executable>
       <inquire>…</inquire>
       <publish>…</publish>
       <parameter name="…" value="…"/>

       …

    </start-registry>

    …

  </registries>
  <components>
    <component name="jagent" implementation="java"
wsdl="jagent.wsdl" service="jagents">
       <executable>…</executable>
       <parameter name="…" value="…"/>
       <parameter name="…">

          …

       </parameter>

       …

    </component>

    …

  </components>
  <settings>
    <property name="…" value="…"/>

    …

  </settings>

  …

</hive>
```

all-pervasive use of Web services as a means of communications between individual components allows us to build the core HIVE system around a very small kernel with extensible core components that are independent of programming language and specific implementation. Overall, this works in analogy to the Microkernel approach for operating systems.

Launcher Configuration

Configuring and starting a HIVE server is actually very simple: The basic configuration actually describes the components to start (e.g., start the Agent Server here but no Data Store), gives some information about their implementation, and requires all components to register at a list of given registries. Additionally system services are started to monitor the component services and restart them if they should fail. A sample XML configuration (greatly simplified to account for length restrictions of this chapter) might look like in Figure 3.

When starting up the HIVE launcher, the launcher loads the configuration file and executes the following steps (note that the launcher can be implemented in any possible programming language; all external communication is based on Web services and thus we do not care for the details of the programming language):

1. Execute a Web service call "exchangeHIVERegistryInfo" to all (UDDI) registries for which this launcher is configured to connect. A list of the known connectable registries is transmitted with this call. The locally known registries are stored with the called registry and a list of locally unknown registries is returned. This step is cyclically repeated as defined in the settings to keep the list of known and working registries up to date.

2. All locally requested registries are started by looking up the implementation type and searching for a file called impl-desc.cfg which specifies the way to create instances of the given implementation type on the local system. All parameters are given to the registry to allow flexible configuration of each registry.

3. The list of known other registries is exchanged with each local registry.

4. Start each given component in the same way as described for registries.

5. Start a system- and launcher-specific service for each registry and component that checks if the component is still available under the given service name and otherwise restarts the component if it is no longer running.

6. The WSDL file for each component is published to all known registries.

    Please note that the actual configuration and start-up process is more involved. The details are beyond the scope of this chapter and will be expanded in future research papers. Under current research are aspects like hot-swapping service implementations, priority rules for service calls (see Agrawal, Bayardo, Gruhl, & Papadimitriou, 2001, for more ideas about this).

Figure 4.

```
<launch>
  <script>
    ...
  </script>
  <call>d:\jdk1.5.0\bin\javaw -classpath ... %P %E</call>
  <pardef>-D%N=%V</pardef>
</launch>
```

Implementation-Launcher Configuration

For each implementation type, a system-specific launch configuration is provided. Again, a (simplified) example is provided in Figure 4.

For each implementation type, an (optional) script is defined that is executed before the actual call to initialize the component is executed. The defined call contains a placeholder %P representing the whitespace-concatenated expanded parameter list (see below) and a placeholder %E to take the executable value given for the registry or component in the hive configuration file.

The parameter definition contains two placeholders %N (for the name of the parameter) and %V (for the value of the parameter). To create the value for placeholder %P all parameters from the hive configuration file are concatenated with whitespace and inserted for the %P placeholder.

Since components and registry parameters are intended to be platform-independent further placeholders are provided and expanded to allow flexible parameter definition (e.g., %basedir% for the base directory for all installed applications and %config% for the base directory for all configuration files).

Extensibility

Since no hard assumptions are made about the way services are implemented, a flexible configuration approach similar to the descriptions in Agrawal et al. (2001) is possible. Since, for example, a HIVE Agent Server can either be an actual implementation for an agent server or a rather simple façade for a dispatcher that distributes incoming calls among a specialized list of registries not publicly available, the distribution and scaling of HIVE installations becomes very simple. Additional façades are possible: data caches for the HIVE data store, caches for external resources, load balancer for component types, and so on. This allows for flexible resource distribution and performance adaptation.

Model-Driven Software Development for the Semantic Web

In this final section, we will give a short overview of the new trends that could help to leverage the inherent powers of the Semantic Web and bring its blessings to a larger audience. So far, we have talked about how to simplify the development of Semantic Web based systems and this is the classical perspective of most approaches available today.

Now we would like to concentrate on a new way of approaching software development. Model driven architecture (MDA) and model driven software development (MDSD) both strive to simplify software development by automatically generating executable code from models (Stahl & Völter, 2005). This approach seems to be very well suited for Semantic Web development considering the implied semantic definitions of models, agents, and ontologies, for example, provided by DAML. Nonetheless, one inherent weakness is left unconsidered by these approaches: Both MDA and MDSD require a sound understanding of the underlying technological and theoretical foundations, combined with a good amount of experience about how to model systems in the best way. This does not really help in transferring the conceptual knowledge that software customers possess into software systems as the developers still concentrate on building sound technological models and keeping all the minute details under control.

We thus propose the next step in model-driven technologies that we have named *conceptual model-driven software development (CMDSD)*. The basic idea is to model systems through intuitive models on the conceptual level. These models are not based on one global theory (like MDA with the Meta Object Facility) but rather on the most pragmatic theoretical foundation possible for the problem at hand. Additionally, the model should abstract as much as possible from the technological details of the system and focus on the conceptual facets possible. Models are aggregated into models that are more complex while great care is taken to provide a simple transformation from the individual model to the runtime system representation of the model. This allows software developers and architects to work together with customers and concentrate on the business side of the system—a simple and effective transformation from business problem to system representation is assumed. Existing design patterns support this notion.

How does this help with Semantic Web development? As explained in the sections above, one of the research directions currently actively investigated is the research in semantically rich descriptions for Web services. Now imagine a development system that can understand existing semantic descriptions of services load them and generate definition and aggregation interfaces for such services. Suddenly, developers and customers can work together in a semantically rich environment to model the business side of systems and—by using a framework like the WASP framework—can mostly ignore the technological side as the underlying framework handles configuration and assembly.

Currently systems are still far from this state but current research indicates that CMDSD might very well be the next logical step in software development—getting away from the technological perspective by consequently relying on existing designs, frameworks, and patterns and focussing on the actual business models with the simplest representations possible.

Background Information

This chapter is based on published and well-accepted papers by the authors as well as their continuing research in the areas of Semantic Web, agent systems, and model-driven software development, among them Biskup et al. (2005), Biskup and Marx Gómez (2004a, 2004b), and Biskup and Marx Gómez (2005).

References

Agrawal, R., Bayardo, R. J., Gruhl, D., & Papadimitriou, S. (2001). *Vinci: A service-oriented architecture for rapid development of Web applications.* Paper presented at WWW10, Hong Kong.

Benjamins, R. (2003). *Agents and the Semantic Web: A business perspective.* Paper presented at the Agent Technology Conference (ATC 2003), Barcelona, Spain.

Benjamins, V. R., Fensel, D., & Asunción, G. P. (1998). Knowledge management through ontologies. *PAKM-98*, 5.1-5.12.

Berners-Lee, T. (1998). *Semantic Web roadmap.* Retrieved February 12, 2006, from http://www.w3c.org/DesignIssues/Semantic.html

Berners-Lee, T. (2000). *Weaving the Web.* London, UK: TEXERE Publishing Limited.

Berners-Lee, T., Hendler, J., & Lassila, O. (2001). *The Semantic Web.* Scientific American.

Biskup, T., & Marx Gómez, J. (2004a). Building blocks of a Semantic Web framework —Requirements analysis and architectural implications. In *Proceedings of 3rd International Workshop on Web Semantics—WebS'04 in conjunction with the*

14th International Conference on Database and Expert Systems Applications DEXA 2004, Zaragoza, Spain (pp. 214-218).

Biskup, T., & Marx Gómez, J. (2004b). Component requirements for a nuiversal Semantic Web framework. *Semantic Web and Information Systems, AIS SIG-SEMIS Bulletin October Issue 1*(3), 25-28.

Biskup, T., & Marx Gómez, J. (2005). *Building a Semantic Web framework with reusable and configurable core technologies.* Paper presented at IRMA 2005, San Diego, CA.

Biskup, T., & Marx Gómez, J., & Rautenstrauch, C. (2005). The WASP framework—bridging the gap between the Web of systems, the Web of services and the Web of semantics with agent technology. *International Journal of Intelligent Information Technologies (IJIIT), 1*(2), 68-82.

Bray, T., Paoli, J., Maler, E., Sperberg-McQueen, C. M., & Paoli, J. (Ed.) (2000). Extensible markup language (XML) 1.0. *W3C Recommendation.* Retrieved February 12, 2006, from http://www.w3.org/TR/REC-xml

Brickley, D., & Guha, R. V. (Ed.) (2000). Resource description framework (RDF) schema specification 1.0. *W3C Candidate Recommendation.* Retrieved February 12, 2006, from http://www.w3.org/TR/RDF-schema

Christensen, E., Curbera, F., Meredith, G., & Weerawarana, S. (2001). Web services description language (WSDL) 1.1. *W3C Note.* Retrieved February 12, 2006, from http://www.w3.org/TR/wsdl

Ciancarini, P., & Wooldridge, M. J. (Ed.) (2001). *First international workshop on agent-oriented software engineering* (LNCS 1957). Berlin, Germany: Springer.

Dale, J. (2002). *Exposing Web services.* Paper presented at Agentcities.NET iD2, Lisbon, Portugal.

DAML+OIL. (2000). Retrieved February 12, 2006, from http://www.daml.org/language/

De Buijn, J., Fensel, D., Keller, U., & Lara, R. (2005). Using the Web service modelling ontology to enable semantic e-business. *Communications of the ACM 48*(12), 43-47.

Finin, T., Labrou, Y., & Mayfield, J. (1997). KQML as an agent communication language. In J. M. Bradshaw (Ed.), *Software agents* (pp. 291-316). Cambridge, MA: AAAI/MIT Press.

Foster, I., Jennings, N. R., & Kesselman, C. (2004). *Brain meets brawn: Why grid and agents need each other.* Paper presented at AAMAS'04, New York.

Gilbert, D., Aparicio, M., Atkinson, B., Brady, S., Ciccarino, J., Grosof, B., et al. (1995). *IBM intelligent agent strategy.* IBM Corporation.

Gottschalk, K., Graham, S., Kreger, H., & Snell, J. (2002). Introduction to Web services architecture. *IBM Systems Journal, 41*(2), 170-177.

Gourley, D., & Totty, B. (2002). *HTTP: The definitive guide.* O'Reilly.

Gruber, T. R. (1993). A translation approach to portable ontologies. *Knowledge Acquisition, 5*(2), 199-220.

Harper, S., & Bechhofer, S. (2005). Semantic triage for increased Web accessibility. *IBM Systems Journal, 44*(3), 637-648.

Heflin, J., & Hendler, J. (2000). Dynamic ontologies on the Web. In *Proceedings of the Seventeenth National Conference on Artificial Intelligence (AAAI-2000).* Menlo Park, CA; Cambridge, MA: AAAI/MIT Press.

Heflin, J., Hendler, J., & Luke, S. (1999). *SHOE: A knowledge representation language for Internet applications* (Tech. Rep. CS-TR-4078 UMIACS TR-99-71). University of Maryland at College Park, Dept. of Computer Science.

Hendler, J. (2001). Agents and the Semantic Web. *IEEE Intelligent Systems, 16*(2), 30-37.

Hendler, J., & McGuiness, D. L. (2000). The DARPA Agent Markup Language. *IEEE Intelligent Systems, 15*(6), 67-73.

Joy, B. (2000). Shift from protocols to sgents. *IEEE Internet Computing, 4*(1), 63-64.

Lassila, O. (2000). The ressource description framework. *IEEE Intelligent Systems, 15*(6), 67-69.

Lin, H. K., Harding, J. A., & Teoh, P. C. (2005). An inter-enterprise Semantic Web system to support information autonomy and conflict moderation. In *Proceedings of IMechE 2005, 219,* 903-911.

McIlraith, S. A., Son, T. C., & Zeng, H. (2001). Semantic Web services. *IEEE Intelligent Systems, 16*(2), 46-53.

Metcalfe, B. (2000). The next-generation Internet. *IEEE Internet Computing, 4*(1), 58-59.

Mitra, N. (Ed.) (2001). SOAP version 1.2, part 0: Primer, part 1: Messaging framework, part 2: Adjuncts. *W3C Working Draft.* Retrieved February 12, 2006, from http://www.w3c.org/TR/soap-part0, http://www.w3c.org/TR/soap-part, http://www.w3c.org/TR/soap-part2

Object Management Group. (n.d.). Retrieved February 12, 2006 from http://www.omg.org

O'Brien, P. D., & Nicol, R. C. (1998). FIPA—towards a standard for software agents. *BT Technology Journal, 16*(3), 51.

Platform for Internet Content Selection (PICS). (n.d.). Retrieved February 12, 2006, from http://www.w3.org/PICS

Stahl, T., & Völter, M. (2005). *Modellgetriebene Softwareentwicklung. Techniken, Engineering, Management.* Heidelberg, Germany: dpunkt.verlag.

UDDI Technical White Paper. (2001). Retrieved February 12, 2006, from http://www.uddi.org

Web services choreography requirements 1.0 (2003). *W3C Working Draft.* Retrieved February 12, 2006, from http://www.w3.org/TR/ws-chor-reqs

Web services transaction (WS-Transaction). (2002). Retrieved February 12, 2006, from http://www-106.ibm.com/developerworks/library/ws-transpec/

Chapter IX

Information Parallax

Franc Grootjen, Radboud University Nijmegen, The Netherlands

Theo van der Weide, Radboud University Nijmegen, The Netherlands

Abstract

To effectively use and exchange information among AI systems, a formal specification of the representation of their shared domain of discourse—called an ontology—is indispensable. In this chapter we introduce a special kind of knowledge representation based on a dual view on the universe of discourse and show how it can be used in human activities such as searching, in-depth exploration and browsing. After a formal definition of dualistic ontologies we exemplify this definition with three different (well known) kinds of ontologies, based on the vector model, on formal concept analysis and on fuzzy logic respectively. The vector model leads to concepts derived by latent semantic indexing using the singular value decomposition. Both the set model and the fuzzy-set model lead to formal concept analysis, in which the fuzzy-set model is equipped with a parameter that controls the fine-graining of the resulting concepts. We discuss the relation between the resulting systems of concepts. Finally, we demonstrate the use of this theory by introducing the dual search engine. We show how this search engine can be employed to support the human activities addressed above.

Introduction

Sharing information is a challenge in situations where we cannot rely on some common underlying body of conceptualization and representation. Ontologies are crucial for enabling knowledge-level interoperation between agents, since meaningful interaction among them can only occur when they share some common interpretation of the vocabulary used in their communication (Farquhar, Fikes, & Rice, 1996).

The often-cited article of Berners-Lee, Hendler, and Lassila (2001) on the Semantic Web and its semantic foundation called "Ontology" inspired many researchers in different fields to contribute to this topic, almost making it a "revamped cross-disciplinary buzzword" (Spynes & De Bo, 2004). In this chapter, we will limit ourselves to Sowa's view on ontologies (Sowa, 1984, 2004):

> *The subject of ontology is the study of the categories of things that exist or may exist in some domain. The product of such a study, called an ontology, is a catalog of the types of things that are assumed to exist in a domain of interest D from the perspective of a person who uses a language L for the purpose of talking about D.*

The construction of ontologies can be done either manually, automatically, or in some hybrid supervised way. Manual construction is difficult and time consuming, but yields verified and rich ontologies. The effort constructing such an ontology may be reduced by using a tool (Farquhar et al., 1996; Noy et al., 2001), or by reusing other ontologies (Gruber, 1992).

Automatically (or fully unsupervised) constructed ontologies will be less detailed and may contain errors but are labor free and may even be evolutionary (adapting to the changing situation). Furthermore, in some application areas small errors and mismatches in the ontology do not lead to dramatic effects. An example of such an area is information retrieval.

This chapter will present a formal, constructive and usable approach to unsupervised generation of concepts (or categories). Just like parallax is used to measure distance between celestial bodies, the dual perspective view on the universe of discourse creates an extra dimension that is visualized by concepts. This is referred to as *information parallax.*

In this chapter, we will study ontologies from the information-retrieval point of view, but the theory can be applied to other fields as well. In the classic retrieval situation there is a searcher with an information need, and a system that is (hopefully) able to supply the information the searcher is looking for.

In order to solve the retrieval problem the system somehow has to determine the relevance of each information item. Of course, without feedback from the searcher the system is only able to do an educated guess about the relevancy. Judging the relevancy of each information item can be simplified by using an ontology, especially if this ontology corresponds with the searcher's view on the universe of discourse.

A searcher can express an information need in several ways: The searcher may select or present a relevant information object (also referred to as a document), or formulate the information need by a combination of search terms (a query). In practice, searchers find it difficult to provide a proper query formulation, but have no problems in recognizing a document as being relevant. According to Taylor (1968), the following levels of information need may be distinguished:

1. **The visceral need:** The searcher experiences unconsciously something is missing. We assume the searcher at this stage is capable of recognizing (at least) some characteristics of what could satisfy this need.

2. **The conscious need:** The searcher is aware of this need, and can judge the relevance of documents. At this stage, the searcher may start to actively search for ways to satisfy the need.

3. **The formalized need:** The searcher has some either implicit or explicit formulation of the need. In case of an implicit formulation, a searcher can judge the relevance of description of the need. This assumption is the motivation for the mechanism of Query by Navigation.

4. **The compromised need:** a compromise of the best product composition from the actual assortment.

It will become apparent that dualistic ontologies can support the searcher on all these levels of information need.

From an abstract point of view, the information-retrieval problem may be seen as a semantics-transformation problem. We assume a searcher to have some mental model of the world. It is within this model that a searcher is aware of a knowledge gap. The searcher will try to find information objects that help the searcher to fill this gap. In order to facilitate finding information objects, a typical solution is to construct a catalogue that offers the searcher the opportunity to have a more directed avenue for search.

Figure 1. Different models of the real world

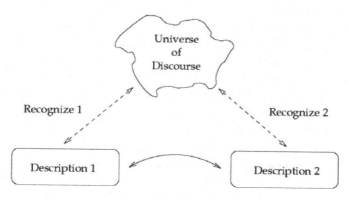

Traditionally (see Salton & McGill, 1983), information-retrieval systems try to relate a set of *descriptors* (or terms) with a set of *information objects* (or documents). Since single terms have only limited descriptive power, IR systems allow individual terms to be combined into bigger semantic units. These units are referred to as *intensional (meaning) objects*. How terms are combined to form intensional objects depends on the actual IR system. Likewise, a combination of documents will be called an *extensional (meaning) object*. We will call an IR system *dual* if it can transform intensional objects into extensional objects, and vice versa. In general, we will use the term *dualistic system* for such a system. To demonstrate the look and feel of a realistic system, we present DUALITY (see Figure 2 and 'The Dual Search Engine').

An example of an intensional object is a query while an example of an extensional object is the outcome of search. We will use the terms *query* and *search result* as alternative terms for intensional and extensional objects respectively. Being a combination of terms, intensional objects can be used to capture the meaning of a document, while extensional objects (being a combination of documents) can be used to capture the meaning of a term. As such, a dualistic system may be seen as a mutual semantics assigning system.

The principle of alternating between the intensional and extensional view of an information need has been employed to some extent in previous work. In the probabilistic model of information retrieval (Führ, 1989), a searcher is offered a sample set of documents. The searcher inspects this extensional object, and the relevant documents are marked. From this marking, the retrieval system derives an intensional view on the information need. The system uses this intensional object to derive (using statistical techniques) a new extensional object, and offers this to the searcher for evaluation, and so on. The probabilistic model may be seen as a one-sided dualistic system.

In Hearst and Pederson (1996) a user interface for information retrieval based on the scatter-gather technique has been introduced. The system makes a limited classification of the collection, and presents this classification to the searcher. The searcher then selects the appropriate classes, after which the procedure is repeated on subcollection consisting of the selected classes. In this procedure, the extensional objects subsets of the document collection, and the intensional objects consist of the summarizations of those classes.

In this chapter, we focus on dualistic systems. In the 'Dual Systems', we show how different views on the real world can be combined to recognize concepts as semantic fixed points. We provide a formal definition and discuss some properties. In 'The Vector Model', we focus on the interpretation of concepts in the context of the vector model, and find a relation with the latent semantic indexing approach (Deerwester, Dumais, Landauer, Furnas, & Harshma, 1990). This approach is based on the singular value decomposition, usually applied when noise removal is an issue. In 'The Set Model', we study concepts in the set model, and find the relation with formal concept analysis (see Ganter & Wille, 1996). This approach is very fine-grained, and can be used to find a needle in the haystack. In 'The Fuzzy-Set Model', the fuzzy-set model and fuzzy logic and the basis the formal concept approach are generalized, to cover some degree of uncertainty. This degree is a parameter steering the trade-off

Figure 2. Initial query

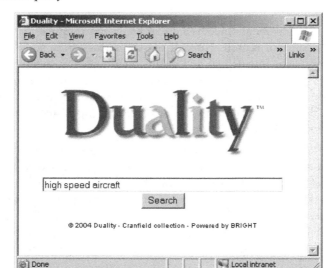

between granularity and (computational) complexity. In 'The Dual Search Engine', we apply this general theory by introducing the dual search engine DUALITY, and show the validity of the approach taken in this chapter. Finally, in the final section, we present some conclusions.

Dualistic Systems

A system that can transform different views on some area of interest is called a *dualistic system*. For convenience, we will refer to these two views as the intensional and the extensional view. In this section, we show that under weak assumptions this connection can be used to introduce a formal notion of concepts. These concepts are the basis for an ontology.

Consider a dualistic system as described in the previous section. Let $\mathbf{I}$ be its set of intensional objects and $\mathbf{E}$ its set of extensional objects. We assume an equivalence relation $\equiv_i$ for comparing intensional objects expressing their similarity, and its counterpart $\equiv_e$ on extensional objects (we will leave out the indices when no confusion is likely to occur). The motivation to introduce similarity relations is to be able to handle for example equivalences that originate from syntactic variety in queries.

The Model

As intensional and extensional objects provide a different perspective on some area of interest, they will be semantically related. This is modeled by assuming that intensional and extensional objects have assigned a meaning in terms of each other. The function *match*: $\mathbf{I} \rightarrow \mathbf{E}$ interprets intensional objects in terms of extensional objects, the function *index*: $\mathbf{E} \rightarrow \mathbf{I}$ does it the opposite way (see Figure 3). The assignment of meaning should be closed under similarity:

DS 1. *Similar queries yield a similar query result:*

$$q_1 \equiv_i q_2 \Rightarrow match(q_1) \equiv_e match(q_2)$$

DS 2. *Similar collections have a similar description:*

$$d_1 \equiv_e d_2 \Rightarrow index(d_1) \equiv_i index(d_2)$$

Figure 3. A dualistic system

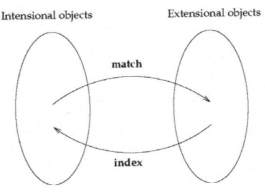

These rules express the intuition that (1) the matching of internal meaning is not dependent on its surface-structure representation and (2) indexing of external meaning handles representation variety consistently. These requirements are referred to as the *similarity closure assumptions*. The resulting dualistic system is denoted as

$$<<I, \equiv_i>, <E, \equiv_e>, match, index>$$

We do not make any special assumptions on the relation between the functions *match* and *index* governing their interaction.

> **Remark:** *The basis <O, A, ~> for formal concept analysis is a formal context, consisting of a set O of objects, a set A of attributes, and a relation ~ over A × O. If for example, we interpret extensonal objects as subsets of a document collection D, and the functions match and index are antigonous in the sense that for all documents d and intensional objects q we have: d ∈ match (q) ⇔ ∃_e [d ∈ e ∧ index (e) = q]. The context relation then is defined as d ~ q ≡ d ∈ match (q). Then <D, I, ~> is a formal context. Note that our approach does not require structure of the intensional and extensional objects and does not require a connection between the functions match and index.*

Proto-Concepts

In general, the meaning assigning functions *match* and *index* are not presumed to be inverse to each other. Consequently, mutual sharing of meaning is a special property. As a first step, we wonder what objects are invariant under *mirroring*, that is, the subsequent application of *index* and *match* in either order. We introduce proto-concepts as objects that have a similar mirror (reflection):

$$\mathbf{Qpc} = \{q| \ index(match(q)) \equiv_i q\} \qquad (query \ proto\text{-}concepts)$$
$$\mathbf{Dpc} = \{d| \ match(index(d)) \equiv_e d\} \qquad (search \ result \ proto\text{-}concepts)$$

If intensional object q has a similar mirror, then this meaning *match* (q), assigned by the dualistic system, will also be a proto-concept. For example, if an intensional object q has a similar reflection from the dualistic system, then the meaning represented by q is also available in the extensional view. In other words, the functions *match* and *index* can be restricted and seen as mappings between these sets **Qpc** and **Dpc** of proto-concepts:

Lemma 1:

1. $q \in \mathbf{Qpc} \implies match(q) \in \mathbf{Dpc}$
2. $d \in \mathbf{Dpc} \implies index(d) \in \mathbf{Qpc}$

Therefore, if a query is similar to its reflection, then the (extensional) meaning is also similar to its reflections. For search results, this is formulated analogously.

> **Proof:** *We will only show the first case. Let $q \in \boldsymbol{Qpc}$, then index(match(q))*
> $\equiv_i q$, *and according to the similarity closure assumption DS1, we conclude:*
> *match(index(match(q)))* $\equiv_e$ *match(q), and thus match(q)* $\in \boldsymbol{Dpc}$.

Furthermore, as a direct consequence of the similarity closure assumptions, these restricted functions respect similarity:

Lemma 2:

1. $q \in \mathbf{Qpc} \land q \equiv_i q' \implies q' \in \mathbf{Qpc}$
2. $d \in \mathbf{Dpc} \land d \equiv_e d' \implies d' \in \mathbf{Dpc}$

Proof: *We show the first case. Let q be similar to its reflection, and q' be an alternative for q, then from the similarity closure assumption DS2 we conclude index(match(q))* $\equiv_i$ *index(match(q')). Using the transitivity of similarity we conclude index(match(q'))* $\equiv_i$ *index(match(q))* $\equiv_i$ *q* $\equiv_i$ *q', and thus q'* $\in$ ***Qpc***.

Proto-concepts thus are stable under the variation covered by similarity relations.

Abstracting from Variation

The similarity relations on intensional and extensional objects may be seen as a mechanism dealing with the variation that is offered by the underlying description mechanism. In this subsection, we abstract from these variations.

It is easily verified that the restriction of the relation $\equiv_i$ to **Qpc** still is an equivalence relation. Let **Qc** = **Qpc**\$\equiv_i$ be the corresponding set of equivalence classes. The equivalence class containing q is denoted as $[q]_i$. The class of $[q]_i$ may be seen as the deep structure of q. The same holds for the restriction of $\equiv_e$ to **Dpc**. The set **Dc** is introduced analogously, $[d]_e$ will denote equivalence class of $d \in$ **Dpc**.

The functions m: **Qc** $\rightarrow$ **Dc** and i: **Dc** $\rightarrow$ **Qc** are the generalizations of the restricted versions of *match* and *index* over equivalence classes. Let $qc \in$ **Dc** be some equivalence class from **Qpc**\$\equiv_i$ then m (qc) is obtained by taking any q from class qc, and taking the equivalence class containing *match* (q). Because of lemma 1, we have *match* $(q) \in$ **Dpc**. Because of lemma 2, the resulting class does not depend on the actual q taken from qc. The function i is introduced analogously:

$$m(qc) = [match(q)]_e \quad \text{for } q \in qc$$
$$i(dc) = [index(d)]_i \quad \text{for } d \in dc$$

This brings us to a main result of this chapter:

Theorem 1:

The functions m and i are inverse functions.

Proof: (1) *Assume qc* $\in$ ***Qc***, *and let q* $\in$ *qc. As q* $\in$ ***Qpc***, *we conclude index(match(q))* $\equiv_i$ *q, and thus qc = [index(match(q))]*$_i$. *Consequently, i(m(qc)) = qc.* (2) *Assume dc* $\in$ ***Dc***, *and let q* $\in$ *qc. As d* $\in$ ***Dpc***, *we* *conclude match(index(d))* $\equiv_e$ *d, and thus dc = [match(index(d))]$_e$. Consequently, m(i(dc)) = dc.*

Concepts

As we are looking in a dualistic system for sharing of meaning, we concentrate on combinations of intensional and extensional objects. Symmetry in mutual meaning assignment for such combinations is a central issue in text and data-mining environments. Such combinations are referred to as concepts.

> **Definition 1:** *A pair (qc,dc) is called a concept if: m(qc) = dc ∧ i(dc) = qc.*

Let **C** be the set of concepts, then the following is a direct consequence of theorem 1:

Theorem 2:

$$\mathbf{C} = \{(qc,m(qc)) \mid qc \in \mathbf{Qc}\} = \{(i(dc),dc) \mid dc \in \mathbf{Qc}\}$$

Concepts consist of an intensional and an extensional part. Concepts may be ordered by the knowledge they reflect, as represented both by their intention and extension. We will not further elaborate on this ordering of concepts, as such an ordering will become meaningful only if some further properties are assumed on the interaction between the functions *index* and *match*. The resulting set of concepts forms the ontology that is implicit for the dualistic system.

Descriptor Approximation

An interesting operator is the approximation of intensional or extensional objects. Let *d* be some extensional object. Then *d* is described by intensional object *index(d)*. It is possible, however, that no intensional object can produce this meaning, or: $\forall_q$ *[match(q) ≠ d]*. The question then is what descriptors are good approximations of the contents of this query result. An intensional object that produces extensional object *d* is called a root of *d*. We call an intensional object *q* an approximation of extensional object *d* if it is root of an intensional object similar to *d*. In other words, the materialization *match(q)* of this descriptor has similar (intensional) meaning as *d* (see Figure 4).

> **Definition 2:** *The set $Approx_e(d)$ of approximations of extensional object d is defined by: $Approx_e(d) = \{q|\ index(match(q)) \equiv_i index(d)\}$*

Analogously, we can introduce the approximations of a descriptor *q* as those extensional objects *d* that have a mirror *match(index(d))* similar to materialization of *q* (see Figure 5):

> **Definition 3:** The set $Approx_i(q)$ of approximations of extensional object *d* is defined by: $Approx_i(q) = \{d|\ match(index(d)) \equiv_e match(q)\}$

Approximations are an important feature in a dualistic system. If a searcher would offer a query result as a typical specimen of the information need, then approximations of this query result can be used as a starting point during the process of Query by Navigation (see 'The Dual Search Engine'), supporting the searcher in finding a proper formulation of the information need.

> **Lemma 3:** *If query result d and query q are approximations of each other, then ([index(d)]$_i$,[match(q)]$_e$) is a concept.*

Figure 4. Projection of an extensional object

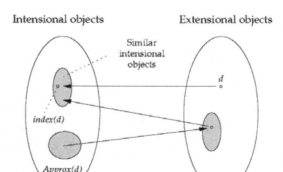

Proof: *Suppose query result d and query q are approximations of each other, or: index(match(q)) $\equiv_i$ index(d) and match(index(d)) $\equiv_e$ match(q). Then match(q) $\in$ **Dpc** and index(d) $\in$ **Qpc** are easily verified. The result then follows from theorem 2.*

In 'The Dual Search Engine', we will demonstrate how a search engine may employ the nature of dualistic systems. Besides the dual view, this system will benefit from descriptor approximation.

Note that our approach does not cover lower and upper approximations, as for example introduced in rough-set theory. The reason is that we do *not* assume an (partial) ordering relation on intensional and extentional objects.

Special Realizations

In this section, we will discuss in three different realizations of dualistic systems: the vector model, the set model, and the fuzzy model. These realizations provide different ways in which the dualistic system can derive its concepts according to the rules of the general model from this section. In the vector model, focus is on finding a minimal set of concepts spanning the conceptual space available in a document collection. With each concept a value is associated that describes the relevancy of that concept in the collection. This provides the opportunity to eliminate concepts that are a consequence of semantic noise. The set model results in a much more refined look, trying to give a complete view on the concepts in the collection, pro-

Figure 5. Projection of an intensional object

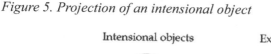
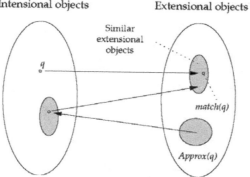

viding an ontology that describes the nature of concepts in terms of generality. This conceptual view will usually be much larger than the conceptual view obtained by the vector model. However, in cases like looking for a needle in the haystack, the searcher actually may be looking for rare information that would be interpreted as noise in the vector model approach. The fuzzy model provides the opportunity to balance between granularity and cost of computation.

The Vector Model

Assume a set **D** of documents and a set **T** of terms, and an *aboutness* function A: **D * T** $\rightarrow$ [0,1]. This function A is usually represented as a matrix. The value $A_{d,t}$ describes the degree in which document d is about term t.

In the vector model, intensional objects are linear combinations of terms, referred to as document vectors. On the other hand, extensional objects are seen as a linear combination of documents. Consequently, both intensional and extensional objects are seen as vectors. The equivalence relations $\equiv_i$ and $\equiv_e$ are straightforward: Two vectors are considered equivalent if they are a (positive) linear combination of each other:

$$x \equiv y \Leftrightarrow \exists_{\lambda > 0} [x = \lambda y]$$

One might say that x and y cover the same topic, but only differ in degree of intensity, which is expressed by the scalar λ.

The functions *match* and its dual function *match* are defined as follows:

$$match(q) = Aq$$
$$index(d) = A^T d$$

These functions satisfy the similarity closure assumptions:

Lemma 4:

1. $q_1 \equiv_i q_2 \Rightarrow match(q_1) \equiv_e match(q_2)$
2. $d_1 \equiv_e d_2 \Rightarrow index(d_1) \equiv_i index(d_2)$

Proof: (1) *Suppose $q_1 \equiv_i q_2$, then $q_1 = \lambda q_2$ for some $\lambda > 0$. Consequently: match $(q_1) = Aq_1 = \lambda \, Aq_2 = \lambda \, match(q_2)$ and thus $match(q_1) \equiv_e match(q_2)$.* (2) *Analogously.*

A value λ such that $Aq = \lambda d$ and $A^T d = \lambda q$ for nonzero vectors q and d, is called a singular value of matrix A. The vectors d and q are called left-singular and right-singular eigenvectors for singular value λ, respectively. Invariance under subsequent application of *match* and *index* leads to the eigenvectors of $A^T A$ and AA^T respectively:

Lemma 5:

1.   **Qpc** $= \{q| \; \exists_{\lambda > 0} \; [A^T A q = \lambda q]\}$
2.   **Dpc** $= \{d| \; \exists_{\lambda > 0} \; [AA^T d = \lambda d]\}$

Finding the eigenvalues and eigenvectors of $A^T A$ for a given matrix A is called *singular value decomposition* (SVD), also referred to as *principal component analysis*. This approach, well known as latent semantic indexing in IR research (Berry, Dumais, & O'Brien 1995; Deerwester et al., 1990), is commonly used to sort out noise and relevant data. The idea behind this decomposition is that eigenvectors with relatively small eigenvalues can be eliminated (set to 0) without essentially disturbing the relevant data.

Figure 6. Projecting an extensional object onto term space

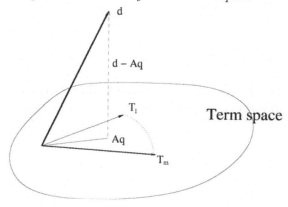

The singular value decomposition of a square matrix A results in the following decomposition:

$$A_n = U \begin{pmatrix} \Sigma_r & 0 \\ 0 & 0 \end{pmatrix} V^T$$

Where:

1. U is the matrix of left singular vectors, $UU^T = U^TU = I$.
2. Σ_r is a diagonal matrix containing of the roots of the eigenvalues, r is the rank of A^TA.
3. V is the matrix of right singular vectors, $VV^T = V^TV = I$.

The set *Approx(d)* of approximations of extensional object d is described by:

$$Approx(d) = \{q \mid A^TAq = A^Td\}$$

In terms of linear algebra, the vector q is the best solution of the equation $Aq \approx d$. Being the best solution means that (see Figure 6) $d - Aq$ is orthogonal on the image space of A (the term space), that is, $A^TA(d-Aq) = 0$. This optimal query q thus is the solution of the equation $A^TAq = A^Td$. Consequently, the set *Approx (d)* consists of the projection from d onto term space.

The Set Model

Assume a set **D** of documents and a set **T** of terms, and assume a relation $\sim \subseteq$ **T** * **D**. We write $t \sim d$ to denote that term t describes document d. For example, $t \sim d \Leftrightarrow A_{d,t} > 0$. The tuple <**T**, **D**, $\sim$> is called a *formal context* (Ganter & Wille, 1996). It will be convenient to overload the similarity relation as follows:

$$t \sim D \equiv \forall_{d \in D} \ [t \sim d]$$
$$Q \sim d \equiv \forall_{t \in Q} \ [t \sim d]$$
$$Q \sim D \equiv \forall_{t \in Q, d \in D} [t \sim d]$$

While the vector model uses vectors as a grouping mechanism, the set model uses *sets* for this purpose. In the set model, intensional objects thus are sets of terms, while extensional objects are sets of documents. Like before, intensional objects represent both queries and document meaning, while extensional objects represent the outcome of a search, or describe the meaning of a term. Similarity on intensional and extensional objects is introduced as set equivalence:

$$x \equiv y \Leftrightarrow x = y$$

The function *index* is introduced as the left-polar function:

$$index(D) = \{t \in \mathbf{T} \mid t \sim D\}$$

The function *match* corresponds to the right-polar function:

$$match(Q) = \{d \in \mathbf{D} \mid Q \sim d\}$$

Due to the simplicity of the similarity relation for both intensional and extensional objects, the similarity closure assumptions DS1 and DS2 are trivially satisfied. Notice that *index* and *match* form a *Galois connection*, a pair of reverse-order functions between two partially ordered sets.

Note the special similarity relation implies that the set **Qpc** and **Qc** are isomorphic, as is the case with **Dpc** and **Dc**.

Before further focusing on the nature of concepts in this case, we summarize some properties that will be needed (for proofs, see Grootjen & van der Weide, 2002). The polar functions introduce mutuality between documents and terms.

Lemma 6:

1. $index(D) \sim D$
2. $Q \sim match(Q)$

Both polar functions are nonincreasing functions as larger sets have more restrictions for sharing than smaller sets: the larger a set, the less the elements have in common.

Lemma 7:

1. $D_1 \subseteq D_2 \Rightarrow index(D_1) \supseteq index(D_2)$
2. $Q_1 \subseteq Q_2 \Rightarrow match(Q_1) \supseteq match(Q_2)$

Mutual sharing of meaning between documents and attributes is a special case. First, we provide a better characterization of this situation. In the next section, mutual sharing of meaning will be the basis for the introduction of concepts.

Lemma 8:

$$Q \sim D \Leftrightarrow D \subseteq match(Q) \Leftrightarrow Q \subseteq match(D)$$

The polar functions can be decomposed in terms of elementary set operations. The following property shows how these operations distribute over the polar functions.

Lemma 9:

1. $index(D_1 \cup D_2) = index(D_1) \cap index(D_2)$
2. $match(Q_1 \cup Q_2) = match(Q_1) \cap match(Q_2)$

Both document class and term class are extensions of their argument set:

Lemma 10:

1. $D \subseteq match(index(D))$
2. $Q \subseteq index(match(Q))$

After these properties, we return to the sets **Qpc** and **Dpc**. From each starting point, these sets are encountered after one step:

Lemma 11:

1. $match(q) \in \mathbf{Dpc}$
2. $index(d) \in \mathbf{Qpc}$

Proof: *We will only prove the first statement; the second is proven analogously.*

From lemma 10:2 we conclude $Q \subseteq index(match(Q))$, and thus by lemma 7 we get: $match(Q) \supseteq match(index(match(Q)))$.

On the other hand, using lemma 10:1, substituting D by $match(A)$, we get: $match(Q) \subseteq match(index(match\ (Q)))$.

As a consequence: $match(index(match(Q))) = match(Q)$.

The set *Approx(d)* of approximations of extensional object d has been introduced as:

Approx(d) = {q| index(match(q)) = index(d)}

Let *index(match(q)) = index(d)*, then also *match(index(match(Q))) = match(Q) = match(index(d))*. So *Approx(d)* is the set containing the intensional object that approximates to the concept determined by intensional object *index(d)*.

The Fuzzy-Set Model

In this section, we consider a fuzzy model for information retrieval based on the construction of a fuzzy formal context. The basis for interpreting information retrieval in terms of many-valued logics is the introduction of a fuzzy implication. In van Rijsbergen (1986), a nonclassical logic is proposed for information retrieval (see also, Crestani & van Rijsbergen, 1995). We will use $\rightarrow_f$ as a generic symbol for fuzzy implementation. Fuzzy implementation is seen as a function with signature $[0,1] * [0,1] \rightarrow [0,1]$. $a \rightarrow_f b$ indicates how certain we are over the validity of the implication given how certain we are over its arguments (a and b respectively). Fuzzy logic provides a logic of vagueness (Hájek, Godo, & Esteva, 1996). Fuzzy logics may be based on a conjunction operator $t(x, y)$ and an implication operator $i(x, y)$. They form an ad-joint couple if $z \leq i(x, y) \Leftrightarrow t(x, y) \leq y$. There are three main variants:

1. Łukasiewicz' logic
   $x \& y = max\ (0, x+y-1)$
   $x \rightarrow_L y = min\ (1, 1-x+y)$
2. Gödel's logic
   $x \wedge y = min\ (x, y)$
   $x \rightarrow_G y = (x \leq y \rightarrow 1; y)$

3.   product logic
$$x \odot y = xy$$
$$x \rightarrow_p y = (x \leq y \rightarrow 1; y/x)$$

In these logics, the constants *true* and *false* correspond to 1 and 0 respectively. As in the set model, we assume a set **D** of documents and a set **T** of terms. The aboutness relation is seen as a fuzzy relation, that is, for each document d and term t the $A_{d,t}$ describes the degree in which document d is supposed to be about term t. This fuzzy relation may be identified with the aboutness matrix from the vector model.

In our fuzzy model for information retrieval, an intensional object is a fuzzy set over terms **T**, while an extensional object is a fuzzy set of documents **D**. Intensional and extensional objects are similar when they are equal. The similarity closure assumptions thus obviously are satisfied.

Indexing a set of documents can be seen as finding for each term the degree in which this term is implied by the (fuzzy) collection being indexed. The result of indexing is an intensional object, or a fuzzy set of terms. This may be expressed as:

$$index(D) = \lambda_{t \in \mathbf{T}} \left[\wedge_d \left[D(d) \rightarrow_f A_{d,t} \right] \right]$$

During matching, it is determined to what degree documents are implied by the query. The result is an extensional object, or a fuzzy document set:

$$match(Q) = \lambda_{d \in \mathbf{D}} \left[\wedge_t \left[Q(t) \rightarrow_f A_{d,t} \right] \right]$$

Small certainty may originate from noise. A threshold ϑ is introduced for the recognition of noise. Scoring above this threshold means acceptance, otherwise the statement is believed to be invalid. In Elloumi, Jaam, Hasnah, Jaoua, & Nafkha (2004), this is effectuated by:

$$match_\vartheta(Q) = \lambda_{d \in \mathbf{D}} \left[\wedge_t \left[Q(t) \rightarrow_f A_{d,t} \geq \vartheta \right] \right]$$

where the outcome of the comparison operator is to be interpreted using the identities: *true* = 1 and *false* = 0. Consequently, the result $match_\vartheta(Q)$ is a set of documents.

Using Gödel's logic, the index operator is further elaborated as follows:

$$index(D) = \lambda_{t \in T} \, [\wedge_d \, [D(d) \to_G A_{d,t}] \,]$$
$$= \lambda_{t \in T} \, [min_d \, (D(d) \le A_{d,t} \to 1; A_{d,t})]$$
$$= (\text{in case } D \text{ is a crisp set}) \, \lambda_{t \in T} \, [min_{d \in D} \, A_{d,t}]$$

Therefore, it seems reasonable to restrict extensional objects to sets of documents. For the match operator we get:

$$match_\vartheta(Q) = \lambda_{d \in D} \, [\wedge_t \, [Q(t) \to_G A_{d,t} \ge \vartheta] \,]$$
$$= \lambda_{d \in D} \, [min_t \, (Q(t) \to_G A_{d,t} \ge \vartheta \to 1 \, ; \, 0)]$$
$$= \lambda_{d \in D} \, [min_t \, (A_{d,t} \ge min \, (Q(t), \vartheta) \to 1 \, ; \, 0)]$$

Thus $match_\vartheta(Q)$ corresponds to the (crisp) set $\{d| \, A_{d,t} < Q(t) \Rightarrow A_{d,t} < \vartheta\}$. Therefore, documents should satisfy sufficient information on each term, except if the term is noise in that document. Note that a drawback of this approach is that documents with noisy terms only, will be retrieved.

In Elloumi et al. (2004), a hybrid approach for matching is taken. The conjunction operator is defined as in Gödel's logic, while the implication is substantiated according to Łukasiewicz' logic. The matching operator then is elaborated as follows:

$$match_\vartheta(Q) = \lambda_{d \in D} \, [\wedge_t \, [Q(t) \to_L A_{d,t} \ge \vartheta] \,]$$
$$= \lambda_{d \in D} \, [min_t \, (min \, (1, 1 - Q(t) + A_{d,t}) \ge \vartheta)]$$

Thus, in this case, $match_\vartheta(Q)$ corresponds to the (crisp) set

$$\{d \, | \, \forall_t [A_{d,t} < \vartheta \Rightarrow (Q(t) - A_{d,t}) \le 1 - \vartheta]\}$$

So if a document would fail the requested supply of some term, then the term shortage for this document should be limited by $1 - \vartheta$.

First we note the special case $\vartheta = 1$. In that case, the limit for term shortage is so strict that uniform term supply is requested:

$$match_1(Q) = \{d \, | \, \forall_t [A_{d,t} \ge Q(t)]\}$$

Lemma 12: *For $\vartheta = 1$ the fuzzy-set model is equivalent to the set model.*

Proof: *For the formal concept we have:* $t \sim d \Leftrightarrow A_{d,t} > 0$. *If we assume* $A_{d,t} \in \{0, 1\}$, *then* $A_{d,t} \geq Q(t)$ *is equivalent with* $A_{d,t} = 1$, *and therefore with* $t \sim d$.

For the case $\vartheta = 1$ all documents will pass the membership test to match the query. The resulting concept lattice thus will contain only 1 concept. The noise threshold may be used to take a position in between. For example, if small variation is not likely to be a consequence of noise, then ϑ could be chosen near 1. If a limited number of concepts is required, then a smaller value should be taken for the noise threshold. In Figure 7, we see how for an example document collection the number of concepts depends on the noise threshold. Note that the figure suggests an almost linear dependency on a logarithmic scale.

The set *Approx(D)* of approximations of extensional object *D* has been introduced as:

$$Approx(D) = \{Q| \; index(match \; (Q)) = index(D)\}$$

Let *Q* be some query, then the associated query result reflects the degree in which the documents support the query. This query result is indexed as:

$$index(match(Q)) = \lambda_t \, [\wedge_d \, [\wedge_t \, [Q(t) \rightarrow_f A_{d,t}] \rightarrow_f A_{d,t}] \,]$$

Figure 7. Granularity of concepts

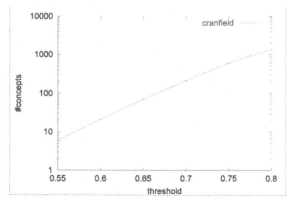

The condition *index(match(Q)) = index(D)* thus is formulated as:

$$\wedge_d [\wedge_t [Q(t) \rightarrow_f A_{d,t}] \rightarrow_f A_{d,t}] = \wedge_d [D(d) \rightarrow_f A_{d,t}]$$

This expression may be further simplified using the rules of the underlying logic.

The Dual Search Engine

In this section, we show how dualistic systems can be used in practice. As an example of the theory, we describe the so-called *dual search engine*. A simple prototype, called **Duality**, is discussed to show its behavior and to provide a flavor of its look and feel.

The general architecture of the dual search engine is presented in Figure 8. The search engine internally uses the standard vector model for document representation. The documents are characterized by keywords. A more challenging test would be to use more elaborated characterizations like index expressions (Grootjen, 2004), which have been shown to perform better as a vehicle for query by navigation than keywords do.

From the document representations, **Duality** constructs the ontologies for the vector-model approach, the set-model approach and the fuzzy-model approach.

A typical state of the dual search engine during interaction with a searcher is an overview that displays both the intensional and extensional object that manifest the searchers' current focus. The relation between these two objects is the consequence of the previous step of the searcher.

From the current state, the engine is ready to process the following kinds of requests made by the searcher:

1.   Shift focus
2.   Refine focus
3.   Shift conceptual view

The searcher may shift focus by either entering a new intensional or a new extensional object as base for further exploration.

Figure 8. Dual search engine architecture

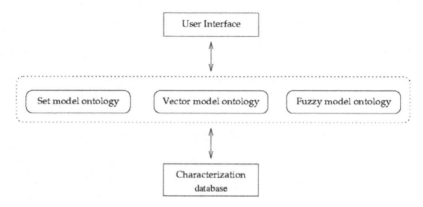

Q1.   After entering a query *q*, the engine evaluates the search result *match(q)*. This
will produce the conventional list of documents, ordered by relevancy.

Q2.   After entering a weighted set *d* of documents, the engine will produce a common description by evaluating *index(d)*. This will produce a list of terms,
ordered by their weight.

Furthermore, the dual search engine makes it possible to refine the current focus by
further elaboration on the results obtained. This feedback process is displayed in
Figure 10. Note that this process has a clear resemblance with the stratified archi-

Figure 9. Interaction state of dual search engine

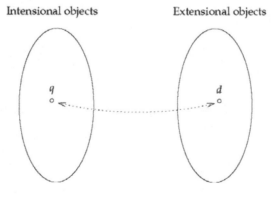

tecture (Bruza & van der Weide, 1992), as this architecture also has a separation in a hyperindex and a hyperbase. The contrast to the stratified architecture is that the primary focus of the stratified architecture is the support of Query by Navigation. The focus of the dual search engine is on exploiting the ability to switch between hyperbase and hyperindex.

R1.   The result r of a *match*-operation may be used to create a new query q ***Op*** *index(r)*. This new query then is evaluated by the dual search engine, producing *match(q **Op** index(r))*.

R2.   The result r of an *index*-operation may be used to create a new weighted set of documents d ***Op*** *match(r)*. This new set is evaluated by the dual search engine, producing *index(d **Op** match(r))*.

During a search quest, it may be profitable to change a conceptual view. For example, from a view directed towards the main semantic components (the vector-model approach) to a more complete view (the set-model approach). This is especially useful in combination with the approximation functions. The reason for approximation is that there will be no 1-1 correspondence between the concepts from the different conceptual views. In case we want to switch from underlying dualistic model, the following steps are useful:

P1.   A query q is approximated by a set *Approx(q)* of extensional objects.

P2.   An extensional object d is approximated by a set *Approx(d)* of queries.

Using these kind of requests, the searcher can employ the dual search engine in several ways.

- **Query by example:** A searcher may offer the dual search engine a document d that is very much alike the kind of documents wanted. The dual search engine determines these documents by evaluating match *(index({d}))*.

  The searcher may also use this for relevance feedback, by selecting a relevant subset from the initial query result.

- **Document contents:** Offering a document (or a set of documents) to the dual search engine may also be done in order to get an impression of its contents.

Figure 10. Feedback loop during searching

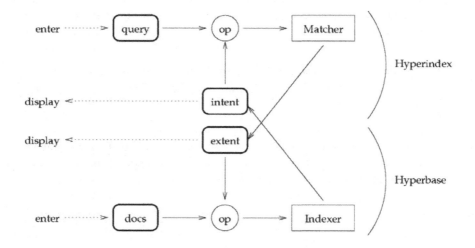

- **Coverage:** After entering a query q, the dual search engine evaluates *match({q})*. After inspecting some document d, the searcher might conclude a partial satisfaction of the information need (van Bommel & van der Weide, 2005). This can be done by requesting the dual search engine to extract the characterization *index ({d})* from the original query q, leading to a new query for evaluation.

In "A Sample Session," we describe the elementary searching process, showing the operations of shifting and refining focus. In "Crossing the Boundary," changing conceptual view is further discussed.

A Sample Session

We now demonstrate how a searcher may perform a search using the dual search engine **DUALITY**. The results are calculated by the **BRIGHT** system (Grootjen & van der Weide, 2004a), a generic tool for experimental information-retrieval research. The underlying collection is the Cranfield Collection (Cleverdon, 1967).

Query by Example

Suppose a searcher wants to know about problems associated with high-speed aircraft. As an initial attempt, the query "high-speed aircraft" is entered into the search engine (Figure 2), which produces a classical ranked list of documents (see Figure 11). Notice that the output of the search engine has two different panels, one called the *Intensional View* containing the (weighted) entered query keywords, and one called the *Extensional View* which shows the set of ranked documents.

After inspecting the document titles and excerpts of the top 10 ranked documents, the searcher assesses the fourth document (d12) to be relevant, and selects the document's checkbox.

Since the selected document covers the desired topic area, the user decides to use 'Query by Example'. This is done in two steps: First, the corresponding Intensional object is created by pressing the index button (the button marked with the symbol >). This will update the Intensional View panel and shows a new list of weighted terms. The second step is to update the Extensional View panel using these new terms. This is done by pressing the match button (the button marked with the symbol <). The result, depicted in Figure 13, shows the new list of documents. Since this query is part of the Cranfield Collection, and therefore accompanied by relevance judgments, we can calculate the performance of the retrieval result. Not surprisingly, the performance improved drastically (see Figure 12). Note that, in contrast to the example, more than one document can be selected when performing Query by Example.

Coverage

In the previous example, a document selection is used to create a new set of terminals, which is directly used as input to a subsequent match call; the original query terminals are *replaced* by the new ones. DUALITY offers the possibility to do more than that: In some cases, we do not want the old terminal set to be replaced (**Op** =). So, two simple operators are implemented allowing the user to add (**Op** +) or subtract (**Op** -) the index or match result to the current set. Another possibility is to modify the resulting terminal list before invoking the index function: The searcher might add or penalize terminals.

These operators can be used to disambiguate the original query: For example, a query about operating systems returns pages about Linux that we want to ignore. Or, when our information need is already partly covered, and we are looking for additional (new, residual) information.

Figure 11. Ranked list

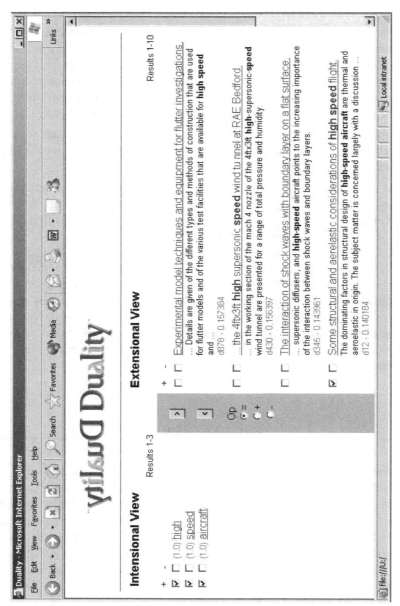

Figure 12. Retrieval performance

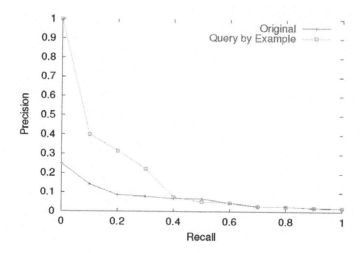

Note that after selecting a relevant document, and invoking index with Op + followed by a match is equivalent to applying the standard Rocchio technique for relevance feedback (e.g., Baeza-Yates & Ribeiro-Neto, 1999).

Crossing the Boundary

We will conclude this example section by showing the benefits of combining two dualistic ontologies: We will show how the vector-space model and the fuzzy model can be combined to yield one powerful search tool.

Suppose a searcher has an information need described as query 173 of the Cranfield collection:

> *References on Lyapunov's method on the stability of linear differential equations with periodic coefficients.*

From the relevance judgment, we know that there are only three relevant documents in the collection. Assume that during (vector space based) browsing the searcher finds the relevant document d532. Instead of using Query by Example

Figure 13. Query by example

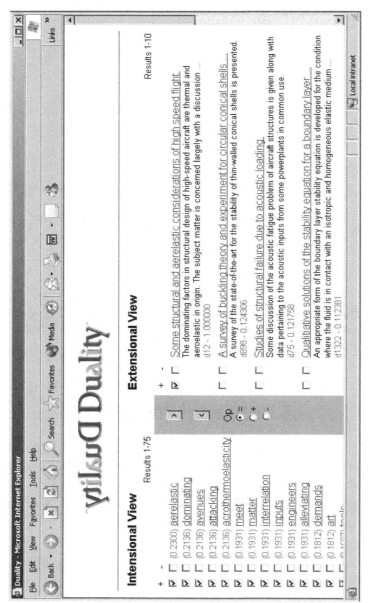

or Relevance feedback, the searcher decides to switch to the fuzzy-concept model (In our example, the fuzzy-concept lattice is generated with threshold 0.775 and contains 993 concepts}.

Using the approximation function **Duality** presents the fuzzy concept containing d532 with its fuzzy-terminal set. One of the extra features of the conceptual model is that the concepts are *ordered*. This enables the user to navigate to related concepts (Query by Navigation). As shown in Figure 14, the searcher can beam down to the bottom concept of the lattice or beam up to three different superconcepts. After inspecting the terminals presented by the concepts, the searcher decides to beam up to the concept containing both d532 and d367 (which happen to be both relevant). The process of beaming up increases the extension and reduces the intention. This is clear when we look at the result (Figure 15): The list of terminals is shorter since it covers two documents. In this new fuzzy concept, the searcher can beam up to the top concept of the lattice, beam down back to the concept containing only d532, or beam down to the concept of document d367. If the searcher switches back to the vector-space model, doing a Query by Example of the two found documents, he will get a ranked document list as extension, with the three relevant documents ranked 1, 2, and 3.

Conclusion

In this chapter, we have introduced the concept of dualistic ontologies, discussed properties of such ontologies, and related them to some well-known retrieval models. In order to demonstrate their usefulness, dual search engines have been introduced and illustrated by a sample session of its prototype **Duality**.

Further research may be directed towards further elaboration of the theoretical framework, and towards large-scale experiments. The prototype **Duality** is based on the **Bright** system (Grootjen & van der Weide, 2004a), which has successfully been applied in a large scale TREC experiment. The construction of a concept lattice can become a limiting factor, especially for the set model, as the number of concepts could possibly grow exponentially (in practice smaller upper bounds seem valid). The fuzzy model seems to be a good candidate to scale between completeness and feasibility in that case.

By using a reference set of documents, the dualistic approach can be used to compare different retrieval models based on their indexing and matching algorithm. We feel that this also may be useful in the context of ontology negotiation (e.g., Bailin & Truszkowski, 2001), where the need for explicit ontologies is crucial for the ontology-negotiation process (ONP).

Figure 14. Switching to fuzzy-concept model

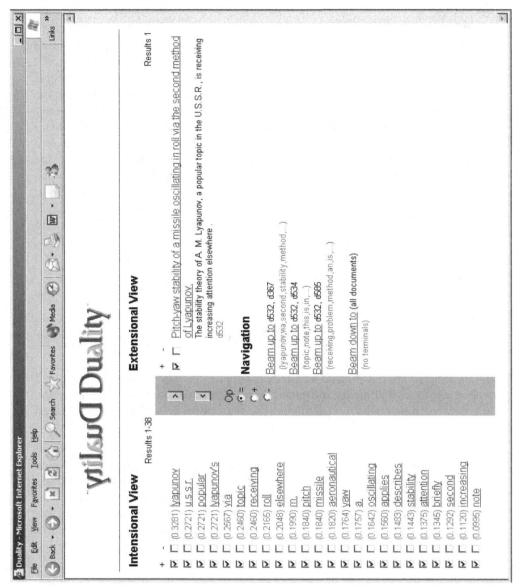

Figure 15. Beaming up

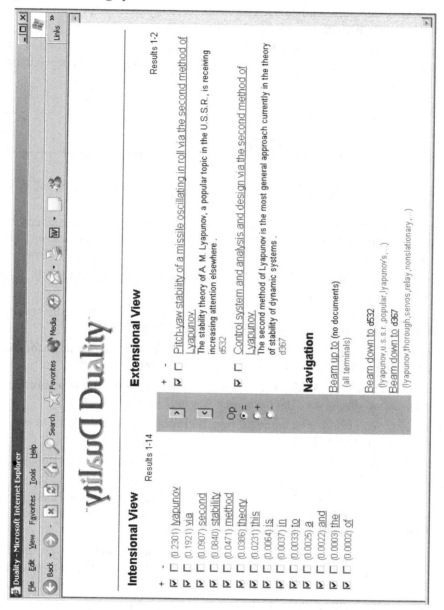

Another application could be in the context of user profiling and collaborative approaches. For example, a dualistic view on customers and purchased products would lead to a conceptual view on customers' taste.

Further investigations might consider the question of how the combination of several dualistic ontologies may offer further opportunities for searchers to improve their retrieval effectiveness.

References

Baeza-Yates, R., & Ribeiro-Neto, B. (1999). *Modern information retrieval*. Addison-Wesley.

Bailin, S., & Truszkowski, W. (2001, July). Ontology negotiation between scientific archives. In *Proceedings of the Thirteenth International Conference on Scientific and Statistical Database Management (SSDBM 2001)*. IEEE Press.

Berners-Lee, T., Hendler, L., & Lassila, O. (2001, May). The Semantic Web. *Scientific American, 284*(5), 35-43.

Berry, M. W., Dumais, S. T., & O'Brien, G. W. (1995). Using linear algebra for intelligent information retrieval. *SIAM Review, 37*(4) 573-595.

van Bommel, P., & van der Weide, T. P. (2005). Measuring the incremental information value of documents. *Information Sciences, 176*(2), 91-119.

Bruza, P. D., & van der Weide, T. P. (1992). Stratified hypermedia structures for information disclosure. *The Computer Journal, 35*(3), 208-220.

Cleverdon, C. W. (1967). The cranfield tests on index language devices. In *Aslib Proceedings* (pp. 173-194).

Crestani, F., & van Rijsbergen, C. J. (1995). Information retrieval by logical imaging. *Journal of Documentation, 51*, 3-17.

Deerwester, S. C., Dumais, S. T., Landauer, T. K., Furnas, G. W., & Harshman, R. A. (1990). Indexing by latent semantic analysis. *Journal of the American Society of Information Science, 41*(6), 391-407.

Elloumi, S., Jaam, J., Hasnah, A., Jaoua, A., & Nafkha, I. (2004, June). A multilevel conceptual data reduction approach based in the lukasiewicz implication. *Information Sciences, 163*(4), 253-262.

Farquhar, A., Fikes, R., & Rice, J. (1996). *The ontolingua server: A tool for collaborative ontology construction* (Tech. Rep. No. KSL 96-26). Stanford, CA: Stanford University, Knowledge Systems Laboratory.

Führ, N. (1989). Models for retrieval with probabilistic indexing. *Information Processing and Management, 25*(1), 55-72.

Ganter, B., & Wille, R. (1996). *Formale Begriffsanalyse, Mathematische Grund-lagen*. Berlin, Germany: Springer-Verlag.

Grootjen, F. A., & van der Weide, T. P. (2002, October). Conceptual relevance feed-back. In *Proceedings of the 2002 IEEE International Conference on Systems, Man and Cybernetics (NLPKE 2002)*, Tunis.

Grootjen, F. A., & van der Weide, T. P. (2004a). *The Bright side of information retrieval* (Tech. Rep. No. NIII). Radboud University of Nijmegen.

Grootjen, F. A., & van der Weide, T. P. (2004b, June). Effectiveness of index ex-pressions. In *Proceedings of the 9th International Conference on Applications of Natural Language to Information Systems (NLDB 2004)* (pp. 165-175). Manchester, UK: Springer.

Gruber, T. R. (1992). *Ontolingua: {A} mechanism to support portable ontologies* (Tech. Rep. No. KSL 91-66). Stanford, CA: Stanford University, Knowledge Systems Laboratory.

Hájek, P., Godo, L., & Esteva, F. (1996). A complete many-valued logic with prod-uct-conjunction. *Archive for mathematical logic, 35*, 191-208.

Hearst, M. A., & Pedersen, J. O. (1996). Reexamining the cluster hypothesis: Scatter/gather on retrieval results. In *Proceedings of SIGIR-96, 19th ACM International Conference on Research and Development in Information Retrieval* (pp. 76-84). Retrieved October 12, 2006, from http://doi.acm. org/10.1145/243199.243216

Noy, N. F., Sintek, M., Decker, S., Crubezy, M., Fergerson, R.W., & Musen, R.W. (2001). Creating Semantic Web contents with Protege-2000. *IEEE Intelligent Systems, 2*(16), 60-71.

van Rijsbergen, C. J. (1986). A non-classical logic for information retrieval. *The Computer Journal, 29*(6), 481-485.

Salton, G., & McGill, M. J. (1983). *Introduction to modern information retrieval.* New York: McGraw-Hill.

Sowa, J. F. (1984). *Conceptual structures: Information processing in mind and machine*. Reading, MA: Addison-Wesley.

Sowa, J. F. (2004). *Guided tour of ontology*. Retrieved from http://www.jfsowa. com/ontology/

Spyns, P., & De Bo, J. (2004). *Ontologies: A revamped cross-disciplinary buzzword or a truly promising interdisciplinary research topic?* (Tech. Rep. No. STAR-2004-20). Vrije Universiteit Brussel.

Taylor, R. S. (1968). Question-negotiation and information seeking in libraries. *College and Research Libraries, 1968*, 178-194.

Chapter X

ADAM:
An Autonomic Approach to Database Management

Sunitha Ramanujam, University of Western Ontario, Canada

Miriam Capretz, University of Western Ontario, Canada

Abstract

In recent years, the emergence of the Internet has resulted in a proliferation of data. This in turn has given rise to increasing demands of organizations to access accurate information swiftly and efficiently. Thus, the scope of functions for databases has expanded more than ever and the complexity of database systems has grown accordingly. Consequently, the burden on database administrators (DBAs) has increased significantly. The objective of this research is to address and propose a solution to overcome this problem of overburdened and expensive DBAs. This chapter focuses on relational database management systems in particular and proposes a novel and innovative multiagent system (MAS) that would autonomously and rationally administer and maintain databases. The proposed multi-agent system tool, ADAM (a MAS for $\underline{a}$utonomous $\underline{d}$atabase $\underline{a}$dministration and $\underline{m}$aintenance), is in the form of a self-administering wrapper around database systems and it addresses, and offers a solution to, the problem of overburdened and expensive DBAs with the objective *of making databases a cost-effective option for small/medium-sized organizations. An implementation of the agent-based system to proactively or reactively identify and resolve a small subset of DBA tasks is discussed and the GAIA methodology is used to outline the detailed analysis and design of the same. Role models describing the responsibilities, permissions, activities, and protocols of the candidate agents, and interaction models representing the links between the roles are explained. The coordinated intelligent rational agent model is used to describe the agent architecture and a brief description of the functionalities, responsibilities, and components of each agent type in the ADAM multiagent system is presented. Finally, a prototype system implementation using JADE 2.5 and Oracle 8.1.7 is presented as evidence of the feasibility of the proposed agent-based solution for the autonomous administration and maintenance of relational databases.*

Introduction

The increasing demands of today's world and the vast variety of both traditional and online services currently being offered, resulting in datasets that are increasing enormously in diversity and volume, have rendered databases an indispensable component of daily life and have increased the complexity of databases significantly. They are no longer viewed as frills affordable only by large, rich organizations, but are now considered a mandatory component of any business, however small, that hopes to succeed and satisfy its clientele. Today, databases play a critical role in almost all areas where computers are used (Elmasri & Navathe, 2000).

Databases are growing rapidly in scale and complexity. With technological developments resulting in rapidly decreaseing hardware and software costs, personnel costs have become the single most important factor contributing to the cost of ownership for database applications. To ensure the appropriate functioning of database systems, database owners are having to rely more and more on the skills of experienced **database administrators** who are, in turn, becoming rarer and more expensive (Lightstone, Kwan, Storm, & Wu, 2002; Lightstone, Lohman, & Zilio, 2002). This has given rise to an increasing need for self-managing, self-administering, and self-maintaining databases.

The key focus of research in the field of databases currently is on making databases intelligent enough to maintain and tune themselves for optimum performance. The objectives of this research are to make databases and the various advantages they offer available to small/medium sized organizations without forcing the organizations to incur the huge costs associated with people required to manage the databases, and to help beleaguered **DBAs** of large (in size or in number) databases by easing some of the burden of **database administration** off their shoulders.

This chapter proposes one such system whose goal is to make databases self-managing. Agent technology is used as the motivation behind the proposed system design in an attempt to replace human **DBAs** with intelligent **software agents** for some of the more mundane **DBA** activities, thereby easing the workload on DBAs and reducing the cost of operation associated with **database management systems**. The **multiagent system** (MAS) for **autonomous database administration** proposed in this chapter builds on the features of proactiveness, autonomy, interaction, collaboration, and negotiation and comprises numerous **intelligent agents** that would automatically schedule and run maintenance and administrative tasks on databases. The agents should proactively monitor the database and autonomously resolve issues, such as abnormal growth of objects or tablespaces, which could result in errors if left unattended. They should interact and collaborate with other agents in the system for services such as backup or recovery of objects or the database, and they should negotiate the terms and conditions of the services depending on time availability and cost requirements. Thus, the ADAM MAS aims at ensuring that the health of the database is monitored and managed efficiently and autonomously.

The organization of this chapter is as follows. A preliminary specification (a subset of the tasks that are part of a DBA's workload) of the autonomous database administration and maintenance (ADAM) **multiagent system** to aid with relational database administration is presented in the subsequent section. This is followed by a description of the methodology and procedures adopted to analyze and design the proposed **multiagent system** and an illustration of the implementation specifics of ADAM with detailed descriptions of the responsibilities and capabilities of each agent type along with their respective activity diagrams. Some of the sample results obtained from the initial prototype of ADAM are presented, and a case for the validation, in a chiefly academic environment, of these sample results is expounded in the subsequent sections. The chapter ends with a discussion of related work and concluding remarks.

The ADAM MAS Specification

One of the many problems that relational **DBAs** are constantly faced with is the object fragmentation issue that arises primarily because of improper object sizing or incorrect growth estimations. In **relational databases**, due to the automatic allocation of incremental space extents, there is potential for an object to grow into a large number of extents if it is not sized appropriately and this, in turn, can cause performance and space problems (Oracle Corporation, 1999a; Oracle Corporation, 1999b). The scope of the proposed agent-based solution to **database administration** is restricted to proactive identification of such fragmentation problems and autonomous resolution of the same through any necessary interactions. The functions provided by this system are as follows:

- autonomously monitoring the database and broadcasting/transmitting any error messages associated with object fragmentation/space issues,
- identifying fragmented objects either through regular monitoring of object statistics or through errors/messages broadcasted/transmitted by the database monitor,
- analyzing object statistics such as current size, growth rate, number of extents currently occupied, and so on and using knowledge gained from past analyses, to decide if the object is a candidate worthy of the defragmentation exercise,
- if defragmentation is required, coordinating and scheduling backups of the concerned object(s),
- upon successful completion of backup, performing the defragmentation exercise and updating information in the module catalog regarding the current health of the database,
- providing status reports to the management through e-mail messages.

The agents comprising the ADAM **MAS** would reside in the agent management reference model framework proposed by FIPA (FIPA, 2004) as shown in Figure 1. FIPA, or the Foundation for Intelligent Physical Agents, is an international, nonprofit organization whose primary objective is to promote the industry of intelligent agents by developing specifications of generic-agent technologies that support a high level of interoperability among heterogeneous agents and agent-based applications. The proposed system, ADAM, adheres to the standards specified by FIPA wherever applicable.

Figure 1. ADAM within the FIPA agent reference model

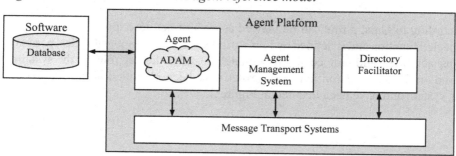

The analysis and design methodology, Gaia, adopted to design the system with the above-mentioned functionalities at the agent level of abstraction is described in the following section.

Analysis and Design of the MAS

Gaia is a methodology for agent-oriented analysis and design proposed by Michael Wooldridge, Nicholas Jennings, and David Kinny (Wooldridge, Jennings, & Kinny, 2000). The motivation behind Gaia is the current lack of support amongst existing methodologies for agents in terms of modeling flexible, autonomous, problem-solving behavior, richness of interactions, and complexity of organizational structure (Tveit, 2001). Gaia comprises of two phases, the analysis phase and the design phase, and enables software engineers to systematically develop a directly realizable design from the requirement statement.

The purpose of the analysis phase is to understand the system and its structure, and to identify the roles of the organization and the interactions between them. The outputs of the analysis phase are the *Role Model*, which identifies and lists the primary roles in the system, and the *Interaction Model*, which depicts dependencies, relationships, and interaction between roles captured in the form of a set of protocol definitions for inter-role interaction.

System Analysis

The objective of this phase is to dissect the system into its component pieces for the purposes of studying how those component pieces interact and work (Ramanujam & Capretz, 2004).

Role Model for the Proposed System Using Gaia

According to Gaia, a role can be viewed as an abstract description of an entity's expected function and is defined by four attributes, namely, responsibilities, permissions, activities, and protocols. A role model identifies the key roles in the system. Based on the above definitions, three roles have been identified in the context of this system and have been detailed in Figure 2.

Figure 2. Role model for ADAM [1]

Role Schema: DBMonitor	Role Schema: Tablespace/ObjectMonitor
Description: The DBMonitor role is responsible for monitoring the health of the database and for keeping track of, and delivering, any error messages generated by the database to the appropriate roles capable of handling those errors.	**Description:** This role is responsible for maintaining and managing the space usage within tablespaces, for monitoring object growth statistics, and for performing maintenance of objects in the event of abnormal growth or space constraints.
Protocols and Activities: MonitorDB, Broadcast, Transmit, UpdateCatalog	**Protocols and Activities:** AcceptDBMessage, MonitorObjects, ScheduleBackup, ReorgObject, UpdateCatalog
Permissions: Read *Database Log Files* Change *Catalog Database* with new/updated error information	**Permissions:** Read *Object Statistics in Database* Change *Catalog Database* with updated object statistics
Responsibilities: DBMonitor=(MonitorDB.Broadcast|Transmit)^w.UpdateCatalog+	**Responsibilities:** ObjectMonitor=(MonitorObjects.ReorgProcess)^w|(AcceptD BMessage.ReorgProcess)*.UpdateCatalog^w ReorgProcess=(RequestBackup.ReorgObject.RequestBack up)

Role Schema: BackupRec
Description: This role is responsible for scheduling and performing backup at the complete database level as well as the individual objects level. It is also responsible for recovery of the database or objects in the event of a hardware/software failure.
Protocols and Activities: AcceptDBMessage, DBBackup, ObjectBackup, OfflineStorage, DBRecovery, ObjectRecovery, AcceptBackupSchedule, AcceptBackupRequest
Permissions: Read *Backup Schedule* Change *Catalog Database* with updated backup/recovery information
Responsibilities: BackupRec=((AcceptBackupRequest.DBBackup|ObjectBackup.OfflineStorage)|(AcceptDBMessage.DBRecovery|ObjectRecovery).Up dateCatalog)^w|(RejectBackupRequest)*

Interaction Model for the Proposed System

Interaction models are used to represent links between roles and consist of a set of protocol definitions. The purpose and processing performed by the protocol definitions used in ADAM are detailed as follows.

Broadcast/Transmit

Purpose	This protocol allows DB messages to be published to all other roles in the system
Processing	The DB Log files are scanned and any errors generated by the database are captured and sent to all other roles or the appropriate role (if known) for resolution.

AcceptDatabaseMessage (AcceptDBMessage)

Purpose	This protocol enables ObjectMonitor or BackupRec role to receive error messages broadcasted/transmitted by the DBMonitor.
Processing	ObjectMonitor/BackupRec claims ownership of the error message and sends an acknowledgement back to DBMonitor confirming receipt of the error.

RequestBackupService

Purpose	This allows the ObjectMonitor to request backup services from the BackupRec role during a defragmentation exercise.
Processing	The ObjectMonitor raises a backup request in response to concerned error messages raised by DBMonitor or in response to abnormal growth patterns or lack of space issues identified during routine monitoring by ObjectMonitor. This request is sent to the BackupRec role which may either accept or reject this request based on its current backup schedule.

AcceptBackupSchedule

Purpose	This protocol permits users to create a backup schedule for the database under question.
Processing	The user specifies the different types of backups he or she requires for the database and the frequency of the backups. This is stored as the backup schedules for the database by the BackupRec role.

Accept/RejectBackupRequest

Purpose	This protocol allows the BackupRec role to accept or reject backup requests received from other roles.
Processing	The BackupRec role checks its schedule and accepts or rejects the request based on its availability and workload.

The attributes of each of the protocols detailed above are listed in Table 1.

Table 1. Attributes of the protocol definitions

Protocol	Initiator	Responder	Input	Output
Broadcast/Transmit	DBMonitor	For Broadcast: All Roles For Transmit: Specific role as obtained from the knowledge component	Error messages from DB Log File	Error Message
AcceptDatabaseMessage (AcceptDBMessage)	ObjectMonitor / BackupRec	DBMonitor	Error Message	Error Receipt Acknowledgement
RequestBackupService	ObjectMonitor	BackupRec	Object to be backup up	Accept/Reject Backup Request
AcceptBackupSchedule	User	BackupRec	Backup types and timings	Backup schedule
Accept/ RejectBackupRequest	BackupRec	ObjectMonitor	Backup request	Accept or Reject request

System Design

System design is defined as the evaluation of alternative solutions and specification of a detailed computer-based solution. During this phase, the basic architecture of how the system will work and what/how each element will satisfy the users' needs will be laid down. Once again, some of the modeling techniques for the design phase have been borrowed from Gaia, specifically, the *services model*.

Agent Architecture

The agent architecture used for the design of the proposed system is the coordinated intelligent rational (CIR) model (Ghenniwa & Areibi, 2002). Agents in this model consist of four components, namely, *Knowledge*, *Problem Solver*, *Interaction*, and *Communication*. Of particular interest in this design are the *Knowledge* and *Interaction* components of the CIR-agent model. The components and roles identified during the analysis phase of this document need to have the ability to learn from experiences, update their knowledge base, and use this knowledge to make better decisions during subsequent processing. The roles would also have to interact and, in distributed environments running multiple agents providing similar functionality, possibly negotiate with each other to achieve their goals in the most optimal manner.

System Architecture

Figure 3 illustrates the components comprising the initial prototype of ADAM, arrived at based on the system analysis and role models developed in the earlier sections. With the use of ADAM, the human **DBA's** activities are greatly reduced and are limited to the definition of a small set of business rules and policies during the initial setup phase. The agents comprising the ADAM **MAS** provide monitoring and automation capabilities on the database and, based on the rules specified by the **DBA**, also take rational decisions, and independent action, on the error resolution techniques that need to be applied in order to rectify encountered problems or proactively avoid possible problem situations. Each of the components' responsibilities, capabilities, and interactions are highlighted and are discussed in further detail in the subsequent sections. In the initial implementation of the ADAM MAS, the functionalities of the two modules, the Tablespace Monitor and the Object Monitor, have been combined into the Object Monitor, the details of which are described in the following sections.

The architecture and conceptual model of the system in terms of CIR agent terminology (Ghenniwa & Areibi, 2002) is illustrated in the following diagrammatic

Figure 3. ADAM prototype system architecture

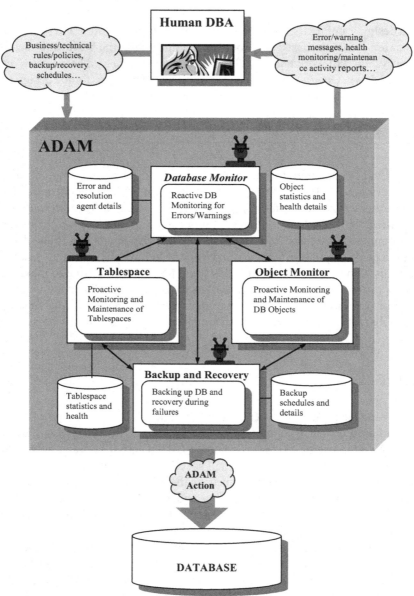

manner. The mapping between roles identified in the analysis phase and agent types is essentially one-to-one since the functionalities of each role are simple enough and do not justify mapping one role into multiple agent types or vice versa. Hence the system has three agent types: DBMonitor, ObjectMonitor, and BackupRec.

The conceptual model, based on the CIR agent architecture, of each of these agent types is presented in Figure 4 below (Ramanujam & Capretz, 2003).

A brief description of the functionalities and responsibilities of each of the above agent types follows:

- **DB Monitor:** This agent type will be responsible for monitoring the database and broadcasting or transmitting any error messages associated with object fragmentation/space issues or backup/recovery problems to the other agents.

- **Object Monitor:** The responsibility of this agent type includes identifying fragmented objects or tablespaces, co-ordinating backups, and defragmenting the objects or tablespaces if required. This agent type would also interact with DB Monitor, claim ownership of any error messages concerning object health that may be broadcasted/transmitted by DB Monitor, and work towards the resolution of such errors.

Figure 4. System architecture for ADAM

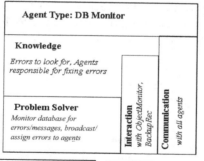

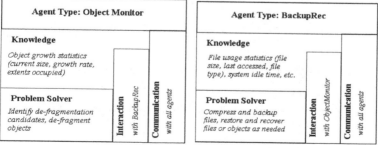

- **Backup Rec:** Within the scope of the ADAM MAS, the Backup and Recovery agent type would be in charge of scheduling and performing regular planned backups of the database or objects and backups of objects that are to be de-fragmented, compressing the backup files, and storing the backup files onto offline storage media. This agent type would also be responsible for restoring the database or objects from backups and recovering the database/objects in the event of a hardware or software loss.

Each of the above agent types can be considered as a micro-DBA, whose tasks are restricted to the local goals assigned to the agent that autonomously achieves these goals.

Services Model

The Gaia services model is used to identify the services associated with each agent type (role), and it specifies the main properties of these services. The services models for each of the roles identified in the analysis phase are as shown in Table 2.

Implementation Specifics

A pilot version of the above design has been implemented using the Java Agent Development Framework (JADE 2.5) (JADE, 2004), a FIPA (FIPA, 2004) compliant platform, with an Oracle 8.1.7 database as the target. The next few subsections dis-

Table 2. Services model for ADAM

DB Monitor Role

Service	Inputs	Outputs	Precondition	Postcondition
Monitor DB Log File	Database Log Files	Errors, if any	DB is up and running	Any generated errors are trapped
Broadcast	All agents' details and error messages	---	Errors generated	Acknowledgement from agent who took ownership
Transmit	Specific agent's details and error messages	---	Errors generated	---
Update Catalog Database	Error message and agent identity	---	Errors generated and acknowledgement received	Knowledge update

Table 2. continued

Object Monitor Role

Service	Inputs	Outputs	Precondition	Postcondition
Accept DB Error Message	Error message	Acknowledgement	Error messages arrived from DBMonitor	Acknowledgement sent to DBMonitor
Monitor objects statistics	Database schema	Fragmented objects, if any	Database up and running, and objects in schema > 0	Fragmented objects trapped
Request backup	Object name	---	Fragmented object exists	Request is accepted or rejected
Reorganize object	Object name	---	Backup of object completed	Object fragmentation resolved
Update catalog database	New object statistics following reorg/monitoring	---	Object monitored or reorganized	Knowledge update

BackupRec Role

Service	Inputs	Outputs	Precondition	Post-condition
Accept DB error message	Error message	Acknowledgement	Error messages arrived from DBMonitor	Acknowledgement sent to DBMonitor
DB Backup	Database name	Backed-up database files	Backup of database requested/ scheduled	Backup Completed
Object Backup	Object name	Backed-up object	Backup of object requested	Backup completed
Offline storage	Backed-up files, storage media	---	Backup of DB/ object completed	Clean-up files from disk
DB recovery	Backed-up database files	Recovered database	DB failure occurred or specific DB version requested	Consistent DB available
Object recovery	Backed-up object files	Recovered object	Object lost or specific object version requested	Object is available for use
Accept backup schedule	Backup types and times	Schedule of backup	---	Backups planned as per schedule
Update catalog database	Backup schedule start/end times	---	Backup completed	Knowledge update

cuss the various capabilities of the involved agent types and include detailed activity diagrams of the system implementation. To recapitulate some of the components of the CIR model, the Interaction module identifies and resolves interdependencies between agent types through coordination. The Communication module is used by the coordination mechanism in the Interaction component as the link media between the agents and enables the sending and receiving of messages between agents and the environment. Due to the close interdependency between the two components, these will be described together, as a single unit, in the following subsections.

Database Monitor (DBMonitor)

DBMonitor – Knowledge

This agent type keeps its knowledge base constantly updated with errors and warnings generated by the database, and it also updates itself with information on the entities that are responsible for the resolution of the encountered errors. This knowledge is used to ease the error propagation process for previously encountered errors.

DBMonitor – Problem Solver

The DBMonitor agent type would periodically and continuously monitor the database log files for error and update its knowledge base with new error information for future reference. It would broadcast the error information to all ADAM agent instances in the system for resolution in the case of new errors and would update itself with information on the agent type responsible for the error. In the case of previously encountered errors, the agent type would use information in its knowledge base and transmit the error details to only the specific agent types responsible for the error.

DBMonitor – Interaction and Communication

The Database Monitor component interacts with all the other modules (human and software) in the system to propagate any errors/warnings (and receive acknowledgement of error-resolution responsibility ownership) it encounters to ensure that the errors are resolved. The flow of operations of an instance of the DB Monitor agent type is illustrated in Figure 5.

The first step is for the agent instance (or simply, agent) to register itself and its services with the yellow-pages service provided by the directory facilitator (DF) in JADE. Once the registration is completed, the agent begins monitoring the database. Each time an error is encountered, the agent checks its knowledge base for information on the error. If no information is found, the error is considered new, the error details are recorded in the knowledge base, and the DF is queried for a list of all ADAM agents in the system. If information is found on the error and the

Figure 5. Activities and interactions of the DBMonitor agent [2, 3, 4, 5]

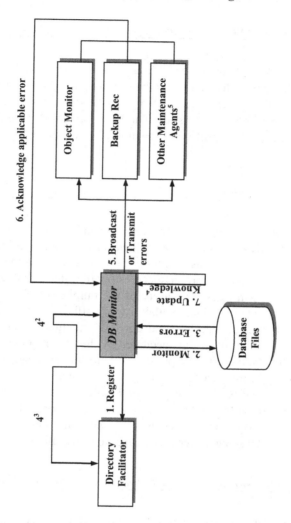

agent responsible for the error, the DF is queried for information specific to only the appropriate agent. The next step is to send the error information to the agents. This is broadcast to all agents or transmitted to a specific agent depending on whether or not the error is new.

The appropriate agent takes responsibility for the error and acknowledges the same to the DBMonitor, which then proceeds to update its knowledge base with information on the agent responsible for the error in the case of new errors.

Tablespace and Object Monitors(Object Monitor)

Tablespace/Object Monitor – Knowledge

These agent types' knowledge bases include constantly updated information about growth of the logical tablespaces, number of files comprising the tablespaces, object growth rates, current number of extents occupied by objects, and object and tablespace fragmentation statistics. The knowledge components also include information regarding the agent types' capabilities in terms of the errors that the agent types are capable of handling and resolving.

Tablespace/Object Monitor – Problem Solver

The Tablespace/Object Monitors' abilities include both proactive as well as reactive maintenance. Proactive action is taken whenever alarming conditions pertaining to an object/tablespace—such as rapidly diminishing space in the tablespace, too much unused space due to incorrect space estimation during tablespace creation, abnormal object growth rates, proximity of the number of object extents to the maximum allowed extents value, availability of sufficient space for the object to grow (next extent space availability), extremely fragmented tablespace/object, and abnormally large number of extents occupied by the object, and so forth—are encountered or anticipated during the periodic monitoring performed by instances of these agent types. The instances of these agent types update their knowledge bases with health statistics pertaining to objects and tablespaces in the database and take preventive actions according to the collected statistics in order to prevent potential failures. Reactive action is taken whenever the DBMonitor agent receives relevant error messages that these agent types are capable of handling.

Tablespace/Object Monitor – Interaction and Communication

These agent types interact with both software as well as human agents. Interaction with software agents is with the DBMonitor agent type for reactive maintenance and error resolution, and with other service providing agent types (such as Backup and Recovery agent type) for services that these agent types cannot perform by themselves. Interaction with human agents is for the collection of certain rules and policies that would govern decisions such as tablespace/object downtimes, defragmentation requirement and schedule, and so forth.

In the current prototype of ADAM, the functionalities of the two agent types have been combined into the Object Monitor Agent type which takes proactive and reactive steps to maintain the health of objects and tablespaces, thereby ensuring optimum utilization of disk space and database performance. Figure 6 below illustrates the sequence of activities and the interactions of the Object Monitor module with the other modules in the system architecture.

The first step, as in the previous case, is registration with the DF. Next, the agent instance (agent) begins monitoring the objects in the database and constantly updating its knowledge base with changed object statistics. Whenever potential risk areas are encountered, if the agent can rectify the situation independently, it does so. If it requires services from other agents in order to proceed with error resolution activities, it engages in the contract-net protocol with the service providers (in the current implementation, they are the Backup Recovery agents). The service providers respond with an accept or reject message and the Object Monitor awards the service to the most appropriate/optimal agent. (Again, the current implementation assumes that at least one service provider will accept the request). Once all capability interdependency issues are resolved, the agent proceeds to rectify the situation. In a parallel process, the Object monitor also constantly listens for any broadcasts or transmits from the DBMonitor agent. Upon receipt of any message, the agent checks its knowledge base and either confirms or disconfirms responsibility for the error. If the error is applicable to this agent, it proceeds to resolve the error following confirmation to DBMonitor.

Backup and Recovery (BackupRec)

BackupRec – Knowledge

The Backup Rec agent type's knowledge base includes information about existing backup/recovery schedules. The agent type also updates itself with new schedules as and when requests arrive from other agents for such services. It updates itself with actual backup statistics (such as the actual time taken to complete the backup, actual backup file size, and so forth) and kinds of backups taken. This knowledge is utilized by the agent type to better estimate and schedule new/special backup requests and to appropriately determine the specific backups required for recovery purposes, thereby resulting in better estimation of service parameters for future requests.

BackupRec – Problem Solver

This agent type's capabilities include establishment of backup procedures and schedules based on availability of system resources and on input gathered from other sources such as the human DBA. It would autonomously execute planned and

Figure 6. Activities and interactions of the Object Monitor agent [6, 7, 8]

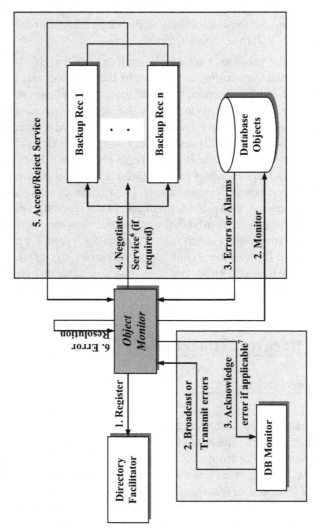

adhoc activities and would manage the compression and storage of backup files onto various storage media. It would also be responsible for the restoration of appropriate files and the recovery of databases in the event of a hardware or software failure.

Figure 7. Activities and interactions of the Backup Rec agent

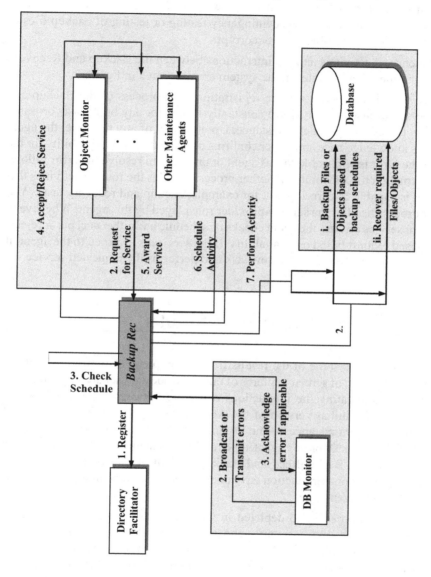

BackupRec – Interaction and Communication

The BackupRec agent type also interacts with both software and human agents. Interaction with software agents is with the DBMonitor agent type for reactive maintenance and with other service-requestor agent types to address and, based on availability, service the requested operations. Interaction with human agents is to obtain an acceptable backup schedule/window and to determine recovery schedules for preplanned activities such as contingency testing or testing of backup files to ensure that they are readable and not corrupt.

The sequence of activities and the interactions between the Backup and Recovery module and the other modules in the system are illustrated in Figure 7.

The first step, as always, is service registration. One process of the Backup and Recovery agent instance (or agent) constantly listens for any broadcasts or trans-mits from the DBMonitor agent instance. Upon receipt of any message, the agent checks its knowledge base and either confirms or disconfirms responsibility for the error. If the error is applicable to this agent, it proceeds to resolve the error follow-ing confirmation to DBMonitor. Another process handles the routine activities that the agent is capable of carrying out, for example, backup and recovery tasks. Yet, another process handles the service-provider role played by this agent. Whenever a request for service arrives, the agent checks its schedule and either accepts or rejects the proposed request based on availability. If the service is awarded to the agent, it updates its schedule to reflect the new task and performs the requested service.

Snapshot of Results

This section presents some of the results from the implementation of the ADAM prototype in the form of screen-captures of output windows, user activity windows, and windows illustrating the interactions occurring between the various agents in the system. The initial version of the ADAM prototype was kept simple and consists of four agent instances—one instance of the DBMonitor agent type, one instance of the ObjectMonitor agent type, and two instances of the Backup Rec agent type, namely, BackupRec1 and BackupRec2. It should be noted that in a real-world scenario or a production environment there could be many instances of each maintenance agent type.

The defragmentation scenario depicted in the snapshots below—while a simple routine **DBA** activity—was primarily chosen to illustrate proof of concept of the ADAM MAS. The chief objective in choosing this very common and mundane **DBA** scenario was to demonstrate and substantiate the feasibility of replacing human DBAs with intelligent, autonomous agents. The ADAM MAS represents a research effort that only skims the surface of what would, if developed to emulate a DBA's duties in totality, be a much more complex industrial product.

The implementation test activities were carried out on a sample user schema called DEMOUSER within the Oracle 8.1.7 database "demodb." (For the purposes of car-rying out the experimentation, both the database under ADAM supervision as well

Figure 8. Message output by the Object Monitor agent

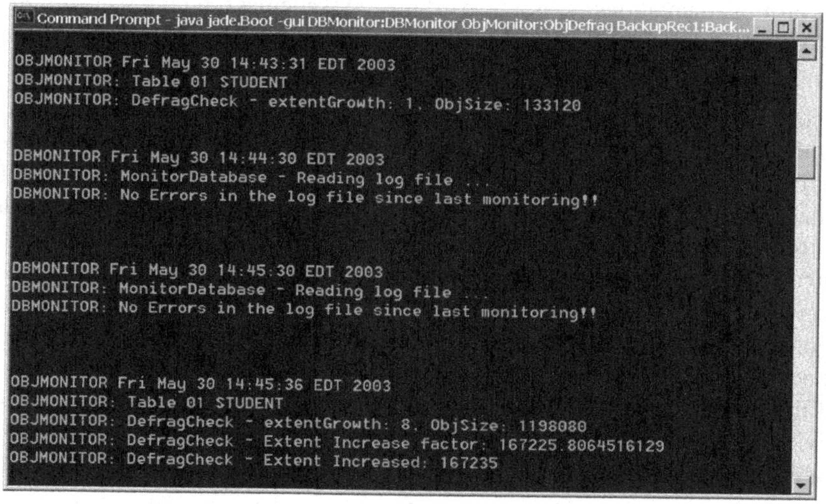

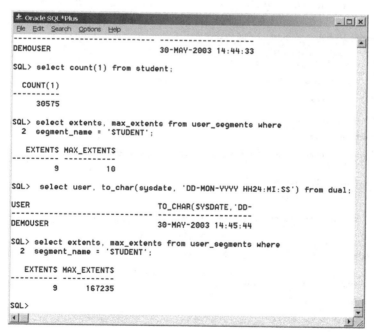

Figure 9. User activity causing proactive action by Object Monitor during proactive monitoring

as the knowledge bases of the various agents reside in the same database. However, production implementations are assumed to house the schemas on completely different databases and, if possible, geographically dispersed locations). The DEMOUSER schema contains a table called STUDENT consisting of four fields.

Four major functionalities were simulated and tested, including proactive monitoring (by the Object Monitor agent), reactive monitoring (by all agents), knowledge update (by all agents), and agent-agent interaction (between all agents). The results pertaining to two of the test cases—that is, to the proactive monitoring functionality and to the capability interdependency problem (agent-agent interaction)—are presented in this section. The SQL*Plus screens capture the user input tasks and commands (applied to the STUDENT table) that are used to simulate the errors and conditions pertaining to the above-mentioned test cases. Figures 8 and 9 illustrate the proactive monitoring abilities of the Object Monitor agent. Figure 8 is a snapshot of the messages output by the Object Monitor during its monitoring process, along with the potential risk areas identified by it and the solutions applied by it to prevent errors in the future.

Figure 9 is a screen-capture of the Oracle SQL*Plus window, which simulates user activity. As can be seen, the EXTENTS value for the sample table STUDENT is fast approaching the MAX_EXTENTS value. The Object Monitor agent observes

Figure 10. User activity window highlighting the fragmentation of STUDENT table

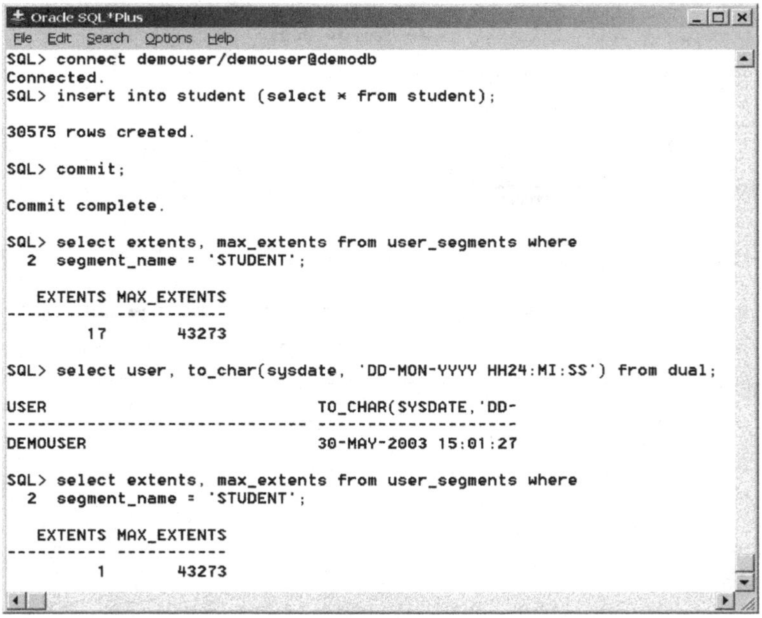

```
Oracle SQL*Plus
File Edit Search Options Help
SQL> connect demouser/demouser@demodb
Connected.
SQL> insert into student (select * from student);

30575 rows created.

SQL> commit;

Commit complete.

SQL> select extents, max_extents from user_segments where
  2  segment_name = 'STUDENT';

   EXTENTS MAX_EXTENTS
---------- -----------
        17       43273

SQL> select user, to_char(sysdate, 'DD-MON-YYYY HH24:MI:SS') from dual;

USER                           TO_CHAR(SYSDATE,'DD-
------------------------------ --------------------
DEMOUSER                       30-MAY-2003 15:01:27

SQL> select extents, max_extents from user_segments where
  2  segment_name = 'STUDENT';

   EXTENTS MAX_EXTENTS
---------- -----------
         1       43273
```

this detail, and proactive actions are taken to increase the MAX_EXTENTS value (the new value as increased by the agent can also be seen in the window) thereby avoiding future errors. The new MAX_EXTENTS value arrived at by the ADAM agent is proportional to the growth rate. The large MAX_EXTENTS value seen in this simulation is due to the insertion of a large amount of data within a very short time period during the test run.

Figure 11. Messages output by the agents involved in the Contract-Net protocol

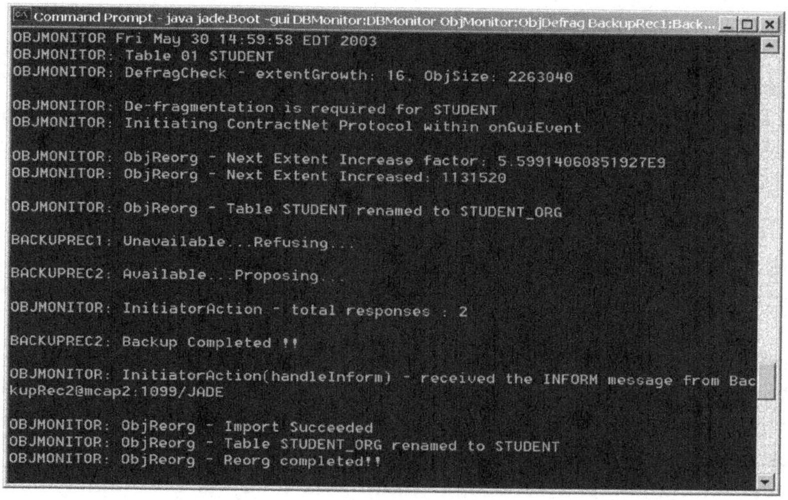

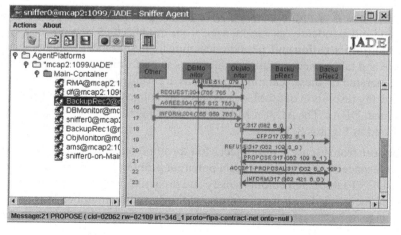

Figure 12. Sniffer Window illustrating the exchange of messages during the Contract-Net protocol

Figures 10 through 12 illustrate the capability interdependency problem between the Object Monitor and the Backup and Recovery (BackupRec) agents and the various interactions that take place in order to resolve this interdependency.

The first half of figure 10 shows the user-activity window with the table STUDENT heavily fragmented (with 17 extents).

Upon identification of the fragmentation problem during its regular proactive monitoring cycle (the first test result presented above), the Object Monitor agent launches the FIPA Contract-Net protocol and begins interaction with all available Backup and Recovery (BackupRec) agents in the system. In the current prototype, there are two such agents: one of them available for service at the time Object Monitor requires it, and the other unavailable due to time-clashes. Figure 11 shows the messages output by all the agents involved in the Contract-Net protocol, and Figure 12 illustrates the actual Agent Communication Language (ACL) messages exchanged between the participants.

Validation of Results

It is a well known fact in the database community that most **DBAs** spend over 80% of their time on performance-tuning activities that include the monitoring and tuning of various statistics such as storage statistics, I/O statistics, query-processing statistics, and fragmentation statistics. One of the primary causes for performance bottlenecks in commercial **relational databases** today is the fragmentation of objects and tablespaces due to incorrect space estimations. As a result, **DBAs** in large organizations, managing large databases, spend a considerable amount of time reorganizing the objects and tablespaces to reduce fragmentation, and consequently improve performance.

The current (and very preliminary) ADAM prototype addresses this issue autonomously and independently as can be seen from the previous section. In a typical **database-administration** unit, periodic scanning for the number of extents occupied by objects and tablespaces within the databases is performed on a daily basis. The reports generated by these scanning operations are studied manually by the human DBAs and any resolution of problem scenarios are suggested/carried out personally by the human DBAs. The ADAM MAS eliminates this load from the human DBAs as illustrated in Figures 8 through 12.

As can be seen from Figure 9, the Object Monitor automatically performs the routine object/tablespace scanning, identifies a potential problem area in a specific object (the STUDENT table), and autonomously and proactively resolves the situation by performing the needed activity of increasing the maximum number of extents that can be occupied by the table. The Object Monitor agent was able, based on certain rules laid down initially by the **DBA** (rules pertaining to object size v/s growth rate ratio), to intelligently decide that the object was not so fragmented as to require a defragmentation exercise and that a simple increase in the MAX_EXTENTS parameter was sufficient in this case (Figure 9).

Similarly, in Figure 10, Object Monitor is able to intelligently infer that the object (STUDENT table) is now too fragmented to be considered for just a MAX_EXTENTS increase. The agent autonomously makes a decision to launch the defragmentation exercises and hence the interaction between the Object Monitor and other service provider agents (BackupRec agents in this case) to complete all the tasks required for this activity.

In all of the above cases, an automated e-mail is sent to the human DBA with a summary of the tasks that have been carried out by the agents, thereby keeping the DBA aware of all changes to the database.

Thus, as can be seen from the above results, one of the most commonly and routinely performed tasks during the course of a human DBA's workday, namely object maintenance and defragmentation, has been completely eliminated from his task list, thereby freeing him for more important tasks at hand.

The initial prototype of ADAM was kept very simple and dedicated to a very small subset of DBA tasks as the primary objective was to illustrate the feasibility of the concept of **autonomous database administration**. The idea behind this research was to establish the fact that intelligent, rational, and autonomous **software agents** can indeed be deployed in the world of database administration to ease the workload on human DBAs. While the initial experimentation and validation was carried out in a largely academic environment as a proof-of-concept, the next step is to enhance the research and the ADAM MAS in order to ensure its deployment in a real-world database application to better validate the viability of this approach. This idea, when developed on a much larger scale to include a variety of other agents such as performance-tuning agents, resource-management agents, capacity-planning agents, and so forth, would be able to eliminate more and more tasks from a DBA's task list and make database management more autonomous than has been made possible by the current, predominantly academic, version of ADAM.

Related Work

Though the database community has made several significant contributions towards autonomic systems that would simplify the lives of developers, little has been done to date to assist the **database administrators** in their tasks. Microsoft's AutoAdmin project is one of the first attempts at easing the burden on DBAs by including self-managing and self-administering features within the database systems. Databases actively auto-tune themselves to be responsive to application needs. This research has led to the introduction of innovative self-tuning server, SQL server (Microsoft Corporation, 2004).

Another effort along the same direction is IBM's SMART (Self-Managing and Resource Tuning) project which aims to make IBM's database product, DB2, autonomic (Lohman & Lightstone, 2002).

Yet another leading database vendor, Oracle, has integrated an intelligent self-management infrastructure with the core database engine of its latest RDBMS product, Oracle 10g (Kumar, 2003). This infrastructure consists of four components—Automatic Workload Respository, Automated Maintenance Task infrastructure, Server Generated Alerts, and Advisory Framework—and, through these components, aims to automate and simplify the day-to-day database management tasks. The Oracle 10g database is also the first RDBMS product to include a self-diagnostic engine called Automatic Database Diagnostic Monitor (ADDM) through which it diagnoses its own performance, detects a variety of common problems, and determines how those problems can be resolved (Wood, et. al. 2005; Dias, Ramacher, Shaft, Venkataramani, & Wood, 2005). It also includes various other enhancements and advisors such as the SQL Tuning Advisor (Ziauddin, Zait, Minhas, Yagoub, & Dageville, 2005) and SQL Access Advisor (Hobbs, 2005), Automatic Shared Memory Management (Lahiri, et. al. 2005), Segment Advisor (Ganesh & Kumar, 2005) which are all aimed at reducing the time and effort required from a DBA.

While several of the objectives of these research efforts are similar to the objectives presented in this chapter, the difference lies in the problem domain. The SMART, AutoAdmin, and Oracle projects deal with algorithms and configurations that are completely internal to the database.

In addition to the above endeavors by the leading database vendors, a plethora of research efforts are underway at various academic institutes in the **self-tuning databases** arena. One such effort is the CORDS algorithm (Ilyas, Markl, Haas, Brown, & Aboulnaga, 2004) developed at Purdue University in collaboration with IBM that aims to automate the identification of statistics to maintain by automatically discovering statistical dependencies and correlations between pairs of columns. The ultimate goal of CORDS is to facilitate, through the automatic maintenance (without DBA intervention) of appropriate statistics, the selection of a minimum-cost plan for accessing data. The work on new indexing schemes suitable for **self-tuning databases** that is presented in Sattler, Schallehn, and Geist (2005) is yet another endeavor towards the goal of **self-managing databases** as is the database indexes' self-tuning methodology presented in (Costa, Lifschitz, & Salles, 2003) where **software agents** have been integrated with **database management systems** to automate the selection, creation, and exclusion of indexes.

The result of these projects would be a database that is intelligent, while this chapter proposes a step towards a tool that would intelligently administer and maintain any database, whether intelligent or not. Systems such as the ones proposed in this chapter would not change the inherent database features, but would proactively and intelligently manage the database. Thus, organizations need not have to go through expensive and risky upgrade procedures to install the latest, intelligent databases. Instead, they could just use the proposed system to act as an intelligent wrapper around a nonintelligent database, thereby acting as a bridge that provides autonomy, rationality, and intelligence to an otherwise non-self-administering database.

Conclusion

An agent-based solution for the autonomous administration and maintenance of **relational databases** has been presented in this chapter, in the form of a multiagent system, ADAM. The motivations behind the conception of the ADAM prototype have been discussed and an in-depth description of the analysis, design, and implementation specifics of the same has been presented. Evidence of how the ADAM agents can take over the role of human DBAs, thereby reducing the workload on them, which is the primary objective of this research, has been presented in the results section.

To reiterate what has been stated in the previous sections of the chapter, the increasing demands of today's world have resulted in databases growing rapidly in complexity. Skilled DBAs are becoming more rare and more expensive. Under such scenarios, the work proposed in this research provides a novel solution to the **database-administration** problem. It integrates the best features of agent technology to produce an autonomous maintenance tool. This tool would take over the responsibilities of the human DBAs thereby reducing and even eliminating the need for them. Thus, it facilitates the realization of the goal of **self-managing databases**.

This research is only one of a very large number of possible applications of agent technology in the database area that can be developed to ease the burden of certain mundane, routine tasks off the DBAs. While the current implementation operates on a single database located at a single site, the true potential of this research would be realized in environments consisting of distributed databases where the agents would administer multiple databases located at geographically dispersed sites and would possibly share resources across these different sites. Under such a scenario, this architecture may be impaired by communication costs due to high degree of distribution. Further, with increasing complexity added to the problem-solver in an attempt to expand the system capability set, additional bottlenecks may be encountered in terms of performance and computational costs. Therefore the right balance between performance and capability will have to be kept in mind while enhancing and expanding the proposed system.

The future directions and visions for this research are immense. Foremost would be an expansion of the "skill-set" of the "virtual-DBAs" comprising ADAM. In the current version, as an illustration of the possibilities offered by this research, only a very small subset of activities has been implemented. The Backup and Recovery agent in particular does not completely justify its nomenclature since it only performs the functionality of the first half, that is, backup. The recovery component of this agent is yet to be implemented. Further, the range of errors and situations that the agents ought to be capable of handling needs to be increased to better serve their purpose as replacements to human DBAs.

Another important aspect that needs to be addressed in the future in order for this architecture to be truly effective is to extend the ability of the proposed system to maintain and administer heterogeneous database systems offered by different vendors. In order to realize this, it will be necessary to support multiple ontologies that capture the terminologies of different, and possibly overlapping, database domains, and map requests expressed in one ontology into requests using terms for another. Hence, in the future, the system could be expanded to include such ontological and mapping services to service a more heterogeneous set of databases.

The size/complexity-of-databases-to-skilled-DBAs ratio is becoming progressively more inversely proportional. Further, the world of ubiquitous computing, where nontechnical end users would have microdatabases within their mobile devices and would need the ability to use such databases without extensive knowledge of the internals and workings of the tasks involved in the maintenance of the same, is right round the corner. Hence, in spite of the above-mentioned limitations, we believe that the work presented in this chapter makes a rudimentary but significant contribution to the field of **database administration**.

References

Costa, R., Lifschitz, S., & Salles, M. (2003). *Index self-tuning with agent-based databases, CLEI Electronic Journal, 6*,(1). Retrieved on January, 2006 from http://www.clei.cl/cleiej/paper.php?id=88

Dias, K., Ramacher, M., Shaft, U., Venkataramani, V., & Wood, G. (2005). Automatic Performance Diagnosis and Tuning in Oracle, In *Proceedings of the Second Biennial Conference on Innovative Data Systems Research (CIDR 2005)*, Asilomar, CA (pp. 84-94).

Elmasri, R., & Navathe, S. (2000). *Fundamentals of database systems* (3rd ed., p.3). Pearson Education, Inc.

FIPA. (2004). *The foundation for intelligent physical agents*. Retrieved November, 2005, from http://www.fipa.org

Ganesh, A., & Kumar, S. (2005). *The self-managing database: Proactive space & schema object management with Oracle database 10g release 2.* An Oracle White Paper.

Ghenniwa, H., & Areibi, S. (2002, July). Agent orientation for evolutionary computation. In *Proceedings of ECOMAS*, New York (pp. 57-64).

Hobbs, L. (2005). *Performance tuning using the SQL access advisor.* An Oracle White Paper.

Ilyas, I., Markl, V., Haas, P., Brown, P., & Aboulnaga, A. (2004). Automatic relationship discovery in self-managing database systems. In *Proceedings of the International Conference on Autonomic Computing (ICAC 2004)*, New York (pp. 340-341).

JADE (2004). *Java agent development framework.* Retrieved on November 2005 from http://sharon.cselt.it/projects/jade/

Kumar, S. (2003). *Oracle database 10g: The self-managing database.* An Oracle White Paper.

Lahiri, T., Nithrkashyap, A., Kumar, S., Hirano, B., Patel, K., Kumar, P., et al. (2005). *The self-managing database: Automatic shared memory management with Oracle database 10g release 2.* An Oracle White Paper.

Lightstone, S., Kwan, E., Storm, A., & Wu, L. (2002). *Automatic configuration for IBM DB2 universal database.* Retrieved February, 2006, from http://www.redbooks.ibm.com/redpapers/pdfs/redp0441.pdf

Lightstone, S., Lohman, G., & Zilio, D. (2002, September). *Toward autonomic computing with DB2 universal database.* ACM Sigmod Record.

Lohman, G., & Lightstone, S. (2002). SMART: Making DB2 (more) autonomic. In *Proceedings of the 28th VLDB Conference*, Hong Kong, China (pp. 877-879).

Microsoft Corporation. (2004). *AutoAdmin: Self-tuning and self-administering databases.* Retrieved January, 2006, from http://research.microsoft.com/dmx/autoadmin/default.htm

Oracle Corporation. (1999a, December). *Oracle8i administrator's guide, release 2 (8.1.6).*

Oracle Corporation. (1999b, December). *Oracle8i concepts, release 2 (8.1.6).*

Ramanujam, S., & Capretz, M. (2003). Augmenting database management: A multi-agent approach, *Journal of Three Dimensional Images*, 17(4), 121-129.

Ramanujam, S., & Capretz, M. (2004). Design of a multi-agent system for autonomous database administration. In *Proceedings of the Seventeenth Annual Canadian Conference on Electrical and Computer Engineering (CCECE 2004)*, Ontario, Canada (Vol. 2, pp. 1167-1170).

Sattler, K., Schallehn, E., & Geist, I. (2005). Towards indexing schemes for self-tuning DBMS. In *Proceedings of the 21ˢᵗ International Conference on Data Engineering (ICDE 2005)*, Tokyo, Japan (pp. 1216-1223).

Tveit, A. (2001). *A survey of agent-oriented software engineering*, First NTNU CSGSC. Retrieved on February, 2006 from http://csgsc.idi.ntnu.no/2001/pages/papers/atveit.pdf

Wood, G., Hailey, K., Gongloor, P., Vaidyanatha, G., Green, C., Dias, K., et al. (2005). *The self-managing database: Automatic performance diagnosis with Oracle database 10g release 2*. An Oracle White Paper.

Wooldridge, M., Jennings, N. R., & Kinny, D. (2000). The gaia methodology for agent-oriented analysis and design. *Journal of Autonomous Agents and MAS, 3*(3), 285-312.

Ziauddin, M., Zait, M., Minhas, M., Yagoub, K., & Dageville, B. (2005). *The self-managing database: Guided application and SQL tuning with Oracle database 10g release 2*. An Oracle White Paper.

Endotes

[1]   For the purposes of conciseness, the Tablespace/ObjectMonitor Role will be known simply as Object Monitor throughout the rest of the document.

[2]   Check Knowledge component for error information.

[3]   Check with the directory facilitator (DF) for all available, or specific (if information existed in the knowledge base), maintenance agents in the system.

[4]   DBMonitor's knowledge component is updated only for new errors.

[5]   Other maintenance agents may include agents such as query performance maintenance agents, cache management agents, resource management agents, capacity planning agents, and so forth.

[6]   Negotiation is based on the FIPA Contract-Net Specification (FIPA, 2004).

[7]   After acknowledgement of relevant error messages to the DB Monitor agent, the Object Monitor then proceeds to perform the steps required to resolve the error (Step 6 in Figure 6).

[8]   The two shaded areas in Figure 6 represent parallel processes. The Object Monitor agent performs the two sets of activities/interactions simultaneously, as separate threads (extending various behavior classes provided by JADE (JADE, 2004).

Chapter XI

Towards Distributed Association Rule Mining Privacy

Mafruz Zaman Ashrafi, Monash University, Australia

David Taniar, Monash University, Australia

Kate Smith, Monash University, Australia

Abstract

With the advancement of storage, retrieval, and network technologies today, the amount of information available to each organization is literally exploding. Although it is widely recognized that the value of data as an organizational asset often becomes a liability because of the cost to acquire and manage those data is far more than the value that is derived from it. Thus, the success of modern organizations not only relies on their capability to acquire and manage their data but their efficiency to derive useful actionable knowledge from it. To explore and analyze large data repositories and discover useful actionable knowledge from them, modern organizations have used a technique known as data mining, which analyzes voluminous digital data and discovers hidden but useful patterns from such massive digital data. However, discovery of hidden patterns has statistical meaning and may often disclose some sensitive information. As a result, privacy becomes one of the prime concerns in the data-mining research community. Since distributed data mining discovers rules by combining local models from various distributed sites, breaching data privacy happens more often than it does in centralized environments.

Introduction

The advancement of technology allows us to store a huge amount of digital data in an efficient but cheaper way. Because of various automation techniques such as barcode readers, smart cards, and so on, organizations often store simple transactions and intend to utilize them for various future activities such as direct marketing, promotion, customer services, and so on. Association-rule-mining algorithms (Agrawal Imielinski, & Srikant, 1993; Agrawal & Srikant, 1994; Klemettinen, Mannila, Ronkainen, Toivonen, & Verkamo, 1994) initially intend to generate association rules from a sequential environment a where dataset is kept in a centralized location. However, modern organizations by nature have many data centers across the country or the around the globe, storing millions of transactions every day. Thus, combing those datasets in a single site for generating association rules from them, is not often feasible because of the size of each dataset.

Although one can combine those datasets in a single site, generating an association from such a dataset perhaps needs substantial processing power that may not be sufficient for a single computer (Cheung, Ng, Fu, & Fu, 1997). Nevertheless, in many cases, data may be inherently distributed and may not possibly combine them into a centralized site for a number of practical reasons such as security, statutory constraints imposed by the law, business competitiveness, fault tolerance, and so on. Therefore, to generate an association rule from such a geographically distributed dataset, a new technique—distributed-association-rule mining—has emerged.

Since distributed-data-mining algorithms need to share local data and discover patterns beyond the organization boundary. However, discovery of such patterns from various participating sites has statistical meaning and may often disclose some sensitive information. For example, suppose two sites S_1 and S_2 have private datasets such as D_1 and D_2. Site S_1 wants to access dataset of site S_2. On the other hand site S_2 would not mind to share its private dataset but sharing its private dataset with site S_1 may allow site S_1 to divulge some of the important statistics and subsequently site S_1 may misuse those statistics for it own profit.

To preserve privacy of each participating site in distributed-association-rule mining, in this chapter we present a secure multiparty communication-based methodology that generates association rules without revealing confidential inputs such as statistical properties of individual sites and yet retains high level of accuracy in resultant rules. The goal of secure multiparty computation in distributed-association-rule mining is to find global support of all itemsets using a function where multiple parties hold their local support counts, and at the end, all parties know the global support of all itemsets and nothing more. In addition, each participating site later on use those global-frequent itemsets and generate candidate itemset for the next iteration. One of the important outcomes of the proposed technique is that, it reduces the overall communication cost.

The rest of the chapter is organized as follows: First, we describe our motivation to carry out this study, then describe the background of distributed-association-rule mining and several privacy-preserving distributed-association-rule-mining frameworks. Next, we present our proposed privacy-preserving ddistributed-association-tion-rules-generation methodology. In the beginning of that section, we outline the assumption we made to maintain the privacy of each participating site. Then we discuss two protocols: (1) obfuscation and (2) deobfuscation. The former protocol obfuscates the private inputs of each participating site using a random number. When the global obfuscate support of all candidate itemsets is generated, then the later protocol is used to deobfuscate and finally each site discover the global-frequent itemset of that iteration. We also illustrate the message-exchange cost and propose an optimized technique in this section. The proposed optimized technique able to obfuscate the support of the candidate itemset using the support of the subset itemset thus the deobfuscation can be done on a single site rather than a participating site passing the global obfuscate support to the adjacent site. Subsequentlym the proposed optimized method is able to reduce the communication cost significantly. Then, we discuss the performance measurements of our proposed method and finally we draw our conclusions.

Motivation

Distributed-association-rule-mining algorithms discover association rules beyond the organization boundary and enable different participating organizations to achieve mutual benefits. However, association-rule mining discovers patterns from various collaborating datasets based on some statistical measurements such as support of an itemset. For that reason, a question arises as to whether private inputs of each participating site are divulged to other sites during the rule-discovery process or not. Let us now illustrate some of the facts that motivate us to carry out this study:

1.   Distributed-association-rule-mining algorithms aggregate local support of various participating sites and generate a global-frequent itemset. However,

support of each itemset has significant statistical meaning, and hence exposure of those supports may disclose corporate information or their transaction
details. Perhaps privacy is a main concern of distributed-association mining;
otherwise, the resultant patterns may reveal sensitive information, and thus,
participating sites may loose their business. Consequently, collaborating organizations will not share their datasets and subsequently will be unable to
get benefits that distributed-association-rule-mining offers.

2.   In recent years, privacy issues have received huge attention from various research communities. However, such attempts often diminish the objective of
distributed-association mining because they increase the overall communication
cost. We are motivated by the fact that privacy-preserving distributed-association-rule-mining algorithms should have an efficient method that is able to
generate rules without increasing the overall communication cost.

Distributed-Association-Rule-Mining Background

Distributed-association-rule mining algorithms generate an association rule in the
same manner as sequential-association-rule mining except it communicates with other
participating sites during the mining process. Thus, all of the distributed-association-
rule-mining methods comprise two components: local association-rule-generation
method and communication. The former component enumerates local support of all
global-candidate itemsets whereas the latter component exchanges messages among

Figure 1. Generic distributed-association-rule-mining framework

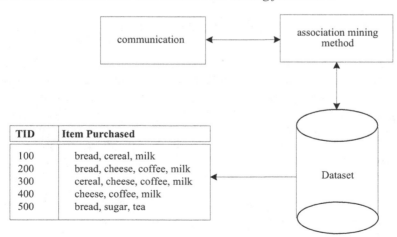

TID	Item Purchased
100	bread, cereal, milk
200	bread, cheese, coffee, milk
300	cereal, cheese, coffee, milk
400	cheese, coffee, milk
500	bread, sugar, tea

participating sites to obtain global support of a global-frequent itemset. A generic framework of distributed-association-rule mining is depicted in Figure 1.

All distributed-association-rule-mining methods first generate the support of local itemsets then exchange them with other sites to find global support of those itemsets. For example, suppose $S_1, S_2, S_3, ..., S_n$ collaborating sites each of them has respective dataset $D_1, D_2, D_3, ..., D_n$. Let each of the datasets have a set of transactions T with a unique transaction ID (tid) and set of items I. Suppose X is an itemset, the local of X in D_1 is the number of the transaction in D_1 where X appears as a subset and can be computed using Formula 1 stated in section 2. The global support of X is the aggregation of all the local support of itemset X of all collaborating sites in the dataset where it appeared.

$$\sigma_{global}(X) = \sum_{i=1}^{n} \{X \in (tid, I) | X \subseteq I\} \tag{1}$$

Global-Frequent Itemset: An itemset X is known as globally frequent if and only if the aggregation of all local support of itemset X is greater than or equal to the minimum support threshold defined by the user.

Since the dataset of each collaborating site may vary in number of transactions, an itemset X is considered as locally frequent if its local support is greater than or equal to the ratio of the global-support threshold.

> **Property 1:** *An itemset X is globally frequent if and only if there is at least one collaborating site S_i ($1 < i < n$) where itemset X and all of its subset itemsets are frequent.*

> **Proof:** *Since global support of X is aggregation of all local support, if X is locally infrequent in all collaborating sites then aggregation of all local support of X will also be infrequent. Thus, the support of X is globally frequent if there exists at least a site S_i where itemset X is frequent. Additionally, if X is frequent at site S_i, it subsequently implies that all of its subset itemsets are also frequent at that site.*

Though the number of local frequent itemsets of various collaborating sites may be less however generating candidate itemset for next iteration from local frequent itemset is not sufficient rather need to generate support of additional itemset to find all global-frequent itemset of next iteration. The rationale is simple that is—an itemset may not be frequent at one of the collaborating site but it does not imply that itemset is globally infrequent.

Property 2: *Global candidate itemset of any iteration is the union of all local candidate itemset of that iteration.*

Proof: *As stated previous property that a global-frequent itemset and all of its subset itemsets are locally frequent at least at one of the collaborating sites.*

Suppose all subset of an itemset X such as $x_1, x_2, x_3, \ldots, x_n$ is locally frequent than itemset X is not only a candidate at that site but also a candidate for global-frequent itemset and subsequently imply all participating sites need to enumerate the support of itemset X if it appears in the local datasets of any sites. Thus, the global-candidate itemset is the union of all local-candidate itemsets.

A *global-association rule* is an implication of $X \rightarrow Y$, where $X \subseteq I$, $Y \subseteq I$ are global-frequent *itemset*, and $X \cap Y = \varphi$ and its global support is equal to $X \cup Y$. Here, X is called antecedent, and Y consequent.

The distributed-association-rules-mining algorithms tasks are similar to the sequential-association-rule mining except it communicates with other collaborating sites and generates global-frequent itemset. Thus, mining global–association-rule tasks can be divided into the following three subproblems:

Enumerating local support: Find support of all global-candidate itemset C from various collaborating-site datasets $D_1, D_2, D_3, \ldots, D_n$. That is generating local support of all global-candidate itemset from various datasets.

Generating global-frequent itemset: At a given user-defined global-support σ, combine all local frequent itemset and find all global-frequent itemset for that iteration.

Association rules: At a given user-specified confidence c finds all association rules R from a set of global-frequent itemset F such that each of the rules has confidence equal to or greater than c.

Related Works

A number of distributed-mining methods have been proposed. Chan et al. outline the number of distributed-mining applications in their recent review. Though there is large number of distributed mining methods but few of them have been proposed for maintaining the privacy of distributed-associationdistributed-association-rules (Atallah, Bertino, Elmagarmid, Ibrahim, & Verykios, 1999; Dasseni, Verykios,

Elmagarmid, & Bertino, 2001; Evfimievski, Srikant, Agrawal, & Gehrke, 2002; Kantercioglu & Clifton, 2002; Rizvi & Haritsa, 2002; Vaidya & Clifton, 2002). Most of these methods dealt with sequential- or centralized-association mining. Mining Association with Secrecy Konstraints (MASK) (Rizvi & Haritsa, 2002) was proposed for a centralized environment to maintain privacy and accuracy of resultant rules (Ashrafi, 2004b). This approach was based on simple probabilistic distortion of user data, employing random numbers generated from a predefined distributed function. However, the distortion process employs system resources for a long period when a dataset has a large number of transactions. Furthermore, if we use this algorithm in the context of a distributed environment, we need uniform distortion among various sites in order to generate unambiguous rules. This uniform distortion may disclose confidential inputs of an individual site and may breach the privacy of data (i.e., exact support of itemsets), and hence it is not suitable for distributed-data mining.

Evfimievski and his colleagues presented a randomization technique in order to preserve privacy of association rules (Evfimievski et al., 2002). The authors analyzed this technique in an environment where a number of clients are connected to a server. Each client sends a set of items to the server where association rules are generated. During the sending process, the client modifies the itemset according to its own randomization policies; as a result, the server is unable to find the exact information about the client. However, this assumption is not suitable for distributed-association-rule mining because it generates frequent itemsets by aggregating support counts of all clients (i.e., sites). If the randomization policy of each site differs from others, we will not be able to generate the exact support of an itemset. Subsequently, the resultant global-frequent itemsets will be erroneous. Hence, we may not able to discover useful rules. Furthermore, this technique individually disguises each attribute, and data quality will degrade significantly when the number of attributes in a dataset is large.

A new technique to preserve privacy of sensitive knowledge by hiding out frequent itemsets from large datasets was presented in Atallah et al. (1999). The authors apply heuristics to reduce the number of occurrences to such a degree that its support is below the user-specified support threshold. Dasseni et al. (2001) extended this work and investigated confidentiality issues of association-rule mining. Both works assume datasets are local and hiding some itemset will not affect the overall performance or mining accuracy. However, in distributed-association-rule mining, each site has its own dataset and a similar kind of assumption may cause ambiguities in the resultant global-rule model.

Vaidya and Clifton (2002) presented a technique to maintain privacy of association rules in vertically partitioned distributed data sources (across two data sources only) where each data site holds some attributes of each transaction. However, if the number of disjoints attributes among the site is high, this technique incurs huge communication costs. Furthermore, this technique designed the environment where there are two collaborating sites, each of them hold some attributes of each transaction, hence it may not be applied in an environment where collaborating sites do not posses such characteristics.

Recently, Kantercioglu and Clifton (2002) proposed a privacy-preserving association-rule mining for horizontally partitioned data (i.e., each site shares a common schema but has different records). The authors propose two different protocols: secure union of locally large itemsets and testing support threshold without revealing support counts. The former protocol uses cryptography to encrypt the local support count, and therefore, it is not possible to find which itemset belongs to which site. However, it reveals the number of itemsets having a common support. Since the first protocol gives the full set of locally frequent itemset, to find which of those itemset are globally frequent the latter protocol is used. It adds a random number to each support count and finds the excess supports. Finally, these excess supports are sent to the second site where it learns nothing about the first site's actual dataset size or support. The second site adds its excess support and sends the value until it reaches the last site.

However, this protocol can raise a collusion problem. For example, site i and $i+2$ in the chain can collude to find the exact excess support of site $i+1$. Furthermore, this protocol only discovers an itemset, which is globally large; not the exact support of an itemset and each site generates rules based on the local support counts.

Proposed Method

In this section, we propose a methodology that maintains the privacy of distributed-association-rule mining. At first let us explain the rational of why each site in distributed-association-rule mining sharing the support count of each itemset with all other sites.

Rationale

First, in the context of distributed-association mining, each participating site needs to know whether a particular itemset is globally frequent or not, in order to generate global-frequent itemsets for the next pass. Without that piece of information distributed-association-rule-mining algorithms are unable to generate global-candidate itemsets for the next iteration regardless of the how efficient distributed-association-rule-mining methods are. Let us illustrate the above fact in the following example:

Example 1: *Suppose there are three sites S_1, S_2 and S_3 as shown in Figure 2 and each of them have datasets D_1, D_2 and D_3. Let us discover all global-frequent itemsets that appeared in the various participating datasets three or more times. In order to find global support of each itemset, all participating sites share their local support candidate itemset with other sites. For example, the global support of 1-itemset 'tea' is 8 however 'tea' appeared only two times in site S_1, thee times in site S_2 and S_3. Thus during the process of aggregation all local support each of the participating site such as S_1, S_2 and S_3 divulge their local support of itemset 'tea' to other*

Figure 2. Distributed-association-rule mining

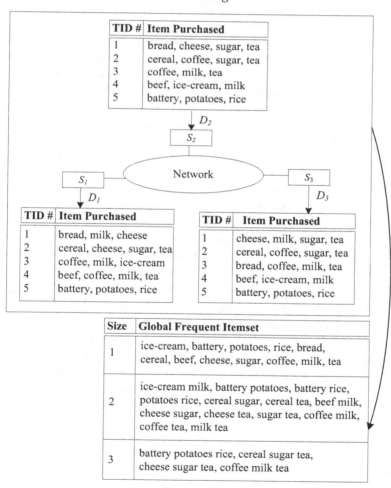

Size	Global Frequent Itemset
1	ice-cream, battery, potatoes, rice, bread, cereal, beef, cheese, sugar, coffee, milk, tea
2	ice-cream milk, battery potatoes, battery rice, potatoes rice, cereal sugar, cereal tea, beef milk, cheese sugar, cheese tea, sugar tea, coffee milk, coffee tea, milk tea
3	battery potatoes rice, cereal sugar tea, cheese sugar tea, coffee milk tea

sites. However, if any participating site does not share its local support of itemset 'tea' with other sites then it is not possible to know whether itemset 'tea' is globally frequent or not. Subsequently, if a participating site generates rules based on their local support then discrepancy (i.e., confidence of rules at different sites may vary) will arise. For example, the rule tea → milk has 50% confidence at site S_1, 33% confidence at site S_2 and 67% confidence at site S_3. Perhaps, because of such confidence discrepancy at one site the rule tea→ milk is considered interesting, in the same time another site may exclude that rule since it has low confidence thus it may not allow the collaborating sites to utilize the common benefits that the distributed-association-rule mining offers.

Since itemset support of each participating site is divulged during the mining process, distributed-association-rule mining mainly relies on how each collaborating site shares its local support of all itemsets with other sites without divulging the exact support of each itemset. To achieve that goal though there are two well known approaches such as (1) randomize and (2) secure multiparty computation however, both of the approaches have some limitations and thus may not be suitable for distributed-association-rule mining. For example, a randomization approach intends to discover association rules from randomized datasets of various sites. It focuses on privacy of an individual site, and it does not reveal original records of one site to other participating sites. To preserve privacy, transactions are randomized by discarding some items and inserting new items into it (Rizvi & Haritsa, 2002). The statistical estimation of original supports and variances given randomized supports allow a central site to adopt the Apriori algorithm (Agrawal & Srikant, 1994) to mining frequent itemsets in nonrandomized transactions by looking at only randomized ones. If each participating site has a large dataset, then distorting the dataset may involve a huge computation. In addition, if each site uses different randomization techniques then the final model may have a number of discrepancies.

On the other hand, the secure multiparty computation (Goldriech, 2001) is the problem of evaluating a function where every participating site has a secret input and it remains secret though each party knows the output (Vaidya & Clifton, 2002). Since the above technique maintains the input of various sites secret thus employing it in mining context allows us to build a data-mining model combining inputs of various local datasets without revealing individual inputs of one participating site to another. To achieve this, it computes a function $f(x, y, z)$, where in this case three parties hold the support x, y, and z of an itemset I, and at the end all parties know about the global support of I and nothing more. When using this model, each participating site is able to generate the association rule. Without using it, however, to generate $f(x, y, z)$ may involve a huge amount of communication. Perhaps communication cost is one of the few issues that distributed-association-rule-mining methods are intended to reduce. Thus, the aim of distributed-association-rule mining will only be attained if secure multiparty-computation-based distributed-association-rule-mining algorithm requires the same amount of communication as it incurs for the state-of-art distributed-association-rule-mining methods.

Though the above two approaches have some drawbacks, however one needs to employ one of these approaches to maintain privacy of each participating site. Since the randomize approach toward each participating site distorts their local datasets, this not only requires additional computation but there is also a possibility that all participating sites may not have the equal support for the same itemset. Thus, here our proposed method employs the secure multiparty communication to maintain privacy of distributed-association-rule mining. Before embarking on the details of our proposed method, let us discuss the basic notations and assumptions of this framework.

Assumptions

As mentioned in the previous section, secure multiparty communication offers some to maintain privacy of distributed-association-rule mining. Since the number of participating sites in distributed-association-rule mining is more than one, let us briefly discuss the nature of each of the participating sites:

Each site participating in distributed-association-rule mining possesses a minimum level of trust. Ideally, it is easier for any distributed-association-rule-mining algorithms to maintain privacy if all computations are done by a trusted third party. However, this kind of solution is not feasible due to various limitations. Due to this reason, we assume that all participating sites are semihonest sites. A semihonest site possesses the following characteristics:

1. Follow multiparty computation protocols completely.
2. Keep a record of all intermediate computation.
3. Be capable of deriving additional information using those intermediate records.

Though we assume that each participating site is semihonest, but the total number of participating sites is an important issue. The aim of this work is to find an exact global support of all itemsets without revealing the exact support counts of each participating site. However, when the number of participating sites is equal to two, it becomes very easy for both sites to find out the exact support counts of the other site, no matter what kind of secure computation we enforce (Vaidya & Clifton, 2002). Hence, we assume the number of sites participating with this framework is equal to n, where $n > 2$.

Figure 3. Proposed methodology

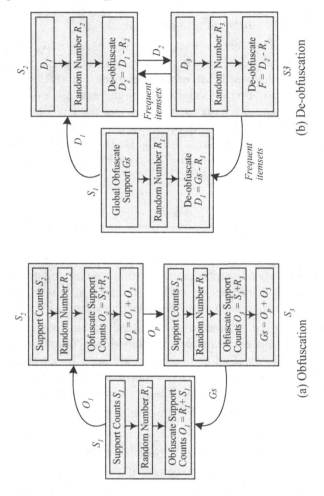

(b) De-obfuscation

(a) Obfuscation

To overcome the above problem, one may think of randomization techniques. However, it is clear that if different sites distort their respective dataset using a non-uniform randomized function or add/drop some of the items from the transaction, the resultant global-rule model will be inconsistent and subsequently diminish the objective of distributed-association-rule mining in the first place.

Methodology

In this section, we discuss how we generate global-association rules without revealing the exact support counts of any itemset to other participating sites. Our proposed method is based on the following analogy—the summation or subtraction of any two numbers S remains private until we know that exact value of any of those numbers. For example, suppose there is a large real number $N \subseteq R$, which is a sum of two numbers such as N_1 and N_2, where $N_1 \subseteq R$ and $N_2 \subseteq R$, $N_1 \neq 0$ and $N_2 \neq 0$ and R is a real number. If the value of N is known, and N_1 and N_2 are unknown, the value of N_1 or N_2 remains private until we know the exact value of either N_1 or N_2.

The proposed method uses the aforementioned technique and considers N_1 as an exact support count of an itemset, N_2 as a random number, and N as a disguised support count of a particular itemset. It has two distinct phases, namely (1) obfuscation and (2) deobfuscation as shown in the above Figure 3a and 3b. Let us now discuss the protocol of each of those phases:

a. Obfuscation Protocol

Input: Each site $S_1, S_2, S_3, \ldots S_n$ has local frequent itemsets $F_1, F_2, F_3, \ldots F_n$.
Output: Global obfuscate candidate itemset support.

1. At every iteration site S_1 obfuscated all of its global candidate itemset (i.e., an addition/subtraction of exact support count and with a random number) and is sent to an adjacent site such as S_2.
2. Each adjacent site S_2 then aggregates its obfuscated support count with the receiving support count, and sends that aggregation to the next site.
3. This sending process continues until it reaches the last site. When it reaches the last site, it aggregates its obfuscated support count with the receiving support count and sends it to the first site where the obfuscation started. We call those support is a global-obfuscated-candidate itemset support.
4. Once the first site (i.e., where the obfuscation process started) receives the global-obfuscate-candidate support, it initiates the deobfuscation phase.

b. Deobfuscation Protocol

Input: Each site S_1, S_2, S_3, S_n has local frequent itemsets OF_1, OF_2, OF_3, OF_n.
Output: Global-candidate itemset support.

3.   Site S_1 initiate deobfuscate phase adding/subtracting by its own generated random number from each of the global-obfuscated-candidate itemset support and sends resultant-candidate itemset support to adjacent site.

4.   Each site adds/subtracts their respective random number, which was previously added/subtracted from local candidate itemset support during obfuscation phase and sends resultant candidate itemset support to the next site until it reaches the last sites.

5.   When the last site adds/subtracts its own generated random number from the global obfuscated support count, the exact global support of those candidate itemset is found. Then, all global candidate itemset supports are checked in that particular site and each nonfrequent global itemset is pruned away.

6.   Finally, all global-frequent-itemset support is sent to all other sites and each site generates global candidate itemsets for the next iteration

c. How Privacy is Preserved

7.   In obfuscated phase, each of the participating sites receives only the obfuscated support from the adjacent site. Thus, the exact support of any candidate itemset is unknown to that site.

8.   During deobfuscation, each site adds/subtracts its own random number from the each of the global-obfuscated-candidate itemset. Since the support of global-obfuscated-candidate itemset is an aggregation of all local support, prevent each participating site to reveal exact support of any candidate itemset of other participating sites when it adds/subtracts its own generated random number from that global-obfuscated-candidate-itemset support. Thus, according to the definition of secure multiparty computation, the support of a global-frequent itemset is computed privately.

Table 1. Obfuscation phase

Local Support at Different Sites			Random Number		O_S	Adjacent Site		
Site	Name	S	Name	R	$S+R$	Site	Name	ΣO_S
S_1	AB	5	AB	100	105	S_2	AB	105
	AC	3	AC	100	103		AC	103
	BC	4	BC	100	104		BC	104
S_2	AB	10	AB	200	210	S_3	AB	315
	AC	9	AC	200	209		AC	312
	BC	1	BC	200	201		BC	305
S_3	AB	5	AB	200	205	S_1	AB	520
	AC	5	AC	200	205		AC	517
	BC	1	BC	200	201		BC	506

To elaborate this process, let us explain using the following example.

Example: Suppose there are three sites S_1, S_2 and S_3. After the first iteration, the global candidate 2-itemsets is equal to {AB, AC, and BC} and local support counts of candidates of site S_1 are equal to {5, 3 and 4}, at S_2 are equal to {10, 9 and 1}, and at S_3 are equal to {5, 5 and 1} as shown in Table 1. Let us consider, site S_1, S_2 and S_3 generate random number $R_1 = 100$, $R_2 = 200$, and $R_3 = 200$ and each site obfuscates its own support count of candidate itemsets by adding the corresponding random number with each support counts. After performing obfuscation, consider site S_1 sends its obfuscated support counts set (i.e., 105, 103, and 104) to site S_2. When S_2 receives this obfuscate support counts, it aggregates its own obfuscate support counts {210, 209, and 201} with the receiving support counts. Since each site shares the same candidate itemset, this aggregation operation can be done on-the-fly. Upon performing these tasks, site S_2 sends obfuscate support counts set {315, 312, and 305} to site S_3 that performs the same task as it does for site S_2 and finishes the obfuscation phase by sending them to the first site S_1.

In the next phase (i.e. deobfuscation), site S_1 receives the global-obfuscated-candidate itemset support {520, 517, and 506} from site S_3. At first, it subtracts a random number R_1 (it adds that number during obfuscation phase) from each itemset as shown in table 9.2. However, this subtraction does not reveal any knowledge to site S_1 as R_1 is subtracted from the global obfuscate-candidate-itemset support. Hence, the exact candidate itemset support of other sites remains hidden to site S_1. After subtracting R_1, site S_1 sends support counts set {420, 417, and 406} to site S_2 that subtracts the random number R_2 and sends support counts to site S_3. After subtracting random number R_3, site S_3 finds the global-support counts {20, 17, and 6} and discovers global-frequent itemsets. Since the global candidate itemset support is an aggregation of all local candidate support counts, it is not possible for site S_3 to discover the exact support counts of the other sites (i.e., S_1 and S_2) from the global support of resultant candidate itemset.

Table 2. Deobfuscation phase

Local Support at Different Sites			Random Number		D_S	Adjacent Site		
Site	Name	ΣO_S	Name	R	$\Sigma O_S - R$	Site	Name	PD_S
S_1	AB	520	AB	100	420	S_2	AB	420
	AC	517	AC	100	417		AC	417
	BC	506	BC	100	406		BC	406
S_2	AB	-	AB	200	220	S_3	AB	220
	AC	-	AC	200	217		AC	217
	BC	-	BC	200	206		BC	206
S_3	AB	-	AB	200	20	S_1, S_2	AB	20
	AC	-	AC	200	17		AC	17
	BC	-	BC	200	6		BC	6

One of the important outcomes of the proposed method is that it minimizes the collusion problem. The collusion problem can be defined as: when several participating parties in the chain collude, to find the private support inputs of the other party. Since our proposed method obfuscates candidate support counts of each participating site with a random number, that random number is added/subtracted from global-obfuscated-candidate itemset support on that particular site, in order to perform deobfuscation, it requires n-1 sites of the chain to collude to find out the exact support count of any site S_i. In compare with of the other method for example, (Kantarcioglu & Clifton, 2004) any two parties such as S_i and S_{i+2} can collude to extract the private inputs of the other site S_{i+1}.

Algorithms

A general distributed-association-mining algorithm has three distinct phases: (1) generates support for local-candidate itemset, (2) sends those candidate itemsets or the local frequent itemset to other sites and (3) generates global-frequent itemset. Our proposed method works in the same manner, but obfuscates and deobfuscate at every step. The pseudocode of the proposed obfuscation phase is shown in the algorithm 1. Let us now discuss various steps of that phase:

- **Step 1:** In the beginning, all sites generate local frequent 1-itemsets based on the enhanced Apriori algorithm presented in the previous chapter. After generating frequent 1-itemset, each site generates a random number $\mathbb{R}$ then to obfuscate it add/subtract $\mathbb{R}$ from the candidate support count. For example, suppose 'A' is candidate 1-itemset and the corresponding support at site S_I is equal to 10. Suppose site S_I generates a random number 100 and to obfuscate the exact support of itemset 'A' it adds that random with that candidate support. Finally sends obfuscated to the adjacent site.

- **Step 2:** The adjacent site receives the obfuscate-candidate support and it adds its own obfuscate support with that and sends it to the next adjacent site. For example, suppose it receives obfuscate support 110 for candidate itemset 'A'. After obfuscating the local support of candidate itemset 'A', suppose obfuscate support of itemset 'A' becomes 220. Then it add these two numbers, now the obfuscate support of itemset 'A' becomes 330 and sends that to the next adjacent site.

- **Step 3:** This procedure continues until the obfuscated supports reach the last participating site; it adds its own obfuscate support with the obfuscate support it receives from the adjacent site. Then it sends that global obfuscated support to the first site where the obfuscation process was started.

Algorithm 1.

```
1.  while (C_k ≠ {}) do
2.      for all transaction t' ∈ T
3.          for all k-subsets X ∈ C_k
4.              if (X ⊆ t')
5.                  X.support++;
6.              end if;
7.          end for;
8.      end for;
        //obfuscate local candidate itemset support
9.      for all itemset e ∈ C_k
10.         R ← generateRandomNumber ();
12.         O ← e ± R;
12.     end for;
        //each site send obfuscate support to adjacent site
13.     for all site s_i ∈ S
14.         O_{s_i} ← { O_{s_i} | O_{s_i} + O_{s_{i-1}} };
15.         sendToAdjacent (O_{s_i});
16.     end for;
        //each site add/subtract its own R from global obfuscate sup.
17.     for all site s_i ∈ S
18.         O_G ← deObfuscate (O_G,R);
19.         sendToAdjacent (O_G);
20.     end for;
        // generates global frequent itemset
21.         GF_k ← { X | X.support ≥ σ }
            broadCast (GF_k);
22.     k++;
        // generates candidate itemset
23.         C_k ← {Candidate k-itemset};
24. end do;
```

- **Step 4:** After receiving global obfuscate candidate itemset support, it starts the deobfuscate phase and adds/subtracts the random number with the global obfuscate support and sends it to the adjacent site. For example, suppose it receives global obfuscate support for itemset '*A*' as 550. Since it adds its own random number 100 with the exact support of local itemset '*A*,' it subtracts that random number from the global obfuscate support and sends it to the adjacent site.

- **Step 5:** This deobfuscation process continues until it reaches the last participating sites. Since all participating sites deobfuscate their own random number with global-obfuscate-candidate-itemset support, it finds the exact global support of each candidate itemset. Subsequently it generates global-frequent itemset. Finally, it broadcasts those global-frequent itemset of all participating sites.

- **Step 6:** After receiving global-frequent itemsets, each site generates a candidate itemset for the next iteration and continues the same process for all different lengths of candidate itemsets until there is no more global candidate itemset.

Message Optimization

In distributed-association-rule mining, exchanging messages among different participating sites are widely considered one of the main tasks (Schuster 2001; Cheung, Ng, Fu, & Fu, 1996; Zaki, 1999). Thus, message optimization becomes an integral part of distributed-association-rule mining algorithms. However, in this chapter we presented a novel secure multiparty computation-based technique that intends to maintain the privacy of each participating site's while they share their private input during global-frequent itemset generation task. To maintain privacy of each participating site, it generates the global-frequent itemset of any iteration in three rounds and in each round each site exchanges messages with other participating sites thus posing communication overhead. To reduce the message-exchange size, we propose further modification of our method, which, does not fully comply with the aforementioned method that is obfuscation and deobfuscation for every iteration. It follows that method only to discover global-frequent 1-itemset. After that, each site uses a function $f(x)$ as shown in formula 1, to obfuscate the candidate itemset support counts by utilizing local subset itemset support count of those global-frequent itemsets, rather than a random number. Since the frequent itemset has a number of subset itemset, and when obfuscation is accomplished using (i.e., added/subtracted from the exact support of a candidate itemset) the local support counts of all subset itemsets of a global-frequent itemset, and sent to the adjacent site then from that obfuscate candidate itemset support the adjacent site unable to drive the exact support of any candidate itemset. For example, suppose 'A' and 'B' are two global-frequent 1-itemsets, and '$A\ B$' is a candidate itemset of current iteration. If any site obfuscate the exact support of '$A\ B$' with the local support of subset itemset such as 'A' and 'B' and sent that obfuscate candidate support to the adjacent site then the adjacent site is unable to discover the exact support of '$A\ B$' itemset.

$$f(x) = O_S \pm C_S \tag{1}$$

where O_S is the exact support count of a n-itemset and C_S is the sum of n number of local support of (n-1)-itemset.

After generating the obfuscated-candidate-support counts, each site sends those obfuscate support counts of all candidate itemsets to the adjacent site in the same manner as the obfuscation phase described in a previous section, until it reaches in the last site such as S_n. When the site S_n receives those obfuscate-candidate supports, it computes the global support of those candidate itemsets using Formula 2 and subsequently finds the global-frequent itemset for that iteration. Finally, site S_n sends back the global-frequent itemset to all other participating sites. Since the last site S_n always discovers all frequent itemsets, for simplicity we named that site as *receiver* and all remaining participating sites as a *sender*. For example, suppose there are four sites such as S_1, S_2, S_3 and S_4 collaborating in distributed-association-rule mining, here we assume the former three sites obfuscate candidate support counts and send those obfuscate supports to an adjacent site as mentioned in the previous section. The remaining site that is S_4, which receives aggregate of obfuscate candidate itemset support from all participating sender sites and generates global-frequent itemset is considered as a receiver.

$$G_S = \sum_{i=1}^{n} f(x) \pm F_S \tag{2}$$

where G_S is the global-support count of a n-itemset and F_S is the sum of n number of global support of $(n-1)$-itemset. The sum of local support of an itemset is equal to the global support of that itemset. So one can easily prove that:

$$F_S = \sum_{i=1}^{n} C_S \,.$$

As a result, when we add or subtract F_S from:

$$\sum_{i=1}^{n} f(x) \,,$$

it gives us the exact global support of an itemset. To illustrate the abovementioned procedure, let us consider the following example:

Example 2: *Suppose there are three collaborating sites such as S_1, S_2 as sender and S_3 as receiver. After the first iteration, suppose it discovers {A, B, and C} as the global-frequent 1-itemsets the corresponding support is shown in the Table 9.3. Then each site generates candidate itemsets and their corresponding support. In order to obfuscate the support count of each candidate itemset, at first site S_1 uses formula 1 (for each candidate n-itemset, C_S is the addition of local support counts of all (n-1)-itemsets, example, local support of itemset 'A' and 'B' for candidate itemset 'AB') and sends those obfuscated support count to the adjacent site S_2. Then* *site S_2 aggregates its own obfuscated-candidate-itemset support with the obfuscated support it receives from site S_1 and sends that to the receiver sites S_3. Since the receiver site receives only the value of $f(x)$, this does not tell the exact support count of an itemset. It is only able to discover the global support of each candidate itemset by using Formula 2. As a result, we will be able to eliminate the deobfuscation phase of our proposed method and reduce the message-exchange size.*

Complexity Analysis

In this section, we analyze the message exchange size of our proposed privacy-preserving distributed-association-rule mining technique. As mentioned earlier, the proposed methods need three rounds to compute global-frequent 1-itemsets. However, after a method generates the global-frequent 1-itemset, it adopts a new technique and when all obfuscate candidate support reaches the last participating site of the chain, that site is able to discover the exact global support of all the candidate itemsets (please note the exact support of the candidate itemset of any participating sites). Thus, that site, also known as the receiver, is able to generate the global-frequent itemsets for that pass. Subsequently, it sends the global-frequent itemset to all participating sites, which are also known as sender sites. Since all sender sites obfuscate the support of each itemset using Formula 1, sends obfuscated support to the receiver sites; the receiver site is unable to generate the exact support of any itemset and it only can generate the global support of all itemsets. The total number

Table 3. Example

Global Frequent k-Itemset		Local Support at Different sites			Candidate $k+1$-Itemset		$f(x)$			Global $k+1$-Itemset		
Name	F_S				Name	O_S	C_S	$O_S + C_S$	Name	$\Sigma f(x)$	G_S
A	150	S_1	A	70	AB	10	120	130			
			B	50	AC	25	105	130	AB	335	60
			C	35	BC	30	85	115			
B	125	S_2	A	40	AB	25	85	110			
			B	45	AC	40	75	115	AC	370	90
			C	35	BC	20	80	100			
C	130	S_3	A	40	AB	25	70	95			
			B	30	AC	25	100	125	BC	315	60
			C	60	BC	10	90	100			

of messages each participating sender site sends to a receiver site is equal to $(1 * |C|)$. We can calculate the total message size using the Formula 3.

$$T_{sender} = \sum_{i=1}^{n} (n-1) * C \qquad (3)$$

where, n is the total number of sites and C is number of candidate itemsets.

Once the receiver site generates global-frequent itemsets, it broadcasts those item-sets to all sender sites. The total number of messages broadcast from the receiver is equal to $(n-1 * |F_G|)$. Thus, the total message-exchange size can be calculated by using the following formula 4:

$$T_{messages} = T_{sender} + (n-1) * F_G \qquad (4)$$

where, n is the number of sites, C is the candidate itemsets and F_G is the global-frequent itemsets.

> **Example 3:** *Suppose there are three sites S_1, S_2, and S_3. After the first iteration, let us consider the set of global-frequent 1-itemsets is equal to {A, B, and C}. Thus, the candidate itemset of the next iteration is equal to {AB, AC, and BC}. If we consider sites S_1 and S_2 as senders and site S_3 as the receiver, then after the second iteration the support counts of S_1 first obfuscated and sent that obfuscated-candidate-itemset support to the site S_2. The site S_2 adds its obfuscate support with the obfuscate support it receives from the site S_1 then sent to the receiver site S_3 where the global-frequent itemset of this iteration will be generated. Consider the global-frequent itemsets of this iteration are equal to {AB and BC}, and site S_3 will then broadcast them to all sender sites. If we calculate the total message size using the Formulas 3 and 4, then we found the proposed method needs only 10 messages.*

Performance Measurement

We have done an extensive performance study on our proposed message-reduction techniques to confirm our analysis of their effectiveness. The client-server-based distributed environment is established in order to evaluate the message-optimiza-

Table 4. Dataset characteristics

Name	Transaction Size avg.	Number of Distinct Items	Number of Records
Cover Type	55	120	581012
Connect-4	43	130	67557
BMS-WEB-View-1	2	497	59602
BMS-WEB-View-2	5	3340	75512

tion technique. Initial evaluation was carried out on four different sites. Each site has a receiving and a sending unit and listens to a specific port in order to send and receive the support counts.

We have also implemented a sequential association-mining algorithm using Java 1.4 and replicate the algorithm to four different sites in order to generate candidate-support counts of each site. Each site generates a random number using a pseudo-random-number generator to obfuscate support counts.

Four real datasets are chosen for this evaluation study. Table 2 shows the characteristics of the datasets that are used in this evaluation. It shows the number of items, the average size of each transaction, and the number of transactions of each dataset. Cover Type and Connect-4 dataset are taken from the UC Irvine Machine Learning Dataset Repository (Blake & Merz, 1998) whereas BMS-Webview-1 and BMS-Webview-2 are real-world datasets containing several months' worth of click-stream data from an e-commerce Web site and are made publicly available by the Blue Martini Software (Kohavi, Broadley, Frasca, Mason, & Zheng, 2000).

To deploy a distributed-association-mining algorithm, we divide all datasets into four different partitions and assign to them four different sites. In order to reduce

Table 5. Accuracy

Dataset	Supports	No of Sites	Total No. of Global Frequent Itemsets		Accuracy
			DMA	PPDAM	
Cover Type	0.2% 0.4% 0.6%	4 4 4	166171 216018 305485	166171 216018 305485	100% 100% 100%
Connect-4	75% 80% 85%	4 4 4	1612127 541591 144751	1612127 541591 144751	100% 100% 100%
BMS-Webview-1	0.068% 0.074% 0.08%	4 4 4	752076 61955 20800	752076 61955 20800	100% 100% 100%
BMS-Webview-2	0.06% 0.067% 0.075%	4 4 4	86391 67072 52678	86391 67072 52678	100% 100% 100%

identical transactions among different sites, each of these partitioned datasets was generated in such a way that each partition has 75% of the transactions of the original dataset.

Accuracy

The accuracy is one of the main objectives of data mining. Our proposed method obfuscates and deobfuscates the candidate itemset support count during the mining process. For simplicity, here we name our methods as privacy-preserving distributed-association-rule mining (PPDAM). Since the obfuscation process distort the original support of each itemset therefore, create new requirements to show whether the PPDAM can generate the same number of global-frequent itemsets when we generate the global-frequent itemsets in traditional distribute association rule mining approach. Table 5 shows the accuracy of our proposed approach in global-frequent itemsets generation. From the table, it is clear that our proposed method generates the same number of global-frequent itemsets as the traditional approaches. Thus, the accuracy of our method is the same as that of the traditional approach.

Message-Exchange Size

Reducing the message-exchange size is one of the main aspects of all distributed-association-rule-mining algorithms and privacy-preserving distributed-association-rule mining indents to reduce overall communication cost. Perhaps, one of the key performance improvements sought in various distributed-association-rule mining algorithms (Agrawal & Shafer, 1996; Cheung et al., 1996) is on message optimization. As these algorithms are based on the sequential Apriori algorithm (Agrawal & Srikant, 1994), or extensions of it, the performance varies due to the message-broadcasting technique. The intention behind distributed-association mining is to reduce communication cost. Hence, those improvements are a significant achievement in the context of distributed-association mining (Ashrafi, 2004a).

In addition, all existing privacy-preserving distributed-association-rule-mining algorithms (Evfimievski et al., 2002; Kantercioglu & Clifton, 2002; Vaidya et al., 2002;) are derived from well-known algorithms such as count distribution (CD) and Distributed Mining Association (DMA) rule (Cheung et al., 1996). Those derived algorithms work in the same manner except those algorithms involved in extra communication to generate a global-rule model. Therefore, the efficiency of our proposed method over those existing privacy-preserving distributed-association-rule-mining algorithms will be clearly illustrated if we compare our proposed PPDAM with the original algorithms where those privacy-preserving distributed-association-rule-mining algorithms have their foundation.

Figure 4. Message exchange size

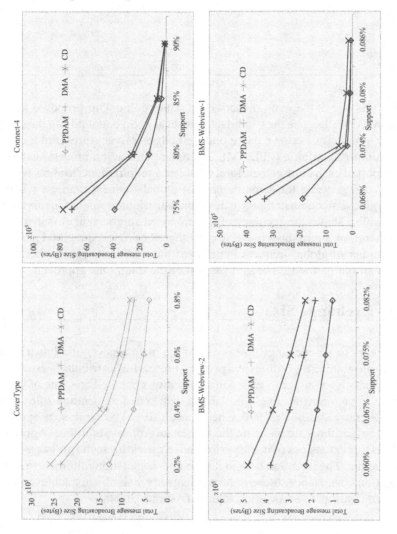

Figure 4 depicts the total size of messages (i.e., number of bytes) exchanged by PPDAM, DMA, and CD in order to generate global-frequent itemsets from different datasets as mentioned earlier. Depending on the characteristics of each dataset, we vary the minimum-support threshold value. To generate a reasonable number of global-frequent itemsets, we use a very high support threshold for a dense dataset and a low support threshold for a sparse dataset. The message size was measured by assuming 4 bytes for each support counts and 2 bytes for each candidate itemset name. Similar assumptions are also made for other distributed-association-rule mining algorithms.

From the above comparison between PPDAM, DMA, and CD as plotted in Figure 4, it is clear that the PPDAM algorithm exchanges fewer messages. Indeed, in all cases PPDAM reduces communication cost by 60-80% compared to CD. The PP-DAM algorithm obfuscates and deobfuscates the candidate itemset support at the initial iteration. However, after the first iteration, it only obfuscates candidate itemset support and does not need deobfuscation. Thus able to generate global-frequent itemset, it sends candidate support to a receiver site where the frequent itemset of that iteration will be generated. Finally, the receiver site will send back only the global-frequent itemset to all sender sites. On the contrary, using a CD algorithm, each site exchanges messages with all other sites after every pass, and hence the message-exchange size increases when we increase the number of sites. In contrast, PPDAM transmits 25-50% less messages compared with DMA. DMA algorithm exchanges more messages because the polling site sends and receives support counts from remote sites. Further, it sends the support count of the global-frequent itemset to all sites. Consequently, it increases the message size. On the other hand, using our proposed method, each site sends its support counts to a single site and receives the global-frequent support count from a single site. Hence, it reduces the number of broadcasting operations. Furthermore, the local pruning technique of DMA effectively works only when different sites have vertically fragmented sparse datasets. However, this will not be able to prune a significant number of candidate itemsets when each site uses horizontal fragmented datasets.

Conclusion

Distributed-association-rule mining has the ability to find out patterns beyond the organization boundaries. However, discovery of such patterns from various participating sites has statistical meaning and may often disclose some sensitive information. Thus, privacy-preserving mining of association rules becomes one of the active research issues in recent years. On the other hand, maintaining privacy in distributed-association-rule mining is more difficult than the centralized approach. To maintain the private inputs of each participating site in this chapter, we propose a methodology that efficiently generates distributed-association rules without revealing the support counts of each site. The proposed method generates global-association rules without revealing confidential inputs such as statistical properties (i.e., support of each item) of individual sites. It employs a secure multiparty computation-based technique that keeps the private inputs of each participating site secret when all participating sites generate the global-frequent itemset.

One of the important outcomes of the proposed techniques is that the private inputs of each participating site remain secure but each site knows the exact global-frequent support of each itemset. Thus, each site is able to generate association rules based on the exact global support of an itemset. The resultant rule model generated by this proposed method is the same as if one generates it using some of the well-known distributed/parallel algorithms. In addition, the proposed method does not distort the original dataset and for this reason, it diminishes the reconstruction problem, which is raised when we distort transactions of a dataset by using different randomization techniques.

The communication cost is an important issue in distributed-association-rule mining. Since distributed-association mining communicates with other participating sites to generate the global-frequent itemsets and the communication cost increase when none of the participating sites divulge their private inputs to other sites. However, our proposed technique is able to discover all global-frequent itemsets without revealing the private inputs of each participating site but incurring minimal communication among the participating sites. Nevertheless, the performance evaluation shows that the overall communication cost incurred by our proposed method is less than those of CD and DMA algorithms.

References

Agrawal, R., Imielinski, T., & Srikant R. (1993). Mining association rules between sets of items in large databases. In *Proceeding of ACM SIGMOD* (pp. 207-216).

Agrawal, R., & Srikant, R. (1994). Fast algorithms for mining association rules in large database. In *Proceedings of the 20th International Conference on Very Large Databases* (pp. 407-419).

Agrawal, R., & Shafer, J. C. (1996). Parallel mining of association rules. *IEEE Transactions on Knowledge and Data Engineering, 8*(6), 962-969.

Ashrafi, M. Z., Taniar, D., & Smith, K. A. (2004a). ODAM: An optimized distributed association rule mining algorithm. *IEEE Distributed Systems Online*.

Ashrafi, M. Z., Taniar, D., & Smith, K. A. (2004b). Reducing communication cost in privacy preserving distributed association rule mining. In *Proceedings Database Systems for Advanced Applications, Lecture Notes in Computer Science Springer-Verlag* (pp. 381-392).

Atallah, M., Bertino, E., Elmagarmid, A., Ibrahim, M., & Verykios, V. (1999). Disclosure limitation of sensitive rules. In *Proceedings of the IEEE Knowledge and Data Engineering Exchange Workshop KDEX*.

Blake, C. L., & Merz, C. J. (1998). *UCI Repository of Machine Learning Databases*. University of California, Irvine, Department of Information and Computer Science. Retrieved January 1, 2005, from www.ics.uci.edu/~mlearn/MLRepository.html

Cheung, D. W., Ng, V. T., Fu, A. W., & Fu, Y. (1996). Efficient mining of association rules in distributed databases. *IEEE Transactions on Knowledge and Data Engineering, 8*(6), 911-922.

Dasseni, E., Verykios, V. S., Elmagarmid, A. K., & Bertino, E. (2001). Hiding association rules by using confidence and support. In *Proceedings of the Intl. Information Hiding Workshop*.

Evfimievski, A., Srikant, R., Agrawal, R., & Gehrke J. (2002). Privacy preserving mining association rules. In *Proceedings of the SIGKDDD* (pp. 217-228).

Goldriech, O. (2001). Secure multipart computation. *Working Draft Version 1.3.*

Kantercioglu M., & Clifton C. (2002). Privacy preserving distributed mining of association rules on horizontal partitioned data. In *Proceedings of ACM SIGMOD Workshop of Research Issues in Data Mining and Knowledge Discovery (DMKD)*.

Klemettinen, M., Mannila, H., Ronkainen, P., Toivonen, H., & Verkamo, A. I. (1994). Finding interesting rules from large sets of discovered association rules. In *Proceedings of the International Conference on Information and Knowledge Management* (pp. 401-407).

Kohavi, R., Broadley, C., Frasca, B., Mason, L., & Zheng, Z. (2000). KDD-cup 2000 organizers report: Peeling the onion. *SIGKDD Explorations, 2*(2), 86-98.

Rizvi, S. J., & Haritsa, J. R. (2002). Maintaining data privacy in association rule mining. In *Proceedings of 20th International Conference on Very Large Databases* (pp. 682-693).

Schuster, A., & Wolff, R. (2001). Communication-efficient distributed mining of association rules. In *Proceedings of the ACM SIGMOD international conference on management of data* (pp. 473-484).

Vaidya, J., & Clifton, C. (2002). Privacy preserving association rule mining in vertically partitioned data. In *Proceedings of ACM SIGKDD* (pp. 639-644).

Zaki, M. J. (1999). Parallel and distributed association mining: A survey. *IEEE Concurrency, 7*(4), 14-25.

Chapter XII

A Generic Internet Trading Framework for Online Auctions

Dong-Qing Yao, Towson University, USA

Haiying Qiao, University of Maryland, USA

Haibing Qiao, FileNet Corporation, USA

Abstract

In this chapter, we introduce a generic Internet trading framework for online auctions. We present the requirements and service of the framework. A generic OR/XOR bidding language that can express different OR/XOR combinations is adopted for Web interfaces. The framework is implemented with free open-source technologies already successfully tested in industries. Researchers can use the platform to implement different electronic-market mechanisms, simulate the market behavior of their interests, and experiment with it. We also provide future directions for the framework design.

Introduction

Due to its distinguishing characteristics such as lower operational cost, long duration, and no geographical limitation, online auction has been a rapidly growing success of Internet technology (Ariely & Simonson, 2003). According to Forrester Research, online auction will account for $54 billion or around 25% of total online retail sale by 2007, and will reach $65 billion by 2010. There are different categories for online auction. For example, Bapna, Goes, and Gupta (2001) categorized online auction into three dimensions: business-to-consumer (B2C), consumer-to-consumer (C2C), and business-to-business (B2B); Based on the number of sellers and buyers, Pinker, Seidmann, and Vakrat (2003) further categorize online auction into four segments, namely bilateral negotiations, Web-based procurements, Web-based sales auctions, and Web-based exchange. The most well-known online auction site may be E-bay, where all different types of products can be auctioned; among them are books, apparel, electronics, computers and software, and more.

It is almost impossible to solve a real online auction problem theoretically due to the complexity of problems. For example, bid award criteria could be multidimensional, not only just the price, but also the other attributes such as quality, lot size, and transportation service. Especially for perishable items such as sports ticketa, or flowers, a decision should be made in very short time. Therefore, many researchers turn to experiments or simulations for online auction study. For example, McCabe, Rassenti, and Smith (1991) tested traditional Vickrey's and other simultaneous multiple-unit versions of the English auction. Ba and Pavlou (2002) examined the data from online experiment and online-auction market to test the trust issue in electronic markets. Banks, Olson, Porter, Rassenti, and Smith (2003) ran an experiment on the simultaneous multiround auction (SMA) to assign spectrum licenses used by FCC, reported SMA's several defects, and compared SMA's results with combinatorial auction. Bapna, Goes, and Gupta (2003) presented a simulation approach to study the decision spaces for both auctioneers and bidders. Their simulation was demonstrated for Yankee auction with the objective to optimize the bidder's revenue. Rafaeli and Avi (2005) used a lab experiment to find the social presence (virtual presence and interpersonal information) has significant effects on online English and Dutch auctions. Vragov (2005) used experiments to study E-bay's online-auction procedures and found that collusive behavior exists among buyers that decrease prices and lower efficiency. Gopal, Thompson, Tung, and Whinston (2005) introduced auction options that enable the sellers and buyers to manage their risks respectively, and they adopted simulation approach for the seller to assess the impacts of these auction options on the online-auction market. Gregg and Walczak (2006) developed an auction advisor agent system to help collect data and make decisions. They used simulation and experiment to validate the auction-advisor-agent system.

A potential problem of these experiments and simulations is that customized auction software has to be developed for each of them. A reusable auction software platform is needed for researchers to quickly design a prototype and develop different auction mechanisms to test and experiment with different ideas. So far, some research auction software has been developed on the Internet. For example, FM 96.5 (Rodriguez-Aguilar, Noriega, Sierra, & Padget 1997) is an electronic auction house that is a complete implementation of the trading conventions of the fish market, which allows for a real-time concurrent operation of the complete fish-market auction process. The Michigan Internet AuctionBot (Wurman, Wellman & Walsh, 1998) is a configurable auction server, where classic auctions such as English auctions, Dutch auctions, Vickery auctions, and sealed auctions can be implemented by different configurations. eAuctionHouse (Sandholm, 2002) is an auction server based on the eMediator server developed by CMU. Instead of implementing the classic auctions, eAuctionHouse focuses more on combinatorial auctions. It also implements the XOR of OR bidding language and includes CABOB algorithm to solve the winner determination problem. Other researchers focus on how to solve the problems that could happen during the auction processes such as those involving security, privacy, trust, and fraud. Secure auction marketplace (SAM) architecture (http://www.ece.cmu.edu/~adrian /projects SAM/ a2.html) is a framework to address such issues.

However all the above products limit users to the auction mechanism that can support. Auction designers cannot define auctions as they want with current auction software. To this end, we introduce a reusable software auction framework and platform in an attempt to run different types of auctions and exchanges. The main purpose of this platform is to provide an auction software platform and framework where researchers can quickly develop, deploy, experiment, and simulate different auction mechanisms.

Requirements and Services of Our Framework

The auction process is a marketing mechanism to discover the market equilibrium. This process sometimes is not efficient if it is done in a single round. For example, FCC uses the simultaneous multiround auction to sell spectrum license. For a multitem auction, it is popular to use multiround in an auction. An auction framework should have built-in multiround auction support.

It will be challenging for an individual auction-software platform to support all different types of auctions. Therefore, instead of implementing configurable auction software as Michigan Auctionbot, we generalize and implement the fundamental auction activities and leave some implementation details to specific auctions. With our approach, the framework only abstracts and implements the general activities. Key elements of a typical auction are summarized in Table 1.

Table 1. Key elements of an auction

Auction Element	Key Function or Responsibility
Auctioneer	Create and run auctions
Bid taker	Add auction items and specify the winning rule
Bid item	The object in the auction
Bidder	One who bids for one or more bid items
Bidding language	Used for expressing the preferences of a bidder's bid, including price and conditions
Auction Mechanism	Specify how to run the auction.
Information Revelation	The mechanism to release different levels of information to bidders.
Winner determination	The algorithm to find the winning bid.
Communications	The interactions between the bidders and bid takers.

Next, we list all key features that an auction platform is supposed to support, which are implemented in our platform:

1. **Bid item:**

   - The platform should support different kinds of auction items. From basketball ticket to air spectrum, all auctions of different kinds of goods should be supported by the platform. Although it is possible to create an auction to sell any items on eBay.com, the item specification cannot be clearly defined. For example, you cannot search two tickets whose seats are next to each other on eBay.com.

   - The platform should support single and multiple auction items. This support is important since the obvious benefit of combinatorial auction has attracted more and more researchers. A simple but powerful bidding language that fits the Internet technology should be developed to let bidder place a package bid easily.

2. **Auction mechanism:**

   - The platform should support multiround auctions. A new round should be trigged in different ways, for example, triggered by scheduled time, specific event, or manual initiation.

   - The platform should be able to specify different auction rules for different auctions or rounds. A different mechanism can be plugged into different rounds.

3. **Bidding language:**

- The platform should support different kinds of bid formats and a flexible bidding language. A flexible, succinct, and expressive bidding language is very important for a generic auction platform.

4. **Winner determination algorithm:**

- The platform should allow different algorithms to be plugged into a clear auction or auction round. It should be able to run multiple algorithms simultaneously to compare the performance among them.

5. **Bidder and bidder taker:**

- The platform should support multiseller and multibuyer exchanges in the same auction.

6. **Information revelation mechanism:**

- The platform should take into account different kinds/levels of information revelation mechanism. Since an auction is a game, different information revelation mechanisms have significant impacts on the bidder's valuation, strategy, and auction efficiency. Therefore, the platform should provide convenient ways for an auction designer to deliver different information to bidders. For example, auction can deliver bid information or results to different bidders at a scheduled time.

7. **Communication:**

- The platform should support bidding through the Web by bidders and bidding through software agent.
- The integration with a current enterprise system may also be needed to provide real-time information.

Additionally, the platform should also provide necessary services so that the auction designer can focus on a specific auction mechanism design instead of dealing with the details of software implementations:

8. **Security and access control:**

- The platform should build in security. Although the security is not of critical concern in this framework, some access control such as bidders' privileges and sellers' access privileges should be defined and implemented.

9. **Data-persistence service:**

- The platform should provide data persistence and retrieval service. The service is important, especially for data analysis and presentation.

10. **Task scheduling:**

   - The platform should provide the capability to let participants schedule different tasks; for example, auction close task can be scheduled to certain time or certain events happen.

11. **Web publishing:**

   - An important driver of the popularity of the auction is Internet technology. It is important that the auction framework should support the quick development and deployment on the Web.

For a multi-item auction, a challenging task is how to place a bid. An auction platform should also provide a simple, expressive, and user-friendly bidding language compatible with Web applications and be easy to use. Again, the bidding language should be generic enough so that auction designers have the freedom to design their own bidding structures. In the next section, we propose our composite bidding language specially designed for Web applications.

Bidding Language for Multi-Item Auctions

For a single item English auction, the bidding language is very simple: A bidder may just specify the price that the bidder wants to pay. For a Dutch auction, a bid just needs to specify whether the bidder will take the item at the current price or not, the auction ends when someone submits such a bid.

However, when an auction includes multiple items, whether the items are identical or nonidentical, a bid can be very complicated if the bidder is allowed to bid combinations of items. The exponential number of the possible combinations will make the computation intractable. Nisan (2000) analyzed different kinds of bidding languages. He defined an atomic bid as one which includes a subset of bid items and the associated price. He also formally defined six bidding languages: OR-bids, XOR-bids, OR of XOR bids, XOR of ORs, OR/XOR-formulae, and OR*-bids. The first four languages are the special types of OR/XOR-formulae. OR*-bids can represent all other types by using phantom items. Sandholm (2002) implemented two auction languages in the eAuctionHouse: the XOR bidding language and the OR-of-XOR, which is more convenient than traditional OR bidding language.

Although these languages can express a bid, sometime it is not succinct enough due to the simple definition of an atomic bid. For example, suppose three items (A, B, C) are totally substitutable, the bidder wants to bid on any two of them at price of 2. If using XOR language, the bid will be as follows:

(A, B, 2) XOR (A, C, 2) XOR (B, C, 2)

If atomic can be defined with more flexible expression, the bid can be easily expressed as:

((A, B, C), 2, 2)

where the first "2" means any two-item set. The second "2" is the price. If the size of the items is large, the benefit is tremendous since it can significantly reduce the size of the expression. Auction designers can interpret the language as they wish because they can normally define such bidding language.

By generalizing the atomic bid, the platform allows richer and more convenient input languages without losing expressive power. Other atomic-bid formats may allow bidders to specify step-wise and continuous curve demand functions.

As a general framework, our platform takes into account this flexibility since the main purpose of the framework is to provide a platform where auction designers can play different auction mechanisms and different algorithms. To implement the OR/XOR-formulae, we introduce the concept of a composite bid and expand Nisan's definition of atomic bid as follows:

An auction designer specifies an *Atomic bid*. It can be different kinds of bids such as a package bid, a matrix bid (Day & Raghavan, 2003), step-wise quantity bid, and so on.

Figure 1. Illustration of a composite bid

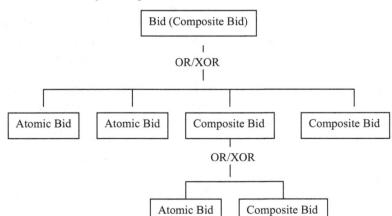

A *Composite bid* is a collection of atomic bids and composite bids, with the relationship (OR or XOR) between the atomic bids and composite bids.

Figure 1 shows the bid structure of the composite bidding language.

From the diagram, we can see that the atomic bid and composite bid can be combined together with different OR/XOR relations. So it can easily implement OR-bids, XOR-bids, OR of XOR bids, XOR of Ors, OR/XOR-formulae bids through different combinations of composite bids and atomic bids.

A composite bid is implemented using a design pattern called a Composite pattern (Gamma, Helm, Johnson, & Vlissides, 1995). Each composite bid has two or more composite bids or atomic bids, and the relationship between them can be defined as OR, XOR, or any kind of relationship that the auction designer defines.

Framework Design

Although there are different types of auctions, some relationships between components in an auction are very static. Figure 2 shows the high level relationship between the components in an auction.

From Figure 2, it can be seen that an auction system has the following components:

Figure 2. High-level component relationship

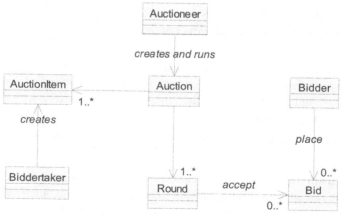

1.   **Auction:** The exchange where the auction takes place.

2.   **Auctioneer:** who creates, runs, and ends an auction.

3.   **Bidtaker:** who places auction items in an auction.

4.   **Bidder:** who places bid(s) on items in the auction.

5.   **Auction round:** An auction may have one or more rounds. An auction round can be a sealed auction or an iterative auction.

6.   **Auction item:** An auction has one or more auction items.

7.   **Bid:** Bidders can place one or more bids on the auction.

The implementation concept of the platform is to specify and implement the high-level relationships, generic attributes, and behaviors of these components, but leave the details of a different auction design including user interfaces to auction designers.

All components include two different kinds of attributes: *general attributes* and *specific attributes*. General attributes are attributes that a component has in most cases, whereas specific attributes are attributes that are unique to an individual or specific auction. For example, auction name and start time are general attributes of auction components while the auction rules such as whether there is a reserve price are different for different auctions.

General attributes are defined as attributes in class components. All specific attributes of these components can be described using XML. The auction developer can extend the components to manipulate these specific data. Good Web interfaces or agent interfaces are needed to create these specific attributes easily.

By using XML, we can describe any specific attributes of an auction item, auction rules, information revelation mechanism, and so on. An auction designer designs the XML schema, understands the meaning of these attributes, and processes these data as needed while the platform has no knowledge of these data, but it can run these auctions according to the high-level activities and rules specified by these auctions.

To facilitate communication, a Web service may be applied, and all components in the auction may register themselves to a central service registry. Before any two components communicate with each other, they may communicate with the registration server through WSDL.

Currently we have defined six framework level activities as shown in Figure 2.

1.   **Create an auction:** An auctioneer can create an auction in the auction container. He or she can specify general auction information, specific auction information, and auction rules. As mentioned above, the auction information is auction specific. It is auction designer's responsibility to describe the information and

digest the information in the later stage. The framework provides the service of storing and retrieving such information. Once the auction is created, the auctioneer can also specify when it becomes available to the bidders. The auction framework also provides the service to automate such kinds of rules.

2. **Create a round and specify round information:** The auction creator can specify the auction round information such as the round numbers, round schedules, round proceeding rules, and so on. Each auction has at least one round. After a round ends, the results or information of the last round should be sent to the bidder. The auction framework provides real time and an off-line message service. In a classroom setting, the students will be notified through an applet running on each browser. If a round takes a longer time, the bidder can be notified through email.

3. **Add auction items:** Sellers can add one or more items to an auction. Again, they can specify general and specific information of an item. Although E-bay also supports the auction of different kinds of the items, it does this through classification. The different information of an item is organized and searched through this classified information. The problem of this method is that it is too rigidand needs huge catalog, which is impossible for our framework. Auction design needs all the flexibility to specify the auction item to meet the requirements of the auction.

4. **Place bids:** Bidders can place one or more bids on an auction. The auction designer should carefully design the bidding language and bidding interface. A generic bidding-language implementation for combinatorial auctions is described in the previous section. The procedures and interfaces have been designed to create a composite bid. The auction designer does not necessarily have to use the bidding language. The platform supports any XML-based bidding language. However, extra efforts are needed to create and translate such bids.

5. **Information revelation:** During the process of an auction, the system can deliver different kinds of information about the scheduled time, upon some event's or bidder's request. The auction designer can determine what information and how to deliver it to the bidder. The platform provides the communication service to release such information.

6. **Clearing:** Clearing may happen at the end of each round or the end of the auction. A different algorithm can be plugged into the clearing activities. How to define and implement algorithms are the responsibilities of an auction designer.

The auction platform architecture is shown in Figure 3.

Figure 3. Architecture overview

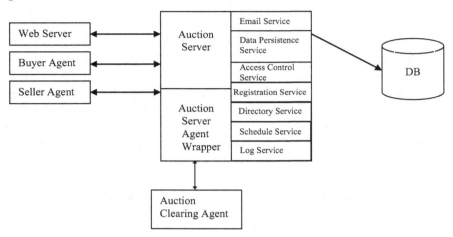

The components of the system are described as follows:

- **Auction server:** handles most basic activities as describe before. It also provides a service interface for the client to communicate with the server. The auction service is implemented as a Web service, as discussed before. The server provides the basic auction service, so it is generic enough to support different types of auctions. Some implementation details are left to different agents or components. The auction designer can plug in different components or services. For example, the clearing details are left to clearing agents. An auction server is responsible for taking information from a buyer agent, seller agent, and clearing agents. The details of how to process the information are delivered to other components in the systems. The auction designer can also register his or her service and implementation as a Web service that may be used by all participating agents or parties.

- **Auction server agent wrapper:** The wrapper provides message-based communication between agents. This wrapper wraps up all functions provided by an auction server. Since the auction server is implemented as Enterprise Java Bean, the buyer agent or seller agent can either use the client API to call an auction server directly or use an auction-server-agent wrapper to communicate with the auction server. Auction server agent wrapper also provides communications from the server to the other agents or components, especially the event notification. For example, a seller can subscribe to a price-change event and get notified from the auction server through the server-agent wrapper.

- **Event handler:** There are many events happening all the time along the auction process. These events include auction started, bid placed, round closed and opened, and round winner and final winner obtained. When such an event happens, all or some parties should be notified and the events are processed accordingly. To centralize the event management, a standard event-handling service such as event definition, notification, and subscription should be provided.

- **Buyer agent:** This agent could be a real buyer or a simulated buyer that simulates the buyer's behavior, the software component represents a buyer to communicate with a server to place a bid or get such information as auction status from the server. The framework just provides high-level communication and event subscription-notification service for these agents. The implementation of these agents depends on different projects and can be implemented using different agent framework such as Cougaar (http://www.cougaar.org), IMPACT, or any other agent framework. Again, the framework provides communication services between these agents and server, but leaves the bidder's logic implementation to a different specific auction project. If the buyer is a real person, then the agent is the only software component to represent the buyer. The communication between the buyer agent and the auction server wrapper is implemented based on a different agent framework. The default implementation is the RMI.

Seller agent: This agent could also be a real seller or a simulated seller. Similar to a buyer agent, the seller agent represents a seller. The underlying logic and the implementation of such agents depend on different projects. The server agent wrapper provides two-way communication between the server and these agents.

Web server: provides Web interface for real buyers and sellers to interact with the auction server. To provide more flexible Web publication, we extend Struts Web publishing framework (http://Jakarta.apach.org/struts) to provide more generic and dynamic Web publishing.

In addition, our framework provides several services that are required to run an auction. These services include an authentication and authorization service, persistence service, log service, registration service, scheduling service, and so on.

The framework abstracts the high-level auction activities and service. However, different auctions have different implementations and requirements, so we provide the XML interface for users and implementers to specify specific auction, round, and item information and so on. All information is specified and managed by the users themselves.

Implementation Consideration
and Demo Implementation

First, we summarize the server open-source technologies used in the platform in Table 2.

The Auction demo software is implemented with the help from several open-source projects such as JBoss for the server-transaction container, Spring Framework for the pluggable service framework, Struts for Web publishing, Xerces for XML processing, Jakarta Slide for access control, log4J for logging, Repast for Agent based simulation, and Jfreechart for chart generation.

The main reason that we choose the above tools is that they are of high quality and freely available. In addition, they have been widely tested and adopted in the industry. This framework is designed to support different research and classroom projects, by avoiding the licensing issue, different applications can be implemented and deployed quickly. By plugging in these tools, we can focus on the design of

Table 2. Server open-source technologies adopted in the platform

Functions	Implementation Technologies	Resource
Auction Container	Jboss J2EE server Spring Framework	http://jboss.org http://springframework.org/
Web server	Tomcat	http://www.apache.org/tomcat
Web publishing framework	Struts	http://www.apache.org/struts
Authorization service	Slide	http://www.apache.org/slide
Log service	Log4j	http://log4j.org
Scheduling service	Java Scheduler	http://java.sun.com
Communication	JAVA RMI	http://java.sun.com
Persistence Service	Java EJB entity bean	http://java.sun.com/j2ee
Web service	Sun JAX-WS	http://java.sun.com/Webservices/jaxws/index.jsp
Development Environment	Eclipse	http://eclipse.org
XML parser	XML4j	http://xml.apache.org/xml4j
Chart Generation	Jchart	http://jfree.org
Agent Framework	IMPACT Cougaar	http://cs.umd.edu/IMPACT http://www.cougaar.org

high-level architecture of this flexible auction framework instead of being bogged down with all the software implementation details that require many years to develop and debug.

The various transactions involved in an auction are implemented in the auction server. The auction server is running in a J2EE-compliant application server. We use JBoss server as the transaction coordinator key to the system and the persistence manager through the Entity Bean mechanism. The transactions coordinator will make sure that each of auction functionalities in the software will be consistent and atomic. For example, when an auction ends, we want the winning bids to persist before declaring the winner. If the winning bid cannot persist due to some reason, we will not close the auction. These standard transactional services are widely used in industries such as financial institutions. This is complex software and is provided by JBoss application server for free.

JBoss application server also provides data-persistence service through the standard J2EE-entity-bean mechanism. With Entity Bean, we do not need to write the SQL statements to retrieve and insert data into the database. Instead, we just need to follow the standard to provide a mapping between the DB tables and our Java objects. The JBoss server also takes care of other aspects for a good persistence manager, such as caching and resource management, as well as seamless integration with transactions service.

For the possible future expansion of this auction software, the JBoss application server also provides transparent scalability. If the auction software needs to process a huge amount of transactions just like any commercial auction site, we can simply add more computers and run more instances as a cluster of auction server. In addition, it is worth noting that all the functionalities we gain from the JBoss application server are not unique to JBoss, they belong to a standard J2EE mechanism. We can also deploy the auction software to other application servers that are commercially available from BEA, IBM, Oracle, and SUN Microsystems.

One of the main requirements for this implementation is the pluggable architecture. We will allow different auction designers to choose different auction modules or design their own auction mechanism and implement their own auction details. The pluggable is the main theme for this auction framework implementation. "Pluggable" comes with two aspects, one is the auction mechanism. This is the main flow of the auction that is controlled by the auctioneer. To start an auction, the auctioneer will use one auction mechanism, such as English or Dutch auction, one round or multiround, and so on. In the first iteration of the implementation, we merely make this mechanism pluggable and implement several standard auction mechanisms. In the future design, we plan to adopt a Workflow engine. The main benefit for the Workflow approach is that auction mechanisms can be expressed through a standard format Workflow language such as BPEL. There will be a graphical user interface to design various kinds of auction mechanisms. This will make it much easier to implement and experiment with various auction mechanisms because there is no need of software knowledge for the auction designer. They can create and modify the auction mechanism through the user interface. Workflow is gaining popularity in the business software mostly for the above reasons, and there are free Workflow engines such as JBoss Workflow engine available and we expect they will be mature in the near future.

The other aspect of the "pluggable" is at the service level. In this implementation, all main functionalities of the auction server and agents are abstracted as a software service. For example, when a bidder submits a bid, it is submitted through the bidding service, the bidding service then calls the persistent service to persist the bid and notifies various agents by calling agent services. Not long ago, to plug different services into software was usually done through proprietary software implementation and suffered bugs and inconsistent software quality. Spring Framework is a free software framework mainly designed to solve this kind of problem. Spring is a lightweight container of software components and can "inject" different software service components in the software without changing the code. In this way, people can "wire" different services together through an XML file instead of hard coding the services in the software. For example, if an auction designer wants to have a special kind of bidding service, he can either implement his own bidding service, obtain another bidding-service component, or change the Spring XML configuration file to tell the auction server to plug-in this service implementation. Spring has become a "container" framework and many other free software components are being built around Spring, such as security, transaction, and persistence.

While Spring and JBoss are independent software, they can be combined to achieve our goal for rapid software development. The result is very encouraging: We have an implementation of a relatively versatile and working auction engine in a short period.

Since we implement the auction engine as a set of services, the client interface to the auction engine is straightforward. The client (usually through the Web interface or the software agent) just needs to obtain the respective service and call the service method. The service presents itself either though the native API or the WebService API. In native API, the client is running as a Java program and usually has the direct access to the auctions server without a firewall. Native API is of high performance but can only be used by the "direct" clients that are running a Java program and are "close" to the auction server. The WebService API is through the standard WebService interface. The WebService API internally transforms the service call and response in the form of XML so that the client does not have to be a Java programmer and does not have to be on the same network with the auction server. The WebService API is usually used by the clients that are not in the same firewall and when integration with other software programs is needed. It is possible to standardize the auction WebService interface as a compliment to other business XML framework.

The demo auction application has been used in an Operation Management course to help business students understand the procurement auction process and make decisions in the gaming environment. The class is divided into several groups, each of which has a different production capacity, production cost, initial inventory, scheduled sales order, and uncertain demand. Therefore, each student group has a different cost of the products, production capacity, and production plan. However, one group has no knowledge of other groups' information (i.e., this is a game with incomplete information). The auction is a multiround auction. The auctioneer (the instructor) can create an auction first, which may have one item and the required quantity. In each round, the auctioneer specifies the price of the auction item based on the bid information of the previous round. Each group places a bid with a quantity that they wish to provide. The auction stops when the total bid quantity is less than the required quantity.

The application includes the following functions:

a. **Create an auction:** The auction administrator can specify the basic auction information such as name, round duration, auction item name, quantity, and so on,

b. **List auction:** shows a list of an auction where the instructor can select an auction to manage or delete.

c. **Manage the auction:** manages the round, start a new round, and clear or close the auction. This is the main function for an auction administrator. The student cannot place a bid until the auctioneer (administrator) starts the auction/create a new round. In addition to the price, the auctioneer can specify some basic rules for the rounds, such as minimum bidding quantity and maximum bidding quantity. The auctioneer can also view current auction status and close the auction so that nobody can place a bid within this auction.

d. **View auction detail image:** The application can also create an image of the auction process dynamically.

e. **Place a bid:** The bidder can place a bid based on his or her previous bid and other auction rules such as he/she cannot place a bid quantity larger than the previous bid or he/she has to place the bid before the end of the round (the system will alert the bidder 30 seconds before the round ends). The bidder will be notified of new events (a new round is created, the auction is closed or cleared, etc.) if the browser's Java plug-in is enabled. A bid cannot be changed after the current round is closed.

We do release some bid information such as the total bid amount in each round to the groups, so each group knows how close they are to their required quantity. We run this auction in a classroom setting, so all groups are in the same classroom. Some interesting bidding behaviors are observed during the auction, such as collaboration and collusion through body languages or expressive words. In addition, we find that although groups have their own preplan bidding strategies, they do change their strategies in the auction since bidding strategies will be adjusted according to other behavior. Some make bid mistakes, since they thought other groups have the same cost factors as theirs. Winner's curse is also observed, since each group wants to win the bid in a competitive environment and forgets the cost. We also run the same auction twice and try to find whether the bidding behaviors change with the knowledge learned from the first auction. The results show that they do change the bidding behavior.

The data including bidding quantity and price for each round are finally stored in an Oracle database through data persistence service, which is implemented as enterprise Java entity bean.

The auction platform is generic and flexible, which can help auction designers quickly design, deploy, modify, and test their auction designs. We have implemented several other auctions using the framework, that is, Day and Raghavan (2003) matrix auction, UM Game ticket auction, an agent-based auction simulation, and so on. Furthermore, we can easily implement other traditional auctions such as English, Dutch, and sealed-bid auctions. As a research auction platform, it can be easily adopted for instructional use, research simulation, and experiment.

Concluding Remarks

The purpose of this chapter is to present a software auction platform framework that can support different kinds of auctions. The platform is implemented using JAVA and many other open-source projects. However, the service and architecture can be implemented using any language. Any researchers can extend the platform and quickly deploy their own auctions. A future extension can build a purely service-based framework. Instead of extending the framework, the researchers can call the service of the auction platform. Researchers still can implement some auction-specific information and processes. The good thing about this is the platform provides a programming-language-neutral implementation.

We present a composite bidding language to enable bidders to flexibly express bid preference. By extending the concept of atomic bidding, researchers are equipped with rich choices of the bidding language. Some default atomic bids can also be implemented for the convenience of implementation. The relationship between atomic bids or composite bids could also be extended beyond the OR/XOR relationship. Although this complicates the implementation, it may improve the flexibility in some cases.

Another value the auction platform could provide is the rule engine: Instead of coding the rules in different places such as agents, a rule engine can provide centralized rule management joined with a process-flow engine. This will also alleviate the auction developer or agent developer the burden of the implementation of these rules.

References

Ariely, D., & Simonson, I. (2003). Buying, bidding, playing, or competing? Value assessment and decision dynamics in online auctions. *Journal of Consumer Psychology, 13*, 113-123.

Ba, S., & Pavlou, P. A. (2002). Evidence of the effect of trust building technology in electronic markets: Price premiums and buyer behavior. *MIS Quarterly, 26*(3), 243-268.

Banks, J., Olson, M., Porter, D., Rassenti, S., & Smith, V. (2003). Theory, experiment and the federal communications commission spectrum auctions. *Journal of Economic Behavior and Organization, 51(3), 303-350.*

Bapna, R., Goes, P., & Gupta, A. (2001). Insights and analyses of online auction. *Communications of the ACM, 44*(11), 42-50.

Bapna, R., Goes, P., & Gupta, A. (2003). Replicating online Yankee auctions to analyze auctioneers' and bidders' strategies. *Information Systems Research, 14*(3), 244-268.

Day, R., & Raghavan, S. (2003). *CAMBO: Combinatorial auctions using matrix bids with order.* Working Paper, University of Maryland.

Gamma, E., Helm, R., Johnson, R., & Vlissides, J. (1995). *Design patterns.* Addison-Wesley

Gopal, R., Thompson, S., Tung, A., & Whinston, A. B. (2005). Managing risks in multiple online auctions: An options approach. *Decision Science, 36*(3), 397-425.

Gregg, D., & Walczak, S. (2006). Auction advisor: An agent-based online-auction decision support system. *Decision Support System, 41*(2), 449-471.

McCabe, K., Rassenti, S., & Smith, V. (1991). Testing Vickrey's and other simultaneous multiple unit versions of the English auction. In R.M. Isaac (Ed.), *Research in Experimental Economics, 4*, 45-79.

Nisan, N. (2000). Bidding and allocation in combinatorial auctions. In *Proceedings of the 2ⁿᵈ ACM Conference on Electronic Commerce* (pp. 1-12).

Pinker, E., Seidmann, A., & Vakrat, Y. (2003). Managing online auctions: Current business and research issues. *Management Science, 49*, 1457-1484.

Rafaeli S., & Avi N. (2005). Special presence: Influence on bidders in Internet auctions. *Electronic Markets, 15*(2), 158-176.

Rodriguez-Aguilar, J. A., Noriega, P., Sierra, C., & Padget, J. (1997). FM96.5: A Java-based electronic auction house. In *Proceedings of the Second International Conference on the Practical Application of Intelligent Agents and Multi-Agent Technology (PAAM'97)* (pp. 207-224).

Sandholm, T. (2002). eMediator: A next generation electronic commerce server. *Computational Intelligence, 18*(4), 656-676.

Vragov, R. (2005). Why is eBay the king of internet auctions? An institutional analysis perspective. *E-Service Journal, 3*(3), 5-28.

Wurman, P. R., Wellman, M. P., & Walsh, W. E. (1998). The Michigan Internet AuctionBot: A configurable auction server for human and software agents. In *Proceedings of the Second International Conference on Autonomous Agents (AGENTS)* (pp. 301-308).

Chapter XIII

Monitoring and Enforcing Online Auction Ethics

Diana Kao, University of Windsor, Canada

Shouhong Wang, University of Massachusetts Dartmouth, USA

Abstract

The online auction has become an important form of e-commerce. Although using a different mode for conducting auction activities, online auctions should abide by the same code of ethics outlined in the face-to-face auction environment. Yet, ethics-related issues for online auctions have not been fully discussed in the current literature. The unique features of online auctions present an opportunity to address how ethical conduct could be supported, monitored, and enforced in an online auction environment. With technology being the backbone of online auction, information systems appear to be a useful tool in facilitating ethics enforcement. This article summarizes ethics-related issues that are particularly relevant in online auctions, and recommends a code of ethics that could be applied to online auctions. Based on this set of ethics, this article proposes a model for an information system that will support and enhance ethical conduct in an online auction environment.

Introduction

After several years of proliferation of e-commerce, online auctions have become an important means of selling merchandise (Klein & O'Keefe, 1999; Reck, 1997; Turban, 1997). Online auctions constitute a $6.4 billion per year industry, with that figure estimated to increase to $15.1 billion per year by 2004 (Albert, 2002). More recently, during the 2005 fiscal year, eBay experienced accelerated growth in many areas. Consolidated net revenues generated by the company nearly exceeded $4.552 billion, representing a 39% increase over the previous figure of $3.271 billion earned in 2004. Confirmed registered users increased by 33% over the previous year to 180.6 million users. Experts are estimating that as the online auction industry continues to grow that eBay's consolidated net revenue could increase to $5.900 billion (eBay, 2005).

Online auctions have been brought about through the synergetic combination of the Internet technology and the traditional auction mechanisms (Bapna, Goes, & Gupta; 2001). In the early development of online auctions, much of the focus was on single-item auctions in isolation from the market context with which they are typically associated. According to Bapna, Goes, and Gupta (2003), the previous limitations of traditional auctions such as space, geography, and time have virtually disappeared with the onset of the online setting. Traditionally, auctions have been used for selling unique and unusual items such as celebrities' personal property and art. Since the Internet became the e-commerce media, online auctions are virtually adopted for all kinds of commodities ranging from low-price books to expensive real estate (Amazon, 2005; eBay, 2005; eShop, 2005). Huge revenues have been generated by online auctions.

Online auctions create virtual auction houses for businesses and consumers. They enhance the cooperative as well as the competitive environment for trading. In addition, they could have a profound implication on participants' behaviours in auctions (Standifird, 2001). Recently, countless reports on fast-growing cases of online auction fraud (Anonymous, 2003; Gatlin, 2003; Keefe, 2003) have brought the attention of law enforcement to the industry. This includes fraud due to the misrepresentation of a product that has been advertised for sale through an Internet auction site as well as nonpayment or nondelivery for those items (Royal Canadian Mounted Police, 2005). While legal cases are often associated with poor morality and ethics in the organizations, ethical issues in online auctions are often overlooked, ignored, or silenced. Little literature on business ethics of online auctions exists. Research concerning this issue is imperatively needed to understand the ethical responsibilities of the different parties involved in online auctions. According to Wieland (2001), there is an interrelated connection between the need for a code of ethics in regards to ethics management systems. Corporate ethics programs must be implemented in order to control, protect, and further develop the integrity of all transactions. There have been many general theories in ethics (Rosenau, 1992). Some argued that developing and enforcing the code of ethics might lead to an abdication of individual moral responsibility (Bauman, 1993). According to this theory, actors who rely on external rules will more likely consider a trade-off between risks and benefits rather than moral impulse. This proposition is true in the sense that ethical issues are not legal issues, and there is no clear moral compass to guide actors through complex dilemmas about right and wrong. Nevertheless, common recommendations offered by experts in addressing business ethics include the adoption of the code of ethics and the enforcement of the adoption (Bayles, 1987; Beets & Killough, 1990).

There are several approaches to enforce ethics. One is using government administrative agencies, such as the Federal Trade Commission, to monitor the conduct of practitioners. An alternative to government regulation is a civilian board elected by the relevant business organizations. Many business organizations have their own ethics enforcement bodies to sensitize their employees to ethical issues and train them to act ethically. Ethics enforcement systems include training-based, auditing-based, and complaint-based systems. At this point, it is unclear which mechanism is the best for online auctions. However, information systems would be a useful tool in facilitating ethics enforcement, given that online auctions are conducted with the support of information systems. Although ethics-related issues for online auction have not been fully discussed in the current literature, we believe that the unique features of online auctions present an opportunity to address how ethical conduct could be supported, monitored, and enforced in an online auction environment. The intention of this chapter is to explore the following questions:

1.   What are the ethical dilemmas existing in the online auction environment?
2.   How can the ethical dilemmas be monitored and governed?

To answer the first question, we first summarize ethics-related issues that are particularly relevant for online auctions, and then explain how these issues have caused ethical dilemmas for the participants. Our attempt to answer the second question is to recommend a code of ethics that could be applied to online auctions. The primary purpose of the code would be to assist in determining a course of action as ethical dilemmas emerge whenever a decision or an action has the potential to impair the well being of an individual or group of people (Davison, Kock, Loch, & Clarke, 2001). This set of code of ethics is further used as the foundation for a model for an information system that will support and enhance ethical conduct in an online auction environment.

This chapter discusses important issues of ethics in online auctions, proposes a code of ethics for online auctions, and suggests use of intelligent information systems to enhance ethical conduct in an online auction environment. The rest of the chapter is organized as follows. In the next section, we describe the ethics-related characteristics of online auctions. The ethical challenges for online auctioneers, online auction sellers, online bidders, and online auction brokers, and in the following two sections, provide theoretical references to support the creation of the ethics articles articulated here. Next, we analyze the need for ethics enforcement information systems (EEIS), and conclude with a summary of the discussions.

Ethics-Related Characteristics of Online Auctions

In general, online auctions provide the opportunity to gain quick and easy access to new markets by means of characteristics that distinguish themselves from the traditional face-to-face auctions. Many characteristics of online auctions have significant ethical implications. This is mainly because the Internet changes the auction environment by mitigating constraints and adding new dimensions, such as the physical absence of products and participants. In this section, we will first outline these unique characteristics, and then explain why these characteristics may cause potential ethical dilemmas for different participants involved in the online auction process.

Physical Absence of Participants

In online auctions, all participants, including sellers, auctioneers, bidders, and auction brokers are physically invisible. There are no physical addresses of sellers and bidders. Anyone can participate in online auctions. For small businesses and individual consumers, trading through online auctions primarily relies on honesty and trust of all parties involved in the auction process. The bid increment has been listed as an important item among control factors that online auctioneers may manipulate and control. These analytical and empirical results obtained by tracking real-world online auctions. In this environment, auctioneers usually play the role of the trusted third party that monitors the auction process. Accuracy on issues such as product description, reliability of delivery, and price are key considerations for those undertaking participating in online auctions. Finally, it is critical that the auctioneer ensures that the highest bidder wins the auction (Davison, Kock, Loch, & Clarke, 2001).

Anonymity

The sellers and bidders usually remain anonymous in online auctions. To protect privacy, identities of individuals are often concealed. There is no common agreement on the approach to the identification structure and binding identities for online auctions. Sellers and bidders use account numbers assigned by the auctioneer. eBay has created an infrastructure which enables buyers to assign and post a rating to the sellers. This feedback ultimately reduces the sellers' anonymity; however, current practices allow an individual to open as many accounts as he or she wishes. This makes it possible for the same individual to appear as a different person for each account opened. It also remains possible for a set of bidders in an auction to collude and form a ring where the members agree not to outbid each other. Although rings are illegal, they are not necessarily unheard of (Kalyanam & McIntyre, 2001).

Diversified Commodities

Virtually anything can be sold through online auctions. The commodities for online auctions could be tangible products or services such as college tuition and plastic surgery (Barker, 2000). Many products are prohibited in online auctions, as they are clearly illegal according to international conventions. Human parts and firearms are examples of illegal products in online auctions. At times, it is impossible to draw a clear line between legal and illegal products or services for online auctions since the jurisdiction issues have become complicated. For example, whether tobacco can be traded through online auctions depends on local government laws.

Physical Absence of Products

Unlike face-to-face auctions, the products remain physically untouchable in online auctions. Although detailed specifications and images of the products for the auction are presented, it is difficult for many products to be accurately evaluated without physical examinations. Examples are the condition of a motor vehicle and the quality of a piece of jewellery.

Long Duration and No Clear-Cut Closing Time

The most popular auction form on the Internet is open-cry (English) auctions. In practice, open cry auctions are usually for one item at a time. At present, online open-cry auctions are primarily asynchronous, and usually take a long period ranging from several days to several weeks. Under these circumstances, bidders may be hesitant to make such an open-ended commitment to buy the item. Although there is a predetermined closing time for an online auction, this closing time can be arbitrarily extended for a reasonable period (e.g., a half hour).

Reverse Auctions Brokers

Online auctions actually provide an open market for online negotiation. Consequently, reverse auctions have been widely used online. A reverse auction refers to an auction where the buyer advertises the intent to purchase a specific product or service and invites sellers to make bids. Not only business buyers request online bidding, but consumers also use reverse auctions to find commodities and services for their needs online. To facilitate reverse online auctions, brokers are used to assist negotiation between buyers and sellers. A typical example is Priceline.com (2005), where a buyer specifies points of origin and destination, travel dates, possible schedules, along with the price he or she will be willing to pay for matching flights. Priceline.com searches the airline databases for a matching itinerary available at a lower price. The auction brokers are rewarded by the discrepancy between the bidding prices and the sale prices.

Use of Software Agents

The technology of software agents is a step toward the solution in the rapid changing business environment of the e-commerce era and has been used in online auctions. Software agents carry out activities similar to that of human agents. Generic intelligent search engines and browsers, learning agents, and knowledge sharing agents have begun to appear in the software market. Software agents bring great benefits for lowering transaction costs and accelerating cycle time for online business (Wagner & Turban, 2002). To survive in the online auction environment, people are increasingly turning to advanced software-agent techniques. However, they sometimes misuse software agents without being considerate about the load on the remote servers and information ownership (Schwartz, 2000).

Summary

The above listed characteristics of online auctions present a unique environment of ethical dilemmas for all participants involved in the process. For example, due to physical absence of participants and anonymity, bidders might submit multiple bids while sellers might be involved in shill bidding (i.e., placing deliberate bids to misleadingly drive up the price of an item on the open auction). Although participants of face-to-face auctions can be physically absent and anonymous sometimes, these conditions are always present in an online auction environment. The third party auctioneer could also manipulate the auction so that he or she would earn a higher commission. These activities might be legal under the online auction regulations. However, the lack of enforcing power of the current system certainly presents opportunities for participants to conduct themselves unethically. Similarly, the lack of physical presence of the merchandise presents an opportunity for misleading potential bidders on the quality and authenticity of the goods. The flexible closing time certainly is unfair to bidders who trusted the auctioneer for closing the auction at the prespecified time. As for the reverse auctions, the dilemma lies in whether the broker actually finds the lowest price for the buyer, given that the commission for the broker is based on the final agreed price of the merchandise.

Some of the above characteristics of online auctions are shared with other online selling methods such as online catalogue sales. While it would be interesting to compare these online commerce approaches, this study is to examine the ethical challenge in online auctions and propose a code of ethics specifically applicable to online auctions.

Ethical Challenges for Online Auctions

There are associations for auctioneers in many countries such as the NAA in the US (NAA, 2005), AAC in Canada (AAC, 2005), NAVA in the UK (NAVA, 2005), AVA in Australia (AVA, 2005), and AANZ in New Zealand (AANZ, 2005). Each association usually has its own code of ethics for auctioneers. However, few codes of ethics are specifically designed for online auctions. Although online auction associations also exist (OAUA, 2005), their codes of ethics rarely fully reflected the characteristics of online auctions. For example, the code of ethics listed on the Web site of the Online Auction Users Association (OAUA) does not apply to auctioneers or brokers, who are major players in online auctions. In fact, the concept and practical application of ethics in online auctions differ from that in face-to-face auctions because of the changes of the environmental setting of auctions. Briefly, individual auction participants are more autonomous and thus are assumed to take responsibilities that are more moral. Also, the behaviours of auction participants are more difficult to monitor.

After searching the literature and surfing the Internet with no success, we felt that a code of ethics that will help eliminate or reduce the ethical challenges discussed in the previous section should be developed. Accordingly, we have developed 12 articles to form the foundation for the code of ethics specifically applicable to current online auctions practices. These articles are developed around the online auction participants: the auctioneers, the bidders, the sellers, and the brokers. Articles 1 to 4 are applicable to online auctioneers; articles 5 to 7 for online auction sellers; articles 8 and 9 for online bidders; and articles 10 to 12 for online-auction brokers. We should emphasize that these articles are not legal requirements and should not be judicial. The 12 articles are presented as follows. Explanations and justifications for each article are presented before the article is stated.

Ethical Challenges for Online Auctioneers

The inevitable temporal and physical separation that online auctions introduce poses new risks that are not anticipated in traditional auction transactions. In order to overcome these risks, Internet technologies can diminish uncertainty through a collectively driven feedback mechanism, which can support online transactions. Several researchers have studied the importance of feedback mechanisms as a trust-building technology that increases prices for reputable sellers. Ba and Pavlou (2001) found evidence that the creation of credibility in online auctions results in price premiums for reputable sellers. In a different research, Lee (1998) finds that cars with an "obscure" history are eliminated from online auctions through technology in Japan's used car markets. To build trust for the online auctions, online auctioneers play a critical role in the auction process. They must be responsible to all parties involved in auctions both in terms of their identities and their behaviour.

> **Article 1.** *An online auctioneer must have an authenticated identity for the auction. The online auctioneer is responsible for timely online communication with all parties involved in the online auction.*

Yahoo! was challenged by French activists for hosting online auctions for Nazi items (Menestrel, Hunter, & de Bettignies, 2002). Although a kidney auction on eBay was eventually shut down with the intervention of eBay's executives (Miller, 1999), the line between appropriate and inappropriate products or services for online auctions has become less clear. Although online auctioneers coordinate the trade market, it is difficult for them to know whether their clients are honest, whether they are capable of selling or buying a product, or whether the seller is the legitimate owner of the product. Nevertheless, online auctioneers should take responsibilities in ensuring that products and services on the auction meet the regulations of the local governments of the seller as well as potential buyers.

> **Article 2.** *An online auctioneer shall take responsibility of protecting the global public's interests before permitting a product or service to be auctioned online.*

There are control factors that auctioneers may set before an auction. According to Bapna et al. (2003), these factors may potentially influence the outcome of the auction process. Current practice reveals that controls may include the opening bid, the bid increment, as well as the time span of the auction. Given the limitations of the current form of online auctions, auctions are not truly real-time. The auctioneer controls the actual closing time. Upon close examination, the listed finish time of the auction does not appear to be a critical area of the auction process. At this time, all auctioneers employ an additional interval of time allowing an actual closing time to occur once new bids have not occurred for a predetermined time interval. In order to be fair to the bidders and the seller, the actual closing time should be revealed to the public.

> **Article 3.** *The auctioneer shall disclose the actual closing time along with the final auction outcome on the Web upon the completion of an auction.*

Given that online auctions have no real human faces attached to them, it would be easy for an online auctioneer to play dual or even triple roles in the auctions by also participating in bidding and selling at the same time. This undesirable behaviour presents a conflict of interest that may compromise the interest of the clients.

> **Article 4.** *An online auctioneer shall not be involved in any bidding or selling activity in the auction.*

Ethical Challenges for Online Auction Sellers

It would be easy for an online auction seller to participate in shill bidding (or bid shielding, i.e., biddings on behalf of the seller to artificially inflate the price) because of the indirect nature of the interactions between participants.

> **Article 5.** *An online auction seller shall not be involved in any shill bidding or bid shielding activity in the auction.*

The products or services for online auctions are not physically present during the auction process. It is the responsibility of the seller to provide accurate information about the product or service for the auction. In eBay's auction arrangement, the current standing of the item is always posted following the description of the item. The bidding history on the item, including unsuccessful bids, is also posted and available for the users (Bapna et al., 2001).

> **Article 6.** *An online auction seller shall provide accurate and complete descriptions of the product or service for sale, including full disclosure of all flaws and possible risks for the buyer, as well as all charges involved.*

Many online auction houses, such as eBay, post the comments of their sellers and buyers. In general, if a seller receives positive evaluations from the buyers, this seller is perceived to be trustworthy. Ideally, this type of comment would help the online-auction community to build an ethical auction environment (Stein, 1999). However, under the current practice, a seller who received negative comments can easily change its identity by registering many accounts. This practice results in compromising the effectiveness of an ethical auction environment.

> **Article 7.** *An online auction seller shall use a single identification for an auction house, and shall make its best effort to deliver the product or service to the buyer upon receiving of the payment.*

Ethical Challenges for Online Bidders

A common online bidding pattern is called sniping. The bidders use sniping technology that essentially automates the process of placing bids during Internet auctions. That is, the bidders do not make the bidding until immediately before the closing time in order to capture the chance of a good deal. Given that the duration of the current open-cry auction is relatively long and bidding competitors are invisible, sniping sometimes is unfair to bidders who participated in the entire duration of the online auction process. It is easy to see snipers at work, particularly in the last few minutes of an auction. It is common for a buyer to see bids jump by more than 50 percent in the closing seconds (Wang, 2002).

> **Article 8.** *An online auction bidder shall not use the sniping technique in online open-cry auctions.*

Similar to buyers commenting on the sellers, sellers also can post their comments about the buyers in many online auction houses. The evaluation comments will reveal the buyers' behavioural profile to the public. Current online-auction systems allow a bidder to change identification by registering many accounts, which makes it difficult to trace unethical buyers.

> **Article 9.** *An online auction bidder shall use a single identification for an auction house, and shall pay for the items upon winning an auction item.*

Ethical Challenges for Online Auction Brokers

Consumer-to-business online reverse auctions are a new phenomenon in e-commerce. Air-ticket reverse auction is a typical example. Other types of reverse auctions might emerge in the near future. In consumer-to-business online reverse auctions, the buyer sends the specifications of the desired commodity and offers a price to the broker. The broker then searches all potential sellers and finds a matching commodity for the buyer. The broker should be unbiased in selecting the sellers, to ensure an ethical reverse-auction environment. The broker should be independent of all potential sellers, which means that the broker has no conflict of interest in dealing with the seller and the buyer.

> **Article 10.** *An online auction broker shall be independent of all potential sellers.*

An online reverse auction broker receives the discrepancy between the buyer's offering price and the sale price of the commodity as a commission. Problems arise when price is not the only factor for a reverse auction. A broker sometimes asks the buyer to provide a range of specifications for the needed commodity. For instance, in air-ticket reverse auction, a buyer is usually asked to provide a flexible schedule and connections. The broker can either find the worst acceptable flights for the buyer and receive a high commission, or find the best matching flights but receive a lower commission.

> **Article 11.** *An online auction broker shall provide commodities best fitted to the buyer's specifications, and shall exercise all due diligence in protecting the buyer's interest.*

Online auction brokers often use mobile software agents to search the databases of auction houses to collect information for potential bidders. With the open nature of the Internet, the technology of software agents should be promoted. In general, software agents consume the resources of the remote servers and collect information from the auction houses. Appropriate use of software agents is beneficial to all parties of online auctions. However, aggressive use of software agent might adversely affect the performance of the host site. It might also violate the ownership of intellectual property by excessively collecting privileged data. Nowadays, techniques of detecting mobile software agents are becoming widely available (Messmer, 2004); however, criteria used for the judgment of aggressive behaviours can never be clear, and depend upon the consent of the owner of the remote computing resource.

Article 12. *When using software agents, the online auction broker shall avoid unfair use of the computing resources and information provided by the remote host sites.*

These 12 articles are articulated based upon the literature survey. They are neither comprehensive nor necessary for reducing ethical challenges. These articles are a useful catalyst for both researchers and practitioners to formalize ethical requirements for online auctions. By closely monitoring the online auction process and enforcing these ethical principals, participants of online auctions would have less opportunity to make a choice between an ethical act and an unethical practice. In other words, many of the ethical dilemmas will no longer exist because of the clear rules that govern the proper behaviour.

Needs for Ethics Enforcement Information Systems

Ethics are crucial for business to succeed. However, the boundary between ethical issues and legal issues is fuzzy. To examine moral and ethical concerns in postmodern organizations such as those virtual organizations of online auctions, the development of enabling systems through applying the principles of affirmative ethics is perhaps the best way to provide mechanisms for interactions and dialogue among stakeholders (Yuthas & Dillard, 1999).

Many online auction sites, such as eBay, have written auction rules. However, those rules are more likely to be online official documents and less likely to be monitored rigorously (Smith, 2003). Nevertheless, many online auction houses have already developed an environment to promote ethics enforcement by posting comments about the sellers and buyers. Such an environment can be expanded through an ethics enforcement information system that will support the adoption of the comprehensive code of ethics that we have proposed. For example, Websites for online auctions should require auctioneers to identify themselves in order to participate in the process. Verifiable information such as driver's license or credit-card information could be used for tracking. Ideally, this process could be further supported by regulations of all governments involved that will prosecute those who provide deceitful information about their identities. Clearly, this becomes another debatable issue of trade-off between protecting the privacy of personal information and enforcing ethics, as well as the fuzzy boundary between ethical issues and legal issues. Nevertheless, ethics enforcement models will always have such limitations.

Features could be built into an ethics enforcement information system to prohibit the auctioneer from representing more than one party in the auction process. The outcome of the auction should also be automatically revealed to the public to ensure the credibility of the auctioneer and the online-auction process. We also believe that every auctioneer should have a feedback section that will help buyers obtain a better idea of the behaviour pattern of the auctioneer. Internet technology can be used to accumulate information about the past trading behaviour. An ethics-enforcement system will ensure that the same person cannot register different names under the same address. This would help the host better identify the auctioneers and the sellers in case there is a problem in the auctioneering process. Similarly, Web-based technology can provide a mechanism to prohibit unethical behaviours of other parties. For example, a bidder who makes biddings right before the closing times constantly in many auction sessions is considered a sniping bidder and might be suspended from participating in the future auctions.

Model of Ethics Enforcement Information Systems (EEIS)

In this section, we will propose a model of EEIS that can be used for detecting the violation of the code of ethics in online auctions. Note that an EEIS is not intended for online-auction policing; rather, it is a consulting agent for a buyer, a seller, or an auction house, depending on where the system is installed, and who it serves.

The major roles of EEIS are to check all auction processes for compliance with the code of ethics and to handle complaints. The final outputs of EEIS will include reports for the responsible actors and for the public. To design a model of EEIS, we first determine the system requirements by interpreting the code of ethics in the context of business processes. Then, we identify object classes that are essential for EEIS, and synthesize these object classes into a network by identifying major messages between them. The 12 articles proposed earlier are used to demonstrate this process.

Interpretation of the Code of Ethics for System Design

In this section, each of the 12 articles proposed is described as a business process that can be supported by the EEIS automatically.

To enforce the code of ethics for online auctioneers:

> **Article 1.** *The EEIS keeps formal registration data of each auctioneer, including business identification, true name, office address, and the IP*

address used for the business. It also keeps a log of auctioneer's communications to other parties, and examines whether the communication messages are timely for all transactions or events.

Article 2. *The EEIS justifies the legitimacy of each product for the auction when posted by the seller, and reviews all complaints from the public regarding the legitimacy of the products.*

Article 3. *The EEIS makes disclosure documents for each auction session available to all parties, including the actual closing time and the outcome of the auction.*

Article 4. *The EEIS warrants that no bidding and selling activities are directly related to the auctioneer by checking auction transactions against the registration data.*

To enforce the code of ethics for online sellers:

Article 5. *The EEIS keeps formal registration data of each seller, including registered identification, true name, IP address, office address, and bank accounts for the auction. It crosschecks all bidding transactions and seller registration data to ensure that no bidding activity is directly related to the seller.*

Article 6. *The EEIS keeps detailed specifications of the product on auction. In case the buyer files a complaint about the purchased product, the EEIS produces a review report indicating whether dishonesty was involved.*

Article 7. *The EEIS monitors all payment and shipping transactions, and produces reports to examine whether all transactions are conducted in a timely manner.*

To enforce the code of ethics for online bidders:

Article 8. *The EEIS keeps all bidding records, and examines whether there are undesirable bidding patterns.*

Article 9. *The EEIS keeps formal registration data of each buyer, including registered identification, true name, IP address, home/office address, and credit card accounts for the auction. It also examines whether the buyer makes the payment in a timely manner.*

To enforce the code of ethics for online auction brokers:

Article 10. *The EEIS keeps formal registration data of each broker, including registered identification, true name, IP address, office address, and bank accounts for the auction. It crosschecks all auction transactions and broker registration data to ensure that no selling activity is directly related to the broker.*

Article 11. *The EEIS keeps a log of reverse auction search made by the broker and examines whether the broker makes inferior offers to the client.*

Article 12. *The EEIS keeps all records of software agents' usage, and examines whether the software agents are used appropriately.*

Object Classes of EEIS

According to the frameworks of object-oriented business information systems developed by Wang (1999), an information system can have three fundamental types of object classes: *physiomorphic*, *event*, and *document*. Based on the system requirements for EEIS, these object classes are defined as follows.

1. **Physiomorphic objects:** The objects of physically existing entities in an online auction system include *Auctioneer, Seller*, *Buyer*, *Broker*, and *Product* of the auction. For EEIS, these actors are represented by their registration data stored in the system.

2. **Event objects:** The event objects represent the online auction business process, and implement the interaction between all parties in online auctions. *Bidding*, *Shipping*, and *Payment* constitute typical auction transaction process events. The objects of *Complaint* from buyers, sellers, and public represent events that trigger the ethics review process. The event objects *Complaint Review*, *Periodical Review*, and *Transaction Review* represent three ethics review processes for handling complaints, periodical evaluation, and crosschecking auction transactions, respectively.

3.   **Document objects:** Electronic document entities used in EEIS are docu-
     ment objects. *Disclosure* documents of online auctions, reverse auction, and
     software-agent usage are the major document objects used for ethical review
     processes. The *Ethics Review Report* object represents the final output of the
     EEIS.

A metamodel of the EEIS is depicted in Figure 1. For simplicity, the synthesis of
individual object classes through messages is not shown in the figure. The connections between the metaclasses symbolize the activation of the ethics-review
processes and the information provision for those processes. The business rules for
ethical review are encapsulated in the disclosure-review object classes and ethics-
review reports. These ethical-review reports reveal violations of ethical codes. An
intelligent software agent, which will be described in the next subsection, can be
hired to generate ethics-review reports. This model can be viewed as an extension
of existing online auction systems. Its structure fits general online auction models
that have been prototyped in Wang (2002) and Liu, Wang, and Teng (2003).

As previously suggested, the proposed EEIS should be used to support the monitoring of ethical conduct in an online auction environment. Although the system is
not just a database, it does have the capability of collecting a tremendous amount
of data about the process and the participants. There is always a possibility that
private and confidential information being violated in the monitoring process. The
development and adoption of EEIS should be subject to the auditing of the auction
bodies. Ideally, EEIS should be developed and operated by a third party, independent of the auctioneers, the sellers, the bidders, and the auction brokers. This third
party will send exception reports to the relevant parties for corrective actions. One
should note that although the implementation of a system such as EEIS or any other
policies that ensure transparent auction operations, it is unlikely that these tools
will prevent collusion between parties completely. In addition, given the volume
of the auction transactions, it is also unrealistic to assume that all transactions will
be captured by an EEIS system.

Intelligent Information Technologies Enabled EEIS

In the EEIS context, the major burden of information processing is located on monitoring the intensive auction activities. Intelligent information technology (IT) is a
step towards the solution in such a dynamic e-commerce environment (Sugumaran,
2005). The software agent techniques have been proposed for online auctions (e.g.,
Dumas, Lachlan Aldred, Governatori, & Hofstede, 2005). The use of agents for EEIS
is a natural extension of these online-auction-agent techniques. An agent for EEIS
is a super object class that accomplishes its mission of monitoring online auction

Figure 1. Model of ethics enforcement information systems

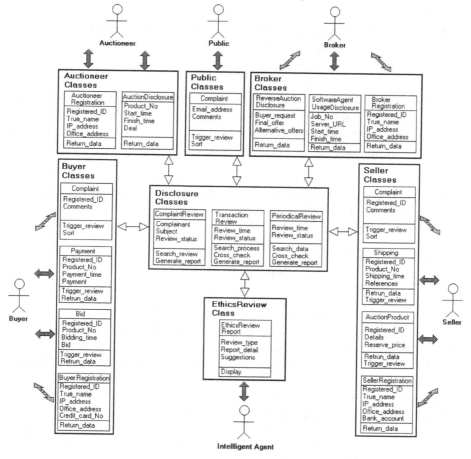

ethics. According to the framework of online auction agents (Liu, Wang, & Teng, 2000), the agent for EEIS includes the following six major components:

1. **Goal:** The core element of the agent is the goal of generating ethics-review reports.

2. **Operational task:** The agent performs basic operational tasks to achieve the goal. These tasks include collecting information of auction transactions, maintaining a database of auction activities, and surveying public opinions.

3. **Cognizance:** The agent possesses knowledge, or cognizance concepts, about online-auction ethics. Specifically, the knowledge base is a set of cognizance

objects representing the interpretation of ethics rules described in the previous subsection.

4. **Mnemonic instrument:** One of the missions of the software agent of EEIS is to reduce information overload. An intelligent agent needs several types of mnemonic functions, such as information filtering and mining online auction patterns.

5. **Decision instrument:** The intelligent agent makes decisions such as what should be included in disclosure-review reports and ethics-review reports and when these reports could be released.

6. **Interface:** Interface aids the dialogue between the user and the EEIS.

Again, the software agent is a consulting agent for a buyer, a seller, or an auction house, depending on where the EEIS is installed, and whom it serves.

Summary

There are two opposite ideological positions in terms of monitoring and governing online auctions. One position is that "Good comes by itself," and the online auctions should not be constrained. The other is that "Bad occupies void," in which online auctions must be forcefully regulated. Most people agree to navigate between the two. We believe that the online auction industry cannot maintain high public interest as well as profits without imposing high ethical standards. A common code of ethics has to be accepted by all parties in online auctions and to promote healthy online auctions. Based on this belief, we developed a 12-article code of ethics specifically for online auctions. These 12 articles provide behaviour guidelines and rules for participants to act ethically. Furthermore, we believe that new business models of e-commerce, such as online auctions, will require a new paradigm of management. A model of an ethics-enforcing information system was developed as an example of how information systems can be used to meet the challenge of information-technology-enabled e-commerce management. This model conceptualizes various aspects of ethics for online auctions by virtually connecting auction parties and public, auction processes, the code of ethics, and ethics enforcement management.

This research is meant to be a catalyst to stimulate further discussions on formalizing ethical requirements for online auctions. For researchers, issues surrounding the balance between less constraints and strong enforcement are always intriguing. Future empirical studies would provide a better understanding of how the online auctions industry evolves. Furthermore, only the practitioners can rectify the applicability and effectiveness of the proposed code of ethics. The proposed information-system model could be applied in many commercial as well as governmental online auctions. It would be also interesting to see more IT applications developed to address the ethical issues in business transactions other than online auctions.

Acknowledgments

This chapter was previously published as an article in the *IJIIT*. Subsequent changes were made to incorporate the most recent literature and suggestions of the book editor. The authors would also like to thank the editor of *IJIIT* and two anonymous reviewers for their valuable comments and the detailed annotation in the manuscript.

References

AAC. (2005). *Auctioneers Association of Canada.* Retrieved January 10, 2005, from http://www.auctioneerscanada.com/abouteth.html

AANZ. (2005). *Auctioneers Association of New Zealand Inc.* Retrieved January 10, 2005, from http://www.auctioneers.org.nz/membership.asp

Albert, M. R. (2002). E-buyer beware: Why online auction fraud should be regulated. *American Business Law Journal, 39*(4), 575-643.

Amazon (2005). Retrieved January 10, 2005, from http://www.amazon.com

Anonymous. (2003, May 11). Online and out of line. *The Washington Post*, p. F06.

AVA. (2005). *The Auctioneers and Valuers Association in Australia.* Retrieved January 10, 2005, from http://www.avaa.com.au/info.html

Ba, S., & Pavlou, P. A. (2002). Evidence of the effect of trust in electronic markets: Price premiums and buyer behaviour. *MIS Quarterly, 26*(3), 243-268.

Bapna, R., Goes, P., & Gupta, A. (2001). Insights and analyses of online auctions. *Communications of the ACM, 44*(11), 42-50.

Bapna, R., Goes, P., & Gupta, A. (2003) Analysis and design of business-to-consumer online auctions. *Management Science, 49*(1), 85-101.

Barker, O. (2000, October 24) Online, operations raise eyebrows many plastic surgeons want to nip budding bidding on the Web. *USA Today*, p. D.9.

Bauman, Z. (2003). *Postmodern ethics.* Oxford, UK: Blackwell Publishers.

Bayles, M. D. (1987). Professional power and self-regulation. *Business and Professional Ethics Journal, 5*(2), 26-46.

Beets, S. D., & Killough, L. N. (1990). The effectiveness of a complaint-based ethics enforcement system: Evidence from the accounting profession. *Journal of Business Ethics, 9,* 115-126.

Davison, R., Kock, N., Loch, K., & Clarke, R. (2001) Research ethics in information systems: Would a code of practice help? *Communications of the Association for Information Systems, 7*(4), 1-39.

Dumas, M., Lachlan Aldred, L., Governatori, G., & Hofstede, A. H. M. (2005). Probabilistic automated bidding in multiple auctions. *Electronic Commerce Research, 5*(1), 25-50.

eBay. (2005). Retrieved January 10, 2005, from http://www.ebay.com

eShop. (2005). *Auctions.* Retrieved January 10, 2005, from http://auctions.msn.com

Gatlin, G. (2003, May 1). Online fraud compels sweep: Enforcers of law respond to surge. *Boston Herald,* p. 37.

Kalyanam, K., & McIntyre, S. (2001). *Return on reputation in online auction markets.* Santa Clara University and IBM Corporation.

Keefe, B. (2003, May 1). Internet: Online auctions feel gavel crackdown. *The Atlanta Journal – Constitution,* p. C.1.

Klein, S., & O'Keefe, R. M. (1999). The impact of the Web on auctions: Some empirical evidence and theoretical considerations. *International Journal of Electronic Commerce, 3*(3), 7-20.

Lee, H. G. (1998). Do Electronic Marketplaces Lower the Price of Goods? *Communications of the ACM, 41,* 73-80.

Liu, H., Wang, S., & Teng, F. (2000). Real time multi-auctions and the agent support. *Journal of Electronic Commerce Research, 1*(4), 143-151.

Liu, H., Wang, S., & Teng, F. (2003). Multicast-based online auctions. *Benchmarking: An International Journal, 10*(1), 54-64.

Menestrel, M. L., Hunter, M., & de Bettignies, H. C. (2002). Internet e-ethics in confrontation with an activists agenda: Yahoo! on trial. *Journal of Business Ethics, 39*(1/2), 135-144.

Messmer, E. (2004). Vendors showcase security. *Network World, 21*(7), 21-22.

Miller, G. (1999, September 3). Technology: Kidney draws $5.7 million bid on eBay. *The Los Angeles Times,* p.3.

NAA (2005). *National Auctioneers Association.* Retrieved January 10, 2005, from http://www.auctioneers.org/aboutNAA/ethics.htm

NAVA. (2005). *National Association of Valuers and Auctioneers*. Retrieved January 10, 2005, from http://www.nava.org.uk/public/conduct.html

OAUA. (2005). *The Online Auction Users Association*. Retrieved January 10, 2005, from http://www.auctionusers.org

Priceline. (2005). Retrieved January 10, 2005, from http://www.priceline.com

Reck, M. (1997). Trading-process characteristics of electronic auction. *EM-Electronic Markets, 7*(4), 17-21.

Royal Canadian Mounted Police. (2005). Retrieved January 9, 2006 from *http://www.rcmp.ca/scams/online_fraud_e.htm*

Rosenau, P. (1992). *Post-Modernism and the Social Sciences*. Princeton, NJ: Princeton University Press.

Schwartz, J. (2000, February 5). Probe of eBay hinges on rights to data; Territorial disputes on Web. *The Washington Post*, p. E1.

Smith, S. (2003, December 18). EBay pulls the plug on peddling flu shots. *Boston Globe*, p. C.1.

Standifird, S. S. (2001). Reputation and e-commerce: eBay auctions and the asymmetrical impact of positive and negative ratings. *Journal of Management, 27*(3), 279-295.

Stein, H. (1999, October 25). When your reputation is online: Most eBayers trade with honor; If not, everyone will know. *The Wall Street Journal*, p. 23.

Sugumaran, V. (2005). The inaugural issue of the *International Journal of Intelligent Information Technologies. International Journal of Intelligent Information Technologies, 1*(1), i-v.

Turban, E. (1997). Auctions and bidding on the Internet: An assessment. *EM-Electronic Markets, 7*(4), 7-11.

Wagner, C., & Turban, E. (2002). Are intelligent e-commerce agents partners or predators? *Communications of the ACM, 45*(5), 84-90.

Wang, S. (1999). *Analyzing Business Information Systems: An Object-Oriented Approach*. Boca Raton, FL: CRC Press.

Wang, S. (2002). Synchronous online open-cry auctions. *INFOR: Journal of Information Systems and Operational Research, 40*(1), 86-94.

Wieland, J. (2001). The ethics of governance. *Business Ethics Quarterly*, 11(1), 73-87.

Yuthas, K., & Dillard, J. F. (1999). Ethical development of advanced technology: A postmodern stakeholder perspective. *Journal of Business Ethics, 19*(1), 35-49.

Chapter XIV

Mail Server Management with Intelligent Agents

Charles Willow, Monmouth Unversity, USA

Abstract

Amidst the era of e-economy, one of the difficulties from the standpoint of the information-systems manger is, among others, the forecast of memory needs for the organization. In particular, the manager is often confronted with maintaining a certain threshold amount of memory for a prolonged period. However, this constraint requires more than technical and managerial resolutions, encompassing knowledge management for the group, eliciting tacit knowledge from the end users, and pattern- and time-series analyses of utilization for various applications. This chapter summarizes current methods for managing server memory by incorporating intelligent agents. In particular, a new framework for building a set of automated intelligent agents with a neural network is proposed under the client-server architecture. The emphasis is on collecting the needs of the organization and acquiring the application-usage patterns for each client involved in real time. Considerations for future work associated with technical matters comprising platform independence, portability, and modularity are discussed.

Introduction

Integrated information systems for distributed organizations, comprising the information technology (IT) infrastructure and generic business applications such as enterprise systems (ES), supply-chain management (SCM), customer-relationship management (CRM), and knowledge-management systems (KMS) are by far one of the vital assets to sustain competitive edge for an e-economy. Figure 1 illustrates the IT infrastructure and its application systems for a generic e-business, suggested by Laudon and Laudon (2004).

The IT infrastructure serves as the backbone of the entire architecture, and requires high-level expertise for its planning, design, and management on a regular basis. As a consequence, most organizations often rely on a number of external service providers for their IT infrastructure management. Moreover, the majority of management information systems (MIS) research to date has focused on issues associated with information architecture (IA) in Figure 1, often referred to as IT applications in general, relative to those of IT infrastructure.

The IT infrastructure and its real-time interconnections with its applications is the focus of this chapter. A summary of current methods for managing the server memory by incorporating intelligent agents is presented. In particular, a new framework for

Figure 1. Information architecture and technology for e-business

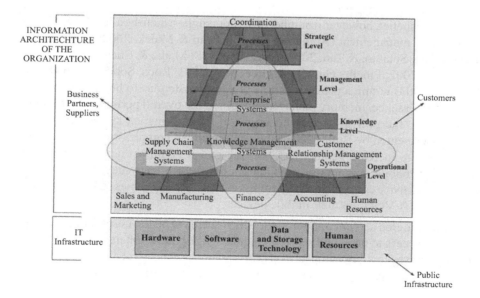

building a set of automated intelligent agents using neural network is proposed under the client-server architecture. The emphasis is on collecting the needs of the organization and acquiring the application usage patterns for each client involved in real time. Considerations for future work associated with technical matters comprising platform independence, portability, and modularity are discussed.

Administrators of IT infrastructure are often confounded with a vast array of management problems, which may be in large classified into:

- Selection and upgrades of hardware platform, middleware, and applications combination
- Information resource management
- Integration of applications
- Security management

This chapter discusses problems associated with information resource management (IRM), and suggests a development framework for reconfiguring the server as well as the clients for moderately large-scale information systems.

Among others, one of the difficulties concerning IRM from the standpoint of the information-systems manager is the correct forecast of overall memory needs for the organization. In particular, the manager is often confronted with maintaining a certain threshold amount of memory for a prolonged period, such as 2 terabytes (TB) for the fiscal year 2006.   One may argue that the cost of memory is declining rapidly, and its management may not be a factor effecting IRM. Contrary to this common misbelief, however, a number of authors suggest there be a certain threshold for memory management (Applen, 2002; Kanawati & Malek, 2002; Kankanhalli, Tanudidjaja, Sutanto, & Tan, 2003; Lansdale, 1988; Mathe & Chen, 1998; Pinelle & Gutwin, 2002; Pinelle, Gutwin, & Greenberg, 2003; Roos, Soodeen, Bond, and Burchill, 2003) within a prescribed time window, analogous to budgetary considerations. In essence, memory management affects the overall performance for both client-server and peer-to-peer architectures of the information system. Based on the ideas presented by Butte (2002), the computational complexity of the problem is expected to increase geometrically, as the global IT infrastructure migrates to distributed mobile computing in which end-users or clients may demand more memory-intensive contents such as wireless e-mails, mobile games, and audio-video on demand (A/VOD) on their mobile devices.

Under multitiered server configuration, which seems to be the norm for most organizations, access to back-end server(s) requires high bandwidth networks (Willow, 2006b). Consequently, the impact of effective memory management is further amplified. Figure 2 represents a general three-tier architecture of the IT infrastructure.

Figure 2. General information technology architecture

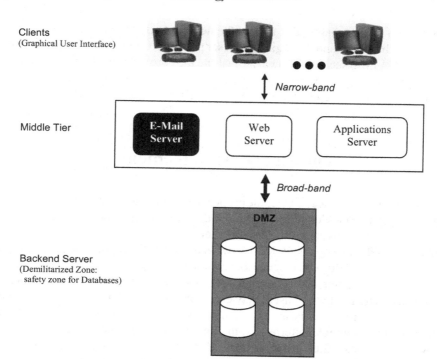

Clients
(Graphical User Interface)

Narrow-band

Middle Tier

E-Mail Server

Web Server

Applications Server

Broad-band

DMZ

Backend Server
(Demilitarized Zone:
safety zone for Databases)

The major focus of this chapter is on building a conceptual framework for developing an intelligent-memory management system for the "mail" server. To tackle the IRM problem more comprehensively, a modular approach is employed. That is, problems governing the mail server and their resolutions are discussed before any others. As e-mails become one of the preferred methods of communications for most organizations, mail-server management indeed requires attention with top priority. A series of forthcoming follow-up research associated with the problems of the Web and application server is discussed in Willow (2006b) and Willow (2006a), respectively.

A major contribution of this chapter lies in the development of a framework for building multiple agents for the mail server, with emphasis on memory management. Agent-based autonomous systems (i.e., automata) have in recent years been adopted as one of the better methods for managing virtual organizations in various applications (Flenner et al., 2002; Kanawati & Malek, 2002; Mathe & Chen, 1998; Murch, 2004; Taylor, 2004). They range from consumer applications such as online travel arrangements to system diagnostics including online data quality audits and remote trouble-shooting.

Organization of this chapter follows. In the next section, knowledge management for eliciting, building, and managing end-user preference and e-mail usage patterns is discussed. A third section follows to illustrate the core system, "multiple agents." Suggestions for (hands-on) construction of the proposed framework are made in the fourth section, subsequently followed by conclusions in the final section.

Knowledge Management

The key to maintaining accuracy of the proposed multiagent system lies in managing highly subjective knowledge for sharing and customizing/personalizing end-user memory usage patterns across the organization. Information tTechnology (IT) may support knowledge management (KM) in two classes: codification and personalization (Kankanhalli et al., 2003). In essence, the codification approach manages structured knowledge, whereas personalization manages unstructured, tacit knowledge. Because e-mail usage patterns for end users may entail both types of knowledge, a separate knowledge base or repository is suggested for the framework of this research. That is, there may be common patterns of e-mail management among end users such as removing messages which are more than 36 months old or organizing their mail folders every 30 days, and so forth on the one hand. On the other hand, each user may have highly subjective patterns that may not be consistent with those codified knowledge. Lansdale (1988) emphasized the need for cognitive interface tools (CITs) to collect, organize, build, and share both types of knowledge for the office system in his early research. However, not many literatures have been dedicated to solving this problem to date.

Markus (2001) describes the general stages of the KM process: knowledge elicitation, knowledge packaging, distributing or disseminating knowledge, and reusing knowledge. To this end, building knowledge bases in conjunction with automatic agents is considered one of the better methods for managing user knowledge associated with e-mail usage in real time.

Attributes for Knowledge Management

This section illustrates the necessary set of attributes to be incorporated into knowledge management (KM). Note that the values of these attributes will be collected in real time from end users for generating patterns of e-mail usage.

As noted in Lansdale (1988), the process of information retrieval in the human mind is fundamentally different from a filing or library system, in which items are accessed by location rather than their meaning. The first notion is that people recall chronological information about information: what else was happening at roughly the same time. Consequently, the "time stamp" of e-mails may be a good source of structured information or knowledge. Association is another means by which humans retrieve information. Each e-mail message is associated with four pieces of tacit information: recipient or sender, event or subject, attachment(s), and significance of the message. Table 1 summarizes the attributes for KM concerning e-mail usage.

A set of six generic attributes associated with e-mails, as described in Table 1, is to be employed in the suggested framework of this chapter. Notice that the first two attributes, time stamp and size, are structured information, which may be available for both the server and clients. By contrast, each client may manage her/his e-mail messages based on one or more of the four tacit attributes: recipient/sender, event/ subject, attachment(s), and significance. Given a certain restriction of memory size, say 100MB per e-mail account holder, one client may choose to either remove or archive (on local memory store) e-mails based on recipient/sender, event/subject, attached file(s), significance, or any combination of the four, so far as tacit knowledge management is concerned. Alternatively, s/he may simply choose to archive or remove e-mails with regards to structured information such as time stamp and/or size. It is precisely this knowledge associated with each e-mail client that is expected to be elicited by the automated multiple agents proposed in this chapter, preferably in real time.

Table 1. Attributes of knowledge-management for e-mail usage

Attribute	Type of Knowledge
Time Stamp	Structured
Size (KB)	Structured
Recipient/Sender	Tacit/Unstructured
Event/Subject	Tacit/Unstructured
Attachment	Tacit/Unstructured
Significance	Tacit/Unstructured

Figure 3. Classification of neural-network models

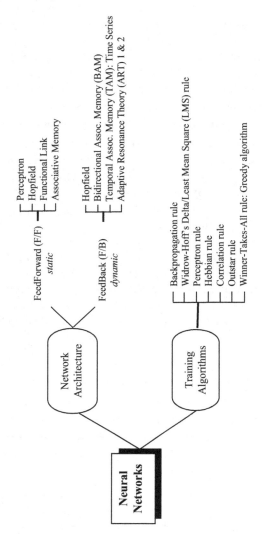

Intelligent Automated Agent

Under a certain memory constraint for each e-mail client, the administrator of the information system (i.e., the mail server) may choose to adopt a "brute-force" approach, based on structured information such as time stamp or size of the message. Consequently, clients—without their consent—may often realize their e-mails unavailable at times, once they have reached the memory quota set by the system. However, this aggressive method is not effective, due to its user-service, if not legal, implications. Thus, an automated system that may *advise* the clients in real time about their e-mail usage patterns is considered as an attractive alternative for information-resource management. Moreover, all clients of the information system may share the workload of managing the memory requirement for the mail server.

Once the client is logged onto the system, the automatic intelligent agent generates a list of e-mail messages that are to be removed, as well as those that are highly likely to be candidates for local archives. In addition, another agent system is suggested for the server to advise the administrator(s) of potential preventative measures. In essence, a conceptual framework for a multiagent system is proposed in this chapter. Similar ideas are being incorporated into the Web and applications servers in Willow (2006a, 2006b) at present.

Neural networks (NN) are employed as the inference engine for the proposed mutiagent system. A neural network typically processes large-scale problems in terms of dimensionality, amount of data handled, and the volume of simulation or neural hardware processing (Willow, 2002). It emerged as an area of artificial intelligence (AI) to mimic the human neurons in both perception and learning. It is interesting to note, however, that a conceivably disparate area within information science classified as "knowledge representation" had brought the attention of researchers to pursue classes of "computing and processing, " such as neural networks. The object-oriented paradigm emerged as one of the better models for knowledge representation. In fact, the motivation for NN research was to seek an improved methodology in *machine learning*, and more specifically, in the area of the *planning algorithm*, thereby augmenting the techniques available at the time. However, as the research progressed, more obstacles in emulating the human neurons were realized. Toward this end, the jargon NN at present is more appropriate if it were to be replaced with *parallel, distributed simulation.* Figure 3 illustrates taxonomic views of NN (Willow, 2002). Notice it is not comprised of an exhaustive list of available NN models to date.

The concept of feedback plays a central role in learning for NN. As illustrated in Figure 3, two different types of learning are to be distinguished: learning with supervision (i.e., training) versus learning without supervision (Willow, 2002).

In supervised learning (Figure 4a), the desired response d of the system is provided by the teacher at each instant of time. The distance $\rho[\mathbf{d}, \mathbf{o}]$ between the actual and the desired response serves as an error measure, and is used to correct network parameters externally. Since adjustable weights are assumed, the teacher/supervisor may implement a reward-or-punishment scheme to adapt the network's weight matrix, $\mathbf{W}$. This mode of learning is pervasive, and is used in many situations of natural learning. A set of input and output patterns called a *training set* is required for this learning mode. Often, the inputs, outputs, and the computed gradient are

Figure 4. Learning modes for neural networks: (a) supervised, (b) unsupervised

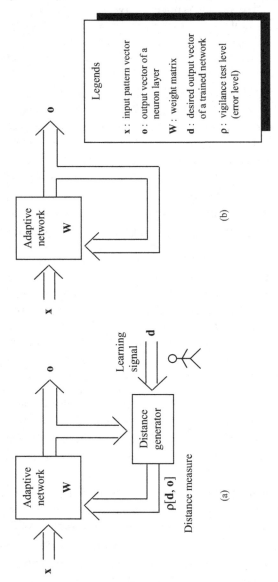

deterministic, however, the minimization of error proceeds over all its random realizations. As a result, most supervised learning algorithms reduce to stochastic minimization of error in multidimensional weight space.

In learning *without* supervision (Figure 4b), the desired response (**d**) is not known; thus, explicit error information cannot be used to improve network behavior. Since no information is available as to correctness or incorrectness of response, learning must somehow be accomplished based on observations of responses to inputs of marginal or at times, no knowledge. Unsupervised learning algorithms use patterns that are typically redundant raw data, having no labels regarding their class membership, or association. In this mode of learning, the network must discover for itself any possibly existing patterns, regularities, separating properties, and so on. While discovering these, the network undergoes a change of its parameters, which is called *self-organization*. Adaptive resonance theory (ART) is a good example of such a class.

Adaptive Resonance Theory

Adaptive resonance theory (ART), as illustrated in Zurada (1992), is a unique *unsupervised* class of neural-network algorithm. It has the novel property of controlled discovery of clusters. Further, the ART network may accommodate new clusters without affecting the storage or recall capabilities for clusters that were already learned, fit for the scope of the problem of this chapter. Figure 5 illustrates the ART architecture (Zurada,).

Nomenclature of the model follows:

Subscripts and Superscripts:

i Subscript for input variable, x; $i = 1, ..., n$.

j Subscript for output clusters, $j = 1, ..., M$.

m Subscript for output neuron, y or neuron of hidden layer; $m = 1, ...j, ...,$ M.

k Superscript for neuron y at layer k; $k \geq 0$.

Parameters:

M Total number of clusters set by the decision maker.

n Total number of variables for input vector/tuple, $\mathbf{x} = [x_1, ..., x_n] = <x_1, ..., x_n>$.

Figure 5. Neural-network architecture for adaptive resonance theory

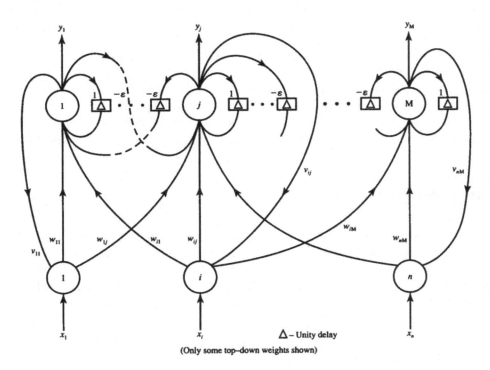

Δ – Unity delay

(Only some top–down weights shown)

Variables:

x   Input vector; $\mathbf{x} = [x_1, \ldots, x_n]$.

w   Weight of the input vector; $\mathbf{w} = [w_1, \ldots, w_n]$.

y   Output vector; $\mathbf{y}^k = [y_1, \ldots, y_M]$.

ρ Controlled vigilance factor indicating closeness of input to a stored cluster prototype to provide a desirable match, $0 < \rho < 1$. The ART net will seek a perfect match for $\rho = 1$ and loosely coupled matches for lower values of ρ.

v   Weight vector for verifying cluster exemplar proximity; $\mathbf{v} = [v_1, \ldots, v_n]$.

t   Update index for weights, **w** and **v**.

Algorithm for ART is summarized as follows (Zurada, 1992):

- **Step 1:** *Initialization*

The vigilance threshold, ρ, is set.

Weights are initialized for n-tuple input vectors and M top-layer neurons. ($M \times n$) matrices **W** and **V** each are initialized with identical

$$W = \left[\frac{1}{1+n} \right] \tag{1}$$

$$V = [1] \tag{2}$$

$$0 < \rho < 1 \tag{3}$$

- **Step 2:** *Input-neuron processing*

Binary unipolar input vector **x** is presented at input nodes, $x_i = 0, 1$ for $i = 1, 2, \ldots, n$.

- **Step 3:** *Matching-score computation*

All matching scores are computed as follows:

$$y_m^o = \sum_{i=1}^{n} w_{im} x_i, \quad \text{for } m = 1, \ldots, M. \tag{4}$$

In this step, selection of the best matching existing cluster, j, is performed according to the maximum criterion, as follows:

$$y_j^o = \max_{j=1,\ldots,M} (y_m^o) \tag{5}$$

- **Step 4:** *Resonance*

The similarity test for the winning neuron j is performed as follows:

$$\frac{1}{\|x\|} \sum_{i=1}^{n} v_{ij} x_i > \rho \tag{6}$$

where, the norm is defined as:

$$\|x\| \equiv \sum_{i=1}^{n} |x_i| \tag{7}$$

If the test as illustrated in equation (6) is passed, the control is passed on to Step 5. Upon failing the test, Step 6 is followed only if the top layer has more than a single active node left. Otherwise, Step 5 is followed.

- **Step 5:** *Vigilance test*

  Entries of the weight matrices are updated for index j passing the test of Step 4. The updates are only for entries (i, j), where $i = 1, 2, \ldots, M$, and are computed as follows:

$$w_{ij}(t+1) = \frac{v_{ij}(t)x_i}{0.5 + \sum_{i=1}^{n} v_{ij}(t)x_i} \tag{8}$$

$$v_{ij}(t+1) = x_i v_{ij}(t) \tag{9}$$

  This updates the weights of the j-th cluster, newly generated or existing. The algorithm returns to Step 2.

- **Step 6:** *Cluster generation*

  The node j is deactivated by setting y_j to 0. Thus, this mode does not participate in the current cluster search. The algorithm goes back to Step 3, and will attempt to establish a new cluster different from j for the pattern under test.

The network itself generates clusters if such clusters are identified in input data and stores the clustering information about patterns or features in the absence of *a priori* information about the possible number and type of clusters. In essence, ART computes the input-pattern-to-cluster matching score (y), which represents the degree of similarity of the present input to the previously encoded clusters. The vigilance threshold, ρ, where $0 < \rho < 1$, determines the degree of required similarity, or "match," between a cluster or pattern already stored in the ART network and the current input in order for this new pattern to *resonate* with the encoded one. If no match is found, then a new class or cluster is created.

Applications of ART to the proposed multiagent system follow in the next two subsections.

Figure 6. ART for the client agent

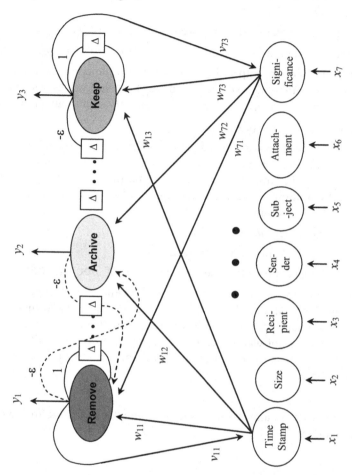

Client-Agent Architecture with ART

This section describes the ART architecture for the suggested client agent. The object of the client agent is to provide real-time knowledge regarding e-mail management for each client end-user. Figure 6 illustrates this.

For each e-mail message, an input vector comprised of the following 7-tuple attribute is produced; $\mathbf{x} = \langle x_1, \ldots, x_7 \rangle$:

x_1 Age of the message. It is automatically computed as system-generated time (TNOW) – (Time_Stamp).

x_2 Size of the e-mail, generally measured in kilobytes (KB).

x_3 Recipient information in smtp address format (To: johndoe@xyz.com).

x_4 Sender information in smtp address format (From: janedoe@xyz.com). Note that x_3 and x_4 are mutually exclusive, and may have null values associated. That is, each message is either received from or strictly sent to an smtp address.

x_5 Subject of the message (character strings).

x_6 Attachment to the message. A unique four-digit code encompassing the number of attachments between 0 and 99 (first two digits) and their file types is assigned for x_6. To simplify the data structure, file types are restricted to the three most common on the Internet; ASCII .txt (1), Microsoft .doc (2), and Adobe .pdf (3). Examples of x_6 values are:

0000   No attachments.

0103   One attachment in .pdf format.

9923   Ninety-nine attachments in mixtures of .doc and .pdf files.

x_7 Significance of the e-mail message, set by the end user. It ranges from 1 to 5, 5 being the most significant, and 1 being the least. Note that this value is applicable exclusively for the *body* of the e-mail. For instance, a message with $x_7 = 1$ does not warrant automatic removal from the mailbox. Instead, the user may choose to archive it due to the importance of its attachment(s), x_6, for example.

A simplified numerical example follows to illustrate. Consider the following three messages for a client:

Message #1 = $<x_1, ..., x_7>$
          = <60, 2000, *jmis@xyz.edu*, null, "publication consideration", 0203, 5>
Message #2 = <02,   20, null, *jdoe@usa.com*, "Greetings",   0000, 1>
Message #3 = <14,   250, *family@home.org*, null, "get together",   0000, 5>

Thus, each message forms an input pattern vector, **x**. Tacit input values are converted into a utility scale of 1 to 5 for neural processing, based on interactions with the knowledge base. This pertains to the attributes, x_3, x_4, and x_5. Consequently, the input vectors are:

$$\mathbf{x}_1 \;=\; <60,\;2000,\;4,\quad null,\;5,\;02,\;5>$$
$$\mathbf{x}_2 \;=\; <02,\quad20,\;null,\;5,\quad1,\;00,\;1>$$
$$\mathbf{x}_3 \;=\; <14,\quad250,\;5,\quad null,\;1,\;00,\;5>$$

When $\mathbf{x}_1$ is presented, the steps of the ART algorithm are:

$$M = 3; \quad n = 7$$

$$w_{ij} = \frac{1}{n+1} = 1/8 = 0.125;$$

$v_{ij} = 1,\; i = 1,\;\ldots,\;7,\; j = 1,\,2,\,3$ for **Remove, Archive, Keep.**

Given a standard vigilance value of $\rho = 0.5$, the left term in inequality (6) is of unity in the first pass, allowing the similarity test to be passed. This results in an unconditional definition of the first cluster, the default being the "Archive." Equations (8) and (9) of **Step 5** produce:

$$w_{32}(2) = \frac{1 \times 4}{0.5 + [4 + 0 + 5 + 2 + 5]} = 0.2424$$

$$w_{52}(2) = \frac{1 \times 5}{0.5 + [4 + 0 + 5 + 2 + 5]} = 0.3030 \quad = w_{72}$$

for the tacit variable set only. Notice x_3, x_5, and x_7 had significant values of 4 or above. The remaining weights $w_{i2} = 0.125$, as initialized in **Step 1**. In addition,

$$v_{32} = v_{52} = v_{72} = 1,$$

as initialized, while the remaining weights are recomputed as $v_{i2} = 0$.

For the second input pattern vector $\mathbf{x}_2$, there are no significance values and the similarity test of equation (6) yields

$$\frac{1}{\|x\|}\sum_{i=1}^{7} v_{ij} x_i > \rho = 0 < 0.5$$

Due to the failure of the vigilance test and the absence of other nodes for further evaluation and for potential disabling, pattern x_2 is treated as another new cluster. Further, a null value for the left-hand side of (6) is classified as the "Remove" cluster.

In essence, the ART-based neural-network processing is expected to advise the e-mail clients of possible action(s) for each (e-mail) message.

Server-Agent Architecture with ART

The adaptive resonance theory (ART) model may also be employed for another set of agent systems dedicated to assisting the e-mail server administrator(s). The two systems of agents, targeting individual clients as well as administrators, may then communicate in real time by accessing the integrated knowledge base. However, the server-agent architecture is relatively more complicated due to differences in network protocols. Two major methods employed are: Internet message access protocol (IMAP) and post office protocol (POP). IMAP integrates messages on the shared mail server and permits client e-mail programs to access remote message stores as if they were local. Thus, the memory burden on the server is far greater for IMAP than for POP. However, complete monitoring of client e-mails is possible under the IMAP scheme. That is, a single server-side agent system may suffice for the IMAP, whereas a single client-agent may fit systems with POP being implemented. Table 2 illustrates this.

A multiagent system, therefore, is expected to be highly useful for managing client knowledge under the IMAP (fourth quadrant in Table 2; mixed) and for managing server knowledge under the POP structure (second quadrant; mixed).

Implementation Agenda

Architecture of the proposed multiagent system, followed by description of its functions and the challenges encountered during systems analysis are discussed in this section.

Sycara, Pannu, Williamson, Zeng, and Decker (1996) has presented a generalized multiagent system (MAS) architecture entitled RETSINA. Three classes of agents are proposed in Sycara et al.: *interface*, *task*, and *information* agents. The major objective of the interface agents is to interact with the clients/users in order to receive user specifications and to deliver the results. They acquire, model, and utilize user preferences to guide system coordination in support of the user's tasks. Task agents perform the majority of autonomous problem solving, and thus are regarded

Table 2. Classes of information availability based on e-mail application protocols

E-mail Protocols Information Process	IMAP *(central)*	POP *(distributed)*
Server-based	Server only	Mixed
User-based	Mixed	Client only

as the "inference schema" of RETSINA. It exhibits a higher level of sophistication and complexity than either an interface or an information agent. Information agents provide intelligent access to a heterogeneous collection of information sources depicted at the bottom of Figure 7.

Having gathered an intuitive understanding of a generalized multiagent system (MAS) architecture in Sycara et al. (1996), the architecture of the proposed MAS for mail-server management is built similar to the RETSINA architecture. Figure 7 shows the proposed architecture, and its components are briefly described below.

In the application domain of mail-server memory management, it is interesting to note that the users or clients themselves act as an information source. That is, the input pattern vector x, to be incorporated into the adaptive resonance theory (ART) algorithm used by the four task agents, represented by shaded hexagons, is collected by each corresponding interface agent for a user. In essence, the interface agents function as both interacting and information agents. There may be as many as m number of interface agents for the n number of clients, where $n > m$, since some users may choose to decline the automated service that tracks and manages their e-mail messages. Instead, they will be liable for managing their memory quota manually. Dashed arrows indicate access to the knowledge repository, in which patterns of e-mail usage for each client are retained in the form of rules.

Three task agents, "Input Weight Vector," "Output Weight Vector," and "Vigilance Factor" dynamically interact with knowledge bases to adjust themselves asynchronously in real time. In effect, the neural network based on ART learns without supervision, and a unique cluster is generated for each e-mail message. Possible clusters were illustrated in Figure 6.

Implementation of the proposed architecture has been initiated with a Dell Power-Edge™ 1850 server with Intel Xeon processor at clock speed of up to 3.0GHz and 1.0GB RAM. At present, a closed proprietary network with two clients is being

Figure 7. Multi-agent system architecture for mail server management

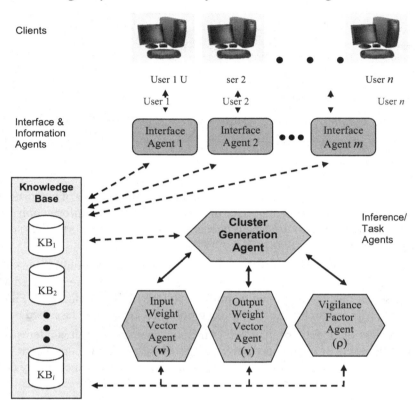

tested for building the prototype multi-agent system. The network operating system (NOS) of choice is Linux, with Visual C++ as the major development platform.

In building a technical infrastructure, the following obstacles are expected, among others:

- **Difficulty of data mining:** Execution of a *spyware* is inevitable on the client machine, which may develop legal implications. At present, cookies are being considered as the quick implementation vehicle.

- **Network utilization:** Running a multi-agent system in real time may decrease the network performance in terms of bandwidth utilization and reliability to a critical level.

- **Portability/Scalability:** There is a constant portability problem of this proposed agent system with respect to an operating systems and/or hardware platforms. Platforms running operating systems other than Linux have to be simulated and tested for, once this prototype completes its pilot run.

Conclusion

A conceptual framework for a real-time multiagent system built with a neural network and knowledge base has been presented in this chapter, with emphasis on information resource management (IRM). Managing client as well as server knowledge concerning e-mails was selected as the scope of this research due to its significance as a major communication vehicle in the e-economy.

Adaptive resonance theory (ART) was the primary algorithm of choice for the neural-network engine due to its capability to achieve *unsupervised* learning. A simplified numerical example was provided to illustrate the effectiveness of ART applied to the problem domain.

Marked differences are discovered for the two major e-mail protocols for the server: IMAP and POP. Consequently, the suggested multi-agents are expected to be most effective for managing client knowledge under the IMAP and for managing server knowledge under the POP structure.

Challenges of implementing the proposed framework include but are not restricted to data mining, network utilization, portability, and security.

References

Ahuja, M. K. (1998). Network structure in virtual organizations [electronic version]. *Journal of Computer-Mediated Communication, 3*(4).

Applen, J. D. (2002). Technical communication, knowledge management, and XML. *Technical Communication, 49*(3), 301-313.

Butte, T. (2002). *Technologies for development of agent-based distributed applications.* ACM Crossroads. Retrieved January 9, 2006, from http://info.acm.org/crossroads/xrds8-3/agent.html

Cohen, F. (2004). *JAVA testing and design: From unit testing to automated Web tests.* New York: Prentice-Hall.

Curran, T. A., & Ladd, A. (2000). *SAP R/3 business blueprint:Understanding enterprise supply chain management, 2/E.* New York: Prentice-Hall.

Davenport, T. H., & Prusak, L. (1998). *Working knowledge: How organizations manage what they know.* Boston: Harvard Business School Press.

Dutta, S. (1997). Strategies for implementing knowledge-based systems. *IEEE Transactions on Engineering Management, 22*, 79-90.

Eales, R. T. J. (2004). A knowledge management approach to user support. In *Proceedings of the Fifth Conference on Australasian User Interface Conference (AUIC2004)* (pp. 33-38). Dunedin: Association for Computing Machinery.

Flenner, R., Abbott, M., Boubez, T., Cohen, F., Krishnan, N., Moffet, A., et al. (2002). *Java P2P unleashed: With JXTA, Web services, XML, Jini, JavaSpaces, and J2EE.* New York: Prentice-Hall.

Gallivan, M. J., Eynon, J., & Rai, A. (2003). The challenge of knowledge management systems: Analyzing the dynamic processes underlying performance improvement initiatives. *Information Technology and People, 16*(3), 326-352.

Gold, A. H., Malhotra, A., & Segars, A. H. (2001). Knowledge management: An organizational capabilities perspective. *Journal of Management Information Systems, 18*(1), 185-214.

Grudin, J. (1988). Why CSCW applications fail: Problems in the design and evaluation of organizational interfaces. In *Proceedings of the 1988 ACM Conference on Computer Supported Cooperative Work* (pp. 85-93). New York: Association for Computing Machinery.

Kanawati, R., & Malek, M. (2002). A Multi-agent system for collaborative bookmarking. In *Proceedings of the First International Joint Conference on Autonomous Agents and Multi-agent Systems: Part 3* (pp. 1137-1138). Bologna, Italy: Association for Computing Machinery.

Kankanhalli, A., Tanudidjaja, F., Sutanto, J., & Tan, C. Y. (2003). The role of IT in successful knowledge management initiatives. *Communications of the ACM, 46*(9), 69-73.

Lansdale, M. (1988). The psychology of personal information management. *Applied Ergonomics, 19*(1), 55-66.

Laudon, K. C., & Laudon, J. P. (2004). *Management information systems: Managing the digital firm.* Prentice-Hall.

Laurillau, Y., & Nigay, L. (2002). Clover architecture for groupware. In *Proceedings of the 2002 ACM Conference on Computer Supported Cooperative Work* (pp. 236-245). Association for Computing Machinery.

Majchrzak, A., Rice, R. E., Malhotra, A., & King, N. (2000). Technology adaptation: The case of a computer-supported inter-organizational virtual team. *MIS Quarterly, 24*(4), 569-600.

Malek, M. (2000). Hybrid approaches integrating neural networks and case based reasoning: from loosely coupled to tightly coupled models. In K. P. Sankar, S. D. Tharam, & S. Y. Daniel, (Eds.), *Soft computing in case-based reasoning* (pp. 73-94). New York: Springer.

Markus, M. L., & Connolly, T. (1990). Why computer supported collaborative work applications fail: Problems in the adoption of interdependent work tools. In *Proceedings of the International Conference on Computer Supported Collaborative Work (CSCW '90)* (pp. 371-380). New York: Association for Computing Machinery.

Markus, M. L. (2001). Toward a theory of knowledge reuse: Types of knowledge reuse situations and factors in reuse success. *Journal of Management Information Systems, 18*(1), 57-93.

Mathe, N., & Chen, J. R. (1998). Organizing and sharing information on the World-Wide Web using a multi-agent systems. In *Proceedings of ED-MEDIA '98 Conference on Educational Multimedia and Hypermedia*. Freiburg, Germany.

Murch, R. (2004). *Autonomic computing*. New York: Prentice-Hall.

Nonaka, I., & Takeuchi, H. (1995). *The knowledge-creating company: How Japanese companies create dynamics of innovation*. New York: Oxford University Press.

Pinelle, D., & Gutwin, C. (2002). Groupware walkthrough: Adding context to groupware usability evaluation. In *Proceedings of the ACM SIGCHI Conference on Human Factors in Computing Systems: Changing Our World, Changing Ourselves* (pp. 455-462). Minneapolis, MN: Association for Computing Machinery.

Pinelle, D., Gutwin, C., & Greenberg, S. (2003). Task analysis for groupware usability evaluation: Modeling shared-workspace tasks with the mechanics of collaboration. *ACM Transactions on Computer-Human Interaction, 10*(4), 281-311.

Roos, L. L., Soodeen, R-A., Bond, R., & Burchill, C. (2003). Working more productively: Tools for administrative Data. *Health Services Research, 38*(5), 1339-1357.

Roseman, M., & Greenberg, S. Building real-time groupware with GroupKit, a groupware toolkit. *ACM Transactions on Computer-Human Interaction, 3*(1), 66-106.

Sycara, K., Pannu, A., Williamson, M., Zeng, D., & Decker, K. (1996). Distributed intelligent agents. *IEEE Intelligent Systems, 11*(6), 36-46.

Taylor, W. A. (2004). Computer-mediated knowledge sharing and individual user differences: An exploratory study. *European Journal of Information Systems, 13*, 52-64.

Turban, E., King, D., Lee, J., Warkentin, M., & Chung, H. M. (2002). *Electronic commerce: A managerial perspective.* Prentice-Hall.

Wiesenfeld, B. M., Raghuram, S., & Garud, R. (1998). Communication patterns as determinants of organizational identification in a virtual organization [electronic version]. *Journal of Computer-Mediated Communication, 3*(4).

Willow, C. C. (2002). A feedforward multi-layer neural network for machine cell formation in computer integrated manufacturing. *Journal of Intelligent Manufacturing, 13*(2), 75-87.

Willow, C. C. (2005). A neural network-based agent framework for mail server management. *International Journal of Intelligent Information Technologies, 1*(4), 36-52.

Willow, C. C. (2006a). *Neural network-based multiple agent system for application server management* (MU WP No. W05-03). Monmouth, NJ: Management Information Systems, School of Business Administration, Monmouth University, NJ.

Willow, C. C. (2006b). *Neural network-based multiple agent system for web server management* (MU WP No. W05-02). Monmouth, NJ: Management Information Systems, School of Business Administration, Monmouth University, NJ.

Ye, Y., Fischer, G., & Reeves, B. (2000). Integrating active information delivery and reuse repository systems. In *Proceedings of the Eighth ACM SIGSOFT International Symposium on Foundations of Software Engineering: 21 Century Applications* (pp. 60-68). San Diego: Association for Computing Machinery.

Zurada, J. M. (1992). *Introduction to artificial neural systems.* St. Paul: West Press.

Chapter XV

Predicting Protein Secondary Structure Using Artificial Neural Networks and Information Theory

Saad Osman Abdalla Subair, Al-Ghurair University, United Arab Emirates

Safaai Deris, University of Technology Malaysia, Malaysia

Abstract

Protein secondary-structure prediction is a fundamental step in determining the 3D structure of a protein. In this chapter, a new method for predicting protein secondary structure from amino-acid sequences has been proposed and implemented. Cuff and Barton 513 protein data set is used in training and testing the prediction methods under the same hardware, platforms, and environments. The newly developed method utilizes the knowledge of the GOR-V information theory and the power of the neural networks to classify a novel protein sequence in one of its three secondary-structures classes (i.e., helices, strands, and coils). The newly developed method (NN-GORV-I) is further improved by applying a filtering mechanism to the searched database and hence named NN-GORV-II. The developed prediction methods are rigorously analyzed and tested together with the other five well-known prediction methods in this domain to allow easy comparison and clear conclusions.

Introduction

Proteins are a series of **amino acids** known as polymers linked together into contiguous chains. In a living cell, the DNA of an organism encodes or *transcribes* its proteins into a **sequence** of nucleotides that are copied to the mRNA which are then *translated* into protein (Branden & Tooze, 1991). Protein has three main structures: (1) *primary structure, which* is essentially the linear **amino-acid sequence**; (2) *secondary structures* which are ɜ helices, β sheets, and coils that are formed when the sequences of primary structures tend to arrange themselves into regular conformations (Kendrew, 1960; Pauling & Corey, 1951); and (3) *tertiary* or *3D structure*, where secondary structure elements are packed against each other in a stable configuration. However, coils or loops usually serve as connection points between alpha-helices and beta-sheets; they do not have uniform patterns like alpha-helices and beta-sheets, and they could be any other part of the protein structure rather than helices or strands. In the molecular-biology laboratory, protein secondary structure is determined experimentally by two lengthy methods: X-ray crystallography method and nuclear magnetic resonance (NMR) spectroscopy method.

Advances in molecular biology in the last few decades, and the availability of equipment in this field, lead to the rapid sequencing of considerable genomes of several species. Several bacterial genomes, as well as those of some simple eukaryotic organisms, have been completely sequenced until now. These large genome-sequencing projects; including human genome projects, generate a huge number of protein sequences in their primary structures that are difficult for conventional molecular-biology laboratory techniques like X-ray crystallography and NMR to determine their corresponding 3D structures (Heilig et al., 2003).

One of the main approaches of predicting protein structures from sequence alone is based on data sets of known protein structures and sequences. This approach attempts to find common features in these data sets, which can be generalized to provide structural models of other proteins.

Prediction Methods

Since Anfinsen (1973) concluded that the amino-acid sequence is the only source of information to survive the denaturing process, and hence the structured information must be somehow specified by the primary protein sequence, researchers have been trying to predict secondary structure from protein sequence. Anfinsen's hypothesis suggests that an ideal theoretical model of predicting protein secondary structure form its sequence should exist anyhow.

Many researchers used the approach of predicting protein structures from sequence alone, which is based on the data sets of known protein structures and sequences, and then deriving general rules for predicting secondary structure. (Chou & Fasman, 1974; Crick, 1989; Krigbaum & Knutton, 1973; Qian & Sejnowski, 1988; Richardson, 1981).

The Problem

A first step towards solving the protein folding dilemma, which is essentially how a protein folds up into its three dimensional structure (3D) from linear sequences of amino acids, is predicting protein secondary structures (helices, strands, and loops). Prediction cannot be completely accurate because the assignment of secondary structure may vary up to 12% between different crystals of the same protein (Cline et al., 2002; Rost, 2001). Now the prediction level of protein secondary structures is still at slightly above the 70% range (Frishman & Argos, 1997; Rost, 2001, 2003).

Multiple **alignment**s of protein sequences are important tools in studying proteins. The basic information they provide is the identification of conserved **sequence** regions. This is very useful in designing experiments to test and modify the function of specific proteins in predicting the function and structure of proteins, and in identifying new members of protein families (Durbin, Eddy, Krogh, & Mitchison, 2002). The objective of this paper is to develop an efficient approach for predicting protein secondary structures by integrating existing techniques and amino-acid sequences.

Prediction Using Neural Networks

Artificial **neural networks** have great opportunities in the prediction of proteins secondary structures. Since the neural network can be trained to map specific input signals or patterns to a desired output, information from the central amino acid of each input value can be modified by a weighting factor, grouped together then sent to a second level (hidden layer) where the signal is clustered into an appropriate class (Frishman & Argos, 1997; Rost, 2001, 2003). Feedforward **neural networks** are powerful tools. They have the ability to learn from example, they are extremely robust, or fault tolerant, the process of training is almost the same for all problems (Haykin, 1999). Thus, neural networks and especially feedforward networks have a fair chance to well suit the empirical approach to protein-structure prediction. In the process of protein folding, which is effectively finding the most stable structure given all the competing interactions within a polymer of amino acids, neural networks explore input information in parallel style.

The feedforward net is the most widely used neural-network architecture in solving problems and accomplishing pattern **classification** and regression tasks. The *feedforward network* is also known as a multilayer perceptron (MLP). One of the most important approaches in **neural networks** is the approach derived from statistical-pattern-recognition theory or probabilistic model (Baldi & Brunak, 2001; Bishop, 1996; Devroye, Györfi, & Lugosi, 1996)

Feedforward networks are often composed of visible and hidden units. The visible units are those in contact with the outside world such as input and output layers while invisible units are those called hidden layer or layers (Baldi & Brunak, 2001). Each network has connections between every node in one layer and every other node in the layer above. Two layer networks, or perceptrons, are only capable of processing first order information and consequently obtain results comparable to those of multiple linear regression.

As an efficient pattern classification tool (Haykin, 1999), a neural network has been used in protein-structure-prediction problems by many researchers (Arbib, 1995; Presnell & Cohen, 1993; Wu, 1997). Qian and Sejnowski (1988) followed by Bohr et al. (1988) greatly influenced the approach of predicting protein structure by their work when first introduced to neural networks in this area. Using an advanced neural-network design, Baldi, Brunak, Frasconi, Soda, and Pollastri (1999) have improved the level of accuracy in predicting beta-strand pairings. Their bidirectional recurrent neural network outperformed the work of many researchers.

Many researchers have described various architectures of artificial neural networks (Baldi & Brunak, 2001; Haykin, 1999; Qian, & Sejnowski, 1988). In this section, we will explore some of the foundational architectures that had been used in **protein secondary-structure prediction**. Inside the neural network (Figure 1), many types of computational units exist; the most common type sums its inputs (x_i) and passes the result through a nonlinear approximation or activation function (Figure 2) to yield an output (y_i). Thus, the output $(y_i) = f_i(x_i)$, where f_i is the transfer function of each unit. This is summarized in equations (1) and (2).

$$x_i = \sum_{j \in N-(i)} w_j \, y_j + w_i \tag{1}$$

$$y_i = f_i(x_i) = f_i\left(\sum_{j \in N-(i)} w_j \, y_j + w_i \right) \tag{2}$$

where, w_i is the bias or threshold of the unit i.

A transfer function may be a linear function like the identity function of the regression analysis, and hence the unit *i* is a linear unit. However, in artificial neural networks, most of the time the transfer functions are nonlinear like sigmoid (Figure 1) and threshold logic functions. Bounded activation functions are often known as squashing functions. When f is a threshold or bias function, then:

$$f(x) = \begin{cases} 1 & \text{if } x > 0 \\ 0 & \text{otherwise} \end{cases} \tag{3}$$

Equation (4) shows a sigmoid-transfer function of type logistic transfer function, which can estimate the probability of a binary event.

$$f(x) = \sigma(x) = \frac{1}{1 + e^{-x}} \tag{4}$$

The simplest way to reduce the network error is by changing the connections according to the derivative of the error with respect to the connections, in a process known as gradient descent. This is often referred to as back-propagating the error through the neural network (Hertz, Krogh, & Palmer, 1991; Muller & Reinhardt, 1990). To avoid being trapped in local minima, in practise, the actual training is

Figure 1. The sigmoid function conventionally used in feedforward artificial neural networks: (a) sigmoid unipolar and its derivative function, (b) sigmoid bipolar and its derivative function

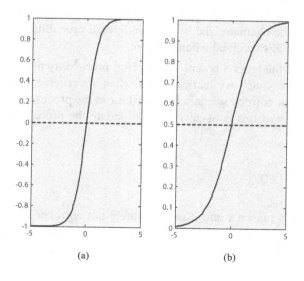

(a)   (b)

typically performed by a variant of the back-propagation algorithm (Rost, 1996; Rost & Sander, 1993).

With enough hidden units, neural networks can learn to separate any set of patterns. Typical applications require them to extract particular features present in the patterns rather than to learn the known examples. A successful extraction of such features permits the network to generalise or also to classify correctly patterns that have not been learned explicitly. As a rule-of-thumb the number of connections should be an order of magnitude lower than the number of patterns to avoid over-fitting the training data, which is also known as overtraining (Rost, 1996; Rost & Sander, 1993).

Prediction Using Information Theory

Information theory is a branch of the mathematical theory of probability and mathematical statistics that quantifies the concept of information. Shannon (1948) explained information theory as a strictly stated mathematical problem in statistics for the very first time. It is concerned with information entropy, communication systems, data transmission, and rate-distortion theory, cryptography, data compression, error correction, and other related fields.

Shannon (1948) defines that entropy $H(X)$ quantifies how much information is conveyed, on the average, by a letter drawn from the ensemble X; that is, it tells how many bits are required to encode such information. The mutual information $I(X; Y)$ quantifies how correlated the two bits are. How much do we know about an event drawn from X^n when we have read about an event drawn from Y^n? This can be explained by an example from the signal communication field. Let a message sent from a transmitter to a receiver, given that the communication channel is noisy, so that the message received (y) might differ from the message sent (x). Then the noisy channel can be characterized by the conditional probability $p(y|x)$ which is the probability that y is received when x is sent.

 Let us assume that the letter x is sent with a priori probability p(x). We would like to quantify that how much we learn about x when we receive y, or simply how much information or entropy we gain to describe x in the process of learning more about x. Bayesian statistics is usually used to update the probability distribution for x; that is:

$$p(x|y) = p(y|x).p(x)/p(y) \qquad (5)$$

However, if for any reason x and y are absolutely not correlated, the information contained in x is zero, and the whole formula in this concept evaluates to nothing.

In the filed of protein structure, researchers have used the information theory approach to analyze the contributions of several traditional amino-acid alphabets (residues) using mutual information (Cline et al., 2002). Interpretation of the reduced representation problem in information-theory terms is straightforward. Mutual information between two variables I and J (representing a grouping of the protein-atom types) is a measure of how much information one variable reveals about the other (Kullback, Keegel, & Kullback, 1987).

GOR Method for Protein Secondary-Structure Prediction

The **GOR** method was first proposed by Garnier, Osguthorpe, and Robson (1978) and named after its authors. The GOR method is based on the information theory described earlier and naive statistics (Garnier & Robson, 1989). The mostly known GOR-IV version uses all possible pair frequencies within a window of 17 amino acid residues with a cross-validation on a database of 267 proteins (Garnier, Gibrat, & Robson, 1996). The GOR-IV program output gives the probability values for each secondary structure at each amino-acid position.

The most-recent version, GOR-V, gains significant improvement over the previous versions of the GOR algorithms by combining the PSIBLAST multiple-sequence alignments with the GOR method. The accuracy of the prediction for the GOR-V method with multiple-sequence alignments is nearly as good as neural network predictions (Kloczkowski, Ting, Jernigan, & Garnier, 2002).

The first version of the GOR method (GOR-I), used a relatively small database of proteins which consisted few residues. GOR-II used a database of 75 proteins containing about 13000 residues (Garnier & Robson, 1989).

The information function $I(S,R)$ is described as the logarithm of the ratio of the conditional probability $P(S|R)$ of observing conformation S, where S is one of the three states: helix (H), extended (E), or coil (C) for residue R, where R is one of the 20 possible amino acids and the probability P(S) of the occurrence of conformation S. The conformational state of a given residue in the **sequence** depends on the type of the amino acid R as well as the neighbouring residues along the sliding window. The information function of a complex event can be decomposed into information of simpler events and then summed up according to the manipulation of the information theory. The GOR-IV method calculates the information function as a sum of information from single residues (*singlets*) and pairs of residues (*doublets*) within the width of the sliding window. In GOR-IV, the first summation is over *doublets* and the second summation is over *singlets* within the window centred round the ith residue. The pair frequencies of residues occurring in corresponding conformations are calculated from the database used for the GOR method. Using the above frequencies calculated from the databases, the GOR-IV algorithm can predict probabilities of conformational states for a new sequence (Garnier et al., 1996).

The GOR algorithm reads a protein sequence and predicts its secondary structure. For each residue *i* along the sequence, the program calculates the probabilities for each confirmation state, and the secondary structure prediction for such states (H, E, or C). Except in very few cases, the predicted conformational state usually corresponds to that with the highest probability. GOR-V version applies the GOR-IV algorithm to multiple-sequence alignments. The GOR algorithm usually skips the gaps in the alignments during the calculation of probabilities of conformation for each residue in the multiple-alignments matrix but the information about position of gaps is kept (Kloczkowski et al., 2002). The main improvement made to GOR-IV was the systematic study of the GOR methods and the utilization of multiple-sequence alignments to increase the accuracy of the secondary-structure prediction. A full description of GOR-V will be presented in the methodology section.

Materials and Methods

The concept of combining models to improve the performance has long been established in statistical framework (Bates & Granger, 1969; Dickinson, 1973; Jordan & Jacobs, 1994). Many accurate methods are currently available to perform protein secondary-structure prediction. Since these methods are usually based on different principles, and different knowledge sources and approaches, significant benefits can be expected from combining them. However, the choice of an appropriate combiner may be a difficult task. In this work, the described neural network architecture is combined with the proposed GOR-V theory to produce a superior protein secondary-structure prediction method. This work is the first to combine the proposed GOR-V method with the neural-network architecture. Full description of the method is elucidated in Figure 2 and explained in this section.

The Stuttgart University neural-network simulator (SNNS) program (Zell et al., 1998) is used in this experimental work. SNNS for UNIX X Windows is used to generate many prototypes of neural networks. In this work, GOR-V method which is based on the information theory and the NN-II method which is based on the work of many researchers in the area of protein secondary structure (Cuff & Barton, 1999; Ouali & King 2000; Quian & Sejnowski, 1988; Rost & Sander, 1993,) are combined to achieve a better prediction method. The new method is further improved by applying a filter mechanism to mask low identity sites in the **sequence** database. This technique is used successfully in PSP-PRED. The "pfilt" program is used to perform this task (Jones, 1999).

Conventional GOR methods used windows of 17 residues. This indicates that for a given residue R, eight immediate nearest neighbouring residues on each side are

Figure 2. A detailed representation for the second version of the improved protein secondary-structure prediction method (NN-GORV-II).

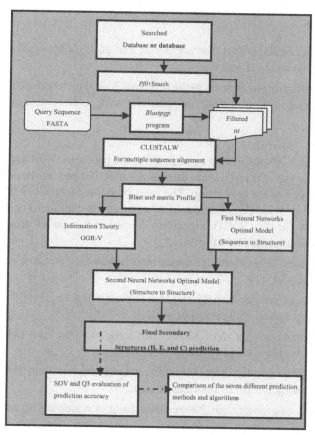

analyzed. If R is considered as R_0, then R_{+8} and R_{-8} are the immediate neighbouring residues. Information theory allows the information function of a complex event to be decomposed into the sum of information of simpler events, which can be written as:

$$I(\Delta S; R_1, R_2, ... R_n) = I(\Delta S; R_1) + (\Delta S; R_2 \mid R_1)$$
$$+ I(\Delta S; R_3 \mid R_1, R_2) + ... + I(\Delta S; R_n \mid R_1, R_2, ... R_{n-1})$$

(6)

where the information difference is written as:

$$I(\Delta S; R_1, R_2, ...R_n) = I(S; R_1, R_2, ...R_n)$$
$$- I(n - S; R_1, R_2, ...R_n)$$

(7)

where *n-S* are the confirmations that are not *S*, that is, if *S* happened to be E then *n-S* is the other two states H and C.

In this experiment, the improvements to the original GOR algorithms are implemented following Kloczkowski et al. (2002) suggestions with considerable modifications as follows:

1.   The database is of 480 proteins compared to the previous GOR database of 267 proteins. The use of this database allows an objective and unbiased calculation of the accuracy of the prediction. The latest version of the GOR-IV algorithm used a window with a fixed width of 17 residues as explained earlier. A resizable window for the GOR-V algorithm is used in this paper according to the length of the sequence as follows:

     a.   Sequences 25 residues or shorter length, a sliding window size of 7 residues is used.

     b.   Sequences greater than 25 and less than or equal to 50 residues length, a sliding window of 9 residues is used.

     c.   Sequences greater than 50 residues long and less than 100 residues, a sliding window of 11 residues is used.

     d.   Sequences greater than 100 residues long and less than 200 residues, a sliding window of 13 residues is used.

     e.   Sequences greater than 200 residues long, a window size of 17 residues is used.

2.   The original GOR algorithms had a tendency to over-predict the coil state (C). The coil state is adjusted so that it will be selected as the predicted state only if the calculated probability of the coil conformation is greater than the probability of the other states by (0.15 for E and 0.075 for H). This approach is known as decision constant or adjustable weights and had been applied successfully in PSIPRED algorithm.

3.   PSIBLAST multiple-sequence alignments for each protein sequence in the database had been used in this experiment. The PSIBLAST program is implemented using the *nr* database with default parameters. The alignments produced by PSIBLAST that are too similar to the query sequence are removed using a *trimmer* program.

The Prediction Methods Studied

To study and analyse the significance of the new prediction method NN-GORV-I and its advanced version NN-GORV-II, other five prediction methods are studied together with these two methods and implemented using the same hardware, platform, data set, and reduction schemes (Subair & Deris, 2006). The methods are:

1. NN-I: this neural-network architecture using the original **sequence** in the prediction process. This method is typically like what was described by Qian and Sejnowski (1988)

2. GOR-IV: as described by the GOR authors.

3. GOR-V: as described by Kloczkowski et al. (2002) with some modifications.

4. NN-II: the same architecture as of NN-I but here multiple-sequence alignment is used to extract long-range information. This is similar to what was described by Rost and Sander (1993)

5. PROF: as described and provided by it authors, Ouali and King (2000)

6. NN-GORV-I: This is the new proposed method in this work as described above in the methodology (Abdalla & Deris, 2005; Subair, Deris, & Saberi, 2005).

7. NN-GORV-II: This is the improved version of NN-GORV-I by using a filtered mechanism to the database (Subair & Deris, 2005).

Assessment of Prediction Accuracies of the Seven Methods

Several measures and methods are used to estimate the prediction accuracy of the several algorithms developed and studied in this research. The methods and measures used to assess the accuracy are further analyzed statistically to observe the significance of each. These methods are discussed in this section.

The Q_3 accuracy per residue which measures the expected accuracy of an unknown residue is computed as the number of residues correctly predicted divided by the total number of residues. The Q_3 measure per the whole protein is also computed using the same definition. The Q_H ratio is defined as the total number of α helix correctly predicted divided by the total number of α helix. The same definitions are applied to Q_E (β strands) and Q_C (coils). The Q_3 factor is expressed as:

$$Q_3 = \sum_{(i=H,E,C)} \frac{predicted_i}{observed_i} x100 \qquad (8)$$

Segment overlap measure (SOV) calculation (Rost et al., 1994; Zemla et al., 1999) is performed for each data set. Segment overlap values attempt to capture segment prediction, and vary from an ignorance level of 37% (random-protein pairs) to an average 90% level for homologous protein pairs. Specifically, the SOV aims to assess the quality of a prediction by taking into account the type and position of a secondary-structure segment, the natural variation of segment boundaries among families of homologous proteins and the deviation at the end of each segment. Segment overlap is calculated by:

$$Sov = \frac{1}{N} \sum_{s} \frac{mnov(S_{obs}; S_{pred}) + d}{mxov(S_{obs}; S_{pred})} \times len(s_1) \qquad (9)$$

Where:

N is the total number of residues,

mnov is the actual overlap, with *mxov* the extent of the segment.

lens_1 is the number of residues in segment s_1.

δ is the accepted variation which assures a ratio of 1.0 where there are only minor deviations at the ends of segments.

The Q_3 and SOV measures are calculated using the SOV program downloaded from the Web site: http://PredictionCenter.llnl.gov/

Matthews' correlation coefficient (MCC) is performed for each of the three states. Calculating the four numbers (p_i, r_i, u_i, and o_i). The formula of Matthews's correlation can be rewritten as:

$$C_i = \frac{p_i r_i - u_i o_i}{\sqrt{(p_i + u_i)(p_i + o_i)(r_i + u_i)(r_i + o_i)}} \qquad (10)$$

Where:

p_i number of correctly predicted residues in conformation.

r_i number of those correctly rejected.

u_i number of the incorrectly rejected (false negatives).

o_i number incorrectly predicted to be in the class (false positive)

$i =$ is one of the confirmation states H, E, or C.

Results and Discussion

In this section, the two proposed methods in addition to five well-known **protein secondary-structure prediction** methods are examined together in a comparative analysis style. The seven methods have been described in the previous section.

Performance of the Seven Methods

Considering the nature of the composition of protein secondary structure, it is worth mentioning that prediction accuracy of about 50% is worse than random guess since the coil composition of most databases is about 50% of the whole database (Baldi, Brunak, Chauvin, Andersen, & Nielsen, 2000).

Table 1 shows the detailed results of the seven methods of prediction. The estimated accuracy for the alpha helices (Q_H), beta strands (Q_E), coil states (Q_C), and the three states together (Q_3) for the seven prediction methods studied in this research are shown in this table with their corresponding standard deviations. The standard deviations for the Q_3 show small estimates compared to the other three states. This result suggests that Q_3 accuracies are estimated from more homogenous and normally distributed

Table 1. The percentages of prediction accuracies with the standard deviations of the seven methods

Prediction Method	Q_3	Q_H	Q_E	Q_C
NN I	64.05±12.68	57.29±30.64	57.39±28.49	74.10±13.36
GOR IV	63.19±10.61	57.02±29.68	51.86±27.36	71.95±12.98
GOR V	71.84±19.63	68.40±33.98	63.68±33.02	78.92±15.08
NN II	73.58±17.82	70.77±31.62	68.72±30.01	78.33±15.18
PROF	75.03±14.74	70.65±31.39	68.29±28.09	79.38±13.68
NN-GORV-I	79.22±10.14	76.56±27.17	68.54±28.22	79.44±12.65
NN-GORV-II	80.49±10.21	77.40±26.53	77.12±24.19	79.99±11.75

Note: Calculations are estimated from 480 amino acids (proteins). Q3 = accuracy for amino acid, QH = accuracy for helices, QE = accuracy for strands, QC = accuracy for coils

data than the other states and hence it is more accurate and reliable estimate.

Figure 3 shows histograms of the performance of the Q_3 prediction accuracies and the segment overlap (SOV) measure of the 480 proteins. It shows that there are almost a negligible number of proteins that score a Q_3 below 50% and there are about 80 proteins score Q_3 predictions below 70% while other proteins scored above 70% with 180 proteins score 80% and about 140 proteins score 90%. This distribution of Q_3 scores have a tendency towards the 80% and 90% scores, making the average Q_3 score of NN-GORV-II method touches the 80% prediction accuracy.

The SOV measure in Figure 3 elucidates that NN-GORV-II method showed a different histogram than that of Q_3 performance. Among the 480 proteins there are about 60 proteins scored below 50% and about 60 proteins scored 100% SOV score. The rest of the proteins achieved score above 50% and below 100% with 120 proteins scored 80% SOV accuracy. This distribution of the SOV of NN-GORV-II method brought down the SOV score to the 76.27 level.

Figure 4 represents a histogram that elucidates the performance (Q3) of the seven prediction methods starting from the 50% level and above.

Figure 4 shows clearly that NN-I and GOR-IV methods predicted most of the 480 proteins at prediction levels near the 55- 65% levels while NN-GORV-II, NN-GORV-I, PROF, NN-II, and GOR-V methods predicted many of the 480 proteins around the 85-90% levels. The new methods NN-GORV-II and NN-GORV-I can be observed

Figure 3. The performance of the NN-GORV-II prediction method with respect to Q_3 and SOV prediction measures

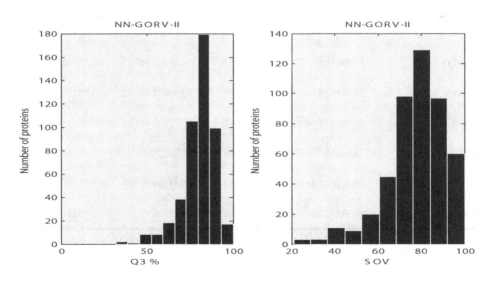

to predict many proteins at the 95-100% levels compared to other methods. This analysis of Figure 4 suggests that generally NN-I and GOR-IV methods are less performance predictors, NN-GORV-II and NN-GORV-I are high performance predictors, while the remaining three methods performed between these two levels.

Figure 5 is a line graph designed to test the ability of the seven prediction methods, and how they behave in the prediction of the 480 proteins. An ideal line for an ultimate predictor is a line parallel to the x axis at the point where y equals 100. When y equals 50 for the same parallel line then the line represents a random guess for the coil-state predictor. A line parallel to the x axis at y equals to 33.3 is as worse (poor) as random guess of a prediction. The figure resembles the reliability index (RI) for predicting proteins similar to that proposed by Rost (2003); that is to show the prediction methods did not only restrict their predictions to the most strongly predicted residues. It is also equivalent to the scale that is discussed by Eyrich et al. (2003), who plotted accuracy versus coverage for subset of 205 proteins.

Figure 5 shows that NN-GORV-II line starts near 40% for Q_3 and steadily increases in accuracy to reach just below 100%, corresponding to the 480 proteins in the database. The NN-GORV-II method line is above all the other six lines of other prediction methods. The NN-GORV-I method line is just below the top line with a small drop in accuracy. From the graph, it can be concluded that the margin between NN-GORV-II line and NN-GORV-I line is the effect of *pfilt* program that masks

Figure 4. Histogram showing the Q_3 performance of the seven prediction methods

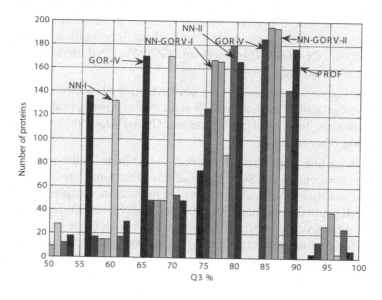

Figure 5. A graph line chart for the Q_3 performance of the seven prediction methods

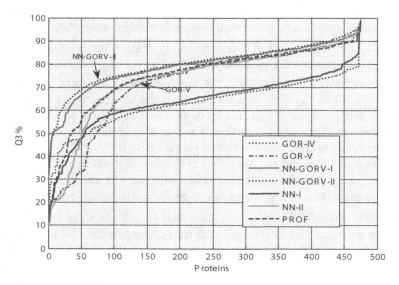

low complexity regions of the data base as explained in the methodology. GOR-IV line is below all the other six lines followed by NN-I method line just above it with very minor margin following a similar pattern indicting that GOR-IV method is the poorest performing prediction method followed by NN-I method. GOR-V method, NN-II method, and PROF method lines are in between the above mentioned four methods. This graph elucidates that these three methods are in between the NN-GORV-I, NN-GORV-II methods and GOR-IV, NN-I methods as far as Q_3 performance is concerned.

To conclude, Figure 5 indicates that the newly developed method (NN-GORV-II) that combines the GOR-V method and NN-II method is superior to all other methods studied in this work. Individual performance of GOR-IV and NN-I proved to be the poorest among other methods.

Figure 6 shows a line graph that illustrates the same lines for the seven prediction methods but representing the SOV measure this time. Since the SOV measure is a measure of quality and reliability rather than performance, this figure shows the quality of each prediction method. NN-GORV-II and NN-GORV-I method lines are above all the other five method lines (Figure 6). The two lines are travelling through the proteins in the same pattern with a very small margin favouring NN-GORV-II method. This confirms the findings that NN-GORV-II and NN-GORV-I methods predictions are the most reliable and of high qualities predictions.

Figure 6. A graph line chart for the SOV measure of the seven prediction methods

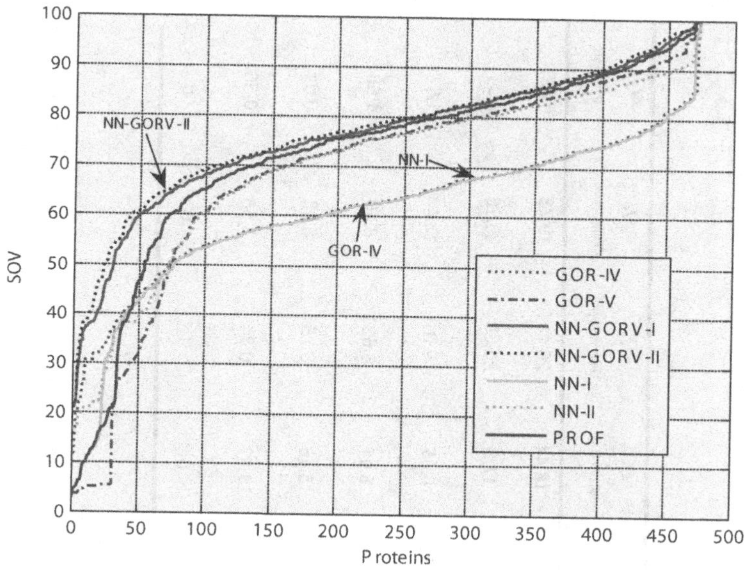

Figure 6 also shows that the PROF line is below the NN-**GOR**V-I and NN-**GOR**V-II lines but above all the other four lines. This indicted that PROF is the third prediction method as far as quality is concerned. The lines in Figure 6 confirm the facts revealed by Figure 5 that the newly developed method in this work (NN-**GOR**V-II) has the highest performance and the highest quality among all the seven methods studied in this work. The NN-GORV-I, PROF, NN-II, GOR-V, NN-I, and GOR-IV methods follow this, respectively.

Improvement of NN-GORV-I and NN-GORV-II Over Other Methods

Table 2 shows the improvement of the prediction accuracy of helices, strands, coils, and all the three secondary-structure states together of NN-GORV-II over the other six methods. The overall Q_3 improvement of NN-GORV-II method over NN-I and GOR-IV is very high which is above 16% improvement. This result is not surprising since the two low-performance predictors (NN-I and GOR-V) did not implement a multiple-sequence-alignment method to make use of the long range interactions of residues in the amino-acid sequences.

Table 2. Percentage improvement of NN-GORV-II method over the other six prediction methods

Prediction Method	Q_3	Q_H	Q_E	Q_C	Q_3 Improvement	Q_H Improvement	Q_E Improvement	Q_C Improvement
NN-I	64.05	57.29	57.39	74.1	16.44	20.11	19.73	5.89
GOR-IV	63.19	57.02	51.86	71.95	17.3	20.38	25.26	8.04
GOR-V	71.84	68.4	63.68	78.92	8.65	9.0	13.44	1.07
NN-II	73.58	70.77	68.72	78.33	6.91	6.63	8.40	1.66
PROF	75.03	70.65	68.29	79.38	5.46	6.75	8.83	0.61
NN-GORV-I	79.22	76.56	68.54	79.44	1.27	0.84	8.58	0.55
NN-GORV-II	80.49	77.4	77.12	79.99	0	0	0	0

The overall improvement (Q_3) of the NN-GORV-II method over the GOR-V method is 8.65%. The reported accuracy of GOR-V is 73.5% (Kloczkowski et al., 2002), which means an improvement of 6.99% is gained. Anyhow, whatever compared to the reported accuracy of GOR-V or the calculated accuracy in this experimental work, the improvement of the NN-GORV-II method performance over GOR-V is high.

NN-II method is also one of the two methods that combined to make NN-GORV-II method. Table 2 shows that the improvements of performance of the NN-GORV-II method over the NN-II method are 6.63%, 8.4%, and 1.66% for the helices (Q_H), strands (Q_E), and coils (Q_C) states, respectively. The improvement of Q_3 of NN-GORV-II over NN-II is 6.91%. Most modern neural-network methods of secondary-structure prediction in the literature reported accuracies from 70.5% and below 76.4% (Cuff & Barton 2000; Riis & Krogh, 1996; Rost, 2003). However, an overall gain of accuracy of about 5- 7% in the NN-GORV-II method over NN-II in this experimental work and other works is a considerably high gain.

Table 2 clearly indicates that the newly developed algorithm that combined the neural networks with information theory of GOR-V method is superior in performance to all the method tested in this experimental work. The improvement in accuracies ranged from 5.5 % to 16.4%, which is a significant gain in the domain of protein secondary structure prediction. The *pfilt* program that masks low complexity regions in the searched database had even boosted the algorithm by 1.27% further.

As defined in the methodology, the SOV measure is a measure of prediction quality and usefulness rather than a measure of prediction performance. Table 3 shows the SOV measures improvements of the NN-GORV-II method over the other methods. The overall SOV improvements of NN-GORV-II method over the GOR-V and NN-II methods that are the two methods that combined the NN-GORV-II algorithm are 6.94% and 5.90%, respectively.

A gain of about 7% in SOV over these two methods is a significantly high gain and proved that combining two different methods of predictions that use different approaches might lead to an exciting improvement in protein secondary structure prediction usefulness and quality.

The improvement of the NN-GORV-II algorithm over the PROF algorithm, which is described as cascaded multiple classifier by its authors (Ouali & King, 2000), is shown in Table 3. In this work, the overall SOV measure of the NN-GORV-II algorithm is increased by 3.53% compared to PROF, which revealed that the NN-GORV-II method is of high quality and useful in the protein secondary-structure prediction.

The improvements in SOV of the NN-GORV-II method over the NN-GORV-I method are small in helices and coil states while it is very high in strand states and reached 9.18% (Table 3). The negative value of SOV_3 (-0.28) in Table 3 suggests that although there is an improvement in the overall performance accuracy (Q_3) of the NN-GORV-II method over the NN-GORV-I method (Table 2), the quality of this prediction is not as good as the prediction of the NN-GORV-I method.

Table 3. SOV percentage improvement of NN-GORV-II method over the other prediction methods

Prediction Method	SOV$_3$	SOV$_H$	SOV$_E$	SOV$_C$	SOV$_3$ Improvement	SOV$_H$ Improvement	SOV$_E$ Improvement	SOV$_C$ Improvement
NN-I	60.94	59.5	57.61	61.53	**15.33**	18.46	22.33	12.82
GOR-IV	62.07	60.81	56.01	62.34	**14.20**	17.15	23.93	12.01
GOR-V	69.33	70.87	64	66.63	**6.94**	7.09	15.94	7.72
NN-II	70.37	71.05	68.47	67.29	**5.9**	6.91	11.47	7.06
PROF	72.74	73.49	69.8	69.75	**3.53**	4.47	10.14	4.6
NN-GORV-I	76.55	76.93	70.76	72.9	**-0.28**	1.03	9.18	1.45
NN-GORV-II	76.27	77.96	79.94	74.35	**0**	0	0	0

Improvement of NN-GORV-II Correlation Over Other Methods

Table 4 shows the improvements in the Matthews correlation coefficients (MCC) of NN-GORV-II method over the other methods. It is important to recall here that

Table 4. Matthews correlation coefficients improvement of the NN-GORV-II method over the other six prediction methods

Prediction Method	MCC_H	MCC_E	MCC_C	MCC_H Improvement	MCC_E Improvement	MCC_C Improvement
NN-I	0.4906	0.4124	0.4448	0.2838	0.2834	0.2053
GOR-IV	0.5283	0.3756	0.4382	0.2461	0.3202	0.2119
GOR-V	0.6859	0.5994	0.5675	0.0885	0.0964	0.0826
NN-II	0.6503	0.5641	0.5304	0.1241	0.1317	0.1197
PROF	0.7102	0.6291	0.5743	0.0642	0.0667	0.0758
NN-GORV-I	0.7736	0.6959	0.6494	0.0008	-0.0001	0.0007
NN-GORV-II	0.7744	0.6958	0.6501	0	0	0

MCC is an index that shows the strength of the relation between predicted and observed values. The closer the coefficient is to 1.0 the stronger the relation is between observed and predicted values. There is significant improvement in the MCC of the NN-GORV-II method over the NN-I and GOR-V methods for all the secondary structure states ranging from 0.21 to 0.32, which indicates that the NN-GORV-II method contains significantly high entropy or more information to describe the relation between predicted and observed values and its prediction has more meaning (Crooks, Jason, & Steven, 2004; Baldi et al., 2000).

Table 4 also shows that the improvements in the MCC of the NN-GORV-II method over the GOR-V and NN-II are ranging from 0.08 to 0.13 for all the secondary-structure states; helices, strands, and coils. There are more improvements in the strand states compared to other states over both the GOR-V and NN-II methods. This result reveals that the new developed algorithm by combining these two algorithms is superior in terms of describing the relations between predicted states and observed ones.

The increment in the MCC achieved by the NN-GORV-II method over its previous version NN-GORV-I is also shown in Table 4. The improvements in helices states and coils states are very small and counted to 0.001 each. Although this is a minor gain in MCC coefficients, it indicates that the improvement in the performance of the NN-GORV-II method over the NN-GORV-I method is accompanied by improvements in the strength of the predictions for the helices and coil states. However, Table 4 also shows a negative number (-0.0001) as the improvement in the MCC of the strand states of the NN-GORV-II method over the NN-GORV-I method. This indicates that the amount of information described in the NN-GORV-I method prediction is more than the information described in the NN-GORV-II method prediction as far as the β strands are concerned.

Conclusion

We have presented the NN-GORV-I and NN-GORV-II prediction methods, which have been developed by combining two different approaches, namely, neural networks and the GOR-V algorithm. The experimental results indicate that our prediction methods performed significantly better in terms of accuracy and quality compared to other prediction methods studied in this work. The NN-GORV-II outperformed the GOR-V methods by 8.7% in Q_3 accuracy and the neural networks method (NN-II) by 6.9%. Also, the SOV measure and the Mathews Correlation Coefficients (MCC) showed that NN-GORV-II significantly outperformed the other prediction methods. Our future work involves further refinement of our approach and conducting additional experimental validation.

Acknowledgments

The authors would like to express their gratitude to Dr El-Mahi Abdalla, Dean of Faculty of Languages, University of Khartoum, Sudan, for proofreading and providing valuable suggestions concerning this work. The authors would also like to thank Al-Ghurair University at Dubai for facilitating the execution of this work.

References

Abdalla, S. O., & Deris, S., (2005, April 9-10). *An improved method for protein secondary structure prediction by combining neural networks and GOR V theory.* Paper presented at the Second Middle East Conference on Healthcare Informatics (MECHCI 2005). Dubai, UAE: Dubai Knowledge Village. UAE.

Anfinsen, C. B. (1973). Principles that govern the folding of protein chains. *Science, 181*, 223-230.

Arbib, M. (1995). *The handbook of brain theory and neural networks.* Cambridge, MA: Bradford Books/The MIT Press.

Baldi, P., & Brunak, S. (2001). *Bioinformatics: The machine learning approach.* MIT Press.

Baldi, P., Brunak, S., Chauvin, Y., Andersen, C. A. F., & Nielsen, H. (2000). Assessing the accuracy of prediction algorithms for classification: An overview. *Bioinformatics, 16*, 412-424

Baldi, P., Brunak, S., Frasconi, P., Soda, G., & Pollastri, G. (1999). Exploiting the past and the future in protein secondary structure prediction. *Bioinformatics, 15*, 937-946.

Bates, J.M., & Granger C.W.J. (1969). The Combination of Forecasts. *Operations Research Quarterly* 20, 451-468.

Bishop, C. (1996). *Neural networks for pattern recognition.* Oxford University Press.

Bohr, H., Bohr, J., Brunak, S.,Cotterill, R. M. J., Lautrup, B., Nørskov, L., Olsen, O.H., & Petersen, S.B. (1988). Protein secondary structure and homology by neural networks: The α-helices in Rhodopsin. *FEBS Lett., 241*, 223-228.

Branden, C., & Tooze, J. (1991). *Introduction to protein structure.* New York: Garland Publishing, Inc..

Chou, P. Y., & Fasman, G. D. (1974). Conformational parameters for amino acids in helical, sheet and random coil regions from proteins. *Biochem, 13*, 211.

Cline, M. S., Karplus, K., Lathrop, R. H., Smith, T. F., Rogers, R. G., Jr., & Haussler, D. (2002). Information-theoretic dissection of pairwise contact potentials. *Proteins: Structure, Function, and Genetics, 49*(1), 7-14.

Crick, F. (1989). The recent excitement about neural networks. *Nature, 337*, 129-132.

Crooks, G. E., Jason, W., & Steven, E. B. (2004). Measurements of protein sequence structure correlations. *Proteins: Structure, Function, and Bioinformatics, 57*, 804–810.

Cuff, J. A., & Barton, G. J. (1999). Evaluation and improvement of multiple sequence methods for protein secondary structure prediction. *Proteins: Structure, Function and Genetics, 34*, 508-519.

Cuff, J. A., & Barton, G. J. (2000). Application of multiple sequence alignment profiles to improve protein secondary structure prediction. *Proteins: Structure, Function and Genetics, 40*, 502-511.

Devroye, L., Györfi, L., & Lugosi, G. (1996). *A probabilistic theory of pattern recognition.* NY: Springer.

Dickinson, J.P. (1973.) Some statistical results in the combination of forecasts. *Operational research quarterly, 24*(2), 253-260

Durbin, R., Eddy, S., Krogh, A., & Mitchison, G. (2002). *Biological sequence analysis: Probabilistic models of proteins and nucleic acids.* Cambridge, UK: Cambridge University Press.

Eyrich, V. A., Przybylski, D., Koh, I. Y. Y., Grana, O., Pazos, F., Valencia, A., et al. (2003). CAFASP3 in the spotlight Of EVA. *Proteins: Structure, Function, and Genetics, 53*(6), 548-560.

Frishman, D., & Argos, P., (1995). Knowledge-based protein secondary structure assignment. *Proteins: Structure, Function, and Genetics, 23*, 566-579.

Garnier, J., & Robson, B. (1989). The GOR method for predicting secondary structures in proteins. In G. D. Fasman (Ed.), *Prediction of protein structure and the principles of protein conformation* (pp. 417-465). New York: Plenum Press.

Garnier, J., Gibrat, J., & Robson, B. (1996). GOR method for predicting protein secondary structure from amino acid sequence. *Meth. Enz., 266*, 540-553.

Garnier, J., Osguthorpe, D. J., & Robson, B. (1978). Analysis of the accuracy and implications of simple methods for predicting the secondary structure of globular proteins. *J. Mol. Biol., 120*, 97-120.

Haykin, S. (1999). *Neural networks: A comprehensive foundation.* Prentice-Hall, Inc.

Heilig, R., Eckenberg, R., Petit, J.L., Fonknechten, N., DaSilva, C., Cattolico., L., et al. (2003). The DNA sequence and analysis of human chromosome 14. *Nature*, (4216923), 601-607.

Hertz, J. A., Krogh, A., & Palmer, R. G. (1991). *Introduction to the theory of neural computation*. Redwood City, CA: Addison-Wesley.

Jones, D. T. (1999). Protein secondary structure prediction based on position-specific scoring matrices. *J. Mol. Biol., 292*, 195-202.

Jordan, M.I., & Jacobs, R.A., (1994). Hierarchical mixtures of experts and the EM algorithm. *Neural computation, 6*, 181-214

Kendrew, J. C., Dickerson, R. E., Strandberg, B. E., Hart, R. G., & Davies, D. R. (1960). Structure of myoglobin. *Nature, 185*, 422-427.

Kloczkowski, A., Ting, K. L., Jernigan, R. L., & Garnier, J. (2002). Combining the GOR V algorithm with evolutionary information for protein secondary structure prediction from amino aid sequence. *Proteins: Structure., Function., and Genetics, 49*, 154-166

Krigbaum, W. R., & Knutton, S. P. (1973). Prediction of the amount of secondary structure in a globular protein from its amino acid composition. *Proc. Nat. Acad. Sci. USA, 70*(10), 2809-2813.

Kullback, S., Keegel, J. C., & Kullback, J. H. (1987). *Topics in statistical information theory*. Berlin; New York: Springer-Verlag.

Muller, B., & Reinhardt, J. (1990). *Neural networks*. Berlin: Springer.

Ouali, M., & King, R. D. (2000). Cascaded multiple classifiers for secondary structure prediction. *Prot. Sci., 9*, 1162-1176.

Pauling, L., & Corey, R. B. (1951). Configurations of polypeptide chains with favoured orientations around single bonds: Two new pleated sheets. *Proc. Natl. Acad. Sci. USA, 37*, 729-740.

Presnell, S. R., & Cohen, F. E. (1993). Artificial neural networks for pattern recognition in biochemical sequences. *Annu. Rev. Biophys. Biomol. Struct., 22*, 283-298.

Qian, N., & Sejnowski, T. J. (1988). Predicting the secondary structure of globular proteins using neural network models. *J. Mol. Biol., 202*, 865-884.

Richardson, J. S. (1981). The anatomy and taxonomy of protein structure. *Adv. Prot. Chem, 34*, 168-339.

Riis, S. K., & Krogh, A. (1996). Improving prediction of protein secondary structure using structured neural networks and multiple sequence alignments. *J Comput Biol., 3*, 163–183.

Rost, B. 1996. NN which predicts protein secondary structure. In E. Fiesler & R. Beale (Eds.), *Handbook of neural computation* (pp. G4.1). New York: Oxford Univ. Press.

Rost., B. 2001. Review: Protein secondary structure prediction continues to rise. *J. Struct. Biol., 134*, 204–218.

Rost, B. 2003. Neural networks predict protein structure: Hype or hit? In P. Frasconi (Ed.), *Artificial intelligence and heuristic models for bioinformatics* (pp. 34-50). ISO Press.

Rost, B., & Sander, C. (1993). Prediction of protein secondary structure at better than 70% accuracy. *J.Mol. Biol., 232*, 584-599.

Rost, B., Sander, C., & Schneider, R., (1994.) Redefining the goals of protein secondary structure prediction. *J. Mol.Biol.* 235, 13-26

Shannon, C. E. (1948). The mathematical theory of communications. *Bell System Technical Journal,* 27, 379-423; 623-656.

Subair, S. O., & Deris, S. (2005). Combining artificial neural networks and GOR-V information theory to predict protein secondary structure from amino acid sequences. *International Journal of Intelligent Information Technologies, 1*(4) 53-72.

Subair, S. O. & Deris, S. (2006, March). *Protein secondary structure reduction methods significantly affect prediction accuracy.* Paper presented at the 4th ACS/IEEE International Conference on Computer Systems and Applications (AICCSA-06). Dubai/Sharjah, UAE: .

Subair, S. O., Deris, S., & Saberi, M. M. (2005). A hybrid classifier for protein secondary structure prediction. *Information Technology Journal, 4*(4), 433-438.

Wu, C. H. (1997). Artificial neural networks for molecular sequence analysis. *Comput. Chem., 21*, 237-256.

Zell, A., Mamier, G., Vogt, M., Mach, N., Huebner, R., Herrmann, K.U., et al. (1998). *The SNNS Users Manual Version 4.1.* Retrieved February 10, 2005, from http://www.informatik.uni-tuttgart.de/ipvr/bv/projekte/snns/usermanual/usermanual.html

Zemla, A., Venclovas, C., Fidelis, K., & Rost, B. (1999) A modified definition of SOV., A segment based measure for protein secondary structure prediction assessment. *Proteins: Structure, function and genetics,* 34: 220-223.

About the Authors

Mafruz Zaman Ashrafi is a PhD student at Monash University (Australia). His research interests include data mining, distributed computing, e-commerce, privacy, and security. He received his MS in computer science from RMIT University.

Narjès Bellamine-BenSaoud is an assistant professor at the University of Tunis and a researcher at RIADI-GDL Laboratory, Tunisia. After obtaining the engineering diploma in computer science (1993) at the ENSEEIHT of Toulouse, she obtained a PhD (1996), from the University of Toulouse I, on computer-supported collaborative work (CSCW) and groupware design. She spent, on 2001, a six-month Fulbright stay at the University of California Irvine. Her main research interests are complex systems, agent-based modeling and simulation of sociotechnical systems, computer-supported collaborative learning, collaborative design and groupware, software engineering, and decision-support systems.

Thomas Biskup studied computer science from 1990 to 1997 at the University of Dortmund. He finished *cum laude* and was granted both the Hans Uhde award and the German Software Engineering Prize of the Denert foundation. After working as an IT consultant, he started to work on his PhD. thesis in 2000. In 2001, he cofounded the QuinScape GmbH (http://www.quinscape.de). He specializes in intranet and extranet systems, model-driven architecture, and model-driven software development. His thesis focuses on agile methods and models in order to simplify requirements for engineering with cooperative rapid prototyping approaches for nontechnicians.

Miriam Capretz has been an assistant professor in the Department of Electrical and Computer Engineering at the University of Western Ontario (Canada) since July 2000. Before joining the University of Western Ontario, she was an assistant professor in the Software Engineering Laboratory at the University of Aizu (Japan). Dr. Miriam Capretz received her BSc and MESc degrees from the State University of Campinas (Brazil) and her PhD from the University of Durham (UK). She has been working in the software-engineering area for about 20 years. Her current research interests include software engineering, software evolution, software maintenance, multiagent systems, service-oriented architecture, autonomic computing, and grid computing.

Safaai Deris received a Deng in computer and system sciences from Osaka Prefecture University, Osaka (Japan) (1998), a MEng from the same university (1989), and a BSc from University Putra Malaysia (1978). Currently, he is a professor in the Department of Software Engineering, Faculty of Computer Science and Information Systems, University Technology Malaysia. His research areas include software engineering, artificial intelligence, and bioinformatics. His current research projects include applications of intelligent techniques in planning, scheduling, and bioinformatics. He is also actively involved with industrial partners for providing solutions and development of systems and applications for manufacturing, healthcare, and plantation industries.

Jorge Marx Gómez studied computer engineering and industrial engineering at the University of Applied Science of Berlin (Technische Fachhochschule). He was a lecturer and researcher at the Otto-von-Guericke-Universität Magdeburg where he also obtained a PhD degree in business information systems with the work *Computer-based Approaches to Forecast Returns of Scrapped Products to Recycling*. In 2004, he received his habilitation for the work *Automated Environmental Reporting Through Material Flow Networks* at the Otto-von-Guericke-Universität Magdeburg. From 2002 until 2003 he was a visiting professor for business informatics at the Technical University of Clausthal. In 2004, he became a full professor of business information systems at the Carl von Ossietzky University Oldenburg (Germany). His research interests include business information systems, e-commerce, material-flow-management systems, life-cycle assessment, ecobalancing, environmental reporting, recycling-program planning, disassembly planning and control, simulation and neurofuzzy-systems.

Franc Grootjen received his master's degree at the University of Nijmegen in 1992 and his PhD in mathematics, physics, and computer ccience on 026 January 2005 at the Radboud University Nijmegen (The Netherlands). He is currently consultant at Edmond Research & Development. His main interest is the broad application of mathematical and informatical techniques in a linguistic environment such as information retrieval.

Christian Heine obtained a master's degree in information systems at the Technical University of Ilmenau and is a research assistant at the University of Hohenheim, Stuttgart (Germany), chair for Information Systems II. He successfully headed the PaGS-project (2000-2001) on partial global scheduling of processes and the ADAPT-project (2002-2003) on adaptive multiagent process planning and coordination. He currently heads the ADAPT II project (2004-2006) on adaptive co-ordination of clinical processes with cooperating software agents. He a is member of the Agent-cities healthcare working group and is specialized in requirements engineering and business process modeling methodologies, especially in the healthcare sector.

Rainer Herrler obtained a master's degree in computer science at the University of Würzburg (Germany) in 2000. Since then, he has been working as a research assistant to the chair of artificial intelligence at the University of Würzburg. His main research objectives are distributed scheduling and agent-based simulation. He was responsible for several joint research projects in cooperation with the University of Hohenheim.

Nils Heyer studied business information systems at the Technical University of Clausthal. Currently he is a PhD student at Carl von Ossietzky University Oldenburg (Germany). His research interests include information systems, agent technologies, Web services, and Semantic Web technologies.

Yasushi Kambayashi is an associate professor in the Department of Computer and Information Engineering at the Nippon Institute of Technology (Japan). His research interests include theory of computation, theory and practice of programming languages, and intellectual property law. He received his PhD in engineering from the University of Toledo, his MS in computer science from the University of Washington, and his BA in Law from Keio University.

Diana Kao (kao@uwindsor.ca) holds an MBA in information systems/finance and a PhD in MIS from McMaster University (Canada). Kao is the associate dean at the Odette School of Business and coordinator of the SAP program at the University of Windsor, where she has taught courses including database, management information systems, and strategic implementation of IT at the undergraduate, graduate, and in the executive MBA programs. She has also developed several distance-education courses. Dr. Kao's research interests are in the areas of systems analysis and design, e-commerce, and ERP adoption and performance evaluation. She has published articles in the *International Journal of Human-Computer Studies*, *Mathematical Modeling and Scientific Computing*, *Industrial Management Data Systems*, and the *International Journal of Intelligent Information Technologies*.

Julie Kendall, PhD, is a professor of e-commerce and information technology in the School of Business-Camden, Rutgers University (USA). Dr. Kendall is the immediate past chair of IFIP Working Group 8.2 and was awarded the Silver Core from IFIP. Professor Kendall has published in *MIS Quarterly*, *Decision Sciences*, *Information & Management*, *CAIS*, *Organization Studies*, and many other journals. Additionally, Dr. Kendall has recently coauthored a college textbook with Kenneth E. Kendall, *Systems Analysis and Design* (6th ed., Prentice Hall). She is also a co-author of *Project Planning and Requirements Analysis for IT Systems Development*. She co-edited the volume *Human, Organizational, and Social Dimensions of Information Systems Development* published by North-Holland. Dr. Kendall is a senior editor for *JITTA* and is on the editorial boards of the *Journal of Database Management* and *IRMJ*. She also serves on the review board of the *Decision Sciences Journal of Innovative Education*. Professor Kendall was a functional editor of MIS for *Interfaces* and an associate editor for *MIS Quarterly*. She recently was both a treasurer and a vice president of the Decision Sciences Institute. Professor Kendall served as a Rand faculty fellow for the Senator Walter Rand Institute for Public Affairs. For her mentoring of minority doctoral students in information systems, she was named to the *Circle of Compadres* of the PhD project, which was begun by the KPMG Foundation a decade ago to increase the diversity of business-school faculty. Dr. Kendall is researching policy formulation for ICTs in developing countries, and agile methodologies for systems development. She and her co-author (and spouse) Ken are currently examining the strategic uses of Web presence and e-commerce for off-Broadway theatres and other nonprofit organizations in the service sector. Her home page can be accessed at www.thekendalls.org.

Kenneth Kendall, PhD, is a professor of e-commerce and information technology in the School of Business-Camden, Rutgers University (USA). He is one of the founders of the International Conference on Information Systems (ICIS) and a fellow of the Decision Sciences Institute (DSI). He is currently the president-elect of DSI. Dr. Kendall has been named as one of the top 60 most productive MIS researchers in the world, and he was awarded the Silver Core from IFIP. He recently coauthored a text, *Systems Analysis and Design* (6th ed., Prentice Hall) and *Project Planning and Requirements Analysis for IT Systems Development*. He edited *Emerging Information Technologies: Improving Decisions, Cooperation, and Infrastructure* for Sage Publications, Inc. Dr. Kendall has had his research published in *MIS Quarterly*, *Management Science*, *Operations Research*, *Decision Sciences*, *Information &*

Management, CAIS, and many other journals. Dr. Kendall is the President-Elect of DSI and the past Chair of IFIP Working Group 8.2. He is an associate editor for the *International Journal of Intelligent Information Technologies*, serves on the Senior Advisory board of *JITTA*, and is a member of the editorial board for *Information Systems Journal* and *Information Technology for Development*, and on the review board of the *Decision Sciences Journal of Innovative Education*. Dr. Kendall has served as an associate editor for *Decision Sciences* and the *Information Resources Management Journal*, and has served as the functional MIS editor for *Interfaces*. For his mentoring of minority doctoral students in information systems, he was named to the *Circle of Compadres* of the PhD project, which was begun by the KPMG Foundation a decade ago to increase the diversity of business school faculty. Professor Kendall's research focuses on studying push and pull technologies, e-commerce strategies, and developing new tools for systems analysis and design. His home page can be accessed at www.thekendalls.org.

Chris Langdon co-founded and chairs the Special Interest Group on Agent-based Information Systems (SIGABIS, http://www.agentbasedis.org) of the Association for Information Systems (AIS). He is affiliated with the Center for Telecom Management of the University of Southern California (USC) (USA) after having been a full-time professor of USC's Marshall School of Business for 5 years. Before joining USC, Langdon was a scientist in the Artificial Intelligence Group of the Beckman Institute for Advanced Science and Technology at the University of Illinois at Urbana-Champaign. His research is focused on IS capabilities and their implications for business strategy using next-generation analytical tools such as agent-based modeling and strategic simulation. Results and insights have appeared in leading publications, including *Communications of the ACM*, *IEEE* journals and the *Harvard Business Review*. Chris Langdon has also been an advisor to Global Fortune 500 companies and governments on digital business development and strategic simulation, first as a consultant with Accenture (formerly Andersen Consulting), and then with Pacific Coast Research Inc., a boutique management advisory firm. He has been educated in the USA and Germany and received graduate degrees in engineering and finance and business economics, and a PhD in economics, all *summa cum laude*.

Jun Liu is a doctoral student in management information systems in the Eller School of Management, University of Arizona (USA). His research interests include data provenance, semantic modeling, business-rules management, ontology, intelligent-data retrieval, heterogeneous-database integration, and agent-based electronic business transactions. He has an MS in management information systems from the University of Arizona.

Haibing Qiao is a consulting engineer in Filenet Corp. California. He has more than 15 years of experience in various disciplines of engineering including recent 10 years in software. He received a BS and MS from Shanghai Jiaotong University (China), and a PhD in mechanical engineering from the University of Maryland College Park (USA).

Haiying Qiao is a research scientist of R. H. Smith School of Business at the University of Maryland, College Park (USA). He also manages eMarkets Lab, which supports both academic research and education. He received his BS in management science from Wuhan Institute of Technology and his MS in systems engineering from Shanghai Jiao Tong University. He received his PhD in operations research from the University of Maryland, College Park. His current research interests are in areas of e-supply-chain management.

Sudha Ram is a professor of MIS in the Eller School of Management at the University of Arizona (USA). Dr. Ram's research deals with issues related to enterprise data management. Specifically, her research deals with interoperability among heterogeneous database systems, semantic modeling, bioinformatics and spatio-temporal semantics, business rules modeling, Web services discovery and selection, and automated software tools for database design. Her research has been funded by organizations such as IBM, Intel Corporation, Raytheon, the U.S. Army, NIST, NSF, NASA, and the Office of Research and Development of the CIA. Dr. Ram has published articles in such journals as *Communications of the ACM, IEEE Expert, IEEE Transactions on Knowledge and Data Engineering, Information Systems, Information Systems Research, Management Science,* and *MIS Quarterly*. Dr. Ram serves on the editorial board for such journals as *Decision Support Systems, Information Systems Frontiers, Journal of Information Technology and Management,* and is an associate editor for *Information Systems Research, Journal of Database Management, Journal of Systems and Software,* and the *International Journal of Intelligent Information Technologies*. She has chaired several workshops and conferences supported by ACM, IEEE, and the Association for Information Systems (AIS). She is a cofounder of the Workshop on Information Technology and Systems (WITS) and serves on the steering committee of many workshops and conferences including the Entity Relationship Conference (ER). Dr. Ram is a member of ACM, the IEEE Computer Society, INFORMS, and AIS. She is also the director of the Advanced Database Research Group based at the University of Arizona.

Sunitha Ramanujam is currently pursuing her PhD in software engineering at the University of Western Ontario (Canada), following the completion of a master's degree in engineering science from the same university in June 2003. She received her BE (Hons.) (electrical and electronics) and MS (software systems) degrees from Birla Institute of Technology and Science, India (1995 and 1998, respectively). She has over 7 years of experience in the field of databases and software development. Her research interests include self-managing databases, agent-based and multiagent systems, and all aspects of autonomic computing.

Fatima Rateb is currently a PhD student at University College London (UK) within the Centre for Advanced Spatial Analysis (CASA). She obtained a BSc in mathematics and management from King's College, London in 1998 (Hons.). She continued studying at City University in London and in 2002 finished an MSc in an information-engineering specialisation in biomedical computing, instrumentation, and informatics. Rateb's MSc dissertation is titled "Analysis of Parameters Generated by Model Predictive Control (MPC) during Clinical Trials on Subjects with Type 1 Diabetes." She was a young visiting researcher at IRIT (Institut de Recherche Informatique de Toulouse) and a young researcher at the University of Granada, both within the European funded project Complexity in Social Science (COSI). Presently, her PhD research is aimed at exploring the propagation dynamics in infectious vector borne diseases such as malaria, using complex system and network theories. Her research interests lie in complex systems, dynamic networks, agent-based simulation, and artificial life.

Kate Smith is an associate professor and deputy head of the School of Business Systems at Monash University (Australia). She holds a BSc (Hons.) in mathematics and a PhD in electrical engineering from the University of Melbourne. Dr. Smith has published over 130 refereed journal and international conference papers in the areas of neural networks, combinatorial optimization, and data mining. She has received around $1.5 million in competitive research funding. She serves on several editorial boards and many program committees for international conferences. She regularly acts as a consultant to industry in the area of data mining.

Saad Osman Abdalla Subair was born on the bank of the river Nile 40 kilometers away from the capital Khartoum. He graduated with a BSc (Hons.) from the University of Khartoum. He obtained a Post Graduate Diploma and MSc in computer science from the University of Technology Malaysia, an MSc in genetics from University Putra Malaysia, and a PhD in bioinformatics from the University of Technology Malaysia. His research interests include bioinformatics, healthcare informatics, data mining, Web technology, and neural networks. He has published several research articles in regional and international journals and conference proceedings. Dr Subair has taught or trained computer science and information technology subjects in several universities or institutes in many countries including Malaysia, Singapore, Qatar,

Saudi Arabia, Oman, and Sudan. Now Dr. Subair is an associate professor and IT department director in Al-Ghurair University at Dubai (UAE).

Munehiro Takimoto is an assistant professor in the Department of Information Sciences at Tokyo University of Science (Japan). His research interests include design and implementation of programming languages. He received his BS, MS, and PhD in engineering from Keio University.

David Taniar holds a PhD in computer science, with a particular specialty in databases. His research areas have now expanded to data mining and warehousing. He has published more than 30 journal papers and numerous conference papers. He has published six books, including the forthcoming *Object-Oriented Oracle*. Dr. Taniar is now a senior lecturer at the School of Business Systems, Faculty of Information Technology, Monash University (Australia). He is in the editorial board of several international journals, and a fellow of the Institute for Management Information Systems (FIMIS).

Vagan Terziyan has been a professor of software engineering since 1994 and the head of the Artificial Intelligence Department since 1997 in Kharkov National University of Radioelectronics (Ukraine). Currently, he is working in Agora Center, University of Jyvaskyla (Finland) as a project leader of the SmartResource TEKES Projects and Head of "Industrial Ontologies" Group. He is a member of IFIP WG 12.5 ("Artificial Intelligence Applications") and PC chair of IFIP International Conference on Industrial Applications of Semantic Web. His research and teaching profile includes intelligent Web applications, which utilise and integrate emerging knowledge-, agent-, machine-learning-, and Semantic Web-based technologies and tools.

Theo van der Weide received his master's degree from the Technical University Eindhoven (The Netherlands) (1975), and a PhD in mathematics and physics from the University of Leiden (The Netherlands) (1980). He is currently a professor with the Institute for Computing and Information Sciences (ICIS) at the Radboud University in Nijmegen (The Netherlands), and head of the Department of IRIS (Information and Knowledge Systems). His main research interests include information systems, information retrieval, hypertext and knowledge-based systems. Natural language-based information modeling in the context of information-system development including the modeling of the temporal evolution of information objects is another strand of his research.

Shouhong Wang is a professor of management information systems. He received his PhD (1990) in information systems from McMaster University (Canada). His research interests include e-commerce, information-systems analysis and design, and artificial intelligence in business. He has published several books and over 80 papers in academic journals.

Charles Willow, PhD (www.monmouth.edu/~cwillow/), is an assistant professor of management information systems (MIS) and management of technology (MOT) in the School of Business Administration at the Monmouth University, West Long Branch, New Jersey (USA). As an engineer-and-computer-scientist-turned-management faculty, Dr. Willow's research agenda has been extensive, ranging from information-systems development to case-driven strategic management issues, systems engineering, and operations research. His current research interests include information systems and network security, neural-network applications, intelligent-software agents, computer-generated graphics, cost-model analysis of Internet-based business, and strategic management of technology. Dr. Willow's papers have appeared in journals such as *ACM Transactions on Information Systems*, *Journal of Intelligent Manufacturing*, and *IEEE Transactions on Systems, Man, and Cybernetics*, among others. He is a member of the IEEE Computer Society, ACM, INFORMS Computing Society, AIS, and the National Society of Professional Engineers (NSPE). At present, Dr. Willow is on the editorial board for the *Journal of Management Information Systems* (JMIS), *MIS Quarterly* (MISQ), and *Information Systems Research* (ISR). Outside academia, he has been an active member of the International Simultaneous Interpreters Society (ISIS) and the International Judo Federation (IJF).

Dong-Qing Yao is an assistant professor of management at Towson University (USA). He received his BS in industrial engineering from Suzhou University and his MS in systems engineering from Shanghai Jiao Tong University (China). He received his PhD in management science from the University of Wisconsin-Milwaukee. His current research interests are in supply-chain management. His publications have appeared in journals such as *International Journal of Intelligent Information Technologies*, *European Journal of Operational Research*, *IIE Transactions*, *International Journal of Production Economics*, and *OMEGA*. He is a member of INFORMS and DSI.

Index

G

GAIA methodology 217
Gaia services model 226
Galois connection 197
general adaptation framework (GAF) 137
general attributes 280
general networking framework (GNF) 137
general proactivity framework (GPF) 137
generic-agent technology 219
generic OR/XOR bidding language 272
geographic information systems (GIS) 70
German Priority Research Program (SPP)
    39
GetAllObjectsOnPosition 46
global-association rule 250
global-frequent 262
global-frequent itemset 249, 250
global understanding environment (GUN)
    123, 135, 137
goal 137, 307
GOR-V information theory 335

H

Haiti 67, 69, 72
healing 69
health 74, 127
heterogeneous 90, 133
hierarchical construction 92
hierarchically structured agent 87
hierarchical structure 93
higher-order mobile agent 87, 103
higher-order property 91
HIVE 153
HIVE data store 166
HL7 39
hospital information system 60
HTTP 93
human population 31, 66, 73
hyperservice 153

I

IBM 285
illustrate scalability 91
imitation 32
individual 39, 69

industrial resource 136
infection 73
information architecture (IA) 313
information function 341
information object 185
information parallax 183
information resource management (IRM)
    314, 331
information revelation mechanism 276
information server 162
information system (IS) 108
information technology (IT) 313
information theory 335, 340
instinct 29
intelligent agent 39, 123, 218
intelligent IT 306
intelligent multirobot system 87, 88
intelligent robot 89, 105
intensional 191
intensional (meaning) objects 185
intensional view 207
inter-ontology relationships manager (the
    IRM) 17
interaction 223
interaction component 228
interaction model 220
interagent migration 92
interdependencies 42
interface 308
inventory 13
IT project 40

J

Java Agent Development Framework 226
Java programmer 286
JBoss application server 285

K

Keep It Simple Stupid (KISS) 69
knowledge 223
knowledge-management framework 154
knowledge-management system (KMS)
    313
knowledge management (KM) 154, 312,
    316